THE WORLD OF
FILM
AND
FILMMAKERS

Editorial Consultant
Don Allen

Consultant
John Gillett

Contributing Authors
Nigel Andrews
Bernard Happé
Gillian Hartnoll
Maurice Hatton
Clare Kitson
Keith Lye
Paul Madden
Tom Milne
James Monaco
David Robinson

Published by Crown Publishers Inc.,
One Park Avenue, New York, N.Y. 10016.
Designed and produced for Crown by
CHRIS MILSOME LIMITED.
Copyright © 1979 CHRIS MILSOME
LIMITED.

Editorial Director
Chris Milsome

Managing Editor
Susan Ward

Project Editor
Tim Dowley

Production Manager
Chris Fayers

Design
Ruth Prentice
Nigel Soper

Illustration
ARKA Graphics
Gordon Cramp Studio
James Marks
Nigel Osborne
Kathy Wyatt

Typesetting by City Engraving, Hull.
Separations by Starf Photolito, Rome and
City Engraving, Hull.
Printed in Italy by New Interlitho SpA,
Trezzano, Milan.

Library of Congress Cataloging in Publication Data

Main entry under title:

The World of Film and Filmmakers

  "A Chris Milsome book."
  Bibliography: p.
  Includes index.
  I. Moving-pictures -- Dictionaries. I. Allen,
Don. II. Dowley, Tim. III. Ward, Susan.
PN1993.45.B57 1979   791.43'02   79-9992
ISBN 0-517-53662-5

THE WORLD OF FILM AND FILMMAKERS

A VISUAL HISTORY

Edited by Don Allen

Foreword by François Truffaut

A CHRIS MILSOME BOOK
Published by
CROWN PUBLISHERS, INC. NEW YORK

Foreword

The inventors of the cinema at the end of the nineteenth century were not immediately aware that they had revolutionized our daily lives. Yet the impact of those early reels, in their purely informative and documentary capacity, is comparable with that of television from the nineteen-fifties onwards.

Initially created in order to reproduce reality, cinema reached the heights whenever it succeeded in going beyond the reality on which it was based, whenever it lent credibility to strange events or people and so established the elements of a mythology based on images.

From this viewpoint the first fifty years of the history of cinema were prodigiously rich. It is very difficult today for a screen 'monster' to compete with *Nosferatu, Frankenstein* or *King Kong;* it is impossible for a dancer to be more graceful than Fred Astaire or for a vamp to be more enigmatic and dangerous than Marlene Dietrich or for a comic actor to be more inventive and amusing than Charlie Chaplin. Sound cinema after some hesitation found its way by filming remakes of the silent films just as today we film remakes in colour of the black and white films.

But at each stage, with every technical advance and each new invention, the cinema loses in poetry what it gains in intelligence, and loses in mystery what it gains in realism. Stereophonic sound, the giant screen, sound vibrations acting directly on the cinema seats, or even attempts at three dimensional effects may help the industry to survive, but none of these things will help cinema to remain an art.

For cinematographic art can exist only by the highly organized betrayal of reality. All the great film directors say 'no' to something. Federico Fellini for example refuses to use real exteriors in his films, Ingmar Bergman refuses to use background music, Robert Bresson refuses to use professional actors, Hitchcock refuses to use documentary scenes. If, after eighty-five years cinema is still in existence, it is thanks to the one thing of which you will fail to find a picture in this magnificent book: a good script, a good story told accurately and inventively. *Accurately* because a film needs to make clear and to grade all the information it gives if it is to hold the attention of the spectator; *inventively* because it is important to stimulate the imagination of the audience if they are to be given pleasure. I hope the use of the word *pleasure* will not shock the reader. Buster Keaton, Ernst Lubitsch, Howard Hawks all thought and worked harder than many of their colleagues, and always with the aim of giving more pleasure.

Today in the universities film is taught alongside literature and the sciences. This may be a good thing as long as teachers do not encourage their students to prefer the dryness of documentary to the flights of fancy of fiction nor to place theory before instinct. Let us never forget that ideas are less interesting than the human beings who invent, modify, perfect or betray them. Some teachers, journalists or even mere observers occasionally set themselves up as the arbiters of what is *cultural* and what is not. You may be sure that they will place *Louisiana Story* in the first category and *Laurel and Hardy* in the second. But I firmly believe that we must reject any hierarchy of genres and call cultural quite simply whatever pleases, entertains, interests us or helps us to live. 'All films are born free and equal' as André Bazin wrote. The most sensuous film director in the world, Jean Renoir, never tired of quoting Pascal's 'What interests man is man'.

This splendid creation, *The World of Film and Filmmakers,* depicts the interactions of machines and men. It is clear on reading and looking at it that the cinema is at its best whenever man-the-filmmaker succeeds in bending the machine to his own desires and so allows us into his dream.

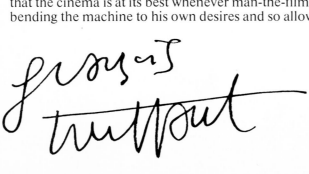

Francois Truffaut
May 1979

CONTENTS

Contributors

The exciting team which produced this work contains some of the most eminent experts in the fields of filmmaking and film criticism. Together they have provided a comprehensive grounding in the history of world cinema, a highly entertaining and readable account of the practicalities of filmmaking, an authoritative introduction to the appreciation of the art of film and a vital reference listing of key actors and directors.

The **Coordinating Editor** is **Don Allen,** Senior Lecturer in Modern Languages and Film Studies at the West London Institute of Higher Education, author of *Truffaut* and a contributor to *Sight and Sound* and the *Monthly Film Bulletin.* He is currently researching the links between the novel and film.

The **contributing authors** are:

David Robinson, film critic of *The Times,* regular contributor to *Sight and Sound* and author of *World Cinema.* His knowledge of film is grounded in a preoccupation with its early history, the subject of his exceptional collection of film ephemera and equipment.

James Monaco, member of the New School for Social Research in New York and a freelance film critic who has lectured widely in colleges and universities. He is author of *The New Wave, How to Read a Film* and *Alain Resnais* and general editor of the *Media Culture* series.

Tom Milne, highly knowledgeable and versatile film critic, with strong enthusiasms and wide experience. Former editor of the *Monthly Film Bulletin* and the *Cinema One* books, his own titles include *Godard on Godard, Rouben Mamoulian* and *Carl Dreyer.*

Nigel Andrews, well-informed and wide-ranging film critic of the *Financial Times,* was formerly Assistant Editor of *Sight and Sound* and the *Cinema One* books and writes regularly for *American Film.*

Maurice Hatton, freelance filmmaker, is best known for his *Praise Marx and Pass the Ammunition* 1968 and also for *Long Shot* – 1978. He has worked as journalist, photographer, producer, director and scriptwriter.

Bernard Happé, former head of Technicolour, is a leading authority on cinema technology and author of such books as *Basic Motion Picture Technology, Film in the Laboratory* and the *Encyclopaedia of Film and Television.*

Gillian Hartnoll, Deputy Head of the British Film Institute's Information and Documentation Section, has contributed to both *The Oxford Companion to Film* and the *International Encyclopaedia of Film.*

Paul Madden, a leading authority on television and the television film, is Television Officer at the British Film Institute.

Clare Kitson, Programme Officer at the National Film Theatre, London, has organized animation film programmes at film festivals in several countries.

Keith Lye, freelance journalist and editor, has had a lifelong interest in film myth and personalities.

THE ORIGINS OF THE CINEMA

For a variety of reasons, the earliest years of the cinema are also the most fascinating. It was in this period that so many of the technical breakthroughs essential to the medium were made. Cinema can be seen evolving from its mechanical and photographic precursors – the magic lantern, the zoetrope, the camera obscura and the other nineteenth-century entertainments.

If the early years of cinema attract for their technical ingenuity and inventiveness, they also foreshadow the themes and styles of the next fifty years of the movies: the Lumière brothers' actuality, George Méliès' film magic, Griffith's editing, the Italian epics, French comedies, Russian political film. It was in this period that Hollywood established itself as the centre of the US film industry, and experienced its first golden years. Finally the breakthrough into sound heralded a new era in movie history.

Magic Pictures:
The Image Moves

The cinema was not the invention of any single man, but the culmination of a long evolution. The urge to create a living image of reality was implicit in man's earliest magic and earliest art–which was often the same thing. We can trace back the ancestors of moving pictures as we know them for more than a century before 1895, when the Lumière brothers gave the first public performance of their *Cinématographe* in Paris.

From the end of the eighteenth century, and with the spread of cheap printing, people increasingly came to look to images for their knowledge of life. The rational spirit of that age produced a passion for visual shows and exhibitions of all kinds. The ancient oriental shadow-show enjoyed a great revival of popularity all over Europe in the 1770s and 1780s. (Significantly the 'Chinese shadow-show' or *ombres chinoises* enjoyed another great craze at the very time the cinema came into being.) There was a great fashion for entertainments which combined painting, theatre and light.

In the 1780s Robert Barker, an Edinburgh landscape painter, invented the Panorama, a *trompe-l'oeil* painting on the inside surface of a great cylinder, which gave a startlingly realistic impression to the audience assembled at its centre. (The name Panorama, coined by Barker from Greek roots, survives in the present-day jargon of the cinema as 'pan'.)

A year or two earlier, the French painter Philippe Jacques de Loutherbourg invented the Eidophusikon. This employed lights to produce dramatic effects upon painted scenes in a small theatre. In the 1820s Louis Jacques Mandé Daguerre, later to become famous as a father of photography, developed Loutherbourg's ideas in his Dioramas, exhibited in Paris in 1822 and in London in the following year. The Diorama audience enjoyed an experience which must have been very much like watching a film. They sat in an auditorium in front of a vast painting, elaborately prepared with translucent portions, so that the atmosphere could be changed dramatically by the varying lights arranged in front and behind.

The magic lantern show

The cinema came still nearer with the magic lantern, a device known as early as the seventeenth century, and already hugely popular throughout Europe in the eighteenth century. Itinerant lantern showmen would travel from village to village, thrilling and alarming their rustic audiences.

The magic lantern attracted a great revival of interest at the close of the eighteenth century. A Belgian showman, Etienne Robertson, thrilled fashionable Paris with his Phantasmagoria. This used a particularly sophisticated magic lantern to produce effects of ghosts and demons in a theatre decorated to appear like a ruined Gothic chapel. By moving the lantern backwards and forwards, whilst carefully keeping his lens focussed, Robertson gave the illusion that his images were magically growing or shrinking. Later in the

Left Like the motion-picture projector, the magic lantern depended on an illuminant enclosed in a lightproof container. From this a beam of light was allowed to pass through a transparent image, which by means of a lens was projected much enlarged onto a screen in a darkened room. Magic lantern slides of the late nineteenth century are mechanical marvels, creating motion in the tiny paintings on glass by the use of sliding panels, levers and ratchets.

Above The Zoetrope, or Wheel of Life. When the cylinder was spun, an illusion of movement was given if the images on the strip inside the drum were viewed through the slits opposite.

Left Phenakistoscope discs. The separate still pictures seem to combine into a continuous moving image when the rotating disc is viewed in a mirror, through slits cut between the individual drawings.

nineteenth century, magic lantern showmen devised other methods to produce movement in their projected images.

But in the motion picture the illusion of movement is produced not by such direct mechanical means, but by applying the physical principle called 'persistence of vision'. The impression of an object received by the retina of the human eye appears to persist for a brief instant, a fraction of a second, after the object itself has been removed from sight. This principle explains why, when we watch a lamp whirled rapidly in the darkness, we see an apparently continuous circle of light.

Philosophical toys

This phenomenon had already been noticed in ancient times. Early in the nineteenth century a number of physicists – including Michael Faraday and Peter Mark Roget in England, Joseph Plateau in Belgium and Simon Stampfer in Vienna – devoted serious studies to the subject. To demonstrate the effect scientists devised a number of 'philosophical toys'. The first was the Thaumatrope, made in 1824 – a disc with matching parts of a single picture on each side. When spun on a string through its axis the two parts seemed to combine in one image.

In 1832 both Stampfer and Plateau designed a disc with pictures of the successive phases of an action (like the frames of an animated cartoon) drawn around its edge. This was known as the Phenakistiscope. Slits in the disc perform the same function as the shutter of a film projector, obscuring the vision while one image replaces the next, enabling the images to be seen as intermittent flashes.

Moving pictures

The Zoetrope was a direct development from the Phenakistiscope. Emile Reynaud, a Frenchman who combined technical skill with exceptional artistic ability, made a significant improvement by replacing the slits of the Phenakistiscope and the Zoetrope with a prism of mirrors at the centre of the drum in his Praxinoscope. In his *Praxinoscope à Projections* Reynaud projected moving pictures onto a screen by combining the Praxinoscope with the magic lantern. With his *Pantomimis Lumineuses*, forerunner of the animated cartoon, Reynaud introduced Parisian audiences to moving pictures three years before the Lumière *Cinématographe*. One element was still missing however: photography.

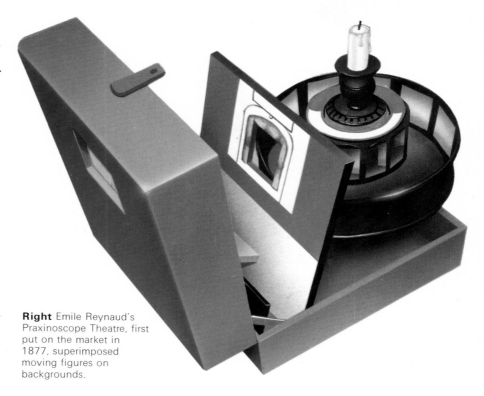

Right Emile Reynaud's Praxinoscope Theatre, first put on the market in 1877, superimposed moving figures on backgrounds.

Above In 1892 Reynaud perfected his masterpiece, the *Pantomimes Lumineuses*. In a specially equipped theatre in the Musée Grévin in Paris he gave an entertainment in which little cartoon figures projected from a continuous band of painted images acted out sketches on scenic backgrounds projected onto the screen.

Below A Zoetrope strip. Cartoon-like illustrations of this kind were placed inside the cylinder of the Zoetrope for viewing.

Capturing Life:
Animated Photographs

In the beginning was the black box. The magic lantern was a light-proof box provided with a lens, and was placed, with a lamp inside it, in a darkened room. The *camera obscura*, a device already known in the sixteenth century, was a light-proof chamber provided with a lens, darkened within, and set to face a brightly illuminated landscape. The magic lantern projected an enlarged image onto a screen outside. By contrast the *camera obscura* projected a reduced image of the scene in front of its lens on to a screen placed inside the box or chamber.

The first photographers

It had already been observed that certain chemicals change – darkening or fading – as a result of the action of light. Now physicists set about finding a chemical sensitive enough to capture the light and shade of an image cast on specially treated paper placed in the *camera obscura*. And then they had to find a way of 'fixing' the image obtained, so that when removed from the 'camera' it would not be further affected by daylight.

The first successful, though crude, photographs were taken in the mid-1820s by Nicéphore Niépce. From the 1840s photography built up a popularity which was never to decline. From the start people were fascinated with the idea of combining the moving pictures of the Phenakistiscope and the Zoetrope with photographs from life. However, the seemingly insuperable problem was that early photography demanded extremely long exposure times. This clearly presented serious problems; the Zoetrope required every second of movement to be broken down into at least a dozen successive images. Showmen and inventors were not completely deterred. Heyl's Phasmatrope, demonstrated in Philadelphia in 1870, produced a brief moving picture of a couple waltzing. It had been made by the agonising process of posing the models afresh for each individual successive image photographed.

Muybridge's move

The problem of making a series of photographs in sufficiently rapid succession to be re-presented to give the impression of movement was eventually solved by people with no initial concern at all in making photographs move. The last quarter of the nineteenth century saw an upsurge of scientific interest in the study of human and animal movement. An ingenious English photographer, who had emigrated from Kingston-on-Thames to

California and changed his name from Edward Muggeridge to Eadweard Muybridge, was commissioned to make photographic studies of race horses. He built an arrangement of twelve (and later more) cameras, arranged along the side of a track. After much laborious experiment, Muybridge perfected his system, to enable him to record all forms of animal and human motion in successive phases of rapidly photographed action.

Above In July 1891 Edison patented the Kinetoscope, a peepshow device in which the images on a continuous film loop were viewed in motion.
Below Some of Eadweard Muybridge's photographic studies of racehorses.

Muybridge's photographs gained him international fame. He came in touch with a physiologist, Etienne Marey, who was working on similar lines in France. They corresponded on the special difficulties of photographing birds in flight. Instead of Muybridge's multiple series of cameras, Marey worked on the idea of making multiple images on a single plate, using a single camera.

Celluloid was the last missing element required to create the modern motion-picture camera. From 1888 it was merely a race to produce the first practicable device to record and project animated photographs in which the illusion of movement was produced by the physical principle of the 'persistence of vision'.

The discoveries of Marey and Muybridge were watched with intense interest by Thomas Alva Edison, the great American inventor. By the late 1880s Edison was dreaming of recording images in the same way that his Phonograph had already recorded sound. In 1888 he entrusted to his brilliant English assistant, W. K. L. Dickson, the task of developing something along these lines. He also began to issue a series of *caveats* to protect his patent interests in any such devices in the future.

By the autumn of 1890 Dickson had succeeded in taking rapid sequences of photographs with a device patented as the Kinetograph. Early in 1893 the world's first film studio was built in the grounds of Edison's laboratories at West Orange. Disrespectfully christened the Black Maria, it was a tar-paper hut with a roof that opened to admit the sun, and a pivot to enable it to be turned to catch the best light. Inside stood the elephantine Kinetograph at one end. At the other stood a little stage on which music hall and circus performers such as Buffalo Bill Cody and Annie Oakley performed. They were the world's first film stars.

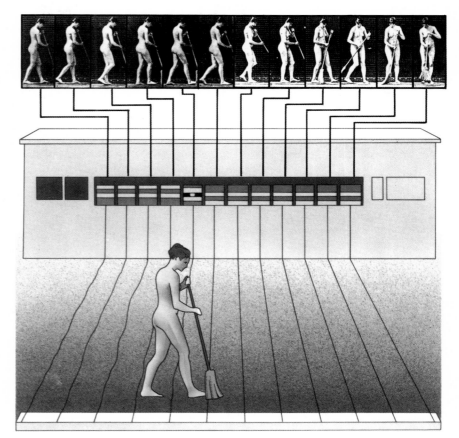

Left In 1881-2 Etienne Marey contrived *a fusil photographique* capable of taking twelve photographs in rapid succession in one second. Its action was suggested by the machine gun.

Top How Muybridge photographed animal and human movement.

Left Etienne Marey's most crucial invention was his *Chrono – photographe,* remarkably similar to the motion-picture camera, which followed the production in 1888 of celluloid-roll film by the Eastman Kodak Photographic Company.

Right Muybridge's Zoopraxiscope projected brief cycles of moving images based on his photographs. In the 1880s he toured demonstrating it, stirring considerable interest.

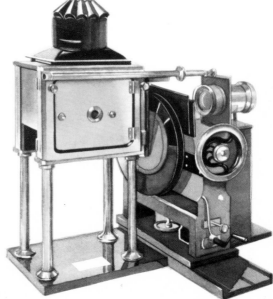

The First Picture Show

The films which Edison shot at West Orange, New Jersey, were designed to be shown in the Kinetoscope. This was a penny-in-the-slot peepshow in which, for a penny, a nickel or ten centimes, one spectator at a time could peer at Annabelle the Dancer, or the Dance of the Seven Veils, or the strong man Eugene Sandow.

Kinetoscope parlours sprang up all over the world. Profitable as these were, it was evident that much more money could be made if more than a single spectator could watch the films. The obvious solution was to combine the moving film with the magic lantern projector. Once again it was a race between rival inventors to perfect the first practical apparatus. This time the winners were the Lumière brothers. They came up with an ingenious multi-purpose device that was camera, film printer and projector in one – the *Cinématographe*.

The coming of the movies

After several months of trials and demonstrations, the Lumières decided to launch the *Cinématographe* as a commercial attraction and set out to exploit systematically what they considered the short-lived commercial possibilities of their invention. They sent agents to every possible part of the world, with the dual role of exhibiting films and selling equipment, and of adding to their repertory of films of exotic places and subjects.

The Lumières soon found themselves faced with rivals. In Britain, Birt Acres (1854–1918) and Robert Paul (1869–1943) – introduced to the business in the first place to make and market copies of the Kinetoscope, which Edison had neglected to patent in England – came up with their own Animatographe, demonstrated within days of the Lumières' *Cinématographe*. In the United States, Edison acquired the patents of the Phantoscope, a projector invented by Thomas Armat and C. Francis Jenkins, and introduced the Edison Vitascope. By the end of 1896 films were flickering on screens across the world from London to Tokyo, and from Moscow to Bombay.

Audiences everywhere were amazed and delighted. They were unconcerned with what they saw so long as it moved. Films were limited to 50 feet – the length of celluloid strip then available – giving a running time of at most as many seconds. The repertoire was similar to that of picture postcards or magic lantern slides – street scenes, rough seas at Brighton, a train entering a railway station.

In North America and Europe the movies found a natural home in the music halls and vaudeville theatres. They took their place alongside the comic singers and serpentine dancers, the jugglers, conjurers, strongmen, cyclists and performing dogs. In Paris the Lumière show played at the Olympia, and in London, where Paul offered opposition at the Alhambra, at the Empire, Leicester Square. But the craze wore off; by the start of the twentieth century the managers of

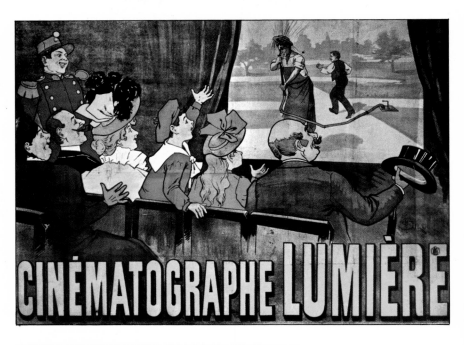

Above A poster advertising one of the early Lumière Brothers' films. Each film lasted only about fifty seconds, and featured either a simple scene, or a basic comedy situation.

Left The Lumière brothers, Auguste and Louis, both worked in their father's photographic materials factory in Lyon, France. Louis made no films after 1898.

Below Thomas Edison's Vitascope in operation at Koster & Bials' music hall in New York in 1896. The earliest films were shown as part of a vaudeville bill.

American non-stop vaudeville shows had taken to relegating films to the end of the bill, as 'chasers' to discourage people from sitting through the programme twice.

The movies suffered a severe early blow to their reputation in May 1897. A *Cinématographe* show had been introduced as a novelty in the great Charity Bazaar organised annually in Paris by the French aristocracy. The projectionist was careless with a naked flame; inflammable film caught light, and fire raged through the flimsy canvas awnings and stalls. 140 people perished, many bearing the most aristocratic names in France. The disaster inevitably received world-wide publicity of the most damaging kind for the cinema. It opened the way for stringent official and municipal regulation of cinema exhibitions in many countries.

The happiest home of the infant cinema in these years was on the fairgrounds. Throughout Europe and America travelling showmen bought projectors and films, and pitched their tents alongside the traditional waxworks and freak shows. They often made their own films as they travelled from town to town: a local street scene was always a sure attraction. At the great fair of Nizhni–Novgorod, the young Maxim Gorki saw the Lumière *Cinématographe* in June 1896. It moved him to prophesy: 'The thirst for such strange, fantastic sensations as it gives will grow ever greater, and we will be increasingly less able and less willing to grasp the everyday impressions of ordinary life.'

Gradually the cinema began to create its own permanent homes. As early as 1900 it was discovered that audiences would happily sit through programmes made up solely of films – when a strike of vaudeville artists in New York obliged some managers to present movie programmes rather than close their doors.

By the early years of the century shops were being converted into little makeshift movie theatres. Such was their success that from around 1905 more and more custom-built cinemas and Nickelodeons were erected. The cinema now took its place in the townscape.

Farce, Magic and History:
Early French Cinema

Right Georges Méliès (1861–1938) with his colleague Emile Cohl. Méliès was a well-known figure in the Paris entertainment world before he turned to film. He set about making films with all the expertise of a professional magician. He soon discovered that by stopping the camera, removing an object or person from the scene, and then restarting the camera, he could perform vanishing tricks. He went on to explore every kind of camera trickery.

Right Trademarks used by Georges Méliès for his movies.

Right No previous film equalled the splendour of *Cabiria* – directed by Giovanni Pastrone. It featured splendid décors, natural settings, sophisticated camerawork and lighting. The scenario was signed by the celebrated poet Gabriele d'Annunzio. It followed the adventures of a slave girl during the Second Punic War. But it proved to be the swan song of Italian cinema's golden age.

For the entire decade after the Lumière show of December 1895, Europe was the world centre of film-making. It was there that the first film-makers began to explore seriously what was at first regarded as a mere scientific novelty. It took time for people to realise that this could be a medium for instruction and entertainment. The father of the Lumière brothers is said to have turned away a prospective purchaser of the *Cinématographe* with the words: 'Young man, you should thank me. This invention is not for sale; but if it were it would ruin you. It can be exploited for a while as a scientific curiosity; beyond that it has no commercial future.' The Lumières' fairly early withdrawal from film-making suggests that they held this view quite seriously.

The young man turned down on this occasion was Georges Méliès, who hoped to add the *Cinématographe* to the attractions of his little magic theatre, the Theatre Robert-Houdin. Undeterred by the refusal, he promptly went to London, bought a camera, and returned to set about making films.

The beginning of narrative

As a by-product Méliès developed the practice of composing action for the cinema. The first film-makers had simply used the camera as a snapshot device, photographing life as they found it. Obvious though the concept of composition now seems, Méliès was the first to work as a director

with cinema. He used actors and scenery, first creating little tableaux, and then series of tableaux, to tell complete dramatic stories.

For a few years Méliès was the outstanding figure in world film production. He soon fell victim to plagiarists and pirates, and by World War I his stage-bound style had been superseded. After 1913 Méliès was forced out of production. He was discovered in the 1920s running a little gift kiosk in the Gare Montparnasse. He died in a home for cinema veterans.

One of the most energetic copiers of Méliès' tricks was Ferdinand Zecca (1864–1947), a one-time vaudeville star who became production head at the growing Pathé studio in 1900. Zecca borrowed shamelessly from every other film-maker. His most successful lifting was the idea of the chase film, first invented and mastered by an Englishman, Alfred Collins, who worked for the London branch of Pathé's rival, the Gaumont Company.

Zecca's chase films – *The Pumpkin Race, The Barrel Race, The Wig Race* and scores of others– achieved heights of mad frenzy. They provided the basis for a brilliant generation of French comic films and clowns. André Deed (1884–193?) trained both in Zecca chases and Méliès' magic films, became the world's first comic star. In his wake followed a whole galaxy of clowns: Charles Prince, Roméo Bosetti, Onesime and the infant comedians Bébé and Bout-de-Zan. The greatest of them all was Max Linder (1882–1925), who took over as Pathé's brightest star when Deed defected to the Italian studios.

Max Linder introduced a new style of comedy. His predecessors had been grotesques, given to frenetic knockabout. The screen Max was urbane and intelligent, elegant and handsome, and his gags were exquisitely composed variations on simple themes. In a rare moment of modesty, Charles Chaplin declared: 'I owe him everything.'

From entertainment to art

Carried on the wave-crest of economic prosperity, French producers developed aspirations to art. In 1908 the new Film d'Art Company premiered *The Assassination of the Duc de Guise.* Later Film d'Art offered Sarah Bernhardt as *Queen Elizabeth* – 1912 and *La Dame aux caméllias* – 1912, and Réjane as *Madame Sans-gene*. These productions were static, stage-bound and over-upholstered. But they profoundly affected attitudes to the infant cinema. Well-known authors and actors in other European countries were similarly persuaded to lend their names to the movies, and notable literary works were adapted. In England Sir Herbert Beerbohm-Tree played King Henry VIII and Sir Johnstone Forbes-Robertson, Hamlet, before the cameras. The social status of the cinema rose by leaps and bounds.

In Italy the influence of Le Film d'Art inspired a school of costume spectacles which brought a brief golden age to the Italian cinema in the years just before World War I. A taste for classical costume

subjects had shown itself as early as 1905 with *The Sack of Rome.* In 1907 followed *Marcus Lycinus* and *Othello.* After the formation of the Film d'Arte Italiana company in 1909, however, spectacle films were produced in great numbers to take advantage of the reliable Italian sunshine and ready-made classical locations.

The peak was reached in 1912 with Enrico Guazzoni's *Quo Vadis?* which boasted thousands of extras, a positive menagerie of lions and a thrilling fire of Rome. The overwhelming success of this Italian film in America changed the course of cinema. Before that time producers had argued that a film was limited in length to a single reel. Audiences, they insisted, could not concentrate for more than fifteen minutes. But audiences sat enthralled through all nine reels of *Quo Vadis?.* The feature-length story film was now inevitable. But World War I put an end to European supremacy. Now came the turn of Hollywood and the American film.

Top Georges Méliès made a careful diagram to guide the construction of 'The Giant of the Pole' – a huge moving figure. His favourite subjects were fairy tales, related in the sophisticated, adult styles of pantomime and ballet, with pretty girls and elaborately painted scenery.

Bottom The French Pathé company set up a special group to film contemporary theatre productions. In 1908 the new Film d'Art Company launched its first production: *The Assassination of the Duc de Guise,* a lavish, over-dressed historical drama.

Film Discovers a Language:
D.W. Griffith

In 1902 Edwin S. Porter (1870–1941), resident director at the Edison studios, made a momentous discovery: separate pieces of film, shot in different places, at different times, from different viewpoints, can be put together like sentences in a book, to complement and modify one anothers' meaning. In *The Life of an American Fireman* – 1903 he brought together already-existing shots of fire brigade practices and acted scenes. This produced an integrated narrative full of dramatic power, which tugged at the hearts of audiences. Next, Porter went one better, telling the story of *The Great Train Robbery* – 1903 in a continuity of no less than fourteen individual shots. Audiences flocked to *The Great Train Robbery*, excited by this film in a completely new way, though probably unaware of the new story-telling technique by which this response had been achieved.

The birth of a director
Soon after this Porter gave a young man his first job in the movies. This newcomer, David Wark Griffith (1875–1948) pushed Porter's discovery to undreamed-of limits. In the summer of 1908 Griffith made his first film *The Adventures of Dollie*. Griffith's care over actors and locations paid off even in this first, insignificant nine-minute drama. The five hundred one-reelers Griffith made in the next five years established him as America's ace director, and Biograph as the nation's undisputed top studio.

Griffith tackled every kind of film: comedy – though humour was never his strong point – melodrama, thrillers, westerns, costume drama

Above right Lillian Gish in a scene from Griffith's masterpiece *The Birth of a Nation* – 1915. Based on a novel about the American Civil War by Revd Thomas Dixon, it shows narrow Southern and racist prejudice. But this cannot detract from its overall achievement, dramatic and spectacular power, and Griffith's rare ability to treat great historic events alongside the private fortunes of individuals.

Right A scene of epic proportions from *Intolerance*. Griffith brought together stories of intolerance from four different periods of history in a film of staggering ambition. The four separate episodes are linked by a symbolic image of a woman rocking a cradle.

and sentimental romance. By his literary tastes he broadened the cinema's range, bringing to the humble nickelodeon audiences the Bible and the works of Browning, Tennyson, Poe, Dickens and Shakespeare.

Griffith as innovator

Griffith's stylistic and technical innovations had even more influence upon the cinema's future. Griffith found that he could split up a scene into small fragments which – though isolated elements, incomplete in themselves – could be assembled so as to control the dramatic form and intensity of the picture. He could provide emphasis through the composition and framing of his images and the placing and movement of the camera. Most important, perhaps, was the way in which Griffith brought together images, and the speed and rhythm with which he cut them.

Before Griffith, directors had used the camera picture as if it were a stage proscenium. The camera stayed more or less fixed in front of a group of actors seen in full length. By contrast Griffith freely mixed close-ups, which revealed significant details of the scene of the action, with vast long-shots, for spectacle and distance. In addition he developed new kinds of actors – fresh young people unhampered by the stage techniques which he recognised as largely irrelevant to work in front of the camera.

Griffith's masterpiece

Griffith poured all that he had learned into his great masterpiece *The Birth of a Nation* – 1915. This film was a sensation everywhere it was shown. It was now no longer possible for intellectuals to dismiss the movies as cheap, second-rate entertainment, the poor man's theatre.

All Griffith's own share of the profits, and much more money besides, was poured into his next picture, the monumental *Intolerance* – 1916. The suspense of the final reels – the apogee of the celebrated Griffith last-minute rescue, tensely built up through cross-cutting and accelerating editing – still thrills modern audiences. But the film was too far ahead of its public. It failed to repeat the box-office success of *The Birth of a Nation*. Griffith never regained his financial stability or his creative independence, though his powers were at first undiminished. He made the great *Broken Blossoms* – 1919 and *Way Down East* – 1920, and *Isn't Life Wonderful?* – 1924, a film about defeated Germany that anticipated Italian neo-realist films of twenty years later. Griffith went on to make two sound films: *Abraham Lincoln* – 1930 and *The Struggle* – 1931, an humiliating failure largely financed by himself. But they fell sadly short of his old master works. By 1931 he was out of films for ever, condemned to spend the remaining years of his life in inactivity and bitterness.

When he died in 1948, his disciple, Erich von Stroheim, wrote a fitting epitaph: 'Griffith put beauty and poetry into a cheap and tawdry sort of amusement.'

Above Griffith's *Man's Genesis* – 1912 was claimed as 'a psychological study founded upon the Darwinian Theory of Evolution'.

Above left Klansmen ford a river in *Birth of a Nation*, one of the most profitable films in history. Its offensive portrayal of the American black made it a controversial film.

Left Griffith with his cameraman Billy Bitzer (left); an innovator and pioneer in lighting and camera work.

Below As the 1920s wore on Griffith seemed more and more a relic of the past. By 1931 he was out of films for ever, condemned to spend his remaining years in inactivity and bitterness.

Movies Become Big Business

The cinema began in the laboratories of scientists such as Edison and industrialists such as the Lumières. Soon it was to be taken over by entrepreneurs, opportunists and businessmen.

In the United States the vast commercial potential of the cinema soon became apparent. The great new urban populations, largely composed of immigrants who were delighted with a cheap form of entertainment which required no great knowledge of the language of their adopted land, took the cinema to their hearts. The pioneer firms were Edison, Biograph (started in 1896 by Edison's former assistant W. K. L. Dickson) and Vitagraph (1899). Soon new film factories sprang up in the urban centres of New York, Chicago and Philadelphia. The making of films was indeed an industry. One-reel dramas and comedies were turned out at the regular rate of one or two a week, according to the size of the factory, with increasingly standardized themes and mechanical formulas for narrative.

Motion picture monopoly

In 1909 a group of companies banded with Edison to form the Motion Picture Patents Company in a bid to monopolize the growing industry. They pooled their patents in motion picture apparatus, and paid Edison a royalty on all films sold, in an attempt to build up a total monopoly of film production. They tried to levy royalties from exhibitors using films and equipment, and to use sanctions to prevent them from showing films made by producers who did not belong to the monopolistic Trust.

The fierce war that followed between the Patents Company and the independents had far-reaching effects upon the development of the American cinema. The independents' search for places where they could make films safe from the reach of the Trust agents led them to California. There they found reliable sunlight for filming, cheap property, exotic locations, and a quick escape over the Mexican border in case of trouble with the Trust.

The coming of the star

The vital struggle to win over exhibitors and their audiences shocked the industry out of the production line mentality. It also won a readier reception for the new ideas and new standards set by D. W. Griffith. In the course of this struggle, film-makers discovered an important asset, hitherto overlooked, which was to dominate cinema economics for the next half century: the star. In the early years of film production in America, the players' identities had been concealed by mutual consent. The actors were happy not to have the indignity exposed, for film work was a sign of having failed in the legitimate theatre. The arrangement suited the producers. But they rightly predicted that once film actors' names were publicized they would follow stage actors in demanding salaries related to their audience-drawing powers.

The public nevertheless identified their favourites in their own way – for example as 'The Biograph Girl', 'The Vitagraph Girl', 'Little Mary' or 'The Girl with the Curls'. When the film actors' anonymity was finally broken down, as a direct result of the Trust war, the star system snowballed. One by one the companies yielded, some more reluctantly than others; and a whole new subsidiary industry – fan magazine publishing – was created.

Among the first generation of stars were the cowboys Broncho Billy Anderson (c. 1883–1971) and Tom Mix (1880–1940). In the move to California, the American cinema had discovered the rich folklore of the West.

Hollywood reigns supreme

By 1914, Europe had entered World War I, removing any significant obstacle to Hollywood's growing domination of the world's film industry. By that time, Mary Pickford, the all-American hero Douglas Fairbanks, (who eventually became her husband) and Charles Chaplin, the London

Top The first great movie magnate was Charles Pathé (1883–1957) who dominated the industry between 1903 and 1909. His closest rival was Léon Gaumont (1863–1946), whose Paris factory is shown here. Their worldwide film empires covered all aspects – from making equipment and filmstock to producing and exhibiting films. Gaumont handed over production of fiction films to his secretary Alice Guy Blaché.

Bottom Little picture houses sprang up everywhere. Audiences often chose films by their trademark rather than their title.

music hall artist who gave the world its best-known comic figure of all time, were earning seven-figure salaries.

Shaping the American cinema, alongside the stars and the great creative contribution of D. W. Griffith, were two dominant producers. These two, Mack Sennett (1884–1960) and Thomas Harper Ince (1882–1924), with Griffith himself, made up the three corners of the Triangle Film Company. Ince was a creative producer who combined organisational gifts with a shrewd anticipation of audience tastes and a unique feeling for the medium. He is credited with the introduction of the scenario. Before his time films were largely improvised.

The feature film arrives

Among the innovations revolutionizing the American film industry at the start of the second decade of the century, was the arrival of the 'feature' film. Until 1912 producers and exhibitors conservatively insisted that a film was limited to a single reel, with a running time of not more than fifteen minutes. When D. W. Griffith found that he could only adequately treat the story of *Enoch Arden* – 1911 in two reels, exhibitors, certain that the audience could only concentrate for one reel, insisted (till the public demanded otherwise) on releasing it as two separate parts.

But films of two, three and even more reels were already arriving from Europe. In 1912 Adolph Zukor achieved startling success with the release in the States of the French four-reeler, *Queen Elizabeth*, starring Sarah Bernhardt. He then launched into production of a series of feature-length 'Famous Players in Famous Plays'. Other producers were encouraged by Zukor's lead, and by the remarkable success of an Italian film, *Quo Vadis?* – 1913, which ran for two hours. The feature film had conquered the US.

Top left Florence Lawrence was the first star whose name was revealed to the public, by Carl Laemmle, an independent director.

Far left Mack Sennett, of the Keystone Studios, was a wayward Irish Canadian who created a new and distinctive vein of slapstick comedy that has become part of American popular culture.

Left Mary Pickford, as 'America's Sweetheart', won a universal popularity that possibly no human being had ever enjoyed before. She recognised her financial value and her enormous bargaining powers.

Generation of Monsters:
The German Expressionists

The end of World War I saw a new balance of power in the world of international cinema. Before the war France, Scandinavia and Italy had been leading powers in the world's film industry. Notable work was done by the Danish director Benjamin Christensen (1879–1959), the Finnish Mauritz Stiller (1883–1928) and the Swede Victor Sjöstrom (1879–1960). But by 1918 America had achieved a domination which she was never afterwards to lose. Another new power had emerged in a quite unexpected quarter – defeated Germany.

The cinema was scorned by pre-war German intellectuals – serious stage actors were professionally forbidden to work for the screen. Its quality was low apart from a few exceptional works such as Paul Wegener's *The Student of Prague* – 1913 and Max Mack's *Der Anderer* – 1913. War-time isolation however had forced the German studios to step up the quantity and quality of films produced. After the war there was new and even more important propaganda work for the cinema: fighting the almost world-wide hostility to all things German.

The German cinema had made great technical strides since 1914. The first German films to gain an international audience were a cycle of costly and handsomely-mounted historical costume pictures, styled *'Kolossal'*. The genre was inaugurated by Joe May's *Veritas Vincit* – 1918. But May was soon eclipsed by the former slapstick comedian Ernst Lubitsch (1892–1947) who brought style, wit and modern psychology to the *'Kolossal'* with *Madame Dubarry* – 1919, *Anna Boleyn* – 1920 and *Das Weib des Pharaohs* – 1921.

Artistic revolt
The immediate post-war period, however, was a period of intense political, social and artistic ferment. This so-called *'Aufbruch'* took the shape, too, of rebellion against outworn artistic forms. Among the competing 'isms' of the time, Expressionism was strongest. The basic aim of Expressionism, to seek out the most expressive form of an object or an image, clearly had immediate relevance to the style and methods of the silent cinema.

Expressionism met film in *The Cabinet of Dr Caligari* – 1919. Pommer entrusted direction of the film to Robert Wiene who in turn engaged as designers three painters active in the Munich Expressionist group: Hermann Warm, Walter Röhrig and Walter Reimann. These three put into practice Warm's theory that 'Films must be drawings brought to life.'

The strange, artificial, angular images of Caligari had no direct successors. But the film served to reveal how a limited kind of Expressionism was natural to the silent cinema's method. Images could be used to reflect and interpret psychological states and interior action. The lesson was taken to heart by a whole generation of German film-makers. The immediate legacy of *Caligari* was a feeling for the use of visual detail for 'psychological' illumination, a claustrophobic tendency to studio production, and a taste – always lurking in the German temperament – for horror, fantasy and twilight monsters.

Giants of Expressionism
The two outstanding German directors of the 1920s, Murnau and Lang, both passed through an Expressionist period. But for his last German film, *Tartüff* – 1925 and *Faust* – 1926, Murnau returned to the *'Kolossal'* genre of costume film. However, his style here, and in his subsequent brief Hollywood career, continued to bear the mark of the Expressionist vision.

Fritz Lang began his career as a script writer and a director of detective thrillers. After *Destiny* Lang went on to make three astonishing films that have become part of twentieth century mythology.

Above *Nosferatu* – 1922, by the German director Friedrich Wilhelm Murnau, was his own unauthorized adaptation of *Dracula*. Several of his earlier expressionist films were based on scripts by Carl Mayer and Hans Janowitz – notably *Der Januskopf* – 1920, a Jekyll and Hyde story.

Left Fritz Lang's *Destiny* – 1921, was a key work for expressionist cinema. This doomladen medieval legend about a girl trying to wrest her loved one from 'weary death' was photographed in luminous visions of light and shade.

Above right A powerful poster for Lang's *Metropolis* – 1927.

Right Lang's *Metropolis* – 1927, gave a prophetic vision of a city of the future. The director had a generous budget for the film. It centred round a futuristic city where the worker-slaves revolt against their rich masters.

Above Expressionism met film in *The Cabinet of Dr Caligari* – 1919. Jointly written by an Austrian Expressionist, Carl Mayer, and a Czech, Hans Janowitz, *Caligari* was the outcome of their joint memories of psychiatric clinics, fairgrounds and sensational murders. The plot told of the mysterious Dr Caligari and a sleepwalker who carried out murders.

Dr Mabuse der Spieler – 1922, an ominous thriller about an omnipresent master-criminal; *Die Nibelungen* – 1924, a two-part retelling of old national legends, and *Metropolis* – 1927.

Expressionism vanishes

As if by magic, all the monsters of Expressionism faded away after 1924, the year that the Dawes Plan brought economic – and political – stability to Germany. It seemed as if the stabilized society felt a new ability to set aside the escapist phantoms and face reality once again. The tough, contemporary subjects of G. W. Pabst's films *Joyless Street* – 1925, *Secrets of a Soul* – 1926, *The Love of Jeanne Ney* – 1927 and *Pandora's Box* – 1928, seemed to relate closely to the work of the painters and writers of the *Neue Sachlichkeit* (New Objectivity) school. One celebrated painter of this school, Heinrich Zille, even gave his name to a series of 'Zille Films', whose themes were rooted in the Berlin street life which had provided the material for his series of very popular drawings and paintings.

The German cinema was to prolong the glories of this post-war decade into the early days of sound. But already Hollywood had begun a policy of pillaging European talent, and Lubitsch and his star Pola Negri, the directors Paul Leni, Murnau and the writer Mayer were all lured to the New World. In later years other German artists such as the directors Robert Siodmak, William Dieterle, Fred Zinneman, Billy Wilder and Fritz Lang, forced out of their homeland, were to contribute immeasurably to the shaping of American film.

Revolution:
Soviet Film in the 1920s

In the new Soviet Russia, the cinema gained a status it had never before enjoyed. For the first time it was *wanted*. Around 1920 Lenin made his famous declaration: 'For us the cinema is the most important of all the arts.' In 1919 the Soviet film industry was nationalized. Film schools were set up. *Agitki* – short propaganda and agitational films – were a crucial part of the earliest re-education programmes.

The years which followed the Civil War (1918–1920) were a period of unparalleled artistic fever in all fields of culture – literature, painting, theatre and cinema. The way was dramatically cleared for the new and young. In the heady atmosphere of these times, the newcomers felt a religious need to destroy the old and the past, and to create a new kind of art that should be truly revolutionary.

Revolutionary editing
Although they rejected the past, the men who most deeply influenced the new Soviet cinema had all made their first essays in film before the Revolution. Mayakovsky had been involved in a crazy avant garde experiment, *Drama in Futurist Cabaret No. 13*, as early as 1913. Vsevolod Meyerhold, the greatest figure in twentieth century Russian theatre, had made two films, *The Portrait*

of *Dorian Gray* and *The Strong Man* in 1915.

In 1917 an 18-year-old film designer, Lev Kuleshov (1899–1970), had written his first articles on film theory for a Moscow cinema magazine. In 1920 this young man was given a 'Workshop' to study film methods with a group of students. By 1922 he was able to demonstrate the so-called 'Kuleshov Effect'. D. W. Griffith had shown how pieces of film could be assembled to serve narrative and drama. Kuleshov showed how by altering their juxtaposition the very significance of pieces of film could be changed. Kuleshov's theories were put into practice in a series of films made by his own collective. But they appeared most notably in the work of his pupil Vsevolod Pudovkin in the great revolutionary film dramas *Mother*, – 1926, *The End of St. Petersburg* – 1927 and *Storm Over Asia*, (or *The Heir to Jenghis Khan*) – 1928.

Though Meyerhold never again worked in the cinema after the revolution, Grigori Kozintsev (1905–1973), one of the teenage artists of the 1920s who remained a leading figure in Soviet film-making for over forty years, said: 'The Soviet cinema learned much more from Meyerhold than the Soviet theatre.' Many of the directors who were to create the Soviet silent cinema fought for places in Meyerhold's Workshop. Among them

Below The energy and power Eisenstein generated through his images and editing were a revelation wherever *The Battleship Potemkin* was shown. It was made in 1925 to commemorate the 1905 revolution, and was based on the story of a mutiny on the *Potemkin*. The cast included the people of Odessa and sailors from the Red Navy.

was the most influential figure in Soviet cinema, Sergei Mikhailovich Eisenstein (1898–1948). Eisenstein in fact rather quickly grew restive working under another genius.

Eisenstein's theories of montage – clearly influenced by Meyerhold's theories of theatre – conflicted with those of the Kuleshov–Pudovkin school, providing one of the violent debates which spiced Soviet cultural life in the 1920s. The Kuleshov–Pudovkin school held that montage was a *linkage* of details. Eisenstein preferred to use editing for collision and shock.

The people as hero
The electrifying results of this approach were demonstrated in Eisenstein's first film, *Strike* – 1924, the first classic Soviet revolutionary film. It abandoned conventional story structure, mixed artificial and eccentric imports from the theatre and circus with the actuality of streets, factories and tenements, and replaced the 'hero' as protagonist with 'the mass'.

Eisenstein was next commissioned to make a great chronicle film to commemorate the twentieth anniversary of the revolutionary movements of 1905. In the event a single incident grew to make up the whole film: *The Battleship Potemkin* – 1925. Its revolutionary content was thought so potent that for years it was forbidden to be exhibited in many countries.

The revolutionary cinema found many routes and forms. Yutkevich and Kozintsev joined forces with another youngster, Leonid Trauberg, as FEKS (The Theatre of the Eccentric Actor) and brought to films the exuberance and eccentricity of their theatrical experiments. Their first extravagances were to mature into such a work as *New Babylon* – 1929, a sophisticated and sardonic interpretation of the Paris Commune of 1871.

The director Dziga Vertov (1896–1954) rejected all theatricality and artifice, He applied to cinema the ideas of Constructivist art. A forerunner of *cinéma vérité*, Vertov's argument for a cinema of unadulterated actuality was in fact undercut by his own intense and inescapable artistic intervention, even in what were apparently straight newsreels *Kino-Pravda (Film Truth)* – 1924, *Kino-Glaz (Film Eye)* – 1924.

From the Ukranian studios emerged Alexander Dovzhenko (1894–1956). He became one of the cornerstones of Soviet film. Having run through careers as teacher, diplomat and painter, Dovzhenko was a relatively mature man of 32 before he embarked on film-making. In *Zvenigora* – 1927, a wild mixture of folklore, magic and legend, *Arsenal* – 1929, and the majestic *Earth* – 1930, Dovzhenko revealed the possibility of using film with the concentration and exhilaration achieved in poetry.

Around these giants there was fevered activity and a whole generation of gifted directors – Esther Shub, with her creative compilations of old archive actuality, Abram Room, Boris Barnet, Viktor Turin, Yakov Protazanov and Mikhail

Kalatozov. But the enchanted era barely outlasted the decade. Lenin had died in 1924; Mayakovsky committed suicide in 1930. The heroic age of revolutionary art ended, but its legacy remained.

Above *October* – 1928, was made by Eisenstein to celebrate the tenth anniversary of the 1917 Revolution. In it he pursued to the limits his ideas on intellectual montage and screen imagery. Public hostility and official disapproval of his formalism and intellectualism mounted, so that he only completed three more films in Russia. Later a score by Dmitri Shostakovish was added to the film.

Left Dovzhenko's *Arsenal* – 1929 gave a dense, lyrical view of the revolutionary struggles of 1918. It looked particularly at the class struggle in the Ukraine in the Civil War which followed.

Hollywood's Golden Era:
The 1920s

For the American cinema, World War I of 1914–18 was the great watershed. The war effectively removed European economic competition. By 1918 the cinema had risen to the ranks of America's major industries.

The old pre-war film manufacturers had mostly merged into larger conglomerates or disappeared entirely from the scene. The firms that were to rule for the next half century were the giants – MGM, Fox, Paramount, Universal, Warners. All of them were dominated by men who not so long before had arrived in the New World as penniless immigrants from Europe, such as Louis B. Mayer, Sam Goldwyn (formerly Goldfish), William Fox, Adolph Zukor, Carl Laemmle and the Warner brothers. The energy of their rise was reflected in the organisation of the industry. The early 1920s witnessed cut-throat competition to gain control of exhibition outlets, which were now clearly the key to industrial domination.

Film technique and production values became much more elaborate. The great new picture palaces, culminating in Rothapfel's monumental 1927 Roxy (where he wanted 'to make a truck driver and his wife feel like a king and queen') changed the social standing of the movies. The film habit now spread to the middle classes.

A new world

Even apart from this social shift, the post-war audiences were different. There was a feeling of a new morality and of new times. In a phenomenally brief period the life and the face of the US were transformed by the automobile, the radio, the tabloid press, advertising, big business.

The post-war generation demanded sophistication, sex and entertainment appropriate to the Jazz Age. Nevertheless, however frivolous and amoral, the Jazz babies and dancing mothers of the 1920s films always tend to end up repentant and marrying the boy next door.

Even so the romantic sentiments, the stories of humble lives and the rewards of virtue, the Griffith heroines haloed in the curls of childhood innocence, were ousted. Sex had already reared its head in dramatic fashion during the war, when producer William Fox launched Theda Bara, building up a great structure of exotic and erotic myth around a quiet girl from Cincinnatti. But sex had now come to the movies. In 1927 Clara Bow starred in *It*, becoming a sex symbol for the period.

No one gauged the new mood more accurately than Cecil B. DeMille (1881–1959). Throughout his long career he revealed a genius for responding to the spirit and level of prevailing public taste. With *Old Wives for New* – 1918 DeMille introduced a series of comedies of manners, soon to be imitated throughout the industry. They reflected the post-Freudian fascination with sex and the general sense of social liberation. The American audience was introduced to a fictitious but glamorous world of country clubs, speakeasies, night clubs, wealth, leisure and moral frivolity – and tried its best to live up to it.

DOUGLAS FAIRBANKS AS THE GAUCHO

·UNITED ARTISTS PICTURE·

Right The cinema card for *Little Annie Rooney* – 1925, an early film starring Mary Pickford. Mary Pickford was famous for the young, ringleted innocents she played.

Left Douglas Fairbanks appears in *The Thief of Bagdad* – 1924, an exotic costume picture. It set new standards in opulence, as well as introducing accomplished 'magic' and 'flying carpet' effects.

Right The greatest and most legendary spectacle of the silent era was Fred Niblo's *Ben Hur* – 1925. The film was based on Lew Wallace's best-selling novel. Ben Hur was played by Ramon Novarro.

Right Theda Bara featured as the femme fatale in *Cleopatra* – 1917. Her real name was Theodosia Goodman; her professional name an anagram of Arab Death. The term 'vamp' (from vampire) was also invented for her.

Left Douglas Fairbanks in another dashing role in *The Gaucho* – 1927. He even dared mock the western.

Other darker aspects of the age were reflected in films. The gangster film, suggested as early as D. W. Griffith's *The Musketeers of Pig Alley* – 1912, came into its own in the late 1920s with the films of Josef von Sternberg (*Underworld* – 1927, *The Drag Net* and *The Docks of New York* – 1929).

Meanwhile a spirit of light-hearted scepticism entered comedy. The films of Harold Lloyd and Harry Langdon parodied American mores. The earliest successes of Douglas Fairbanks characteristically mocked at hallowed movie myths.

Yet it seemed that audiences wanted to delight in the new world and the brief euphoria that lasted until the Wall Street Crash, and at the same time to escape into nostalgia for lost innocence. Paradoxically at the same time as the western suffered the parodies of Fairbanks and Will Rogers, the genre entered its most epic and romantic phase. Masterpieces appeared – such as King Baggot's *Tumbleweeds* – 1925 (the last film of the old western hero W. S. Hart), John Ford's *The Iron Horse* – 1924 and *Three Bad Men* – 1926 and James Cruze's *The Covered Wagon* – 1923 and *The Pony Express* – 1925. Exploration of more innocent and primitive worlds, such as Robert Flaherty's *Nanook of the North* – 1922 and *Moana* – 1926 and Cooper and Schoedsack's *Grass* – 1925 and *Chang* – 1927 evidently stirred some instinct of escapist romanticism in the American audience.

At the height of its riches and extravagance, too, Hollywood made its most spectacular romantic and exotic costume-pictures. After *The Mark of Zorro* – 1920, Douglas Fairbanks abandoned for his screen characters the elegant lounge suit which had made him an all-American hero. He became in turn *Robin Hood* – 1922, *The Thief of Bagdad* – 1924 and *The Black Pirate* – 1926. DeMille, quick to sense a change of taste, moved on to the great biblical spectacles which were always to be associated with his name – starting with *The Ten Commandments* – 1923 and *King of Kings* – 1928.

The Men Who Made The Movies

It was a new generation of great creative figures who made Hollywood's golden era of silent films, between 1918 and the coming of sound. Some, such as the directors Allan Dwan and Herbert Brenon, had established themselves in the last days before the war. But few of the major figures of the first generation survived into the 1920s. The great Griffith himself was at the peak of his fame at the end of the war. He went on to make new masterpieces – *Broken Blossoms* – 1919, *Way Down East* – 1920 and *Orphans of the Storm* – 1922. But by the end of the decade, at 55 years old, Griffith had become an embarrassing survival from the past.

DeMille, who had come from the theatre, was a leader of the new generation. But the greatest figure to emerge at the end of the war was Erich von Stroheim (1885–1957). An immigrant from Vienna, he encouraged the story that he was an army officer of noble family. Stroheim started his film career under Griffith as an actor and assistant. His own trilogy on the theme of adultery (*Blind Husbands* – 1918, *The Devil's Passkey* – 1919 and *Foolish Wives* – 1921), his Viennese triptych (*Merry-go-round* – 1922, *The Merry Widow* – 1925 and *The Wedding March* – 1926) and his monumental realist study of small-town America, *Greed* – 1923, brought to the screen a depth of psychological realism, a perception of the darker areas of sexuality and a genius for *mise-en-scène* far different from the surface sophistication of a De-Mille. This wayward, uncomfortable and uncom-promising genius, however, found it especially difficult to accomodate the commercial establishment. One after the other Stroheim's films were taken out of his hands. The studio cut *Greed* to a fraction of its finished length. After 1930 Stroheim was able to direct only one film, *Walking down Broadway* – 1933.

Looting Europe

It was a deliberate policy of the ascendant American cinema to plunder talent from Europe. This had the valuable dual effect of enriching Hollywood studios and impoverishing commercial rivals. The Swedish cinema, for instance, was irreparably damaged when its greatest directors, Victor Sjöström (1879–1960) and Mauritz Stiller (1883–1928), along with Stiller's protegée Greta Garbo, were lured away to the States.

Leading French directors such as Léonce Perret – noted for his very advanced *L'Enfant de Paris* – 1913 – and Alice Guy-Blaché – the world's first woman director – arrived to work in Hollywood. The French comedian Max Linder had a brief, disastrous career in America. The rise of a new reactionary régime in Hungary brought men such as Alexander Korda (1893–1956), Michael Curtiz (1888–1962) and Béla Lugosi (1888–1956). Soon no film's credits would be without its quota of Austro-Hungarian names. When the Hollywood musical was born in the 1930s, the influence and heritage of the Viennese operetta was to be strongly marked.

Below Rudolph Valentino's acting in *The Sheik* – 1921 brought him an unprecedented popularity. He followed this with *Blood and Sand* – 1922 and *Son of the Sheikh* – 1926. He projected a bold, but fundamentally romantic, sexuality. His funeral was marked by scenes of mass hysteria.

Recruitment from Germany began in 1923, as the old hostilities were cooling. Lubitsch was brought to Hollywood by Mary Pickford. Although their partnership was difficult, within the year *The Marriage Circle* – 1924 had launched Lubitsch on a series of films whose visual wit and 'Continental' sophistication in their treatment of sex and society made 'The Lubitsch touch' famous. Other German directors had less luck. Paul Leni made several excellent comedy thrillers before his early death. But, after one masterwork, *Sunrise* – 1927 – the true apogee of the German Expressionist cinema – F. W. Murnau and Carl Mayer met only frustration. Mayer left for England; Murnau was killed in a car accident before the première of his last film *Tabu* – 1931.

Home-grown talent

The immigrants also of course included the Viennese Josef von Sternberg and the London-born Chaplin, who made *A Woman of Paris* – 1923 and *The Gold Rush* – 1925. There was also a group of native directors who harnessed individuality and supreme craftsmanship to the needs of the commercial cinema. Many of these men dominated Hollywood production for the next two decades.

John Ford (1895–1973) became the unequalled poet of the western. King Vidor (b.1896) was the most versatile of directors, ranging from melodrama (*La Bohème* – 1925) to the war epic (*The Big Parade* – 1925) and from comedy (Marion Davies in *The Patsy* – 1927 and *Show People* – 1928) to the realism of *The Crowd* – 1928. Clarence Brown's taste and authentic romanticism made him an ideal director for stars as different as Rudolph Valentino (*The Eagle* – 1926) and Greta Garbo (*Flesh and the Devil* – 1927, *Woman of Affairs* – 1928 and *Anna Christie* – 1930).

Tod Browning (1882–1962) was a master of the bizarre and horrific, in films which frequently starred the inimitable Lon Chaney. Frank Capra (b.1897), a Sicilian emigré with a sharply critical eye for the manners of his new homeland, developed out of his brilliant silent comedies starring Harry Langdon the whimsical vein of social comedy that was to reach its peak in the sound era. Rex Ingram's taste for exotic adventure launched Valentino's career as a star in *The Four Horsemen of the Apocalypse* – 1922. Meanwhile Buster Keaton brought silent screen comedy to a peak of cinematic and choreographic achievement, with films such as *The Navigator* – 1924 and *The General* – 1926.

Hollywood in the 1920s seemed to be one of the true golden periods in art. The industry, the public and the creators – including stars ranging from goddesses to babies and such strangely gifted creatures as the dog-star Rin-tin-tin – were briefly in a magical balance and harmony.

Meanwhile in Britain by 1925 probably ninety-five percent of screen time was taken by American films. Home production revived with the Cinematograph Films Act of 1927, and the earliest films of Alfred Hitchcock.

Left Buster Keaton in *The Love Nest* – 1923. The main elements to his comic appeal were an insistence on avoiding the impossible or ridiculous, and his own emotional restraint, which sets up a basic calm amidst the wildest events.

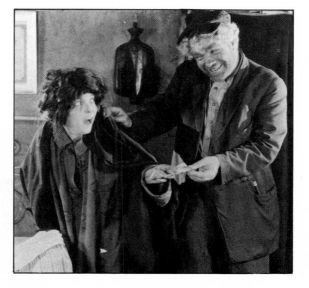

Above F. W. Murnau made the memorable *Sunrise* – 1927, with its theme of universal poetic tragedy. Though some of his aims were altered from economic considerations, the film was technically and aesthetically remarkable.

Left Erich von Stroheim's *Greed* – 1923, was originally ten hours long. It was edited down by a series of processes to two and a half hours, leaving only a shadow of its director's powerful intentions.

France Resurgent:
Impressionism and Surrealism

The end of the war found France's once supreme film empire in ruins, and commercial production in a state of creative atrophy. Yet paradoxically in this economically depressed period, France was to make its most significant contributions to the art of silent film, generally through pictures made for little or no money, and outside the commercial establishment. The first inspiration came from a writer and critic, Louis Delluc (1890–1924) who died aged only 34, at the peak of creative activity. Delluc rejected most predominant French film traditions. He pointed to the achievements in the American cinema of Griffith, Ince and Chaplin, as well as to the German Expressionists and the individualist work of the Scandinavian directors Victor Sjöström and Mauritz Stiller.

French impressionists
Delluc himself passed from theorizing to making his own films. A number of young film makers grouped round him. They included Germaine Dulac (who directed Delluc's first scenario *La Fête espagnole* – 1919, Jean Epstein and Marcel L'Herbier. This group took the name 'Impressionists'. A former Symbolist poet, L'Herbier's aestheticism led him consciously to introduce into films influences from the plastic arts. His first films, *Rose France* – 1919 and *L'Homme du large*, were literally Impressionist in their visual style. In *Don Juan et Faust* – 1924 he adopted cubist design; while *L'Inhumaine* – 1924 was designed by the painters Fernand Léger and Mallet Stevens.

L'Herbier's flirtations with more firmly established arts were good for both morale and reputation. 'This group of men,' wrote the French historian Georges Sadoul, 'was the first in Europe to assert the stature of the film as an art – the equal (or even the superior) of music, literature and the theatre – and to obtain recognition for it as such . . . Henceforward the cinema became a subject of dinner-table conversation like the novel or the play and there emerged a group among the intellectual élite for whom it was a major artistic preoccupation.'

The 'Impressionists' became known as France's 'First Avant-Garde'. The Second Avant-Garde, too, was stimulated by contact with literary and artistic movements of the 1920s. The artists of Dada eagerly embraced the cinema. Man Ray premièred his *Le Retour à la raison* at the famous Dada assembly, *Le Cour à la barbe* – 1923. The following year the young René Clair made his first film *Entr'acte* as an interlude in the Dada ballet *Relâche. Entr'acte* and Clair's first feature film *Paris qui dort* – 1924 belong perhaps to the last stages of Dada. Clair was soon to contribute heavily to the revival of France's commercial cinema with his sparkling comedies *An Italian Straw Hat* – 1927 and *Les Deux Timidies* – 1928 and the new style of musical films he made in the early sound period

Out of the Dadaist *Cour à la barbe* assembly emerged the Surrealist movement. Germaine

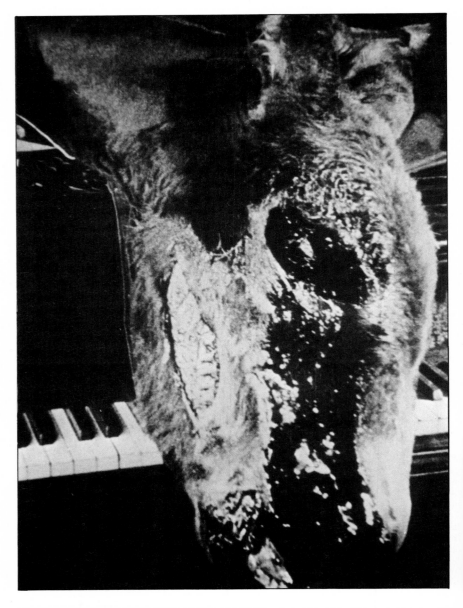

Dulac's *La Coquille et le clergyman* – 1928 (The Seashell and the Clergyman), with a scenario by Antonin Artaud, was claimed as a surrealist film. So too was Jean Cocteau's very personal and symbolic sound film *Le Sang d'un poéte* – 1930. André Breton, high priest of Surrealism, dismissed Dulac's film as 'an aesthetic essay'. In Britain it was refused a certificate by the censors: 'This film is so cryptic as to be almost meaningless. If there is a meaning, it is doubtless objectionable.'

Only after seeing *Un Chien andalou* – 1928 would Breton declare: 'Yes, *this* is surrealism.' It was the work of two young Spaniards in Paris,

Luis Buñuel and Salvador Dali. They conceived the scenario out of the dreams which they related to each other every morning. Its images of brutality and horror (an eye slashed with a razor, an ants' nest in the palm of a hand) seem truly to emerge from the subconscious.

One-man avant garde
Standing apart from the official avant-gardes, Abel Gance, throughout a phenomenally long career, has been his own avant-garde. Born in 1889 and already a film actor in 1909, he was still in 1978 planning films he dreamed of making. In *La Folie du Dr Tube* – 1915 he used the camera subjectively four years before *Caligari*. In *J'Accuse* – 1919, a pacifist statement, he introduced actuality material into a fictional narrative. The impassioned editing of *La Roue* – 1922 was an undoubted influence on Eisenstein and Soviet film theory. Gance's masterwork *Napoleon* – 1927 employed mobile and hand-held camera techniques decades ahead of their time.

Towards the end of the silent period, the interest of the Second Avant-Garde moved in new directions, influenced perhaps by the realist lessons of the Soviet film. Marcel Carné (b.1909), who was to become the outstanding figure in French cinema in the late 1930s and early 1940s, and Alberto Cavalcanti (b.1897), who was shortly to become a major feature director in France and Britain, both made their débuts with outstanding documentaries drawn from Parisian daily life: respectively *Nogent, eldorado du dimanche* – 1929 and *Rien que les heures* – 1926. *À Propos de Nice* – 1930 marked the début of Jean Vigo (1903–1934) as a director. In a tragically brief life and career he established himself as the French cinema's incomparable poet. The avant gardes of the 1920s were impoverished and often reviled. But they were preparing the ground for the triumphant renaissance of the French cinema in the next decade.

The Sound Revolution 1

The movies were never silent. From the very beginning, music played an essential part in building up the emotional response of the audience. Emile Reynaud's *Pantomimes Lumineuses* had a specially composed musical score by Gaston Paulin. The Lumière brothers advertised that a saxophone quartet would accompany the pictures at their little theatre in Paris' Boulevard St Denis in 1897. Camille Saint-Saens was commissioned to write a special score for the prestigious *Assassination of the Duc de Guise* – 1908. The impressionist score compiled by Joseph Carl Briel for Griffith's *The Birth of a Nation* – 1915 was played at the première by seventy performers from the Los Angeles Symphony Orchestra. Even the most modest flea-pit had its resident pianist. Apart from the music, the more ambitious theatres also had sound effects departments to provide the clatter of hooves, the crack of gun shots and the wail of angel choirs.

The first whispers

The search for a mechanical means of providing sound accompaniments went back to the earliest days of the cinema. Edison, indeed, had only been attracted to the idea of moving pictures as a complement to his Phonograph, first devised in 1877. His first Kinetoscopes incorporated sound apparatus. The ambitious Lumières took out a patent for synchronizing cinema and the Phonograph. At the 1900 Paris Exposition no less than three sound film systems competed. At the *Expositions Phono-Cinema-Theatre* for instance, you could see *and hear* Sarah Bernhardt in the duel scene from *Hamlet*, the music hall comedian Little Tich in his Dance of the Big Boots, and a variety of other theatrical celebrities of the day.

Experiments continued throughout the first quarter of the century. Chief among the problems which faced the intrepid inventors were reducing the sizes of the vast horns required for acoustic recording, synchronizing the sound with the image, and amplifying the volume sufficiently to fill large picture-theatres.

Research intensified after World War I, and with the development of radio in the 1920s. By 1925 Dr Lee de Forest (who had invented the Audion amplifier twenty years earlier) made and showed a whole series of 'Photophone' shorts. They were seen and heard at the British Empire Exhibition at Wembley in 1925.

But even though sound films had become a reality by the mid-1920s, the Americam film-makers did not rush to make them. The introduction of sound would mean that their magnificent studios would be made obsolete, as new equipment and sound-proofed stages became necessary. The installation of sound systems in movie theatres would cause a costly upheaval and a period of chaos – not least since the various available sound systems were mutually incompatible. The silent film was an international medium, whereas talkies would restrict markets to countries speaking the same language. The stars

Left A special Vitaphone gramophone record with music to accompany *The Lady of the Rose*. This sound process was introduced in 1926 by Warner Brothers.

Right The Vivaphone was another early method of providing film sound.

Below An attempt to record sound and film simultaneously at Edison's Black Maria studio in 1894.

Bottom A very early method of providing sound for the movies: the Chronophone of 1904.

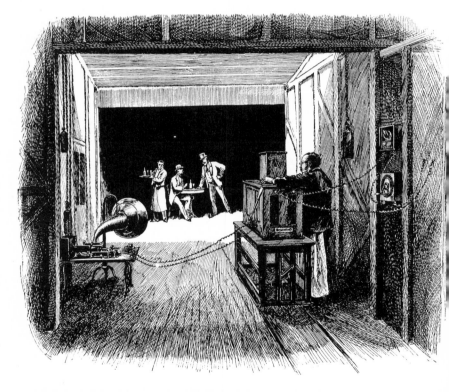

The Sound Revolution 2

who had achieved universal fame in the silent days were trained in the art of mime. It was uncertain how any of them would cope with the difficulties of spoken drama. The movie industry had too much to lose.

The talkies take over

There was one company, however, which at that moment had little or nothing to lose. The Warner brothers were first-generation Polish Americans who had gone into the nickelodeon business in 1903. They built their first studio in 1919, but by 1926 had fallen behind in the race to gain control of distribution outlets. As a last chance gamble, they built a great new Hollywood theatre, acquired the old Vitagraph company, with its fifteen cinemas, and established a new subsidiary, Vitaphone Corporation, to develop synchronized sound films.

The first Vitaphone programme was premièred on 6 August 1926. It consisted of *Don Juan*, starring John Barrymore, in the most lavish production Warner Brothers had yet made. It featured synchronous sound effects and a specially composed score by William Axt. The main feature was accompanied by eight classy short films, featuring such distinguished musical personalities as Giovanni Martinelli and the violinist Mischa Elman.

Don Juan failed to create the sensation for which the Warner brothers had hoped. But their second synchronized sound feature revolutionized motion pictures. The Warners decided to film *The Jazz Singer*, a musical stage success of 1925–26 which had starred George Jessel as the cantor's son who wants to become a jazz singer. Jessel's fee was too high; so instead the Warners engaged Al Jolson, also a major star, but eager to get the part. The director was Alan Crosland, who had previously made *Don Juan*.

The Jazz Singer was premiered in New York on 6 October 1927. Public and critics alike were enchanted. Jolson sang six songs including *Toot Toot Tootsie Goodbye* and *Mammy*. But the greatest thrill was to hear him speak his catchphrase: 'You ain't heard nothin' yet.'

After this there was no turning back. The Warner brothers put Jolson under contract (*The Singing Fool* was to outdo the success of *The Jazz Singer*) and embarked on a hasty programme of talking pictures. The other companies were forced to keep pace. Fox launched its Movietone newsreel, and made a part-talkie, *The Air Circus*. Universal ruined Paul Fejos' marvellous *Lonesome* – 1928 by grafting a clumsy track onto it. Paramount did a better job with their audio addition to *Beggars of Life*. MGM cautiously and cunningly awaited the development of improved techniques; in 1929 they released *Broadway Melody* which inaugurated a new Hollywood genre, the musical.

By 1930 the silent film was as extinct as the great auk. The effect on the film world was spectacular. Players and directors were imported from

Broadway. The new Hollywood names of the early thirties included Paul Muni, Edward G. Robinson, Spencer Tracy, Clark Gable, Humphrey Bogart, James Cagney and Bette Davis. Silent stars lacking the ability of a Gary Cooper or a Wallace Beery to adapt to the requirements of the new medium, rapidly slipped from view. After an uneasy period of play-adataptions and non-stop talk, new genres – such as the musical and gangster film – began to appear.

FIFTY YEARS OF SOUND CINEMA

On 6 October 1977 the sound cinema celebrated its fiftieth birthday. For on that day fifty years earlier *The Jazz Singer* had opened at New York's Warner Theater, and introduced the moviegoing public to the wonders of synchronized sound.

The cause of sound was fought and won long ago. More interesting is the development of sound cinema, over fifty speaking years, as a medium of entertainment, of art, of education and of propaganda. For the cinema takes in all four elements, often in hybrid confusion, and until television arrived in the early 1950s no medium of communication had ever rivalled film in the breadth of its appeal or the versatility of its performance.

This section of the book conducts the reader decade by decade through the sound cinema's history. Different countries and different movements have dominated that history at different times. French cinema and the work of Renoir stood out during the 1930s; Italian neo-realism emerged as a powerful force in the post-war 1940s; in the 1950s Western filmgoers 'discovered' Japanese cinema; in the 1960s the French New Wave broke upon the movie world; and in the 1970s television styles dramatically changed feature film making.

Several things, however, remain constant. Film is film whether projected in the grandeur of 35mm in 3,000-seat cinemas or shown on a small television set in your own living room. The essential virtues of film stay the same: immediacy, accessibility, the most graphic representation of reality 'as he knows it' that man has yet produced.

The Thirties 1

The key factor in the cinema of the 1930s was of course the sound revolution. By 1930 virtually all films made in Hollywood and Western Europe were talking pictures; by 1934 even Russia and Japan, slower to make the necessary technical conversions, had fallen into line. And as the moving picture suddenly mislaid its ability to move, as stars and directors fell by the wayside, temperamentally or technically ill-equipped to deal with the problem of dramatic dialogue, intellectuals and theorists gloomily predicted the end of the art of cinema.

Curiously, amid the general ferment while the major Hollywood studios reorganized, re-equipped and rethought, only the film-makers themselves seem to have realised that nothing need have changed – aesthetically and theoretically at least. The characters in silent pictures had always talked; directors like Erich von Stroheim and F. W. Murnau had always lamented the need to illustrate what was said either by written titles or by explanatory mime (or both); and synchronized sound was now simply filling that long-felt gap.

The movies freeze

Given the phenomenal public response to sound, however – all the early talkies were hugely successful at the box office, even when mocked for their poor quality – the studios decreed that films should become 'all talking, all singing, all dancing'. Broadway was rifled for stars, directors and writers, plays were taken over wholesale, and the musical was born. At the same time – as so often mistaking today's news for tomorrow's sensation – Hollywood also decreed that audiences must not feel cheated; they must *see* the actors deliver their synchronized lines word-by-word. The result was that style regressed to the theatrical 'tableau' of the primitive days before it dawned that an actor's feet need not necessarily be included in the shot.

Many of the early sound films were incredibly stilted, with cumbersome cameras pinned to the studio floor while actors laboriously enunciated screeds of dialogue taken over whole from some Broadway hit. A myth persists that all American films of this period were equally bad – simply marking time while film-makers such as René Clair in France and Alfred Hitchcock in England kept the flag of cinema flying by experimenting in the non-realistic use of sound. This myth is simply not true.

Rouben Mamoulian's *Applause* – 1929 not only used sound both tactfully and inventively, but did so without sacrificing any of the silent cinema's fluid visual techniques. Mamoulian, a successful Broadway director brought in to apply theatrical methods to films, instead became fascinated by the cinema's own potential. Refusing to be tyrannized by the sound camera or to be dominated by dialogue, he evolved a graceful, flowing style. His films were studded with experiments designed to increase the talking picture's vocabulary – notably by using subjective sound (*City Streets* – 1931) and non-realistic sound (*Love Me Tonight* – 1932).

Above This poster for Rouben Mamoulian's *Applause* – 1929 – reflects the fluid and rhythmic style which marks his films. For *Applause* he put the entire filming booth on wheels to achieve mobility.

Below 42nd Street – 1933 was the first of Busby Berkeley's spectacular musicals for Warner Bros. In this number, '42nd Street', the Manhattan skyline itself dances – each chorus-girl carrying a sky-scraper. The star, Ruby Keeler, descends the stairs.

Mamoulian's chief contribution, however, was what he has called his 'principle of integrating all theatrical elements into one stylized rhythmic pattern.' In other words, music and dialogue were made to move as much as the visual elements. The result was a series of films which seem to be choreographed as much as directed, because the camera sets a pace (variable in its rhythms) to which the sound-track is rigorously tailored. *Love Me Tonight* – shot to a pre-recorded score by Rodgers and Hart, with the actors' movements echoing its rhythms, and dialogue scenes evolving subtly into musical numbers (and vice versa) – was a landmark in the history of the 'total' film musical. The lesson was not fully absorbed until Arthur Freed's MGM musicals in the 1940s.

Meanwhile, something like the same result was reached by Howard Hawks (b.1896) and William Wellman (b.1896), who had begun directing towards the end of the silent period. They made the transition to sound simply by ignoring its supposed problems. Wellman's *Other Men's Women* – 1931 is a typical example. In a period dominated by play adaptations in stagey sets, it is remarkable for the almost documentary detail with which it portrays a sleepy backwater town with its quiet suburbs and, nearer to its vast complex of railway lines, shunting yards and engine sheds, a grimy hash-joint and a steamy little dance-hall. Above all, it has *pace:* a rich cinematic drive that never loses its grip after the dynamic opening sequence in which a railwayman leaps off his train as it passes the hash-joint, tears inside for some snappy backchat with the waitress, gulps his food, busily counting all the time, and leaps out again just catching the last coach as it rattles by.

Studio style

Warner Brothers musicals perhaps reached their finest flowering in the highlit and surreal choreographic fantasies of Busby Berkeley. *42nd Street* – 1933 was a fierce and funny depiction of backstage anxieties and jealousies. *Gold Diggers of 1933* included the number 'My Forgotten Man', a moving, passionate statement of resentment at the Depression.

Meanwhile Paramount excelled in light comedy of all types, possibly due to the influence of Ernst Lubitsch. Comedy ranged from the sophisticated brand of Lubitsch himself to the broader versions of the Marx brothers, W. C. Fields and Mae West. Other Paramount stars included George Raft, Ray Milland, Fredric March, Cary Grant, Dorothy Lamour and Carole Lombard. 'If it's a Paramount Picture, it's the best show in town' was the studio's slogan. Some of their 'best' shows were the Marx Brothers' early films, *Monkey Business*–1931, *Horse Feathers* – 1932 and *Duck Soup* – 1933. Mae West displayed a unique combination of sex, humour and suggestiveness in films, which had to be toned down when censorship increased in the mid–1930s. Her most celebrated innuendo was: 'Come up and see me sometime.'

Left *King of Jazz* – 1930 was an all-star musical with extravagant set-pieces such as this, where Paul Whiteman's orchestra plays from the top of a giant piano. The film also included Bing Crosby, Gershwin's 'Rhapsody in Blue' and a brief animated sequence.

Below Busby Berkeley choreographed the musical *Golddiggers of 1933* – 1933, directed by Mervyn LeRoy. Here Renee Whitway plays her illuminated violin.

The Thirties 2

The gangster movie successfully established itself as a new genre, introduced very largely by Wellman (*Public Enemy* – 1931) and Hawks (*Scarface* – 1932). They provided the racy visual style that went with the rattle of machine-guns, chases and whiplash dialogue. With their hair-raising speed, their stylized violence, and their through-the-looking-glass morality (battling against society, the criminal was just as much a hero as Chaplin's 'little fellow'), the gangster movies joined the Marx Brothers in filling an anarchic gap vacant since the demise of slapstick comedy.

Sound was mastered very quickly – even though the embryonic musical could do little better than imitate lavish stage revues, and adapted plays had their casts languishing in theatrical groupings. Roland West's *Alibi* – 1929 made extraordinarily effective use of dramatic silence, broken only by noises off. King Vidor's *Hallelujah* – 1929 had a remarkable sequence: a pursuit through a swamp, accompanied only by the sounds of panting breath, twigs snapping, water lapping and birds twittering. In *The Front Page* – 1931 Lewis Milestone matched a mobile camera to rapid-fire dialogue (he cut within scenes, and had the actors speak twice as fast as usual), allotting dialogue much the same function as a sight gag. Above all Walt Disney, in his first Mickey Mouse cartoons and Silly Symphonies, showed how music and dialogue could be used to counterpoint the images, giving them a wit, rhythm and dramatic impact they might otherwise have lacked.

Making dreams

In other words, by 1932 Hollywood was ready to enter its most prolific period of productivity as the Dream Factory, flooding the world with a dazzling stream of superbly crafted light entertainment. With the spectre of the Depression lurking just around the corner, escapism was the order of the day. With the best cameramen and designers at its disposal, Hollywood created a glittering never-never land in which stars played shopgirls wearing exclusive fashion gowns, virtue was threatened but rarely succumbed, and a happy ending was the rule and the goal towards which all paths led.

There were of course 'serious' films: for instance the social conscience series, spearheaded by Warner Brothers and dealing with such subjects as chain gangs, lynching, prison reform, juvenile delinquency and the Ku Klux Klan; or the historical biographies in which Paul Muni played Pasteur fighting for science, Zola fighting for Dreyfus, and Juarez fighting for Mexico. The pills were always cunningly sugared, however, and by staunchly implying that a little goodwill and common decency will conquer a lot of social ills, they differed very little from Frank Capra's enormously successful series of folksy fairy-tale comedies, in which the whimsical, grass-roots integrity of the hero (Gary Cooper in *Mr Deeds Goes to Town* – 1936, James Stewart in *Mr Smith Goes to Washington* – 1939) is enough to set civic

Left Matt Doyle (Edward Woods) is cut down by a hail of bullets from a rival gang in *Public Enemy* – 1931. The film told in recognizable detail the story of the contemporary urban gangster Hymie Weiss. The film's spare script and economical visual style hinted at the social deprivation in which such gangsters thrived. *Public Enemy* starred James Cagney as Tom Powers and Jean Harlow as Gwen, with Cagney excelling in his role of arrogant, edgy gangland leader.

Below The family offers thanks in Frank Capra's Oscar-winning *You Can't Take it With You* – 1938. The director put his lovable characters into topical situations – and provided an optimistic solution. This helps account for his great success in the Depression years. This film has a complex plot hinging on Grandpa Vanderhof's decision to retire early and enjoy life, and builds up to a hectic and riotous climax.

corruption and political chicanery tumbling like a pack of cards.

Even *Fury* – 1936, Fritz Lang's first film in America, had to pull its punches – not so much in its treatment of the psychology of a lynch mob as in the chain reaction that ensues. The innocent victim (Spencer Tracy) survives and turns himself into a one-man lynch mob thirsting for vengeance even more horribly because he does it in cold blood; but he has to have a change of heart in time for the happy ending, thus negating the story's most chilling implications.

The creation of Hollywood's air-conditioned dream-world was only possible because location-shooting – rife if not the rule during the silent period – now became very much the exception. Reality rarely reared its head. The dream world, a sort of collective wish fulfilment, became viable given the superlatively skilled collaborative talents of the creative team of actors, writers, directors, cameramen, designers and composers.

Hollywood auteurs

Not that Hollywood in the 1930s had no auteurs: Josef von Sternberg, with his series of glittering erotic fantasies starring Marlene Dietrich as the incandescent object of man's pain and desire, is sufficient evidence to the contrary. But Sternberg's closed universe, maintained even without Dietrich and the baroque embellishments that accompanied her mystique, was in fact his idiosyncratic variation on one of the patterns patented by Hollywood. Other film-makers were less fortunate; the studio system kept them sternly in

place as employees, often typecasting them in genres where they had been successful but in which they had no particular interest, or assigning them to routine chores where their opportunities for personal expression were minimal.

John Ford (1895–1973) – now inseparably associated with the Western – in fact made only one during the 1930s: *Stagecoach* – 1939. Nothing Ford made during this period was without interest – even his Shirley Temple vehicle, *Wee Willie Winkie* – 1937. Sometimes he achieved a quality entirely his own, as with his trio of loving forays into small-town America starring the comedian Will Rogers (*Dr Bull*, *Judge Priest* and *Steamboat Round the Bend* – 1935).

After a phenomenal success with *Frankenstein* – 1931, James Whale (1889–1957) was coerced into reluctantly adding to it three more horror film classics: *The Old Dark House* – 1932, *The Invisible Man* – 1933 and *The Bride of Frankenstein* – 1935. What makes these films so remarkable, quite apart from the impeccable visual flair with which Whale handles the gothic elements, is that they are also devastatingly funny comedies of manners. They not only inquire with sympathetic interest into the private lives of the monsters, but analyze the perverse mixture of social savoir faire and role-playing displayed by their masters and victims. Whale's forte, in other words, was black humour, based on an acute awareness of how lives are built on lies. Hardly a recommendation for employment in the Dream Factory; and Whale's career, despite some excellent films made against the grain, gradually faded into oblivion.

Above The famous moment in William Wellman's *Public Enemy* when James Cagney pushes a grapefruit into Mae Clarke's face. The film stands as a good representative of the Warner Brothers' gangster movies of the 1930's.

Above Cecil B. DeMille's western *The Plainsman* – 1937 was loaded with action, and starred Gary Cooper and Jean Arthur.

The Thirties 3

Right James Whale's *Frankenstein* – 1931, gave Universal a reputation for horror films. Boris Karloff was the monster that ran amok, created by the scientist named Frankenstein. Whale's film, based on Mary Shelley's novel of the same title, was chilling but not gruesome in its evocation of terror.

Below *Steamboat Willie* – 1928 was the first of Walt Disney's Mickey Mouse cartoons to use sound. Music was an intrinsic part of its visual structure; the animal concert during which the cow's teeth became a xylophone, and its udder a bagpipe is the first example of Disney's visual orchestration.

Some major Hollywood directors found themselves condemned either not to work at all (Erich von Stroheim) or, like King Vidor (b. 1896 –) and Frank Borzage (1893–1961), to return only intermittently to their preoccupations with, respectively, social commitment and a gently doomladen, romantic *angst*. William K. Howard (1899–1954), who showed alarming tendencies towards intellectualism (his *The Power and the Glory* – 1933 in some ways prefigured *Citizen Kane* – 1941), found work increasingly hard to come by. Rowland Brown resented interference to the point of reputedly hitting a front office executive. His three highly promising films (*Quick Millions* – 1931, *Hell's Highway* – 1932 and *Blood Money* – 1933) showed unmistakable signs of suggesting that crime might very well pay and that justice is anything but infallible; after this, Brown could find work only as a scriptwriter.

Yet repressive as it was, the studio system had its compensations. Overall, Hollywood films of the 1930s had a technical skill and a stylish

elegance never equalled before or since by any other national cinema. The novelists and play-wrights imported to deal with sound might lament that they had sold their souls to the devil, but they also mined a seemingly inexhaustible vein of dazzling verbal wit streaks ahead of anything the scenario-writers of the silents could provide. The film-makers, following the lead offered by such men of flair and theatrical experience as Mamoulian, Whale and George Cukor, soon learned to sift these outpourings and subject their brightest nuggets to the discipline of movement.

Screwball to spectacular

This period was above all marked by its sophisti-cated comedy. This sophistication was trans-formed, by way of spiralling fantasy and an increasingly frenetic pace, into the 'screwball' comedies (Leo McCarey's *The Awful Truth* – 1937, Howard Hawks' *Bringing Up Baby* – 1938) that were the glory of the day. Though they frequently resorted to elements of slapstick, such films nevertheless remained worlds apart from the silent slapstick comedies because their main ingredient – sophisticated verbal wit – erected a sort of class distinction. The best exponents of screwball comedy were performers usually associated with rather more dignified proceedings – for example, Katharine Hepburn, Irene Dunne, Melvyn Douglas and Cary Grant.

If one had to pick a single film-maker repre-sentative of all that was best in Hollywood at this time, it would probably have to be George Cukor (b.1899). It was Cukor who directed Garbo in the exquisite *Camille* – 1936, W. C. Fields in the delightful *David Copperfield* – 1934 and Katharine Hepburn in the wonderfully tender and touching *Little Women* – 1934; he brought a highly distinctive intelligence, taste and cinematic style to everything he did. These three films, along with *Holiday* – 1938 and *The Philadelphia Story* – 1940 rank among the decade's masterpieces.

Yet Cukor was also the studio system's para-gon: a brilliant craftsman able to turn his hand to almost anything, primarily an illustrator (his best work is adapted from plays or novels) and not in the least inclined to use his work as a means of personal expression. This partly explains why Cukor was originally assigned to direct the mammoth cooperative venture set up to produce the intelligent, tasteful, stylish and (as a work of art) largely anonymous *Gone with the Wind* – 1939. Cukor was replaced as director by Victor Fleming after several weeks of shooting – which apparently made not the slightest difference to the film's financial or artistic success.

In theory the sound revolution should have stimulated national production elsewhere since it introduced major language barriers. In practice, although Hollywood panicked to the extent of making carbon-copies of its own films in French-German-Spanish- and Italian-speaking versions, events were conspiring to favour Hollywood in several of the major film-making countries.

A decadent decade

In Germany sound got off to a flying start – even the inevitable operettas revealing a delicacy and verve that made the transition from silent days almost imperceptible. Infused with naturalistic settings and performances from the chamber-film (*Kammerspiel*) techniques developed by Murnau and Lupu Pick, Expressionism had become oriented towards the sort of heightened realism that charged Josef von Sternberg's *The Blue Angel* – 1930 and Fritz Lang's twin masterpieces, *M* – 1931 and *The Last Will of Dr Mabuse* – 1932.

Simultaneously an embryonic movement of social awareness and protest was putting out feelers. G. W. Pabst launched moving if slightly simplistic appeals for human brotherhood using the horrors of war (*Westfront 1918* – 1930) and a mine disaster (*Kameradschaft* – 1931). Leontine Sagan's *Mädchen in Uniform* – 1931, set in a boarding-school for girls, attacked tyrannical authoritarianism; Richard Oswald's *The Captain from Kopenick* – 1931 satirized Prussian mili-tarism; *Kühle Wampe* – 1932, directed by Slatan Dudow and scripted by Brecht, criticized the regime from an openly communist standpoint:

Above One of the most famous fantasy scenes: King Kong, the giant ape on the rampage, meets a spectacular death on top of New York's Empire State Building. *King Kong* – 1933 was one of the earliest films to use back-projection.

The Thirties 4

Above The final sight of Greta Garbo in poignant close-up, standing in the prow of her dead lover's ship, in *Queen Christina* – 1934. In this, her ideal role, Garbo played a ruler brought up as a man, but who discovers her womanhood through love.

That the Nazi writing was already on the wall is clearly apparent from the traumatic social decadence of the milieu in *The Blue Angel*, where the sado-masochism is not leavened by the irreality of fantasy as in the American Sternberg-Dietrich films. Similarly the work of Fritz Lang replaced the inner-directed spiritual *angst* of the Expressionist period with a more objective torment. *M* and *The Last Will of Dr Mabuse*, ostensibly thrillers, are both brilliant in their use of sound (for instance the whistled motif, signifying an impulse to kill, that periodically breaks the child-murderer's habitual silence in *M*). Both are also charged with an extraordinary apprehension of evil – the insane lust for power, attended by a will to destruction and a perversion of justice that make one child-murderer's involuntary crimes pale into insignificance.

Fascist film-makers
The Nazi period, dominated by nationalist fervour, anti-Semitic diatribes and turgid cavalcades of German history, is distinguished chiefly by Leni Riefenstahl's records of the 1934 Nuremberg Rally (*Triumph of the Will*) and of the 1936 Berlin Olympics (*Olympia* – 1938). Hymns to the Nazi mentality rather than strict documentaries, both films are breathtaking in the technical skill with which camera angles and movements are used to mass crowds or isolate heroic figures, and

are essentially triumphs of form over content. Once break the hypnotic spell, and the whole edifice crumbles.

Fascism in Italy was even less productive. Virtually bankrupt in 1930, the Italian film industry offered little that merited suppression. One or two able film-makers did emerge. Alessandro Blasetti (b. 1900) specialized in historical reconstructions such as *1860* – 1934; Mario Camerini (b. 1895) was making comedies of middle class life, such as *Il capelle a tre punte* – 1934. Mussolini refloated the industry in grandiose terms in 1935, to alternate propagandist paeans to Mussolini and the Fascist spirit, with mannered period pieces and historical epics.

In Russia, the most significant fact of the 1930s is that Eisenstein – at the very centre of the creative ferment in the new Soviet cinema during the previous decade – completed only one film: *Alexander Nevsky* – 1938. Spectacular but very much in the conventional American mode, it betrays the disfavour into which all experimentation with form had fallen at more or less the same time as the introduction of sound. Dialogue brought even stricter party-line supervision, presumably because it spelled out messages where silence had left at least room for doubt.

Possibly because his bizarre mixture of fervour, folklore and fantasy resulted in an unclassifiable image, Dovzhenko – the great individualist of the Soviet cinema – survived longer than most. *Ivan* – 1932, *Aerograd* – 1935 and particularly *Shchors* – 1939 are every bit as personal in their expression as *Earth*. By contrast *Chapayev* – 1935, directed by the Vasiliev brothers as a tribute to the Bolshevik hero, would not be out of place as a fast-moving western; Mark Donskoi's Maxim Gorki trilogy (1938–9), a sensitive, humanistic account of a boy's discovery of the world, would make its emotional appeal in any language.

British mediocrity
Britain remained very much under Hollywood's thumb, reflecting American product at its less than best: Sir Alexander Korda's successful *The Private Life of Henry VIII* – 1933 and Anthony Asquith's civilized *Pygmalion* – 1938. Only Alfred Hitchcock (b. 1899) offered any real competition. His thrillers, polished, amusing and peopled by a wonderful gallery of eccentrics, invariably knew when to escalate menace by chattering, when by keeping silent. Hitchcock often made striking use of sound: for example in *Blackmail* – 1929 the girl who has stabbed a man is repeatedly 'stabbed' by the word 'knife' as it recurs during a breakfast-table conversation. In these films Hitchcock perfected his gentle art of amusing audiences while scaring them out of their wits because they knew they could expect the worst – witness his ruthless demolition by bomb of the cheery schoolboy in *Sabotage* – 1936. Hitchcock was, of course, whisked off to Hollywood in 1939.

Ironically, Korda's efforts to put British cinema on the map, after the astonishing financial success of *The Private Life of Henry VIII*, merely demonstrated that imported directors – René Clair with *The Ghost Goes West* – 1935, Jacques Feyder with *Knight Without Armour* – 1937, King Vidor with *The Citadel* – 1938 – could make good films without materially affecting the general level of native mediocrity. John Grierson (1898–1972) achieved more lasting results in founding the British documentary movement at this time; less perhaps in terms of its rather scrappy, socially simplistic achievement (though films such as Basil Wright's sophisticated *Song of Ceylon* – 1934 and avant-garde *Night Mail* – 1936 still stand out for their quality) than in the healthy injections of craftsmanship and realism that revived the entertainment industry during World War II.

France resurgent

France was the exception that proved the rule of Hollywood's dominance. Out of the vigorous French avant-garde movement which had encouraged cross-breeding with commercial film-making during the final years of the silent period came three major directors. By 1934 Luis Buñuel had made *L'Age d'or* – 1930 and *Land Without Bread* – 1932. These two explosive surrealist films sent reason tottering by the assault of their savage mockery, not only of conventional moralities but of liberal reactions to social disorders. Jean Vigo (1905–34) had made *Zéro de conduite* – 1933 and *L'Atalante* – 1934, two intensely personal films that wove reality into weird poetic fantasy with an anarchism only slightly less explosive than Buñuel's. And Jean Renoir, with *La Chienne* – 1931, *La Nuit du carrefour* – 1932, *Boudu sauvé des eaux* – 1932 and *Toni* – 1935, had laid the foundation stones for a career that was to make him one of the great film-makers of France and of all time.

Only Renoir maintained this tradition of innovation, provocativeness and personal expression. *Boudu sauvé des eaux* and *Madame Bovary* – 1934 experimented with the use of deep focus long before *Citizen Kane* brought it to public attention. *Toni* evolved neo-realism in a form superior to anything the Italians later produced. *Le Crime de Monsieur Lange* – 1936 turned a charming entertainment into a sharp attack on the corruptions of capitalism. *La Grande Illusion* – 1937 demonstrated that the structures of war are social rather than nationalistic. *La Règle du jeu* – 1939, performed a dance of death that is as sprightly as a Mozart minuet. It neatly dissected French society to expose the decadence that was about to make it lie down and die under the rule of Nazism.

Elsewhere, with a series of charming comedies from René Clair and a string of well-made films from directors such as Jacques Feyder and Julien Duvivier, French cinema differed from Hollywood only in giving an aura of culture. Not for nothing was France for many years the mainstay of an 'art house' alternative to Hollywood entertainment.

Above Marlene Dietrich became a star overnight as Lola in Josef von Sternberg's *The Blue Angel* – 1930. For years the decadence and sadism of this film made it a daring example of sex on the screen.

Right Jean Cocteau's *Le Sang d'un poète* – 1930 explores the process of artistic creation. Although the film has strong dream-like images and explores the mind's subconscious urges, Cocteau denied that it was influenced by Surrealism.

Right *Swingtime* – 1936 was one of the classic Fred Astaire/Ginger Rogers musicals. It included several memorable numbers such as 'The Way You Look Tonight'.

41

The Forties 1

Hollywood reached its peak during the 1940s, full of confidence after ten years of sound film production. It was still the same old Dream Factory, of course, capable of the worst as well as the best. But after ten years of trial and error, directors, writers and stars were increasingly winning the right to gravitate towards their own predilections.

Bette Davis, for instance, had finally shaken off the persistent and misguided attempts to cut her down to size, and could concentrate on getting her teeth into meaty dramatic roles that allowed her to be incandescently mean, moody and magnificent. John Ford, with *My Darling Clementine* – 1946, *Fort Apache* – 1948 and *She Wore a Yellow Ribbon* – 1949, embarked on the long string of superlative westerns that were to make him the unparalleled chronicler of America's pioneer past, not as it was but as it should have been. Joseph L. Mankiewicz (b. 1909), who had spent the previous decade first as screen-writer, then as producer, of a motley assortment of films, emerged as a writer-director of elegantly acid comedy-dramas such as *The Ghost and Mrs Muir* – 1947, *Letter to Three Wives* – 1949 and *All About Eve* – 1950. Mankiewicz unexpectedly and refreshingly gave pride of place in these films to his own strikingly literate dialogue rather than to cinematic effects.

Orson Welles described the Hollywood machine as 'the biggest electric train set any boy ever had' when he arrived at the RKO studios in 1940 under contract, the 'Wonder Boy' of Broadway and radio whom everybody was talking about.

The movie machine

Push the wrong buttons, and you got a hilarious travesty such as *A Song to Remember* – 1945, a biography of Chopin which cruelly exposed Hollywood's pretensions to culture ('Frederic, you must stop this polonaise jangle!'). Press the right buttons, however, and out came Curtiz' *Casablanca* – 1943, legendary as the archetypal 1940s movie, and celebrated thirty years later in Woody Allen's *Play It Again, Sam*. Basically *Casablanca* is the stuff of women's magazines, using the fight against Nazism as mere background to a romance through which dewy-eyed idealism can be born of despair and disillusionment. Its sheen of magic owes less to any creative distinction in either script or direction than to inspired studio packaging. Everything – from discreetly exotic sets and low-key lighting to plaintive musical score and mournful, menacing supporting cast – skilfully conspires to embalm the bitter-sweet romance between Humphrey Bogart and Ingrid Bergman in a sort of caressing study in black and white.

Orson Welles made his début with *Citizen Kane* – 1941, a film that still startles by its originality. He pressed those selfsame buttons: all the elements specifically hailed as daring innovations in *Citizen Kane* – the mosaic structure, the deep focus, the ceilinged sets, the expressionistic lighting effects – were drawn from the Hollywood repertoire and

had been used before more than once. The real innovation was Welles himself, not so much in the electric entertainment value he provided as in the fact that he was using film as a form of personal expression. He assumed that his audience possessed an intellectual awareness and curiosity, as he pursued his thesis that power corrupts (a recurring theme throughout his work). He offered further provocative food for thought by inviting comparisons between his fictional newspaper magnate, Charles Foster Kane, and the real-life William Randolph Hearst.

Social concern

Hollywood was always prepared to crusade against injustices or iniquities provided they were safely in the past (the displaced farmers of the dustbowl and depression years in *The Grapes of Wrath* – 1940), assured of public indignation (the treatment of the insane in *The Snake Pit* – 1948), or carefully kept within acceptable bounds (the cycle of films about anti-Semitism and the colour bar that flourished between 1947 and 1949 – all lamely uncommitted except for Clarence Brown's magnificent *Intruder in the Dust* – 1949, based on the William Faulkner novel.)

Revolutionary rumblings threatening the status quo were a different matter. *Citizen Kane* got itself into all sorts of trouble (not only with Hearst and his newspapers) because, although primarily a

character study of an idealist who wins success, wealth and power only to mourn his lost innocence, the film is also a powerful polemic. It suggests that the American Dream can fall prey to the political machinations of big business.

Welles, in short, was too much of an intransigent individualist, too much of a potential trouble-maker, for Hollywood to stomach. His second film was *The Magnificent Ambersons* – 1942, a nostalgic evocation of turn-of-the-century America viewed through the gradual erosion of an aristocratic family overtaken by industrialism. But it was cut by some forty-five minutes, and a new ending by a different director was added. No longer having the right to make the final cut on his films, Welles no longer controlled his means of expression. He completed only three more films in the 1940s – *The Stranger* – 1946, *Lady from Shanghai* – 1948 and *Macbeth* – 1948. Welles in Hollywood was always bold, exciting and unconventional, but always hampered by interference and by budget limitations. He finally departed to work abroad.

The Forties 2

For Hollywood, 1939 had ended in panic, with the outbreak of World War II and the loss of the European market threatening a disastrous drop in revenue. Hollywood responded by instituting strict economy measures. Rigorous pre-planning resulted in better scripts and more visual realism (no longer did every shopgirl suffer the privations of poverty in exclusive gowns and apartments the size of palaces). Meanwhile the lost lavishness of extravagant sets and costumes was more than replaced by new lacquers that were developed to give film prints a rich, velvety gloss. Within months the assembly lines were operating at maximum efficiency, serviced by the best technicians in the world.

Hollywood goes to war

Meanwhile war propaganda began to rival the musicals and ubiquitous romantic comedies as a source of inspiration. Before America joined the hostilities, following the attack on Pearl Harbour in December 1941, Hollywood had confined itself mainly to embarrassing tributes to the genteel British stiff-upper-lip (Wyler's *Mrs Miniver* – 1942), equally embarrassing attempts to show how nice Germans had nothing to do with the nasty Nazis (*The Mortal Storm* – 1940), and dazzlingly inept ventures into Occupied Europe. This last group reached its absurd climax with *Above Suspicion* – 1943 where Fred MacMurray played a highly unlikely Oxford don performing highly unlikely undercover espionage in France and Germany. He engages in a classic Hollywood encounter with a German soldier, whose 'Heil Hitler!' is met with 'Nuts to you, dope!' Only major directors such as Fritz Lang with *Man Hunt* – 1941 and Hitchcock with *Foreign Correspondent* – 1940 managed to make the Nazi menace real by relegating it to the background and concentrating on the thriller elements.

After Pearl Harbour, Hollywood began to deal directly with the progress of the war in a flood of films. British critics, chauvinistically convinced that the more sober but equally propagandist British war movies were telling it as it really was, dismissed the American contribution as being preoccupied with showing how Errol Flynn won the war single-handed. Certainly it tended to portray the Japanese as inhuman sadists and to inject brash notes of flag-waving optimism. But the string of sobering American defeats in the Pacific led to a batch of fine, excitingly-paced action movies, in which a creditable attempt was made to reenact the unpleasant raw facts: *Wake Island* – 1942, *Guadalcanal Diary*, *Gung Ho!*, *Air Force*, *Bataan* – all 1943, and Raoul Walsh's *Objective Burma* – 1945.

Hollywood also has the distinction of having made the most honestly downbeat wartime films about the war: William Wellman's *The Story of GI Joe* – 1945, John Ford's *They Were Expendable* – 1945 and Lewis Milestone's *A Walk in the Sun* – 1945. These dealt less in heroics than with the boredom, fear and misery of war. *A Walk in the*

Above Anna Magnani resists German soldiers in *Rome, Open City* – 1945, one of the most powerful films to come out of war-torn Europe. It was planned secretly by director Roberto Rossellini during the German occupation of Rome.

Below Our heroes sit out the Fascist salute. A romantic view of the war in *Above Suspicion—* 1943.

Sun was unique in suggesting that, no matter how patriotic or courageous he might be, a soldier's first concern was his own survival. One soldier still alive after his platoon is cruelly decimated while making a marginal contribution to the Salerno beachhead, sits down to compose a letter in his head: 'This morning we captured a farmhouse. It was easy . . .'

On the home front

Tearful tales of the home front also proliferated. But the most authentic portrait of war-time America came in Preston Sturges' brilliant slapstick comedies, *The Miracle of Morgan's Creek* – 1944 and *Hail the Conquering Hero* – 1944. Here Sturges satirizes all pretensions to heroism and patriotism with merciless glee, in small-town settings that capture startlingly accurately the entire wartime ethos of GI Joes and pin-up girls, service canteens and war-bond campaigns, overseas leave and jitterbug Saturday nights. In *The Miracle of Morgan's Creek*, for example, heroine Betty Hutton does her bit for the war effort by kissing six soldiers goodbye at a dance. She then marries one of them (but which one?) in a drunken stupor, and subsequently causes all sorts of consternation by giving birth to sextuplets. Finally her timid childhood sweetheart (Eddie Bracken), hitherto despised as a 4F weakling denied military glory, demonstrates courage beyond the call of duty by accepting the children's paternity.

Unwarranted euphoria reigned in Britain in the same period. During the war feature film makers were infiltrated by a number of John Grierson's documentarists, leading to what was hailed as an

exciting new realism. In practice, most British war movies were either sober, somewhat dreary reconstructions, such as *Western Approaches* – 1944 or grotesquely stilted and embarrassingly class-bound, like Noël Coward's *In Which We Serve* – 1942. Launder and Gilliat's *Millions Like Us* – 1943 dealt with the home front. Only two directors escaped the prevailing note of sober mediocrity: Humphrey Jennings, inspired by the war to express his love of Britain in a series of superb cine-poems (*Listen to Britain* – 1942, *Fires Were Started* – 1943 and *A Diary for Timothy* – 1945), and the Michael Powell-Emeric Pressburger team with their series of lavish, weirdly fascinating fantasies and/or eccentricities (*49th Parallel* – 1941, *The Life and Death of Colonel Blimp* – 1943, *A Canterbury Tale* – 1944, *I Know Where I'm Going* – 1945, *A Matter of Life and Death* – 1946).

Left A poster for *In Which We Serve* – 1942. Directed by Noël Coward and David Lean, this film brought some of the strengths of British documentaries to feature film making. It told, by means of flashbacks, the background stories of the various crew members of a wartime destroyer.

Below left London firemen struggle against the elements during the blitz. 1930s documentary director Humphrey Jennings turned his hand to wartime subjects in such films as *Fires were Started* – 1943. This film follows twenty-four hours in the life of a fire-station.

Below Betty Grable, favourite pin-up of the US forces during World War II. She won enormous popularity in such films as *Million Dollar Legs* – 1939, *Down Argentina Way* – 1940 and *Coney Island* – 1943.

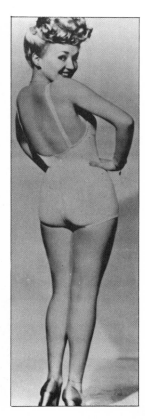

The Forties 3

Preston Sturges' films, though ostensibly variations on the old screwball comedies, are in fact wholly idiosyncratic. Even while faithfully reflecting contemporary manners and customs, they are simultaneously tinged with a quaint period flavour. His characters are as timeless as the playwright Ben Jonson's. Their contemporary idiom is persistently laced with reminders of a more gracious culture from Sturges' own past – as a child he was taken along by his mother, a friend of the dancer Isadora Duncan, on extended tours of cultured Europe.

At its simplest, Sturges' dual viewpoint gives us the sleazy dosshouse in *Sullivan's Travels* – 1941 with the delightfully untimely reminder on the wall: 'Have you written to Mother?'; at its best, a dazzlingly close encounter between Oscar Wilde and slapstick, when the butler in the same film, disapproving his master's decision to become a tramp in order to gather material for a film about the realities of misery, discreetly drives a nail into the project's coffin by remarking: 'The poor know all about poverty, and only the morbid rich would find it glamorous.'

Sturges crammed eight brilliantly successful comedies in this vein into the five years between 1940 and 1944, in a career frequently described as meteoric. From then till his death in 1959 he added only four more, received with something less than enthusiasm, although *Unfaithfully Yours* – 1948, strangely close to slapstick tragedy, certainly deserves a fresh look.

Like Joseph L. Mankiewicz, Sturges had been a scriptwriter since the early 1930s. This relatively new breed, the writer-director, was increasingly to make its presence felt in Hollywood. Val Lewton, for instance, started as a novelist, and became David O. Selznick's story editor and script doctor for eight years. In 1942, as producer of low-budget B-movies for RKO, Lewton initiated a series of horror films – *The Cat People* – 1942, *I Walked with a Zombie*, *The Leopard Man* and *The Seventh Victim* – 1943, *The Curse of the Cat People* – 1944. These brought new life and a breath of poetry and grace to a genre which had largely fallen into disrepute since the great days of James Whale because it kept repeating the same old shopworn themes. Lewton insisted that horror should be suggested rather than shown; a lesson still not properly learned. The literacy and intelligence behind these films have rarely been equalled. Lewton never took a script credit, but his films are faithful images of his own private fears and obsessions. For *The Seventh Victim*, a film

haunted by the lure of death, Lewton chose an epigraph that could stand equally well for the whole series: 'I run to Death and Death meets me as fast' (Donne).

The coming of the thriller

Two other writer-directors, Billy Wilder (b.1906) and John Huston (b.1906), provided major impulses in the extraordinary proliferation of the *film noir*. In *The Maltese Falcon* – 1941 Huston virtually created the thriller as we now know it. He introduced not only a perverse sense of humour but a distinct whiff of perversion, by surrounding its tortuous plot with a darkness scarcely penetrated by any ray of light, and by ending on a note of disillusioned despair that left the audience with a sense of pervading dread. Similarly, Billy Wilder dispassionately turned over stones to examine the darker, grubbier, untrustworthy side of the human soul. *Double Indemnity* – 1943 invited brutish murder into demure suburban lives, and *The Lost Weekend* – 1945 exposed a dipsomaniac's private hell to the city streets.

The *film noir* quickly became almost synonymous with 1940s Hollywood. A response to the prevailing sense of unease, it afforded an irresistible opportunity to explore what Robert Warshow described as 'the dangerous and sad city of the imagination'. A veritable labyrinth opened up, romantic and menacing; murder and violence lurked in dark alleyways fitfully lit by flashing neon-signs, where street lamps fought a losing battle with encroaching shadows. Distinguished expatriate directors such as Fritz Lang (*Woman in the Window* – 1944 and *Scarlet Street* – 1945) and Robert Siodmak (*Phantom Lady* – 1944, *Christmas Holiday*, *The Killers* – 1946) brought discreet tinges of German Expressionism to the closed, tormented worlds they created, where the rancid smell of viciousness, decay and despair held sway. Less distinguished film-makers such as Jules Dassin (b.1911), (*Brute Force* – 1947, *Naked City* – 1948 and *Thieves' Highway* – 1949) and Edward Dmytryk (b.1908), (*Murder My Sweet* – 1945, *Crossfire* – 1947) contributed to the mass of neat, taut, superbly atmospheric thrillers that seemed to spring up on every side.

The *film noir* was, in a very real sense, a last triumph for the Hollywood machine. Neither Dassin nor Dmytryk ever made anything half as good when left to their own devices, released from Hollywood's clutches by the McCarthy witch-hunts, and exiled to work abroad in comparative freedom. Meanwhile the studios were beginning to lose their grip: receipts fell after the boom-years of the war. Hysteria spread when the House Committee on Un-American Activities raised its head in 1947; and the menace of television was looming.

Escapism, as ever, was Hollywood's chief watchword – now justified by a war-weary world that was even readier to forget realities. These were prodigious years for the musical. Colour added the magic ingredient: bright and garish at Twentieth Century-Fox, rich and muted at MGM.

The Forties 4

The total musical was being born; hesitantly in the elegantly stylized fantasy of *Cabin in the Sky* – 1943, triumphantly in the richly nostalgic Americana of *Meet Me in St Louis* – 1944, both produced by Arthur Freed and directed by Vincente Minnelli. These two films achieved a superlative flair and invention. Drama, design, choreography, camerawork and individual skills were fused together with breathtaking virtuosity. The peaks in the catalogue of Freed's successes remain unmatched: *The Harvey Girls* – 1945 (George Sidney), *Summer Holiday* – 1947 (Mamoulian), *The Pirate* – 1948 (Minnelli), *Take Me Out to the Ball Game* – 1949 (Busby Berkeley) and *On the Town* – 1949 (Stanley Donen–Gene Kelly).

The British renaissance

Britain emerged from the war in a state of high hopes. She had directors such as Anthony Asquith, David Lean, Carol Reed, Alberto Cavalcanti, Laurence Olivier, Thorold Dickinson, Michael Powell, Emeric Pressburger and the Boulting brothers. The few years immediately after the war saw some notable films. David Lean made magnificent period adaptations of *Great Expectations* – 1946 and *Oliver Twist* – 1947. Laurence Olivier followed *Henry V* – 1945 with his elegant *Hamlet* – 1948. Carol Reed made *Odd Man Out* – 1946, with its reminders of German Expressionism and French fatalism, and *The*

Third Man – 1949, a haunting vision of corrupt post-war Vienna. Towards the end of the decade came the Ealing comedies, which produced one masterpiece – Robert Hamer's devastatingly elegant black comedy, *Kind Hearts and Coronets* – 1949, and several whimsical comedies about 'little people' (notably *Whisky Galore* – 1949 and *The Man in the White Suit* – 1951, both directed by Alexander Mackendrick).

Italian bombshell

The bombshell of the decade – in retrospect more of a whimper than a bang – was undoubtedly Italian neo-realism. Italy burst onto the international scene again in 1945 with Roberto Rossellini's *Rome, Open City*. In one sense the ecstatic response to the film was due to a misunderstanding. A tale of resistance and Gestapo reprisals, shot on sub-standard film stock in the streets of Rome under difficult conditions with the Germans barely out of the city, it looked like raw, urgent reality. In fact its excitement sprang largely from the unexpected juxtaposition of an unmistakably authentic atmosphere and setting with highly theatrical performances from actors Anna Magnani and Aldo Fabrizi.

Vittorio De Sica's *Bicycle Thieves* (*The Bicycle Thief* in US) – 1948, even more enthusiastically hailed, seemed to be a perfect embodiment of the kind of cinema sought by the theorist of the movement,

Above *Bicycle Thieves* was shot in the back streets of Rome and criticised the influences which bring people to despair.

Below Alec Guinness, as the Admiral, meets his end with a stiff upper lip in Robert Hamer's very individual comedy *Kind Hearts and Coronets* – 1949. Guinness gave a virtuoso performance as eight different relations, all in turn disposed of by gentleman–murderer Louis, played by Dennis Price.

Cesare Zavattini, as an antidote to Hollywood. Forget about plots, Zavattini urged; look for material in the streets, use non-professional actors, do away with technical expertise.

It sounded a fine challenge in theory, but the fallacies had already appeared in *Bicycle Thieves*. It was as carefully plotted as any fiction film; the child in it may not have been a professional actor but he was pure Hollywood moppet; and 'doing away with technical expertise' amounted to no more than the cutting out of surface gloss in order to increase the sense of poverty and misery. As more neo-realist films appeared, it became increasingly clear that the movement was caught in the trap of assuming that only poor people were real and only social injustices worthy as subjects. It sank further and further into special pleading and patronizing sentimentality.

Rossellini's work suggests that neo-realism might have developed in different directions. He never shied away from theatricality, subjectivity or the discreet problems of the bourgeoisie. Similarly, Luchino Visconti's *La terra trema* – 1948, ostensibly a documentary account of the iniquitous economic system that crippled a Sicilian fishing community, was already tinged by the aesthetic/operatic qualities that marked his later work. The neo-realist movement was effectively killed off by official disapproval, however, though not before leaving its mark abroad (notably in the Hollywood vogue between 1946 and 1948 for location-made thrillers such as *The House on 92nd Street* – 1945, *Boomerang* – 1947, *Naked City* – 1948 and *Call Northside 777* – 1947).

France looks within

The French cinema under the German Occupation could do little but mark time while indulging in aesthetic exercises. It had been robbed of several of its most reliable film-makers (Jean Renoir, René Clair and Julien Duvivier (1896–1967) were all in Hollywood, Jacques Feyder (1887–1948) in Switzerland), and was hampered by strict German supervision of its activities. Paradoxically, the results were by no means harmful. Marcel Carné (b.1909) and Jacques Prévert (b.1900), were forced to abandon their pre-war mood of romantic fatalism (although at the height of its success, it was already exhausted). They retreated first into medieval fairy-tale fantasy with the rather drearily beautiful *Les Visiteurs du soir* – 1942. Then, as though imagination had been liberated by this enforced change of pace, they embarked on their masterpiece, *Les Enfants du paradis* – 1945, a rich, bustling, incomparably vivid human comedy. Set within a wide-ranging evocation of nineteenth-century French theatre, it effortlessly translated philosophical meditations into terms of pure poetic fantasy, as it ranged over love, anarchy, crime, fame, the theatre and the nature of good and evil.

Jean Cocteau, who had abandoned the cinema after making his slightly precious *Le Sang d'un poète* in 1930, took the opportunity to return as a

scriptwriter. Cocteau wrote an enchanting dialogue for *Le Baron fantôme* – 1942 (directed by Serge de Poligny). Meanwhile *L'Eternel Retour* – 1943 (Jean Delannoy), a contemporary treatment of the Tristan and Isolde story, was unfairly accused of being collaborationist because it featured markedly blond Aryan lovers. Neither film is perfect, but Cocteau's dominant role is evident in both of them. Already apparent was the exquisite blend of fantasy and legend that was to make his *La Belle et la Bête* – 1947 one of the cinema's most magical fairytales, and his *Orphée* – 1950, with its mirrors in which poetry and death walk hand in hand, one of its most authentic masterpieces.

In 1943 Robert Bresson made *Les Anges du péché*, followed in 1945 by *Les Dames du Bois de Boulogne*. A major new talent had obviously been born. Both have the crystalline dialogue and the spare, almost abstract imagery already pointing to the intense concentration, transcending reality, characteristic of Bresson's later work.

Bresson, like Cocteau, was subsequently able to find finance for his work only at infrequent intervals. But they were the film-makers who were to keep the flag of French cinema flying through the comparatively bleak years of the 1950s – along with Jacques Becker, Jean-Pierre Melville and Jacques Tati (all of whom made their first features during the 1940s but did their best work later).

Above 'Once more unto the breach...' Laurence Olivier took the name part in his screen adaptation of Shakespeare's *Henry V* – 1944. The spectacular Agincourt battle sequence was shot in Eire.

Below The ever popular, ever powerful *Les Enfants du Paradis* was made during the Occupation of France and is one of Carné's lasting achievements.

The Fifties 1

The 1950s was the decade in which the American cinema went to war against television. Hollywood brought out all its heavy artillery – CinemaScope, Cinerama, 3-D – for the campaign against the small screen. It won many battles, but it lost the war. While the number of TV sets in America trebled during the 1950s, feature films produced fell from around 300 in 1950 to just over 200 in 1960. In the late 1940s Hollywood had flirted with social realism and with the low-budget immediacy of location shooting. But the trend did not last, and soon took second place behind the new Hollywood emphasis on spectacle and lavish overstatement.

Hollywood spectacular

The spectacle was enshrined in the series of epics – Greek, Roman, biblical and whatever – that followed *The Robe* – 1952, the first CinemaScope film. It was also enshrined in the Cinerama phenomenon (also born in 1952) which at first was no more sophisticated than a series of giant wrap-around travelogues. The second tendency – histrionic and sentimental overstatement – was to be found in the high-gloss emotionalism of films by directors such as Nicholas Ray, Minnelli and Douglas Sirk.

This was the decade of the 'woman's picture'. It was also the decade of actors James Dean and Marlon Brando, each representing different aspects of crucified youth; of Marilyn Monroe selling her body and her pathos to movie audiences; of the empurpled sincerity of Stanley

Left Gary Cooper and Grace Kelly starred in *High Noon* – 1952, an intelligent and popular western. Fred Zinnemann directed the film, for which Cooper won an Oscar.

Kramer's social concern films; and of westerns turning psychological.

The great Hollywood directors placidly ignored, or rose above, the dramatic overkill that characterized much of Hollywood's 1950s output. The films Hitchcock made during this period are among his very best: a series of mystery-thrillers exquisitely poised between suspense and comedy, and showing that there is no reason why a great film-maker's style should be cramped by his choice to adhere to a popular genre. From *Strangers in a Train* – 1951 to *Psycho* – 1960 there is hardly a film whose images have not carved themselves on the filmgoer's memory. In the late 1950s *Vertigo* – 1958, *North by Northwest* – 1959 and *Psycho* – 1960 offered an unmatchable trio of masterpieces,

Right Michael Powell directed *Peeping Tom* – 1959, the story of a perverted photographer who kills his models in order to capture their horror-struck expressions.

Below The celebrated chariot race in the 1959 remake of *Ben Hur*, directed in Todd–AO Panavision by William Wyler. This 3½ hour epic used stereophonic sound, and starred Charlton Heston, Stephen Boyd and Jack Hawkins.

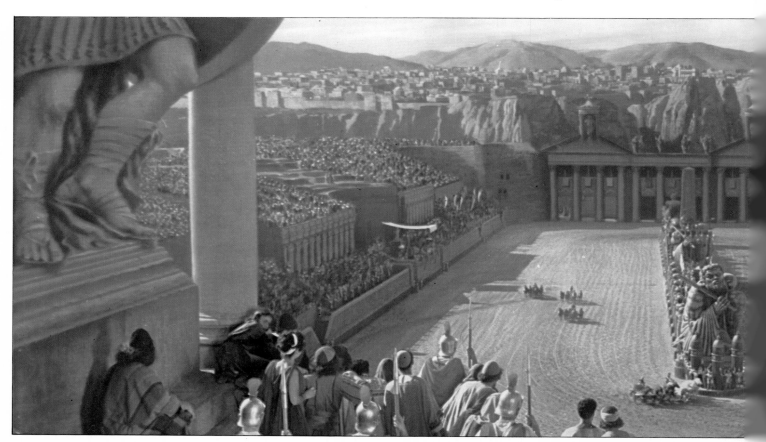

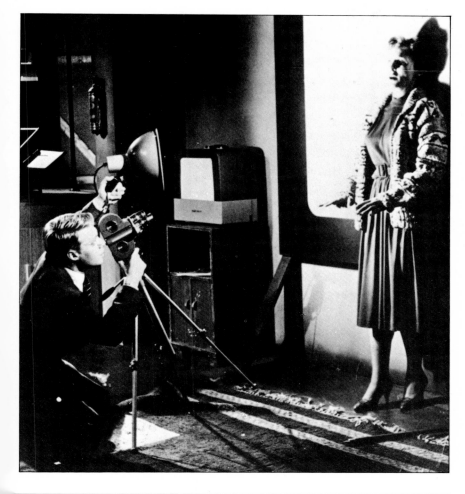

films as remarkable for their variety of style as for their common interest in themes of guilt and confused identity.

For Orson Welles, Howard Hawks and John Ford the 1950s were relatively quiet. Each produced what might be regarded as his late masterpiece – Welles' *Touch of Evil* – 1958, Ford's *The Searchers* – 1956 and Hawks' *Rio Bravo* – 1959.

The creative torch was handed on to a younger breed of directors – particularly in the field of westerns. Budd Boetticher made seven enthralling low-budget westerns starring Randolph Scott. Each explored frontier codes of loyalty and individualism. Delmer Daves, a writer-director with a somewhat syrupy touch in other movie genres, flourished in the western. Films such as *Broken Arrow* – 1950, *3.10 to Yuma* – 1957 and *The Hanging Tree* – 1959 opened up new vistas of both social realism and allegory. The third outstanding newcomer was Anthony Mann (1906–1967). His 1950s westerns with actor James Stewart – among them *Winchester 73* – 1950 and *The Man from Laramie* – 1955 – introduced a fascinating note of hesitancy and circumspection into the four-square ideal of American heroism.

Even in the Hollywood genres maligned earlier, a truly creative director could transcend basically trite or conventional story material. Today's avant-garde critics have seized on the work of film-makers such as Nicholas Ray (*Rebel Without a Cause* – 1955), Douglas Sirk (*Magnificent Obsession* – 1953) and Vincente Minnelli (*Lust For Life* – 1956) to demonstrate how a film's *mise-en-scène* – its decor, colour and camerawork – can add so many layers of meaning to the story and dialogue as virtually to transfigure them.

Some of their examples leave room for scepticism. But Sirk's films are certainly persuasive. His background in the German theatre gave him an insight into dramatic archetypes and dramatic irony that he used brilliantly in his 1950s 'women's pictures'. These films have a sweep and fullness, and a use of precise self-parody (witness the last shot of *Written On The Wind* – 1956: frustrated oil tycoon's daughter Dorothy Malone yearningly clutching a model oil-derrick) that make them perhaps the most interesting and double-edged popular movies in Hollywood's post-war history.

In lighter vein, the American cinema extended its triumphant run of musicals (mostly from MGM) from the late 1940s into the middle 1950s. Some may quibble about Vincente Minnelli's contribution to Hollywood melodrama, but there is no denying him his place as one of the giants of the Hollywood musical. His two best 1950s musicals were *An American in Paris* – 1951 and *The Band Wagon* – 1953. Each displayed a rhythm, a humour and a decorative flair that have few equals in the movie musical's history. (The 'jazz ballet' at the climax of *An American in Paris* – choreographed by Gene Kelly – was set against backdrops variously styled after the painters Dufy, Rousseau and Toulouse-Lautrec.)

The Fifties 2

Above *Dr Cyclops* revived the 'shrunken people' idea used in the 1936 science fiction film *The Devil Doll*. It went to elaborate lengths to achieve its special effects.

Right Monsieur Hulot, the amiable character who clumsily blunders through events, bringing chaos in his train. In *M. Hulot's Holiday* – 1951, director and leading actor Jacques Tati uses a succession of visual gags and delightful incidents to build up an affectionate and hilarious entertainment.

Stanley Donen and Gene Kelly also continued into the mid-1950s a working partnership begun in the late 1940s with *On the Town* – 1949. Their most famous collaboration is *Singin' In The Rain* – 1952, a contender for the best – and most popular – Hollywood musical of all time. The songs and dances were integrated with marvellous ease into a story about the early days of sound cinema. Kelly's acrobatically 'physical' style of dancing was matched stunt for stunt by Donald O'Connor, whose knockabout number 'Make 'em Laugh' almost steals the film.

In America in the 1950s there was surprisingly little 'alternative' cinema. Perhaps Americans were still settling into composure after World War II (or struggling with their silent discomposure during the Korean War). There were rumblings of satire and disaffection in the best of the popular films (*Rio Bravo*, for example, takes a bash at the simple-minded heroism of *High Noon* – 1952), but largely it was a decade of plush, expensive, apolitical complacency. With a few rare exceptions, such as Kenneth Anger, the cinema's 'underground' movement did not emerge until the 1960s.

Comic subversion

Subversion was to be found, if anywhere, in the comedy department. The outstanding film-maker here was Billy Wilder (b.1906). He began the decade with *Sunset Boulevard* – 1950 – a comedy in the guise of a melodrama, with an unforgettable movie-queen performance from Gloria Swanson – and went on to make *The Seven Year Itch* – 1955 and *Some Like It Hot* – 1959. The latter saw the decade out with a well-aimed kick to the backside. It made rude noises about everything from political integrity to sexual orthodoxy, and was irresistibly funny in the process.

But Wilder was a voice laughing in the wilderness. Apart from him, Hollywood in the 1950s wore a sober face and her prestige films all bore the Good Capitalist's Seal of Approval: money spent in huge quantities on hugely worthy subjects. Stanley Kramer's blockbusting movie sermons – *The Defiant Ones* – 1958, *On The Beach* – 1959 – wore their consciences on their sleeve. For all their serious intentions, they offered no more real food for thought, and considerably less entertainment, than the epics which Hollywood sent trundling out like armoured tanks to do battle at the box office. Possibly the worst of these (chariot race apart) was William Wyler's *Ben-Hur* – 1959; one of the best Vidor's *War and Peace* – 1956. But common to them all was the unarguable claim that the one province in which cinema had unchallenged superiority over television was that of size and showmanship.

Italy after neo-realism

In the 1950s the threat from television was less make-or-break in Europe than in America. For a while at least, Italy had time to continue exploring the neo-realist trail blazed in the late 1940s by

Rossellini and De Sica. De Sica added to his neo-realist series two more self-financed films, *Miracolo a Milano* – 1951 and *Umberto D* – 1952. But then he drifted slowly and dispiritedly into commercial film-making.

Meanwhile Rossellini made a series of films with his then wife, Ingrid Bergman, which have come in for much critical scorn in the years since. The best known of these, *Viaggio in Italia* – 1952, has been described as a 'clumsy film, with embarrassing dialogue and bad acting. . .' In fact it looks better with each viewing: an effortless, intricate study of the social and psychological forces that break and then heal a marriage. The location shooting and the simple, unbeautified black-and-white photography indicate the heritage of neo-realism.

Francesco, Jester of God – 1950, Rossellini's first film of the decade, was co-scripted by an aspiring young director, Federico Fellini. Fellini made his own first feature in the same year and went on to produce the most fascinating work of any Italian director during the 1950s. Beginning as a talented apprentice in the neo-realist workshop, with films

such as *I vitelloni* – 1953 and *La strada* – 1954, Fellini gradually forged his own style. By the end of the decade he had made the two films that confirmed his reputation as a brilliant individualist, a poet bringing together the realistic and the fantastic. The first was *White Nights* – 1956, the second *La dolce vita* – 1960.

Operatic flamboyance

Luchino Visconti, whose first venture into neo-realism (*La terra trema* – 1948) had a distinctly operatic touch, transformed that touch into an all-pervading style in *Senso* – 1954. This made an all-colour, all-costume, all-flamboyance break with his neo-realist past and it heralded the decorative glories of *The Leopard* – 1963 and *Death In Venice* – 1971. Three years after *Senso* Visconti returned to black-and-white, and to a smaller sphere of action, in his Dostoevsky adaptation *White Nights* – 1957. But the film seems cramped and airless, as if the new Visconti had somehow got trapped in the old austerity, and when it was shown it received a hostile reaction.

Above *Singin' in the Rain* – 1952 combined judicious amounts of satire and nostalgia. It was set in Hollywood at the beginnings of sound cinema. Its title song provided the occasion for Gene Kelly's magnificent song and dance routine through a rainstorm.

The Fifties 3

There was one new Italian director with no roots in neo-realism – Michelangelo Antonioni. He turned his back on the social preoccupations of that movement. It no longer seemed important, he said, 'to examine the relationship between the individual and his environment [but] to examine the individual himself.' Antonioni's middle-class heroes and heroines, wan, restless and spiritually undernourished, are the opposite of De Sica's and Rossellini's. The neo-realist heroes were engaged in a basic struggle for survival against war, poverty and injustice. But Antonioni's heroes have long ago won the battle for survival and are now wondering how to give that survival meaning.

Antonioni's work in the early and middle 1950s was steady and intriguing: *Cronaca di un amore* – 1950, *Le Amiche* – 1955 and *Il grido* – 1957. But it was with *L'avventura* – 1959 that the revelation came. The film was howled down at Cannes and appeared upon the European art movie scene more momentously than any other film in post-war history. In a movie magazine poll of the early 1960s it was voted one of the five best films of all time, in company with such films as *Citizen Kane* and *La Règle du jeu*.

Why the extremes of response? One reason is that *L'avventura* is supremely a movie of doubt. Audiences want certainty – whether it be the certainty of heroism, the certainty of the 'happy ending' or the certainty of boy-meets-girl. In *L'avventura* nothing is certain: neither in the plot (a girl inexplicably disappears from a remote, rocky island), nor in the relationships, nor in the characters' values. The film presents and explores that disconcerting freedom where everything is possible and there is no infallible higher authority – God, parent or country – to whom the individual can refer his decisions. It is the definitive existentialist movie, showing the individual alone in the universe, with no compass but his own mind and will to guide him.

1959: year of the film
To describe 1959 as a watershed year is an understatement – 'floodgate' would be a more appropriate word. The following European films were all made in 1959: *La dolce vita*, *L'avventura*, *Breathless*, *Les Quatre Cents coups*, *Hiroshima mon amour*, *Le Signe du lion* (Eric Rohmer's first film), *Les Cousins*, *Pickpocket*, *Les Yeux sans visage* and *Le Dejeuner sur l'herbe*. All but the first three were made in France. 1959 was that country's *annus mirabilis:* the 'springboard' for the New Wave, and the year in which European cinema's revolutionary forces gathered themselves for the assault on the 1960s.

Earlier in the decade Max Ophuls had come from Germany, via America, to make his last four films (1952–55) in France. Robert Bresson had made three films between 1950 and 1959, Jacques Tati two, and Louis Malle five. Alain Resnais' *Nuit et brouillard* appeared in 1955, and in 1958 François Truffaut made *Les Mistons* and Claude Chabrol *Le Beau Serge*.

54

The outstanding French director during this prelude was Robert Bresson. *Journal d'un curé de campagne* – 1950 was the first film in which Bresson largely set aside professional actors to pursue his own highly personal ideal of cinematic truth. Based on a novel by Bernanos, it peels away decoration and superfluous theatricality from the story of a young dying priest. The same austerity is evident in *Un Condamné à mort s'est échappé* – 1956, the story of a French prisoner's escape from the Germans. In addition to his unwavering exploration of the human soul, Bresson also developed a fascination with the minor aspects of human activity – gestures, clothes, sounds – that finds expression in *Pickpocket* – 1959, an adaptation from Dostoevsky. Here is a film so purged of narrative suspense, of 'actor-ish' characterization and of any other hook to catch the filmgoer's attention that the viewer sometimes wonders whether Bresson has left anything behind at all. But a great artist should be allowed his follies – time often proves them masterpieces.

The funniest Frenchman?
There is nothing austere or forbidding about the films of Jacques Tati. *Monsieur Hulot's Holiday* – 1954 established this human version of the Leaning Tower of Pisa as probably the funniest comedian France has produced. His grasshopper walk, inquisitive pipe, and air of deranged and unflappable politeness were here enshrined in a film of effortless comic charm and precision.

Max Ophuls' last four films were a fitting swansong to his career. Viennese kitsch blended with Parisian cynicism to produce a unique bitter-sweet flavour in *La Ronde* – 1950, *Le Plaisir* – 1952 and *Madame de . . .* – 1953. Few directors have ended their careers with such an enviably grandiose folly – widescreen, sweeping camerawork, spectacular decor – as *Lola Montés* – 1955.

The Fifties 4

Above James Dean, as a teenage rebel. Nicholas Ray's best-known film, *Rebel Without a Cause* – 1955, follows twenty-four hours in the lives of three violent adolescents. The film was carefully researched to illuminate the problem of juvenile delinquency. It is largely for this role that Dean is remembered.

Opposite: Marlon Brando's brooding arrogance made *The Wild One* – 1954 a trend-setter for 1950s youth. He plays Johnny, leader of a motorbike gang which invades a small American town and creates havoc. The film's violence was deplored at the time; it was banned from Britain for several years.

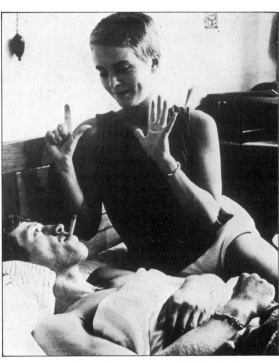

Above Jean-Paul Belmondo as a tearaway young criminal in *Breathless* – 1960. In this revolutionary film, Jean-Luc Godard broke numerous film-makers' traditions. He shot the film entirely on location, told his actors not to learn their lines, and tried to retrieve the directness of the American gangster movie.

By the mid-1950s the machinery of artisti revolution was beginning to whir in France. Th rallying cries had already sounded in the critica writings of the film magazine *Cahiers du Cinéma* among whose leading contributors were Jean-Lu Godard, François Truffaut, Eric Rohmei Jacques Rivette and Claude Chabrol. It was a impressively bloodless revolution. Most *Cahier* critics did not scorn the first generation of Frenc film-makers. Indeed they venerated Renoir, eve during the creative drought of his work in th 1950s, when he made a series of films – includin *Le Carrosse d'or* – 1953 and *Élena et les hommes* 1956 – some of whose thickly encrusted sty concealed an increasingly hollow centre.

If the French critics were rebelling again anything, it was against the glossy unadventurou ness of some French cinema during the 1950s. place of the sophisticated sentimentality directors such as Claude Autant-Lara and Andr Cayatte the *Cahiers* critics demanded a ne vitality both of style and of subject matter.

It was no surprise that they admired the critica writings of André Bazin, founder of *Cahiers c Cinéma* and prophet of film realism, and the film of Roberto Rossellini. These men were th standard-bearers of low-budget immediacy i film-making. More surprisingly, the *Cahiers* criti admired – indeed were totally infatuated with post-war Hollywood cinema. 'Cinéma *is* Nichola Ray,' Godard once wrote. He similarly praise such directors as Minnelli, Sirk, Robert Aldric and Hawks. As for Truffaut, Rohmer an Chabrol, they venerated Hitchcock. (The last tw even wrote a book about him.)

The *Cahiers* critics turned from preaching t practice with astonishing confidence. 1958 came i like a lamb and went out like a lion. Truffaut's *L Mistons* and Chabrol's *Le Beau Serge*, the advanc guard of the new movement, were both made i that year. Neither film is particularly innovatory i style – except for a looser, freer shaping of th narrative. But the tone is quite new: a sort o barbed, defiant amorality. They refused to lead th filmgoer by the hand through the jungle of huma motives and emotions.

The calm breaks

So these critics and theorists had prepared th ground for 1959: the new French masterpiec literally tumbled over each other in their haste t reach the public. There was Alain Resnai *Hiroshima mon amour*, re-mixing past and presen sound and image, in a kaleidoscopic study of woman's emotions. There was Franju's *Les Yeu sans visage*, orthodox in style but wildly ur orthodox in content, with its theme of huma vivisection. There was Rohmer's *Le Signe du lic* and Chabrol's darkly comic *Les Cousins*, fa surpassing his first film. Its town mouse/countr mouse story told of a pair of cousins whos temperamental differences cause first hostility an finally murder and served to establish th director's preoccupation with darker themes.

The Fifties 5

Most important of all the fims of 1959 were Godard's *Breathless* and Truffaut's *Les Quatre Cents coups*. The first turned movie story-telling conventions on their head, in showing how a young car thief played by Jean-Paul Belmondo meets, beds (and holds lengthy conversations with) American-girl-in-Paris Jean Seberg. Godard flouted every film-making 'rule', from chronological clarity to consistent character motivation. At the same time he paid tribute to almost every movie god adored by *Cahiers* – from Humphrey Bogart to French director Jean-Pierre Melville (who appears in the film). *Breathless* is not so much a masterpiece in its own right (Godard himself went on to make much better films later) as a blueprint for an irresistibly vital and inventive new cinema.

The idea for the story of Godard's film was supplied by François Truffaut. Truffaut's own first feature film was characteristically more humanist, and less tub-thumping, than Godard's. The juvenile-delinquent hero of *Les Quatre Cents coups* is Truffaut himself writ small. The contrasting yet convincing facets of his character are vividly conveyed by Truffaut's direction and Jean-Pierre Léaud's performance. Truffaut's camera moves about more freely (particularly in the famous last tracking-shot to the sea) than in his later films.

Elsewhere in Europe the decade was less productive. Great Britain turned out a meagre ration of Ealing comedies, war movies and Olivier-in-Shakespeare films. One late-in-the-day masterpiece (again in the year 1959) was Michael Powell's *Peeping Tom*. This superlative horror film was also a characteristic Powell allegory about the Englishman's inability to come to terms with his own emotions.

In Germany World War II still cast a shadow so dark that it seemed to blot out all artistic enterprise in the cinema. Denmark produced a single majestic masterpiece in Carl Dreyer's *Ordet* – 1955.

Seriousness and satire

Two giants stood out in Europe in the 1950s: Ingmar Bergman and Luis Buñuel. Bergman's output in this decade was formidable: some thirteen feature films, of which four – *Sawdust and Tinsel* – 1953, *The Seventh Seal* – 1957, *Wild Strawberries* – 1957 and *The Face* – 1958 – saw Bergman extending his artistic reach from the comic-naturalistic style of *Summer Interlude* – 1950 into realms of allegory. Unfortunately Bergman's work became known for its knotty, anguished obscurity – a favourite target for movie sceptics and satirists. *The Seventh Seal* – 1957 in particular has not worn well. Its grandiose and literary symbolism compares poorly with Bergman's 1960s films, in which symbolic motifs

Above *The World of Apu* examines changing life in India.

Below The Knight (Max von Sydow) plays for his life and the lives of humanity against the monk-like figure of Death, in Ingmar Bergman's *The Seventh Seal* – 1957. Bergman derived much of his inspiration from medieval art and life – particularly the Dance of Death.

are deftly woven into realistic stories. But Bergman was the greatest North European director of his age, seeing in modern psychological neuroses the symptoms of a larger spiritual crisis.

Buñuel's 'seriousness' as a film-maker took a different form than Bergman's. There is never a hint of solemnity in the Spanish director's work. Buñuel set himself to track down and destroy, with a mixture of humour and venom, the false idols of past creeds. 'Thank God I am still an atheist,' he once said – gratitude that comes over clearly in films such as *El* – 1952, *The Criminal Life of Archibaldo de la Cruz* – 1955 (both made in Mexico) and *Nazarín* – 1958. The last film combines malice with compassion in its tale of a priest stubbornly clinging to his faith in the face of innumerable disillusionments. Buñuel began the decade with *The Young and the Damned* – 1950. This vivid story of an anarchic band of urchins in the slums of Mexico City was his first international success after a fifteen-year period of self-imposed silence in the cinema.

East of Suez

Meanwhile India discovered a notable new talent in Satyajit Ray. *Pather Panchali*, the first part of Ray's Apu trilogy, appeared in 1955 and promptly won a prize at Cannes. Then came *Aparajito* – 1956, *The Music Room* – 1958 and *The World of Apu* – 1959. Ray's delicate, sad humanism is not for all tastes (François Truffaut walked out of *Pather Panchali*). But Ray has remained India's outstanding director for over twenty years.

Although Japanese cinema reached its first peak in the 1920s and 1930s it was practically unknown in the West until 1951, when Kurosawa's *Rashomon* was screened at the Venice Film Festival. *Rashomon* won the Grand Prix there and opened western filmgoers' eyes to what was virtually the cinema's lost continent. The films of Ozu (hitherto considered too Japanese for export) and of Mizoguchi started to appear at European festivals. Kurosawa's own 1950s work, including *The Seven Samurai* – 1954 and *The Throne of Blood* – 1957, established him as a master of the dramatic-panoramic style, Japan's answer to John Ford. Kurosawa also had a flair for more thoughtful, miniaturist work, as he showed in *Ikiru* – 1952, the story of a timid, elderly government clerk who learns that he is dying of cancer.

There were a remarkable number of important directors at work. One of Kurosawa's leading rivals in the 1950s was Kon Ichikawa, an animator turned director. His films have a passionate realism seen at its best in *The Burmese Harp* – 1956 and *Fires on the Plain* – 1958. But it was the discovery of Ozu and Mizoguchi for which western filmgoers had most to be grateful. In the 1950s, the love of intimate family subjects evident in Ozu's early work reached its fullest expression in a series of exquisite domestic miniatures which included *Early Summer* – 1952, *Tokyo Story* – 1953, *Early Spring* – 1956 and *Good Morning* –

1959. His flair for comedy gradually subsided into resignation and 'sympathetic sadness'.

Mizoguchi's career also reached an inspired climax in the 1950s. In four years he produced four abiding masterpieces: *The Life of Oharu* – 1952, *Ugetsu Monogatari* – 1953, *Sansho the Bailiff* and *Chikkamatsu Monogatari* (both 1954). These films are remarkable not only for their epic period sweep but for their precise and critical examination of the role of women in feudal society.

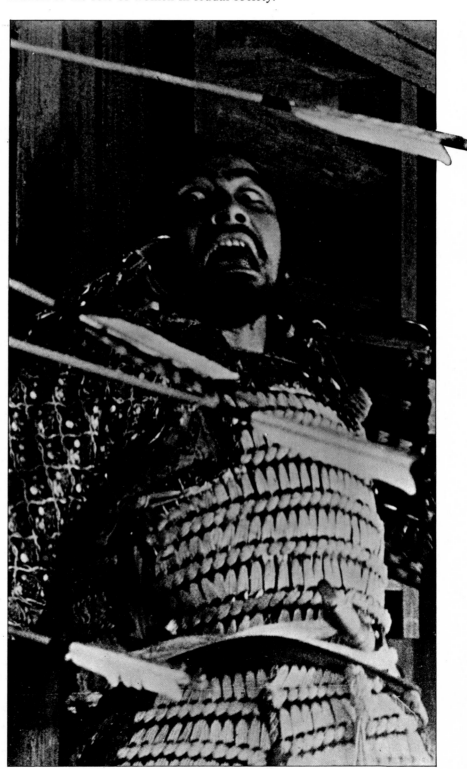

Below Kurosawa adapted Shakespeare's *Macbeth* for *The Throne of Blood* – 1957, and introduced some specifically Japanese elements, particularly from Noh theatre.

The Sixties 1

The 1960s were the autumn of Hollywood: the old directors – Ford, Hawks, Walsh – were making their last, or almost last, movies. The big-money pictures such as *El Cid* – 1961 and *The Fall of the Roman Empire* – 1964 were exiled to Spain and Italy to save on production costs. But the 1960s were also the spring of the new American cinema. The 'underground' movement began in virtually the first year of the decade. John Cassavetes' *Shadows* was first seen in 1960. It blazed a path for such hitherto frowned-upon practices as improvisation and hand-held camerawork.

The Hollywood epic became an exercise in financial ingenuity and brinkmanship. Independent producers such as Samuel Bronston and Sam Spiegel set down their film crews in Madrid and points east. They knew that if they made the same films with the same resources in California they would be bankrupt. Rome's Cinecittà studios welcomed the most notable band of fugitive Americans in 1962: those making Twentieth Century-Fox's *Cleopatra*.

Hollywood in recession

Meanwhile Hollywood's veteran directors seemed relieved at having to cut down their panoramic visions to fit the economic cloth available. Ford's final feature film, which followed the majestic *Cheyenne Autumn* – 1964, was the studio-built melodrama *Seven Women* – 1965. Though its story is rather sentimental and improbable it is highly regarded by many Ford enthusiasts. Raoul Walsh's *A Distant Trumpet* – 1964 closed a marathon movie career on a modest note, but Hawk's *Red Line 7000* – 1965 and *El Dorado* – 1967 were virtuoso productions, despite being more modestly budgeted than their predecessors. The US director Henry Hathaway brought the decade to an end with *True Grit* – 1969, an autumnal homage to the western's greatest star, John Wayne.

Down-beat westerns were to be found everywhere in the 1960s: for example *Lonely Are the Brave* – 1962, *The Professionals* – 1966 and *Monte Walsh* – 1969. One director made westerns with no

Below A colourful sequence from Anthony Mann's *El Cid* – 1961. This three-hour epic spectacle sustained interest throughout. It laid emphasis on pictorial splendour, and starred Charlton Heston and Sophia Loren. The story concerned a Spanish knight who helped drive the Moors from his country in the eleventh century.

nostalgic sentiment, but with a tough modernity. He was Sam Peckinpah, whose film *Ride the High Country* (*Guns in the Afternoon* in Britain) – 1961 was a taut, combative tribute to the sunset of the American frontier period. He followed with *The Wild Bunch* – 1969, a film of savage brilliance which hauled the western into the 1970s.

One reliable Hollywood veteran in a very different stamping ground was Alfred Hitchcock. Hitchcock's first film of the decade was *Psycho* – 1960, a movie with a blood-curdling first impact contrasting with a lasting subtlety. *The Birds* – 1963 and *Marnie* – 1964 were both thrillers which undercut America's New World optimism with wit and cunning. Hitchcock was less on form in his cold war spy thrillers *Torn Curtain* – 1966 and *Topaz* – 1969.

Some of the sharpest American films of the 1960s were made by directors who had graduated from television: for example Sidney Lumet, John Frankenheimer and Sidney Pollack. Frankenheimer's *The Manchurian Candidate* – 1962 was a political thriller with a fierce cutting edge and its own form of macabre wit. The ideal of tense, low-budget cinema represented by these directors' films came as a backlash against the Technicolor over-sell of so many 1950s Hollywood films.

The underground reaction

The backlash also came through in the films of John Cassavetes from *Shadows* onwards, in Dennis Hopper's hippie odyssey *Easy Rider* – 1969, and even in an outstanding American film of the decade, Arthur Penn's *Bonnie and Clyde* – 1967. Penn's film is in many ways an 'intimate' gangster thriller, though shot in colour and wide screen. It is as concerned with the inner thoughts and feelings of its characters as with the outward fireworks of violence.

The American underground movement formed the most obvious shift from Hollywood-style big spending. Its supporters argued simply that a low budget meant more creative freedom for the film-maker, since he had to bow to fewer outside interests. 8mm and 16mm film-making were favoured, and technical skills and professionalism were discounted in favour of 'the artist's vision'. Unfortunately the artist's vision was sometimes almost invisible since the films were made with a vaunted lack of craftsmanship. In untalented hands underground cinema tended to become wayward and indulgent doodling.

There were some more talented hands. They belonged to directors such as Jack Smith – *Flaming Creatures* – 1962, Kenneth Anger – *Scorpio Rising* – 1964, Stan Brakhage – *Dog Star Man* – 1959–64, Jonas and Adolfas Mekas – *Guns of The Trees* – 1961, Michael Snow – *Wavelength* – 1966–67 and Andy Warhol – *Chelsea Girls* – 1966 and *Lonesome Cowboys* – 1968. The styles varied so much as to make 'underground cinema' an almost meaningless blanket term. The three key areas of the movement were non-narrative or formalist

cinema (recently dubbed 'Structuralism'), the rough-grained, anything-goes realism of directors such as Warhol, and the fantasy cinema of film-makers such as Anger and Smith.

Left *Dr No* – 1962 was the first of the James Bond film-extravaganzas. Sean Connery took the part of Bond, caught up in a mortal struggle with a fiendish would-be world-ruler. Successive Bond films took the technical gadgetry and sexual flamboyance to exaggerated lengths.

Below A horrific moment in Hitchcock's *The Birds* – 1963, as a flock turns on the children. As usual the master comes up with startling photographic special effects to achieve his suspense.

The Sixties 2

Meanwhile in Britain there was another, much more tentative, 'new wave'. England's cinematic revolution took the form of an emphasis on the provinces. It was implied that regionalism equalled realism. British filmgoers were treated to an intensive diet of films about working-class life in the industrial North, the suburban South or the faceless Midlands. The best-regarded of these films were Lindsay Anderson's *This Sporting Life* – 1963 and Karel Reisz's *Saturday Night and Sunday Morning* – 1960. The films were almost invariably adapted from plays or novels, and the British cinema's old sickness of an over-dependence on literary originals was not cured by directors such as Tony Richardson, John Schlesinger, Anderson, Reisz and Richard Lester.

Britain was infiltrated by foreign film-makers in this period. The Hollywood studios sent emissaries to London to invest in British production. Albert Broccoli and Harry Saltzman, two travelling Americans, founded and financed the lucrative James Bond series. There were also film-making visits from such famous Europeans as François Truffaut (*Fahrenheit 451* – 1966),

Roman Polański (*Repulsion* – 1965 and *Cul-de-sac* – 1966), Jean-Luc Godard (*Sympathy with the Devil* (or *One Plus One*) – 1968) and Michelangelo Antonioni (*Blow-up* – 1967). The most distinguished 'British' work of the decade also came from foreigners: the Americans Stanley Kubrick and Joseph Losey. Kubrick made the political black comedy *Dr Strangelove, or How I Learned to Stop Worrying and Love the Bomb* – 1963 and the majestic space opera *2001: A Space Odyesey* – 1968. Losey was at his peak with films such as *The Servant* – 1963 and *Accident* – 1967. In them he recorded the faltering pulse of the British middle-class more accurately and sardonically than any other director.

The French New Wave

Across the Channel there was yet another flowering of new talent, the French New Wave – 'Nouvelle Vague'. This was the most revolutionary and influential cinematic movement of the decade, perhaps of the whole post-war era. The first stirrings had been seen in 1959; but it was in the 1960s that Godard, Truffaut, Chabrol, Resnais

Below The gang 'rumble' in *West Side Story* – 1961, screen adaptation of the stage musical hit. Some of the dynamic dance sequences were filmed on location in New York City. The musical transplanted *Romeo and Juliet* to New York's West Side slums, and set it to Stephen Sondheim's lyrics, and Leonard Bernstein's music.

Below An image for the 1960s.' Paul Newman – apparently cool, his ironic detachment masking a certain idealism. He was for a time promoted as Marlon Brando's successor, because of his acting style and facial similarities. Here he appears in a characteristic pose in *Hud* – 1963.

and the rest came into their own.

The unofficial rallying cry of the New Wave was Godard's celebrated statement: 'A film should have a beginning, a middle and an end, but not necessarily in that order.' The storyline was chopped, scrambled and otherwise broken up. A new realism was achieved in actors' performance and by on-location shooting. A miscellaneous series of styles was added – for example chapter headings, a literary off-screen narrator and quotations from other movies.

Godard's work in the early 1960s was brilliant. He examined carefully different sections and sub-sections of French society – prostitutes in *It's my Life* (*My Life to Live* in US) – 1962, terrorists in *The Little Soldier* – 1960, the army in *Les Carabiniers* – 1963 and the idle rich in *Contempt* – 1963. He carried out his analysis with a skill and wit unrivalled by any of his fellow-countrymen. Godard made three acclaimed masterworks in the mid-1960s: *Pierrot-le-fou* – 1965, *Alphaville* – 1965 and *Weekend* – 1967. But then he evidently decided that he had been playing to the bourgeoisie too long. He 'went underground' and made a series of films at different ports-of-call: *Sympathy with the Devil* and *British Sounds* in England, *One American Movie – 1 am* in America. They were remarkable for their daring style and ingenuity, and for the hectoring dogmatism of their left-wing views.

Truffaut, after beginning as an innovator, went in the opposite direction. *Shoot the Pianist* (*Please Don't Shoot the Piano player* in US) – 1960 is like a Hollywood *film noir* reflected in a broken mirror. It is a beautifully jumbled collage of gangster themes built around the sad, still centre of Charles Aznavour's hero. But after *Jules et Jim* – 1961, more conventional in form but still with a sprightly and subversive theme, Truffaut seemed to become gradually the prey of glossiness and orthodoxy. *The Bride Wore Black* – 1967 is an uninspired Hitchcockian film; *Stolen Kisses* – 1968, a bland comedy of adolescent love; *La Sirène du Mississippi* – 1969, an American-type thriller lacking style. His best film in the late 1960s was *L'Enfant Sauvage* – 1970. This austere film was eloquent and touching, endorsing the virtues of education.

Chabrol revived with his late 1960s trilogy *Les Biches, La Femme infidèle* – both 1968 – and *Que le bête meure* – 1969, after spending a period in the semi-commercial wilderness producing B-movie hokum. With his unique alchemy he transformed the murder thriller into a biting satire on the bourgeoisie and its moral contortions. Another French director, Jean-Pierre Melville, was equally skilled at turning 'pulp thriller' material into art. *Second Breath* – 1966 is an autumnal *film noir*, superbly shot in black and white, with subtle underlying themes of loyalty and betrayal. Other notable Melville films of the decade included *Léon Morin, prêtre* – 1961 and *L'Armée des ombres* – 1969.

Two new French directors distinguished by their surrealist leanings were Alain Resnais and Georges Franju. Resnais' *Last Year in Marienbad* – 1961, based on a script by the French novelist Alain Robbe-Grillet, was a virtuoso film. In *Muriel* – 1963 and *Je t'aime, je t'aime* – 1968 Resnais' talent for undermining our notions of time and memory was employed in a richer context. Franju's work swung between outright fantasy, in *Judex* – 1963 and a sort of twilight realism in *Thérèse Desqueyroux* – 1962.

The Sixties 3

The older directors were still active in France in the 1960s. Luis Buñuel returned to the country to make *Diary of a Chambermaid* – 1964, *Belle de jour* – 1966 and *The Milky Way* – 1969. Comedy-maker Jacques Tati produced *Playtime* – 1967. Meanwhile Robert Bresson continued to hymn the uncomfortable virtues of stoicism, suffering and suicide in films such as *Au hazard, Balthazar* – 1966 and *Mouchette* – 1966.

Other outstanding French film-makers of the decade included Claude Lelouch, Jacques Demy, Louis Malle, Alain Robbe-Grillet, Agnès Varda, Chris Marker, Jacques Rivette and Eric Rohmer. Rivette's films *Paris nous appartient* – 1960 and *La Religieuse* – 1965 gave little hint of his avant-garde flights of invention to come in the 1970s. But Rohmer's *La Collectioneuse* – 1966 and *Ma Nuit chez Maud* – 1969 were among the earliest and wittiest of his series of six moral tales.

New Italian talent

Although there was no cinema movement in Italy concerted enough to earn the term 'New Wave', the country boasted much new talent in the 1960s. The outstanding newcomer was Pier Paolo Pasolini. Pasolini seemed to rejoice in opposing extremes of temperament. He was a puritan and a pleasure-seeker, a pessimist and an optimist, a Marxist fascinated by Christianity. In later years the contradictions seemed to tear him and his work apart. But in the 1960s they fuelled the raw energy of *Accatone* – 1961, the bare primitivism of his *The Gospel According to St Matthew* – 1964, the grandeur of *Oedipus Rex* – 1967 and the rich

ambiguities of *Theorem* – 1968 and *Pigsty* – 1969.

Directors Bertolucci and Bellocchio both brought the thick, heady melodrama of Italian theatre into the cinema. Bertolucci's *Before the Revolution* – 1964 and *Partner* – 1968 both combine stylized drama bordering on the operatic with an obscure radical style borrowed from Godard. Bellocchio's first film was the powerful *Fists in the Pocket* (*A Fist in his Pocket* in US) – 1966, in which epilepsy is a symbol for the moral and psychological break-up of an Italian family.

More direct in their approach as political film-makers were Francesco Rosi and Gillo Pontecorvo. Pontecorvo's *The Battle of Algiers* – 1965 was a feature-film re-creation of events from the Algerian war, done with the immediacy and power of a newsreel. Rosi favoured a similar style, but with a more complex structure. His first noteworthy film was *Salvatore Giuliano* – 1962, a vivid mosaic of episodes from the life of the Sicilian bandit leader of its title. He followed it with *Hands over the City* – 1963 and *The Moment of Truth* – 1964, about the rise of a bullfighter.

Other talented new directors in Italy included Ermanno Olmi and Sergio Leone. Olmi's *Il posto* – 1961 and *I fidanzati* – 1963 extended the tradition of neo-realism into an area of gentle tragi-comedy. Leone made 'spaghetti Westerns' with Clint Eastwood.

Of the older film-makers in Italy, some continued to grow and develop, while others tended to depend on exaggerated personal style alone. Rossellini, always an intelligent and evolving artist, made worthy historical films for French and

Below Malcolm McDowell machine-guns the guests at the public school in Lindsay Anderson's *If ...* – 1968. The film's theme of rebellion at an English public school was intended to stand as a metaphor for society at large.

Below right *Bonnie and Clyde* – 1967 retold with nostalgia and psychological insights the story of two small-time criminals in 1930s US The threat of bloody retribution mounts as the film progresses, and the film almost exults in its realistic violence. Warren Beatty and Faye Dunaway took the name parts, and Arthur Penn directed.

Right Jean-Luc Godard's *The Little Soldier* – 1960, was banned for three years by the French government – probably as much for its torture scenes as for its political content. It dealt with the confused situation during the Algerian war, when both left and right resorted to extreme methods.

Italian television, most notably *La Prise de pouvoir par Louis XIV* – 1966. Fellini's work swung between high brilliance and high kitsch. *8½* – 1963 comes in the first category, *Juliet of the Spirits* – 1965 in the second, *Satyricon* – 1969 in between.

Visconti became more operatic with age. He made a last autumnal stab at neo-realism in *Rocco and his Brothers* – 1960 and ended the decade with the theatricality of *The Damned* – 1970. In between came *The Leopard* – 1963, *Of a Thousand Delights* – 1965 and *The Stranger* – 1967. The best work from an older director was that of Antonioni. In *La notte* – 1961 and *L'eclisse* – 1962 he gave a bleak, thin poetry to the restlessness of the Italian middle classes, lost in a jungle of glass-and-concrete apartment blocks, cold parks and bare city streets.

In Germany, after two decades of stagnation, film revived with the first works of the soon-to-be-celebrated new German cinema. Alexander Kluge's *Yesterday Girl* – 1966 borrowed from Godard, with its jumpy, multi-styled political parable centred around a heroine who is a 'victim-of-her-time'. But the film gave Germany a new voice. The late 1960s ushered in the first, highly original, films by Rainer Werner Fassbinder (*Katzelmacher* and *Why Does Herr R Run Amok?* – 1969), Werner Herzog (*Signs of Life* – 1967) and Jean-Marie Straub. Straub's work was genuinely revolutionary, and is still considered too challenging or difficult to be shown in most commercial cinemas. His *Chronicle of Anna Magdalena Bach* – 1967 used direct sound, long takes and monotone performances by professional musicians.

The Sixties 4

Swedish cinema in the 1960s was again dominated by Ingmar Bergman. He began the decade with a trilogy – *Through a Glass Darkly* – 1961, *Winter Light* – 1963 and *The Silence* – 1963 – which explored the loneliness of modern man, starved of faith in God. These films seemed to be Bergman's final exorcism of his religious preoccupations. In *Persona* – 1966, *Hour of the Wolf* – 1968, *Shame* – 1968 and *A Passion*(*The Passion of Anna* in US) – 1969 he looked for an explanation of humanity's emotional sickness not in Christianity or its decline, but in private trauma, personal relationships and the institutionalized cruelty of war. Freed from religion Bergman's work became more personal and political – and far more directly powerful than ever before.

Other Swedish directors briefly caught the attention – for instance, Bo Widerberg with *Elvira Madigan* – 1967 and *Adalen '31* – 1969. Vilgot Sjöman with *I Am Curious–Yellow* – 1967 and Mai Zetterling with *Night Games* – 1966. But Bergman towered above his contemporaries.

Denmark and Spain each produced a solitary masterpiece: Dreyer's *Gertrud* – 1964 and Buñuel's *Viridiana* – 1961. Dreyer's last film is a long, majestic meditation on human love. It is the story of a woman who sacrifices 'all' – her marriage, her wealth, her reputation – for the love of a young composer. It is directed in slow, statuesque takes, whose uneventfulness drives some filmgoers to fury or despair. But in Dreyer still waters run deep; the film's quiet intensity and shining wisdom richly reward patient attention.

No less rewarding is Buñuel's *Viridiana* – 1961. The film is an assault on Catholic Christianity by the cinema's most devoted atheist. Its best-known sequence is the burlesque version of the Last Supper, with the twelve disciples replaced by twelve corrupt and lecherous beggars. But the film is witty and malicious throughout. It is no surprise that Buñuel's first film-making visit to his native Spain for thirty years was also his last for another nine. *The Exterminating Angel* – 1972 and *Simon of the Desert* – 1965 were both made in Mexico.

Movement in the East
Meanwhile there were rustlings of activity in Eastern Europe. Czechoslovakia's cinematic renaissance lasted only until 1968, when the Russian tanks came in to roll it flat. But until then it gave good value: a series of gentle, funny and compassionate films on provincial life by directors such as Miloš Forman, Jiří Menzel, Ivan Passer and Veřa Chytilová. Some consider Chytilová the most original, with the wacky surrealism of *Daisies* – 1966. But the most popular was Forman with *A Blonde in Love* – 1965 and *The Fireman's Ball* – 1967. He soon found himself packing his talent and taking it to Hollywood.

In Russia the two directors who produced outstanding work in the 1960s were Sergei Paradjanov (*Sayat Nova* – 1969 and *Shadows of Our Forgotten Ancestors* – 1964) and Andrei Tarkovsky (*Andrei Roublev* – 1966). Tarkovsky. has had difficulties with the regime over showing some of his later films.

Below *Viridiana* – 1961 sums up the anti-establishment and anti-clerical attitudes of its director, Luis Buñuel. This scene, which reconstructs Leonardo da Vinci's *Last Supper* using a disreputable collection of cripples and beggars, is typical of his outspoken attack. The film was banned in Spain – but is generally regarded as one of Buñuel's most powerful and subversive. The film tells how the convent novice, Viridiana, is misled and ill-treated by everybody.

sconti used an operatic
yle to portray the
rrupt roots of Nazism in
ermany in *The Damned*
1970. His rich use of
lour, music and
amatic settings
mbined to present a
ntal attack on fascism –
t betray a fascination
th decadence. The film
ces the impact of
azism through the family
rtunes of the Essenbeck
eel dynasty. Among the
m's international cast
ere Dirk Bogarde,
elmut Berger and Ingrid
ulin.

The Sixties 5

In Hungary Miklós Jancsó found fame with *The Round-Up* – 1965, *Silence and Cry* – 1968 and *The Confrontation*—1969. These political fables were choreographed in rich dance-like movement. Jancsó was the most original stylist the cinema discovered in the 1960s. He matched his political theory of 'perpetual revolution' to the perpetual-motion methods of his camera work and settings.

In Poland Andrzej Wajda followed his famous war trilogy of the late 1950s with a series of increasingly stylized allegories including *Everything for Sale* – 1968 and *Hunting Flies* – 1969. Two other Poles, Roman Polański and Jerzy Skolimowski left the country after directing the films that made their names: *Knife in the Water* – 1962 in Polański's case, *Walkover* – 1965 and *Barrier* – 1966 in Skolimowski's. Polański went to England to make two macabre and stylish films in black-and-white – *Repulsion* – 1965 and *Cul-de-sac* – 1966 – then to America to make the all-colour Satanist shocker *Rosemary's Baby* – 1968. Skolimowski went to Belgium to make one of his most endearing comedies-of-obsession, *Le Départ* – 1966.

The Indian cinema continued to lean heavily, if not exclusively, on the Bengali Satyajit Ray for its reputation abroad. Ray's work was best in an enclosed 'apolitical' setting, delicately etching the portrait of a family, a village or a couple, injecting them with his warm, Renoir-like humanism. His more important films came early in the decade: *Devi* – 1960, *Kanchenjunga* – 1962, *The Big City* – 1963 and *Charulata* – 1964. Meanwhile new talents emerged elsewhere in India.

In Japan the film-making boom of the 1950s slowed down dramatically during the 1960s. Mizoguchi had died in 1956, Ozu died in 1963,

Above *Diary of a Shinjuku Thief* – 1968 was directed by Japanese film-maker Nagisa Oshima. He rejects the accepted methods of film narrative, and instead use film to analyze Japanese political and cultural values.

Left Jancsó's *The Round-Up* – 1965 was based on political events in Austro-Hungary in 1868. But the director deliberately made the buildings, costumes and setting timeless. The film presents a brooding menace and a cold beauty.

fter completing his serene and masterful swan-
ong, *An Autumn Afternoon* – 1962. Neither
urosawa nor Ichikawa made any films in this
ecade after 1966. Before that, Kurosawa made
ojimbo – 1961, *Sanjuro* – 1962 and *Red Beard* –
965 – further sumptuous evidence of his mastery
f action and the widescreen. Ichikawa's versatile
utput included a Kabuki-style melodrama – *An
ctor's Revenge* – 1963 – a tale of eccentric
eroism, *Alone on the Pacific* – 1963 and *Tokyo
lympiad* – 1965.

The new heir apparent to the Japanese cinema
oon appeared. He was Nagisa Oshima, a director
ith a strong political sense. His films were the
ost successful mix of narrative realism with
olitical allegory since Godard. Oshima's strong,
llusive, piercingly intelligent style was seen at its
est in *Death by Hanging* – 1968, *Diary of a
hinjuku Thief* – 1968 and *Boy* – 1969.

The new radicalism evident in Oshima's films

was also strongly evident in cinema from the Third
World. For instance, the 1960s saw the flowering
of *Cinema Novo* in Brazil, with outstanding work
from Nelson Pereira dos Santos (*Vidas Secas* –
1962), Ruy Guerra (*Os Fuzis* – 1963) and Glauber
Rocha (*Black God, White Devil* – 1964 and
Antonio das Mortes – 1969). Journalist Glauber
Rocha's films were an exotic mixture of allegory,
tribal ritual, costume melodrama and direct
political propaganda.

Other notable South American directors of the
1960s included the Bolivian Jorge Sanjines with his
Blood of the Condor – 1969, Miguel Littin and
Aldo Francia in Chile and Fernando Solanas in
Argentina with *The Hour of the Furnaces* – 1969.
Meanwhile in Cuba, carrying the torch of re-
volutionary cinema, were Tomás Gutiérrez
Alea (*Memories of Underdevelopment* – 1968),
Humberto Solas (*Lucia* – 1969) and the documen-
tary film-maker Santiago Alvarez.

Below The geometrical
gardens and endless
corridors which dominate
Alain Resnais's *Last Year
at Marienbad* – 1961
reflect its attempt to
explore memory and
imagination. The narrator
tries to persuade a
woman at an elaborate
mansion that they have
met before. The film has a
haunting dream-like
quality, and a certain icy
beauty.

The Seventies 1

The 1970s have seen the renewal of Hollywood. American film had been caught in the economic doldrums in the early 1950s by the meteoric rise of television and the film industry's failure to meet the new challenge. Artistic stagnation also occurred as old Hollywood hands were slow to transfer power to a new generation.

This situation began to change gradually in the late 1960s. Independent film-makers began to show that films made outside the traditional Hollywood assembly-line system could win critical praise *and* reward financially. At the same time, conglomerate investment corporations discovered the movies. They began to buy up the old Hollywood companies as cores for their growing leisure entertainment divisions.

The major Hollywood studios no longer directly controlled production. Each new film was an independent project, distributed and financed wholly or in part by the studios but organized most often by independent producers. The studios continued to dominate film distribution, and still tightly controlled the whole film system, without the considerable investment in plant and equipment required for production and exhibition.

In fact, with one or two exceptions, the so-called 'studios' no longer operated as such. One by one the companies followed the example of United Artists (which had never owned its own production plant) and sold off their Hollywood property. Far more films were now made on location. Most of the others were made in rented production facilities on an ad hoc basis. Only Universal and Walt Disney's Buena Vista continued to run extensive factory-like plants. Both companies were heavily involved in television production, whose regular production schedules permitted sensible spreading of investments in plant and equipment. The studios also cut down their large payroll commitments to staff, actors and technicians. They preferred instead to hire freelance casts and crews for each film.

Hollywood renewed

There were two major results from these changes. First, more power was now in the hands of producers, directors and – especially – actors. Now, each 'property' – original screenplay, novel or stageplay – has to be 'packaged' with its own box office stars, director, and marketing strategy. This allows a few actors with proved value – such as Steve McQueen and Marlon Brando – to demand the equivalent of fifty per cent of a film's budget.

Right A driver's nightmare. *Duel* – 1971 is the story of a car pursued by a giant petrol tanker. The suspense of the chase is sustained to the violent finish in this early made-for-TV movie by Steven Spielberg.

Below left *Superman – the Movie* produced by Walter Suskind and directed by Richard Donner, one of the last major box office hits of the 1970's.

Below right Steven Spielberg's blockbuster *Close Encounters of the Third Kind* – 1977 was always destined to break box office records. Almost magical in its special effects, it restored a sense of mystery and wonderment to the cinema. Here the extraterrestrial craft is landing.

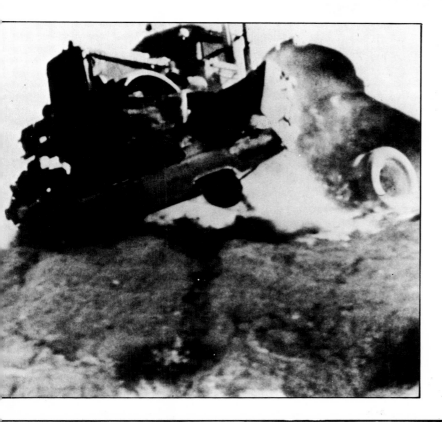

The functions of film workers are no longer rigidly separated. The actor-producer, director-producer, writer-producer, actor-writer and so on is becoming more and more common. The authorship of a film, never very clear, is now even more complicated. Secondly the financiers of American movies, the old studios, with no continuing investment in plant, equipment and regular staff, can now produce as many or as few films each year as they think will be profitable.

When the conglomerates moved to take control of the American film industry in the late 1960s and early 1970s there was a brief flurry of artistic excitement. Executives new to the film industry trod softly at first. There was an explosion of talent as new film-makers found backing for what might previously have seemed risky projects.

This resulted in streams of essentially exploitative films about young people and blacks in the early 1970s. Both genres were briefly popular and profitable. They ceased by 1974, when it had been decided that the future lay with the blockbuster marketed to massive audiences. Occasionally low-budget films such as *American Graffiti* – 1973 and *Rocky* – 1976 proved that it was still possible for a movie to become successful without the overwhelming exaggeration of publicity.

The Seventies 2

The so-called Hollywood Renaissance is a *rebirth* of traditionally successful genres. More of the same, only 'bigger and better' than ever before. A number of the brightest directorial talents in Hollywood in the 1970s have devoted themselves to producing profit-making entertainment machines. Steven Spielberg, the most successful, with two major blockbusters, *Jaws* – 1975 and *Close Encounters of The Third Kind* – 1977, is a good example. His films are never particularly personal statements. Spielberg has admitted in interviews that he may have spent too many of his thirty years committed to the craft of film-making rather than to studying the lives and ideas films might be *about*. But his films entertain with a clear good humour that sets them apart from the general run of chase and suspense films.

William Friedkin, who made *The French Connection* – 1971 and *The Exorcist* – 1973, is another very able technician who knows how to make a film work on an audience. So is George Lucas, whose first success was the low-budget *American Graffiti*. He has since produced *Star Wars* – 1977, the most profitable film of all time.

Peter Bogdanovich had an early success with a seemingly personal film, *The Last Picture Show* – 1971. He has had less luck with more recent imitations of the old Hollywood genres. His screwball comedy *What's Up, Doc?* – 1972 was successful, as was *Paper Moon* – 1973. But his 1930s-style musical *At Long Last Love* – 1975 was an expensive disaster, as was his tribute to early movies, *Nickelodeon* – 1971. Bogdanovich, a former journalist and interviewer, appeared to be the new American director closest to the European model of the 1970s. But his admiration of old movies has not been enough to sustain him.

Martin Scorsese also began with personal films – *Who's That Knocking at My Door?* – 1969 and *Mean Streets* – 1973 – which were highly praised. He went on to produce more traditional copies of old genres such as *Alice Doesn't Live Here Anymore* – 1974 and *New York, New York* – 1977 with varied success. Brian De Palma, like Scorsese with roots in New York, has had a similarly chequered career. He started with personal films such as *Greetings* – 1968 and *Hi Mom!* – 1970. After this he settled into the commercial mimicry of the suspense/horror genre with *Sisters* – 1973, *Carrie* – 1976 and *The Fury* – 1978.

All these directors started in independent projects in the late 1960s. More recently, the most fruitful source of film talent has been the large group of young screenwriters who supply scripts for the blockbusters; for example John Milius, Gloria Katz and Willard Huyck, Robert Towne, Robert Getchell and most notably Paul Schrader.

Independent survivors

At the same time, a handful of film-makers has managed to continue to produce and direct movies that are clearly personal statements, and which sometimes reach audiences as large as the more calculating blockbusters.

John Cassavetes is the father of this group. He has been an independent film-maker on the edge of Hollywood for almost twenty years. *Husbands* – 1970, *Minnie and Moskowitz* – 1971 and his other films have kept up a highly individual style partly because Cassavetes has provided his own finance and even runs his own distribution company.

Robert Altman has been less cut off from the Hollywood establishment. The prolific Altman produces most of his films through his own company, but releases them through the normal channels. Although none of his films since *M*A*S*H* – 1970 has made a significant profit, he has released more than one film a year since 1970. They include an intriguing variety of essays in style, from *The Long Goodbye* – 1973 to *Three Women* – 1977, from *California Split* – 1974 to *Nashville* – 1955 and *Quinter* – 1979.

Francis Ford Coppola has made small, sophisticated and personal films such as *The Rain People* – 1969 and *The Conversation* – 1974, as well as true

Below *Saturday Night Fever* – 1977 was a box office hit. Its star, John Travolta, was a 'local boy' with whom young audiences could identify. It was quickly followed by another film in the same mould – *Grease* – 1978.

blockbusters such as *The Godfather* – 1971 and *Apocalypse Now* – 1978, without losing his own vision. *The Godfather* and *The Godfather, Part II* – 1974 is arguably a perfect combination of personal concerns and commercial values. Other directors who have maintained cinematic identities while at the same time learning to live with the current system include Paul Mazursky with films such as *Bob and Carol and Ted and Alice* – 1969, *Next Stop, Greenwich Village* – 1976 and *An Unmarried Woman* – 1978, and Michael Ritchie with *The Candidate* – 1972, *Smile* – 1975 and *Semi-Tough* – 1977. Both are satirists in the best Hollywood tradition, extending back to Preston Sturges and Lubitsch. Woody Allen is in the same tradition. With *Annie Hall* – 1977 he began to move from the topical parody which had characterized his earlier films to more general satire.

The black film

The black film, once promising so much, has been eliminated from the Hollywood production schedules. As a result film-makers with refreshing and promising talent, such as Melvin Van Peebles, Gordon Parks and Bill Gunn, have found it difficult or impossible to pursue their craft in the last few years. Women also find it extremely difficult to find creative employment either in front of the camera or behind it. Despite some interesting experiments with the music film, perhaps inspired by the increasing importance of videocassettes, there have been no new genres of any lasting importance developed in the 1970s.

Above left Woody Allen's Oscar-winning *Annie Hall* – 1977 marked a milestone in his career. The hilarious film traces his zanily awkward, but truthful, affair with Annie Hall, played by Diane Keaton. As usual with Allen, the film is full of verbal and visual gags.

Left *Blazing Saddles* – 1974 was one of Mel Brooks' series of parodies on classic movie genres. Here he sent up the western in a series of wildly funny and fast-moving episodes. Elsewhere he parodied the horror film, the silents and Hitchcock.

The Seventies 3

Film industries in some countries have been all but wiped out. In Britain, the brief period of activity in the 1960s came to an abrupt halt in 1970 when American companies began pulling out their investments. The British film industry is now little more than a subsidiary to television.

In France, cinema attendance decreased each year. Despite such singular milestones as Marcel Ophuls' *The Sorrow and the Pity* – 1970 (made originally for television) and Jean Eustache's *The Mother and the Whore* – 1973, the directors who have come to the fore in the 1970s have excited no particular critical interest. Ironically one of the more popular new directors is Bertrand Tavernier, who has worked closely with veteran screenwriters Aurenche and Bost. These were the very men Francois Truffaut had singled out, when a young critic twenty years earlier, as the main exponents of the *Cinéma du Papa* against which the New Wave of the 1960s was rebelling.

Among the more interesting film-makers of this 'second wave' have been Claude Miller, André Techine, Pascal Thomas, Pierre Barouh, Yves Boisset, Michel Drach, and especially Maurice Pialat and Jean-Louis Bertucelli. Miller, who made *The Best Way To Go*, was formerly Truffaut's production manager and has continued in Truffaut's humanist vein. The prolific young Pascal Thomas (*Les Zozos* – 1973, *Don't Cry With Your Mouth Full* – 1974) has also proved that the traditions of poetic realism still have some life in them. Yves Boisset and Michel Drach have been among the main exponents of the muckraking film, while André Techine in *French Provincial* and *Barrocco* has experimented with narrative.

New European cinema

Maurice Pialat is responsible for a number of the most interesting French films of the 1970s. They include *We Won't Grow Old Together* – 1972 and *La Gueule ouverte* – 1975, respectively about marriage and death, probing human feelings with uncommon sensitivity and intelligence. Pierre Barouh's *Ça Va, Ça Vient* suggests the development of a new political realism in France. Jean-Louis Bertucelli (*Ramparts of Clay* – 1970, *Mistaken Love Story* – 1974, *L'Imprecateur*) has combined these two emphases – the political and the humanist – to form a very interesting body of work. Yet, while French films are again being aggressively marketed abroad, most lack critical interest.

The situation in Italy during the 1970s is similarly disappointing. As in France, the general level of cinema is competent. But film has lost the singular energy that attracted worldwide attention in the 1950s and 1960s. This was hardly surprising in the light of the deaths of several leading film-makers including Visconti, De Sica, Rossellini, Germi and Pasolini. Film-makers such as Bertolucci and Scola continue to produce interesting films, but it is hard to discern a new generation for the 1970s. Lina Wertmüller's films had a brief vogue in the US.

In Spain, however, the quiet disappearance of

Left *American Graffiti* – 1973 recreated the experience of being a teenager in a small Californian town in the early 1960s.

Below One of the early Hollywood successes of the 1970s was *The Godfather* – 1972. Conceived in epic-proportions, it outclassed the novel on which it was based. Francis Ford Coppola directed Marlon Brando and Al Pacino in a gangster story about the ageing head of a Mafia clan in New York.

ascism has resulted in an exciting new cinema, although it is still too early to tell which film-makers will prove of lasting importance.

In Eastern Europe, Hungarian cinema, with Marta Meszaros, and Polish cinema, with Krysztof Zanussi, have shown some new signs of life. Meanwhile Jerzy Skolimowski made *Deep End* – 1970 in the US and East Germany, and *The Shout* – 1978.

In Europe, only the German and Swiss film industries have been renewed. The new cinema movement of the early 1970s was centred in Munich. It is best represented in the work of Rainer Fassbinder, Werner Herzog, Wim Wenders, Alexander Kluge, and Volker Schlöndorff, each of whom brought new outlooks to the rebirth of German film.

Kluge has been the 'godfather' of this very loosely knit group. *Occasional Work of a Female Slave* – 1974 and *Strongman Ferdinand* – 1975 show him perceptively reworking Bertolt Brecht's theories of political theatre to make a cinema which is both political and emotionally powerful. Volker Schlöndorff (working generally with his wife Margaretta von Trotta) is, like Kluge, essentially concerned with practical politics. *A Free Woman* – 1972 was a major feminist film and *The Lost Honour of Katharina Blum* – 1975 a powerful and effective attack on neo-fascist stirrings in Germany. The critics have given more attention to the prolific Fassbinder, and to a lesser extent Herzog and Wenders, perhaps because their work is more evidently experimental, at least in terms of style.

Below *Cabaret* – 1972 was a musical based on a Christopher Isherwood book about life in Germany between the wars. Superlative performances by Liza Minnelli and Joel Grey raised the movie above most rivals. Director Bob Fosse dealt with the background to the rise of Nazism with integrity and style.

The Seventies 4

Rainer Fassbinder is noted for his prolific productivity. He is also noted for his camp attachment to the melodramatic forms of the 1950s which he has tried to revive, as well as the directness and compression of his films. Herzog is the mystic of New German Cinema. *Kaspar Hauser, Aguirre-Wrath of God*, and *Heart of Glass* seek to push back the boundaries of the psychological space of cinema. Wim Wenders with *Kings of the Road* – 1975 and *The American Friend* – 1977 is less colourful, but perhaps a more important artist in the long run. Like Fassbinder he is aware of the uses to which the old cinematic forms can be put; like Herzog he is interested in extending the frontiers of cinematic language. The result is a curious amalgam, but one that has attracted the attention of contemporary German audiences. Meanwhile, attention has shifted to about a score of younger directors, based mainly in Berlin, who may prove the main source of German cinema in the 1980s.

In Switzerland, such film-makers as Alain Tanner, Claude Goretta and Michel Soutter have with difficulty continued the work they began in the 1960s. All have been forced into co-productions partly financed with French money and starring French actors. Yet Tanner's *The Middle of the World* and *Jonah, Who Will Be 25 in the Year 2000* are telling, well-developed films.

Arab films may soon influence world markets, and Filipino blood epics and Hong Kong martial-arts movies continue to make their financial mark beyond native borders.

Chilean cinema, one of the most promising in the world in the early 1970s, was destroyed by the coup of 1973. Brazilian films have recently discovered a new popularity. Perhaps the most hopeful developments in Third World cinema in the 1970s have taken place in Cuba. A small but lively native industry continues to grow and mature there. Particularly interesting are the films of Tomás Gutiérrez Alea (*The Last Supper*), Humberto Solas (*Cantata de Chile*) and Manuel Octavio Gomez (*Days of Water*).

New Australian Cinema

Australian Cinema has developed remarkably since 1970. The industry woke after forty years inactivity to emerge as an international film-maker. The Australian government under prime ministers Gorton and Whitlam provided money for the revival. The boom not only helped production but also boosted audience attendance. Australia became an important film market.

Talented Australian directors have appeared, including Peter Weir, Fred Schepsi, Ken Hannam, Bruce Beresford, Michael Thornhill, Donald Crombie and Tim Burstall, as well as creative writers such as Joan Long, David Williamson, Cliff Green and John Dingwall, and charismatic stars such as Helen Morse, Jack Thompson and Barry Humphries.

Below *1900* – 1976, Bertolucci's epic-length treatment of the rise of fascism in Italy. Its colourful, operatic style and heightened emotions echo aspects of his previous films. Italian peasant women test their passive resistance against a squad of horsemen..

Left Rainer Werner Fassbinder is noted for his prolific output, *The Bitter Tears of Petra von Kant* – 1972 centres round the unrequited love of two lesbians. The film is set within the fashion-design world.

Below Peter Weir's *Picnic at Hanging Rock* – 1975 was one of Australia's recent internationally successful films. A party of boarding-school girls go on a Valentine's day picnic, but some never return. The film was noted for its evocative photography and suspense.

Television and Film 1

The relationship between movies and television is curious. On the one hand the younger medium, TV, has closely followed patterns set by its predecessor. Types of television entertainment continue the traditions of the movies. TV genres more or less parallel the film genres of the 1930s and 1940s: action, comedy, drama, police and detective stories, westerns, gangsters, musical variety and occasional ambitious dramas. Even sports and news, so much better done on television, owe their origins as a form to newsreels. The influence of movies on TV extends even to the dimensions of the screen: the 4 by 3 ratio bequeathed by the film industry – which then went on to adopt wide-screen ratios.

The basic form of TV is not the single programme but the series, a continuing framework using the same characters and situations for perhaps hundreds of individual episodes. With this form we come to know characters far better than we ever could in cinema film, the stage or even long novels. In fact we often come to know them far more intimately than we want to, especially in the static situations which characterize most American series.

New formats

Throughout the 1950s and 1960s and well into the 1970s the long-run series dominated American TV. But recently there has been a shift towards new formats: the serial (which tells a continuing and developing story, and aims at an ultimate end), the 'short-form series' (meant specifically for a limited run) and the 'novel-for-television'. This trend should bring American television as a form closer to cinema film.

The development of television formats took place gradually. In the 1950s TV was either live or filmed. Live broadcasts naturally suggested stage shows, and the result was the 'golden age' of drama showcases such as *Studio One* and *Playhouse 90*, which weekly presented different plays, most specially written for television. Before this the variety comedy had shown exceptional promise, especially in *Your Show of Shows*, starring Sid Caesar. This show featured, or was written by, most of the people who dominate Hollywood comedy in the 1970s, from Neil Simon and Carl Reiner to Mel Brooks. 'Sitcoms', half-hour filmed comedies, were also among the highlights of the 1950s, especially those of George Burns, Gracie Allen and Jack Benny. Lucille Ball's *I Love Lucy* was easily the most influential American TV programme of the early years.

In the 1960s, as videotape became available, American television genres settled down into a quite rigid pattern of hour-long adventure/action such as cop shows and doctor shows, and unmemorable half-hour sitcoms. Recordings were still used sparingly for variety shows and specials rather than for regular series.

By the 1970s television producers had realized tape's potential. On television, tape gives a more brilliant picture than film, though until very

Above Lucille Ball in a knife-throwing sequence from one of her long-running US television series *I Love Lucy*, which began in 1951. Her fine comic timing, strong voice and enormous energy contributed to her success. For several years she controlled one of Hollywood's largest TV production companies.

recently it was more difficult to shoot and edit. Series television in America in the 1970s was dominated by two production companies: Norman Lear's Tandem, responsible for series taped before a live audience, such as *All in the Family*, *Maude* and *Good Times* and the Mary Tyler Moore-Grant Tinker partnership which specialized in 'live-on-film' comedies, most notably the Mary Tyler Moore and Bob Newhart shows.

Both *All in the Family* and *The Mary Tyler Moore Show*, the most significant series of the 1970s, were ended while they were still quite popular and long before they had run their commercial course. Two other influential series, the hour-long *Kojak* and the longer *Columbo* lasted for relatively short runs. Creative attention in American TV was switching to the new forms.

In the early 1960s the networks, hungry for material, turned to the libraries of the film studios and began to schedule feature films regularly in prime time. They were without exception highly-rated and by the late 1960s at least one feature was available each night of the week. The library stocks, however, were running low. NBC began experimenting with the 'made-for-TV-movie' in

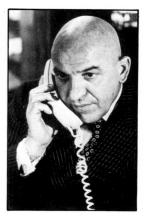

Above Kojak—the bald, lollipop-sucking New York cop, played in MCA television's series by Telly Savalas. He is noted for his earthy moralizing and laid-back dialogue.

Left John Michael Glazer and David Soul in the West Coast cop show *Starsky and Hutch*. Violence in these programmes has been reduced following criticism – now all is sweetness and light.

1966. Shaped to fit hour-and-a-half time-slots (because of commercials the films actually ran 75 minutes or less) and produced on relatively small budgets, they early proved worthwhile. Modern-day equivalents of the B-movie programmers of the 1930s, they were artistically unexceptional, but worked commercially.

Featured on television

However unlike the cinema features they were not presold by extensive publicity and previous cinema runs. To counteract this problem, programme executives such as Barry Diller, who pioneered the form at ABC and later became president of Paramount Pictures, turned increasingly to newsworthy subjects, films about historical characters or current events. By the mid-1970s these highly popular films were being called 'docudramas'. Produced cheaply on short shooting schedules, such films could sometimes be broadcast within months of the event on which they were based.

Brian's Song – 1971, directed by Buzz Kulik and written by William Blinn, was one of the first docudramas. This approximately true story of a famous American football player's death from cancer has become a classic of the genre. *The Missiles of October* – 1974, directed by Anthony Page and written by Stanley Greenberg, *The Autobiography of Miss Jane Pittman* – 1974, John Korty and Tracy Keenan Wynn, and *Fear on Trial* – 1975, Lamont Johnson and David Rintels, were among the notable docudramas that followed. The first retold the events of the Cuban missile

crisis of 1962; the second was the semi-fictional saga of a slave who survived to triumph in the civil rights movement of the 1960s; the last dramatized John Henry Faulk's long battle against the McCarthy period blacklist.

The emphasis in docudramas was often more on drama than facts, and the genre often verged on complete fiction. Some telefilms did not pretend to historical accuracy but dealt with issues of social importance. Boris Sagal's *A Case of Rape* – 1974, written by Robert E. Thompson; Sam O'Steen's *I Love You, Goodbye* – 1974, written by Diana Gould; and Lamont Johnson's *That Certain Summer* – 1972, written by Richard Levinson, William Link concerned themselves with, respectively, sexual assault, feminism and homosexuality in a serious way that never would have been commercially acceptable in cinema films.

Above Lee Majors as Steve Austin, the 'Six Million Dollar Man' – a series figure who is largely built of mechanical parts, and who performs superhuman feats.

Above left Jason Robards in the nine-hour film special *Washington Behind Closed Doors*, a tale closely based on the events behind the fall of President Nixon, with some strong characterisation.

Television and Film 2

A number of directors have specialized in telefilms while still shooting occasional features–notably Sagal, Johnson, O'Steen and Korty. Others, such as Steven Spielberg (*Duel*–1971), John Badham (*The Law*–1974) and Donald Wrye (*Death Be Not Proud*–1975), have used telefilms to train for careers in features. Telefilms can be more directly relevant than feature films, although they are often rushed, and hampered by limited budgets. They do not have to be blockbusters, and they can thus deal with issues in a lower key.

By the mid-1970s the made-for-television movies concept was expanding, and the series concept contracting. The two met on the middle ground of the mini-series, or novel-for-television. The telefilm was also useful as a pilot for a projected series. It paid for itself, and was often lengthened for release as a cinema feature abroad, so that the series concept could be tested with little financial risk.

In 1973 Lorimar Productions tried a new approach. Joseph Wambaugh's novel *The Blue Knight* was filmed in four parts, broadcast on successive nights on NBC. It proved successful–and later became a series. The next year ABC telecast a film of Leon Uris' novel *QB VII*, whose separate parts totalled more than five hours. In January 1977 the eight-part (ten-hour plus) mini-series of Alex Haley's *Roots* set startling ratings records, and accelerated the move to mini-series.

Television formats

At present there are more television formats than ever before. A property can be packaged as a made-for-television movie broadcast in a single ninety minute, two- or three-hour slot; as a dramatic 'special' taped to fit any of those slots; as a two-part telefilm of two, four or six hours; as a three – four – or more part mini-series broadcast on consecutive evenings or weekly; as a short-run series with the possibility of expanding to full series (shot either on film or on tape); as a closed-end series or serial; or as a traditional open-ended series which will survive so long as its ratings justify.

Right Ken Russell, something of an *enfant terrible* of British film-making, began his career with BBC television, making a series of films on composers. He returned to television in 1978 with characteristically idiosyncratic films on the English poets William Wordsworth and Samuel Taylor Coleridge.

Below right Filming part of the BBC TV series *The Forsyte Sage* – 1967, first of a long line of British exports.

Below The long-running Granada TV series *Coronation Street* is a soap opera based on the life in a working class community in Lancashire, England.

The development of videotape for home use will continue to make links between the previously separate forms of cinema movies and television. It is becoming possible for a producer of a film (or tape) to ignore both traditional means of distribution, cinemas and television, and to distribute cassettes direct to consumers.

The television film in Britain

Although a flood of filmed programmes is produced by the BBC and the commercial ITV companies, the ninety-minute American-style made-for-TV movie as yet barely exists in Britain.

In comparison with studio-recorded videotape, location-shot film is an expensive medium for drama. British dramas, unlike their American counterparts, cannot hope to cover costs in the small domestic market. But since both the BBC and ITV are essentially public-service networks and recognize a primary duty to the home audience, they have been able to dramatize British subjects on film. The cinema industry judges such subjects of limited appeal internationally.

TV fiction films

British TV fiction films often come disguised as one-off plays. Jack Rosenthal's wartime drama *The Evacuees*–BBC, 1975, directed by Alan Parker (of *Bugsy Malone* fame) was undoubtedly a fine film. But it was firmly within that British tradition which emphasizes the spoken word and character development—a literary quality associated with theatre, vastly different from the bang-bang action story of the average American telefilm.

As early as 1952 fiction films aimed at the lucrative North American TV market were being shot in British film studios by independent producers, but were usually half-hour series. Commercial television, launched in 1955, demanded more pre-recorded (and therefore pre-filmed) material, increasing the production of telefilm series.

Video-tape and TV

Video-tape recording, introduced into Britain from the US in 1958-59, did not immediately revolutionize drama production techniques, since it was clumsy to edit. The revolution started in 1964, when the BBC opened a second channel and found itself with too few videotape machines to cope with demand. Programme-makers were given the opportunity to record dramas in the studio electronically on 35mm film – for long the practice for pre-filmed exterior scenes inserted into live and videotaped productions.

Thus they acquired a taste for film's flexibility. Impatient with old forms and outdated technology, they urgently wanted to reflect the rapid social change sweeping Britain. The possibilities were shown in the abrasive realism of *Z-Cars* – BBC, 1962, which was set in the tough seaport of Liverpool. It shattered the cosy image of previous police series and was a pacemaker for further developments.

Television and Film 3

Television licences

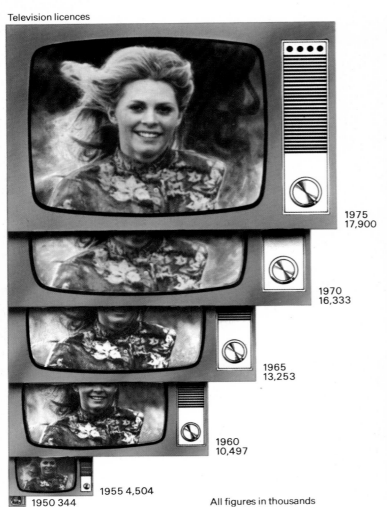

1975
17,900

1970
16,333

1965
13,253

1960
10,497

1955 4,504

1950 344

All figures in thousands

Cinema attendances

All figures in thousands

1975
116

1970
198

1965
316

1960
500

1955
1,181

1950
1,395

But first the superior quality of 35mm film had to be ditched because of its bulky equipment. News and documentary film-makers were already exploiting the portability of 16mm film equipment. Immediacy was prized perhaps above all else by the new drama-makers. Peter Watkins demonstrated the use of 16mm brilliantly in his *vérité* documentary reconstruction of an infamous battle *Culloden* – BBC, 1964, shot in the style of TV news reportage, mixing 'actuality' with interviews.

Two plays directed by Ken Loach memorably exploited 16mm. *Up The Junction* – BBC, 1965, was a kaleidoscope of young London working class life, and included a controversial abortion scene. *Cathy Come Home* – BBC, 1966, was a relentless exposé of homelessness. *The Wednesday Play* (under whose heading they were transmitted) won its notoriety for hard-hitting, almost sensational, contemporary drama. But despite their seamless appearance as films, parts of both plays were recorded electronically in the studio. It was not until 1967 that Union agreements permitted TV plays to be filmed entirely on location.

The BBC, with its two channels, has committed a significant part of its drama output to film. But the ITV companies have been less adventurous, damning the one-off drama film as too expensive and unattractive to large audiences.

TV feature films

Thames, one of the London ITV companies, founded a subsidiary, Euston Films, in 1972. They produced drama series on film, and TV features transmitted under the title *Armchair Cinema*. As in America, feature films suitable for the TV screen were threatening to become scarce, as bad language, excessive violence and frank sex became increasingly common. *Regan* – .1974, one of Euston Films' first efforts, was virtually a pilot for the later successful filmed series, *The Sweeney*, about Scotland Yard's Flying Squad. After 1975 ITV profits dropped in the recession; when the films failed to achieve American sales, Euston concentrated on film series. Oddly Thames' most successful TV film, *The Naked Civil Servant* – 1975, directed by Jack Gold, the autobiography of a flamboyant homosexual, was produced outside the Euston Films set-up.

The BBC has produced such films as *Rogue Male* – 1976, directed by Clive Donner at a reported cost of £175,000, as co-productions (films co-financed by TV companies with foreign partners). Similarly ATV (the most successful British company at penetrating the American market with consciously 'Transatlantic' programmes) produced *Jesus of Nazareth* – 1977, directed by Franco Zeffirelli.

Above The impact of television. Between 1950 and 1975 the number of television licences issued annually in the UK rose from 344,000 to 17,900,000. Meanwhile cinema admissions fell from 1,395,828,000 in 1950 to 116,300,000 in 1975.

THE DREAM INDUSTRY

By the early 1930s, Hollywood had come to dominate world cinema. The history of cinema virtually *meant* the history of Hollywood. Hollywood was already firmly established, and rapidly assimilated sound processes. It plundered Europe for film makers and actors. Its studio system ensured firm control of every stage of the film process – production, distribution and exhibition.

Talk of a 'Dream Factory' is no mere hyperbole. The studios were run on a production-line basis: properties were bought, designed, produced and released. Technicians, executives, artists and directors all worked regularly and intensively. But the results were not mere 'assembly-line' products. Hollywood produced some of its most legendary films: *Gone With the Wind*, *King Kong*, *Modern Times*, *Dracula*, *Queen Christina*, *The Scarlet Empress* . . . The list is endless.

Meanwhile Hollywood itself acquired an image of luxury, scandal and ostentation. Its own publicists magnified this vision, and its stars provided heroes for a film-going populace.

Hollywood:
The Rise of The Studios

Two years before the Lumière brothers' first public movie performance in Paris that famous day in December 1895, a less celebrated, but scarcely less momentous, event occurred in the USA. Thomas Edison built the world's first film studio: a barn-shaped building nicknamed (because of its tar-paper covering) the 'Black Maria'.

In the earliest days of cinema it was realised that high-quality, high-definition film-making required the laboratory-like conditions of the indoor studio. Rather than continuing to mean a room in which the artist shuts himself away to work, 'studio' in film terms now means an organization of creative and administrative forces gathered together to encourage, sometimes to dragoon, its member-artists into working to maximum productivity and profitability.

The studio system, in this sense, was born in the second decade of this century. The American film companies had been based in New York. They now crossed the country to California and set up permanent home there. The companies could now afford to assemble a permanent group of artists and technicians. Property and labour were cheap, sunlight was limitless and film-makers were more or less safe from the raids of the notorious Patents Company based in New York. In short, a hitherto semi-nomadic industry was now able to settle down in peace in what was to become virtually its own artistic capital.

The first Hollywood studio was built in 1911 by the short-lived Nestor Company. In 1913 Cecil B. DeMille came to Hollywood to make *The Squaw Man*, and founded what became known as Paramount Studios. Of the other major companies, Universal was born at about the same time, the Fox Company two years later (merging with 20th Century Pictures in 1935), United Artists in 1919, and Warner Brothers, MGM and Columbia all in the early 1920s.

The men who made the studios

The studios undoubtedly took much of their early character as film-making units from the men who founded them. Carl Laemmle at Universal combined a prophetic belief in the possibilities of the star system with a fondness for a varied output of lively, not-too-expensive movies. By contrast, the keynote at Paramount was glitter – influenced partly by its president, Adolph Zukor's, taste for European sophistication (Valentino and Pola Negri were on his payroll), and partly by Cecil B. DeMille's stock-in-trade extravagance.

The seven major Hollywood studios established their dominance rapidly and with assurance, and have retained it ever since. This achievement is a tribute to the entrepreneurial energy that seems an integral part of American life and culture.

To a great extent each studio preserved its own dynasty as well as its name. Jack L. Warner was at Warner Brothers until 1969, escorting it through a prosperous period in the 1930s (their first sound films were prodigiously successful) and coaxing it through more troubled years from the mid-1950s

onwards. The Laemmles, father and son, ruled Universal for 25 years. Louis B. Mayer remained a power at MGM until 1951. Harry Cohn of Columbia Pictures was unchallengeably in command there until 1958.

Studios in decline

Since the early 1950s the profitability of the feature film has declined. The Hollywood studios have had to shore up their finances with a number of outside projects – chiefly by undertaking the making of television films.

The studio system in Hollywood has triumphed by applying the strategies of industry to a branch of the art and entertainment world. Undoubtedly, if a single factor has made America supreme as a film-making nation, it is the studio system. It can permit success on a grand scale and it can swallow failure on a grand scale. The large size of the major studios is their strength. They can create styles and genres independently of the single artist (Warner Brothers' gangster films, MGM's musicals). They

Right The studios of First National at Burbank, California, in the early 1930s. At that time they figured among the best-equipped. The sound stages are housed in the bow-roofed buildings, behind which, in the back lot, some sets can be seen. The studio administrative offices are situated in the left foreground.

Below Studio shooting in progress for the complex finale to the Warner Brothers' *This is the Army* – 1943. As well as the proscenium stage, actors and orchestra, the large technical crew involved in such an elaborate scene are clearly visible.

Top Carl Laemmle set up Universal Pictures in 1912. He soon moved from New York to California, setting up a studio on a 236-acre chicken ranch in the San Fernando valley. It was created an independent city devoted to film-making in 1915: Universal City.

Bottom Thomas Edison's 'Black Maria' studio at West Orange, New Jersey. Covered in tar-paper, it had a roof which opened to the sun, and a pivot to turn it to capture the best light. It contained a little stage for performers inside.

can give security to people in a notoriously insecure profession.

The equivalent of the Hollywood studio has never existed in Europe, the East or the Third World. Cinecitta in Rome, grand as it is, is a studio merely in the bricks-and-mortar sense. It has no resident company of artists. The nearest non-American equivalent to Hollywood was Germany's UFA, the studio which in the 1920s had a regular group of actors, directors and technicians. The resources of large-scale studios continued to be felt in the 1930s and 1940s. UFA created virtually single-handed the Expressionist movement in the cinema. Japan's Toho Company, a big studio conglomerate, from the 1930s onwards helped to produce some of the greatest Japanese films. Similarly Indian studios, notably those in Bombay, produced a steady stream of studio-made spectaculars. On a humble scale, Britain's Ealing Studios are a fine example of how a building, a company and a style can merge successfully, the style that of English domesticity.

Putting on Style:
The Hollywood Studios

Critics today argue furiously about how we should judge individual films. Should it be in terms of the director who made them, or in terms of the genre to which they belong? Is it more productive to discuss *Singin' In The Rain* – 1952 as a musical or as a Stanley Donen/Gene Kelly film?

The debate will no doubt go on raging. But one 'context' so far glaringly neglected is the studio. Could we not also judge *Singin' In The Rain* as a highly characteristic and significant example of the MGM studio style? Should not the studio which has created the conditions, the resources and the artistic policy which helped to make the film be credited with its success – or blamed for its failure?

Tasteful extravagance

Metro-Goldwyn-Mayer is an excellent example to begin with. MGM was a studio with a more readily definable house style than any of the others. 'Tasteful extravagance' is the best thumbnail description of MGM's style. Its tone was set in the late 1920s and early 1930s by 'boy wonder' Irving Thalberg. He is said to have been a man cursed by 'good taste' and is the model for Scott Fitzgerald's Monroe Stahr in his novel *The Last Tycoon*. The plush period respectability of many of Thalberg's projects, for instance, *Camille* – 1936 and *Romeo and Juliet* – 1936, is not favoured today. But undoubtedly he formed MGM's taste for elegant, glamorous theatricality, which lasted into the 1940s and 1950s with the splendid series of musicals directed by men such as Gene Kelly, Stanley Donen and Vincente Minnelli.

MGM and Paramount both loved expensive sophistication. But there was a lively hint of European decadence in Paramount's early films, by directors such as Ernst Lubitsch, Rouben Mamoulian and DeMille. They boasted such stars as Pola Negri, Marlene Dietrich and Claudette Colbert. In the 1930s and 1940s Paramount showed a flair for comedy in films from Preston Sturges, Mitchell Leisen and Billy Wilder. Their slogan in the 1930s was 'If it's a Paramount picture it's the best show in town.' Later landmarks in this pursuit of high-quality showmanship included the invention of VistaVision in the 1950s and the release of *Love Story* – 1970 and *The Godfather* – 1972 in the 1970s.

At the opposite end of the spectrum from Paramount and MGM were Warner Brothers. Jack L. Warner's unspoken motto was: 'Money should not only be saved, it should be seen to be saved.' So at Warners low-budget, fast-action movies (and stars on low, long-term contracts) were the rule. Their most famous house-genre was the gangster film: that irresistibly dynamic series of low-life thrillers starring such actors as Humphrey Bogart, James Cagney, George Raft and Edward G. Robinson. Many of Bette Davis' finest (and cheapest) films were made at Warners. In later years Warners showed a shrewd flair for profitable co-productions with other studios such as *My Fair Lady* – 1964 with First National and *The Towering Inferno* – 1976 with 20th Century-Fox.

Left After her immense success in *The Blue Angel* – 1930 Marlene Dietrich was signed on by Paramount, who remodelled her. They relaunched her in a series of films by Josef von Sternberg. In *Desire* – 1936, she played a glamorous jewel-thief who has to seduce her naive accomplice to win back a stolen necklace. Sternberg changed her into an aloof, talking mask, beautiful and perverse.

Below A typically anarchic scene from the Marx Brothers' *Monkey Business* – 1931. For a period the famous comedy team worked for Paramount Pictures, before being invited to Metro-Goldwyn-Mayer by Irving Thalberg in the mid-1930s. In *Monkey Business* the brothers were stowaways on board ship.

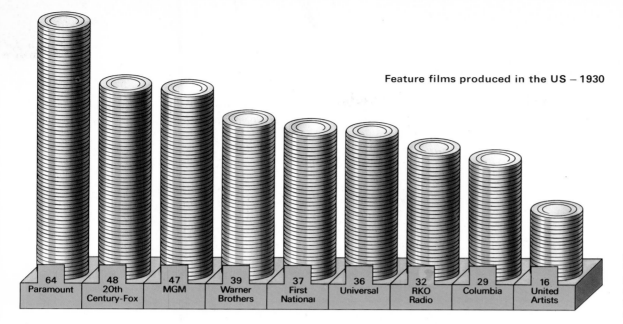

Feature films produced in the US – 1930

| 64 Paramount | 48 20th Century-Fox | 47 MGM | 39 Warner Brothers | 37 First National | 36 Universal | 32 RKO Radio | 29 Columbia | 16 United Artists |

Left Nine major studios dominated Hollywood in the 1930s. This diagram shows the total number of features produced by the major US film companies in 1930.

Below Adolph Zukor (1873 – 1976), who formed the Famous Players film production company in 1912, to develop it into Paramount Pictures. A shrewd businessman, he was among the first to see the possibilities of the star system, and invested huge amounts in stars' salaries. Among the stars he attracted were Mary Pickford, Douglas Fairbanks, Gloria Swanson and Rudolph Valentino.

Guided by Darryl F Zanuck and Spyros Skouras, 20th Century-Fox majored in westerns, musicals, religious epics and generally anything 'big' and likely to splash headlines across newspaper film-pages. It was Fox who introduced CinemaScope in the early 1950s, and who produced the notorious *Cleopatra* – 1963 ten years later. Recent landmarks have included *The Sound of Music* – 1965 and *Star Wars* – 1977.

Open policy

Universal and RKO deserve to be bracketed together as the least dictatorial and artistically most open-minded studios in Hollywood. Universal had a wonderfully indulgent studio-head in Carl Laemmle. Their resourceful production policy paid dividends in such movie genres as the horror film (Universal initiated both the Dracula and the Frankenstein series), and the 1950s 'women's pictures'. Lately Universal has reaped the financial rewards of its generous and flexible approach. The success of *The Sting* – 1973 and *Jaws* – 1975 have turned the studio into the most prosperous in present-day Hollywood.

RKO Pictures had a shorter, but equally glorious, history. Founded in 1928, the studio lasted for twenty years. In that time RKO produced many of the Hollywood films that have become household names: *Bringing Up Baby* – 1938, *King Kong* – 1933, *Citizen Kane* – 1941, Hitchcock's *Suspicion* – 1941, Ford's *The Informer* – 1935 and no less than nine Fred Astaire – Ginger Rogers musicals. Like Universal, RKO had a remarkable *laissez-faire* attitude towards its directors. Under their non-interfering patronage Val Lewton produced his superb series of mini-budget horror films in the early 1940s – among them *The Cat People* – 1942 and *The Body Snatcher* (*The Body Snatchers* in Britain) – 1945.

Columbia and United Artists have a less definable character artistically than the other major studios. Columbia's studio head Harry Cohn had a flair for backing his own hunches – which included Frank Capra and Rita Hayworth. The studio had an especially fine light comedy record in the 1930s. After a lean period in the 1940s, Columbia rallied with a policy of supporting independent producers and directors, among

them Sam Spiegel, David Lean and Otto Preminger. But Columbia has always tended to be a big, prosperous, enterprising studio lacking a consistent style.

United Artists did not have a permanent studio or a permanent company of stars. They tended to flourish in partnership with other production companies. Alexander Korda enjoyed a ten-year association with UA, and the Mirisch Brothers, a company that financed films by Billy Wilder, Norman Jewison and John Sturges among others, signed a contract with them in the 1950s. But United Artists remain essentially a distribution company rather than a Hollywood studio in the popular sense.

The Independents:
Producers Outside The Studios

Independent producers were few and far between during the heyday of the Hollywood studio system. Between 1920 and 1960, only two great American producers flourished outside, and in defiance of, the major studios: Sam Goldwyn and David O. Selznick. It took money, flair, influence and courage for a lone individual to take on the big companies. Goldwyn and Selznick both had these qualities in large measure. By their success they continued the independent film-making traditions of Thomas Ince and D. W. Griffith in Hollywood's 'pre-history'. They also blazed a path for the recent era of American cinema, during which the independent producer-director has flourished.

The American spirit of self-help has seldom been more notably embodied than in the careers of Goldwyn and Selznick. Goldwyn was associated with two major studios – first Paramount, then MGM – before he cut loose in the mid-1920s to found his own company. Samuel Goldwyn Pictures flourished until 1959, producing some of Hollywood's best-known films. Goldwyn's most fruitful collaboration was with director William Wyler, with whom he made *Wuthering Heights* – 1939, *The Little Foxes* – 1941 and *The Best Years of Our Lives* – 1946.

David Selznick

David O. Selznick's career was even more spectacular. In his early years he worked for three different major studios – Paramount, RKO and MGM. But in 1935 he established his own company, Selznick International Pictures. Four years later he produced the film that has sold more tickets than any other movie in the world: *Gone With The Wind* – 1939. Selznick was not so much an independent producer as a one-man industry. Never content unless he had a finger in every pie, he had a stronger claim than most producers to being artistic 'co-author' of his films. Selznick cast *Gone With The Wind* (gambling on the unknown Vivien Leigh), he shaped its screenplay, he bullied its directors (first George Cukor, then Victor Fleming) and willed its commercial triumph. Later Selznick films never quite repeated the bonanza of this lush Civil War epic; but notable successors included *Rebecca* – 1940, *Spellbound* and *Duel In The Sun* – 1946 and *The Third Man* – 1949.

Another intrepid Hollywood outsider was Walt Disney, who cornered the animation market at an early stage. Disney never allowed his independence to be encroached upon or eroded by the major studios.

Yet another independent was Howard Hughes. Hughes took a controlling interest in RKO in the late 1940s, but before that he enjoyed a characteristically meteoric career as an independent producer. His best-known films in the 1930s included *Hell's Angels* – 1930, *The Front Page* – 1931 and *Scarface* – 1932. Hughes released his films through United Artists, the company whose founding had constituted Hollywood's one significant early attempt to resist the stranglehold of the major studios. United Artists was founded in 1919 by Chaplin, Fairbanks, Pickford and Griffith. It offered a vital distribution outlet to producers and directors who spurned the cosy but unstimulating security of working for one of the big studios.

Since the late 1950s the major studios themselves have concentrated more on distribution and less on production. They have provided money and assured film release. Otherwise they have more or less left their producer-directors to make their own films in their own way.

The change has been due not to some sudden surge of kind-heartedness on the part of the studios, but to the increasing unpredictability of audience response. The studios have realised that

filmgoers are less and less inclined to accept the formula diet provided by studio-policy film-making. The public is more and more attracted to the impromptu and the unusual. *Easy Rider* – 1969 was a milestone in recent American cinema. It overturned box office expectations and set in motion a cycle of youth-movies. It helped prove that outsiders and independents, as well as tycoons at Fox or Warners could sometimes hit the jackpot.

A major feature of recent American cinema has also been the low-budget action picture. Many of today's leading independent film-makers were 'blooded' on these exploitation films or 'Z-movies'. The king of the Z-movie is Roger Corman. Once a successful low-budget horror director, Corman is now an even more successful producer and entrepreneur. Since the mid-1960s he has given an early opportunity for feature-film work to directors as diverse and distinguished as Francis Ford Coppola, Peter Bogdanovich and Martin Scorsese.

Outside America, 'independent' means something rather different. Once again it is money that spells creative freedom. Cinema is an expensive art. Only lack of funds stops every film-maker in the world from being an independent. Movies require outside investment – and outside investment usually comes with strings attached.

Realism versus The Dream Factory

The three Frenchmen who 'founded' cinema neatly divided between them the two main stylistic traditions of the cinema's next eighty years. Louis Lumière, with his brother Auguste, pioneered documentary-style realism. They used the camera as a more-or-less 'passive' recording machine, imprinting on celluloid every casual phenomenon of daily life – from a child crying in its pram to workmen knocking down a wall. By contrast, Georges Méliès was the magician of the cinema. A conjuror turned film-maker, he discovered trick-photography and pioneered the cinema of fantasy and illusion.

A schizophrenic medium

The cinema is a uniquely schizophrenic medium. It can at once accurately reproduce and magically scramble the outward appearance of things. But the cinema's 'realistic' power operates vitally in both areas of film-making – documentary *and* fantasy. The emotional force of the cinema's delvings into the unreal lies precisely in its ability always to make that unreal *seem* real. Witness horror films, science-fiction movies and the surrealist shorts of Buñuel and Cocteau.

Of course the plausibility and 'lifelikeness' of the cinema's stories varies greatly. Clustered at one end of the scale are musicals, cartoons and horror and science-fiction films. All these genres test to the limits how far the audience can suspend its disbelief. These films feel no binding obligation to reproduce accurately the surface of life. (Their extravagances are often prone to satire for that reason.) But at the same time they never quite sever their moorings in everyday reality. The musical often uses a 'backstage' story as a pretext for mounting song-and-dance numbers. The exaggerations of the cartoon are rooted in real details of human or animal behaviour. And how many times in horror and science-fiction films have we had to listen to the doctor's or scientist's 'plausible explanation' of the previous ninety minutes of Grand Guignol and mayhem?

Among the ostensibly more realistic genres are the western, the historical film, the romance and (with exceptions such as Frank Tashlin, Jerry Lewis and some of Chaplin) the comedy. But this is still not kitchen-sink realism. In these films heroism, love and beauty are refined to an unworldly purity, dressed in clothes and settings of a very un-average glossiness.

Not that realism should be confused with shabbiness. The gangster film, for example, had little time for palatial settings or heroines dripping with pearls. But its squalor is, in its way, just as unreal as the lustrous beauty of the more expensive Hollywood genres. After all, the average filmgoer is no more familiar with the slums and speakeasies of Chicago than with life in the Waldorf Astoria. Criteria of realism are difficult to define. But we should not fall into the trap of deciding that everything 'unreal' belongs to the higher end of the income scale.

What the audience wants

Movies are a form of existential window-shopping. The greatest single factor luring the Hollywood film-maker away from a represen-tation of the average, the mundane, the 'merely' real, is the audience's demand for wish-fulfilment.

Below Much of the overwhelming box-office success of Robert Wise's *The Sound of Music* – 1965 must be attributed to its blatant escapism. It spawned newspaper reports of people seeing it time and time again as a refuge from the harsh realities of mid-twentieth century life. Its heart-warming story, homespun concern for the family and religion, simple tunefulness and innocence, and Tyrolean scenery conspire to create an alluring dreamland. The film was based on the stage musical by Rogers and Hammerstein and starred Julie Andrews and Christopher Plummer. The story stemmed from a true incident in the Nazi take-over of Austria.

An audience goes to the cinema to gaze at, and mentally try on, a different life. They go to bask in the warm emotions of a love story, to tremble at the dangers of a gangster story, to shriek at the two-headed creature from outer space, to open up the West with John Wayne.

It is misleading, then, to think of movie realism and movie fantasy as irreconcilable opposites. Dreams are what the movie audience has always wanted; realism is the way in which it has wanted them served. But it is true that the post-war cinema in Europe and in America has capitalized as never before on the photographic immediacy and authenticity of cinema as a medium. There has been an unprecedented thrust towards what could be called 'newsrealism' in the cinema, from the *cinéma vérité* documentaries of Pennebaker to the improvisational vitality of Godard's or Cassavetes' films. This is the realism of news reportage, in which the hand-held camera becomes an expressive instrument as swift, flexible and precise as the writer's pen.

This new style and emphasis has already spread to the commercial cinema. It gives rise to the on-location immediacy of the cops-and-robbers films and the colloquialism of much modern screen dialogue. The directors doubtless hope to persuade audiences that the fictions they are watching are more real than before because the surface tics and idioms are more racy, downbeat and recognizable. But the films still *are* fictions. The cinema's cosmetic modernism merely demonstrates that a dream factory, like any other factory, must adapt to change and keep itself ahead of obsolescence or go into decline.

Left Greta Garbo represents a screen mystery of a unique kind. Her reserve and loneliness were built up into a mystique which provided its own attraction for audiences. By appearing inscrutable, she became the object of the filmgoer's sensuous fantasies. Her real neame was Greta Gustafsson, and her first film appearances were in shop advertisements. It was the Swedish director Mauritz Stiller who transformed her, and eventually took her with him to Hollywood. Her appeal has lasted: re-issues of her films have attracted large audiences, especially in the US.

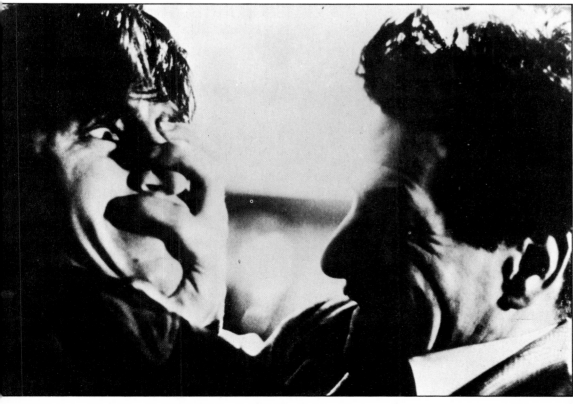

Left John Cassavetes' directorial debut, *Shadows* – 1960 was made on 16mm film with hand-held camera in New York. He had a crew of four people, and the film was totally improvized. It marked a rebellion against the Hollywood system; its grainy vitality presents one concept of 'reality' in cinema.

The Star System:
Screen Idols

'Acting talent is not enough. A star must possess another mysterious quality, which you might call personality, magnetism, glamour. The essence of it is the capacity to stir the imagination of the audience, to make them feel that there is much more to the actor or actress than meets the eye and ear.' This definition of stardom was given in 1967 by Rouben Mamoulian, who directed many of Hollywood's greatest stars.

Until the 1960s the star system was an important part of commercial film-making throughout the world, although it began and reached its peak in the United States. Almost every American feature film from the 1910s to the 1950s reveals its influence. Stories were often chosen and screenplays adapted to fit the personality of a particular star. The novelist Margaret Mitchell has confessed that, while writing her book *Gone With The Wind*, she developed the leading character of Rhett Butler as a mirror image of Clark Gable's screen personality. In due course Gable played the cynical, fascinating hero in the film – and it became his most famous role.

Star quality

The 'star' emphasis went yet further. The cameraman, film editor and director were also often chosen because of their ability to bring out a star's photogenic qualities, acting talent and chosen personality.

The extent of the influence of the star system on film-makers is admitted by, among others, the American director King Vidor. He wrote in 1972: 'It took me years to learn that big stars had established symbols that shouldn't be tampered with ... it was a mistake to try to reshape the character symbolized by the star to fit a different character called for in the screenplay.' But not all directors accepted the star system with such equanimity. Some, including Cecil B. DeMille, Josef von Sternberg and, more recently, Alfred Hitchcock, have expressed misgivings about the stars' influence, and sometimes contempt for stars and film actors in general.

The origins of stardom

The word 'star' was coined in the early 1900s, but before 1909 film companies did not disclose the identities of performers. Inevitably filmgoers became increasingly curious about their favourites, and wrote to the companies requesting information about them. The company heads pursued a secretive policy partly for fear that if the names of performers became known, they would then demand more money, thus reducing their dependence on the companies. At the same time many actors and actresses cherished their anonymity, since they were rather ashamed of their film work, regarding cinema as a poor substitute for the live theatre.

Most early stars were young actors without stage experience – partly because primitive lighting techniques failed to conceal the age of mature performers. In any event, acting styles in

Above Rudolph Valentino – one of Hollywood's earliest heart-throbs. His star potential was first recognized with his performance in *The Four Horsemen of the Apocalypse* – 1922. This decoration was designed for a cigar-box illustration.

Left One of the big box-office star-attractions of the late 1960s was Rober Redford, who first gained attention with his appearance in *The Chase* – 1966. With his open good looks and accomplished acting he jumped to acclaim with his role as co-star with Paul Newman in *Butch Cassidy and the Sundance Kid* – 1969.

lms differed from those required in the theatre. The term 'staginess' came to mean falseness. incerity, youthfulness and restraint, the most dmired features in screen acting, were more vident in younger performers who had little or no age experience.

he popularity of stars

rom 1910 the stars began to realize their nportance and power in the growing industry. an magazines and newspaper gossip-columns ported their activities, and star performers ceived heavy fan-mail. But the enthusiasm of the blic came as a surprise to many of the new idols. Highly-paid stars, including Charles Chaplin, ouglas Fairbanks, Greta Garbo, Lillian Gish, ary Pickford and Rudolph Valentino, became usehold names throughout the world in the 20s. Such stars were often called screen gods and ddesses – a measure of the worship they were corded. Psychologists have diagnosed that stars lect the needs, dreams and fantasies of the ngoing public. But their popularity declined pidly when their personality, image or tech- ques fell out of fashion. The introduction of und, from 1927, proved disastrous for many rs of the silents.

By the 1930s stars were to be found everywhere. e term 'star' had come to mean any performer ose name was billed above the film's title. day, the term has become limited to any former whose appearance is considered to arantee a film's success at the box office.

e modern star system

om the 1960s the star system lost much of its wer as cinema audiences declined and tastes nged. A star no longer guarantees profits. For mple, Julie Andrews achieved star status with tremendous success of *Mary Poppins* – 1964 *The Sound of Music* – 1965. But some of her films, including *Star!* – 1968, were flops. anwhile, other films, without stars, such as *The duate* – 1968 and *2001: A Space Odyssey* – 1968 ved to be great successes. And *Jaws* – 1975, ther starless film, except perhaps for its rubber rk, grossed about $125 million within 78 days ts release.

tar appeal, though less consistent than it once , cannot be written off. Some older stars, such ohn Wayne, still have a following, possibly as a lt of nostalgia. And a few stars still receive onomical fees for their work. Charles Bronson puted to earn $2 million per film and, in 1977, rlon Brando received $2.25 million for ten s' work – as guest performer in *Superman* – 3, a role which occupies no more than ten utes in the final film.

ut stars are created by the public, their status nds on continued box-office success and a e of identification between themselves and the ence. If that link is broken, then our hero is a star in a vacuum – and Hollywood is ed with flawed heroes.

Above Gloria Swanson was signed up by Cecil B. DeMille in 1918. He set about moulding her into a symbol of sensuous extravagance. She was under contract to Paramount Pictures between 1922–26, when she was among the best paid stars. She became notorious for her heavy spending and much-publicized romances.

Left Fred Astaire and Ginger Rogers first featured together in *Flying Down to Rio* – 1933. They achieved acclaim for one number in that film: 'The Carioca', which led to a series of films.

Shaping the Modern Cinema 1

Throughout its history, the size and shape of the cinema theatre has reflected the economic health of the motion picture industry and its position in the field of popular entertainment. In its first years film was a technical novelty, shown in any available space – in disused shops, in local meeting-rooms and fairground marquees, and as an occasional variety theatre act. But as 'going to the movies' became a habit, existing live theatres were often converted.

Film's increasing popularity also called for special halls to be built – the 'Electric Theatre'. This phase spread through all the major industrial countries, reaching its peak roughly between 1925 and 1935. It was then that the large, luxury custom-built cinema became most wide-spread. The escape it offered during the years of industrial depression is reflected in both the decor and the names of the period: 'Palace', 'Ritz', 'De Luxe' and more exotically 'Hawaii', 'Granada' and 'Luxor'. Buildings to hold audiences of 2,000 or 3,000 were found in most major city centres, while the cinema theatres in the suburbs were only slightly smaller.

The addition of sound to the motion picture show involved no major alterations to the majority of existing cinemas, although from then on new buildings were always designed with acoustic requirements in mind.

During World War II and immediately afterwards, theatre building, like much other low-priority construction, practically stood still, although cinema-going was still the leading mass entertainment. When new building was at last permitted it was once again in the form of the large auditorium for a large audience, but now reflected the higher standards of comfort demanded by its patrons. From the mid-1950s the proscenium wall was shaped to accept the new curved wide-screens required by the latest technology.

The shrinking cinema

But even while these developments were going forward, cinema's role in popular leisure activities was already changing, partly as a result of TV's competition as a visual entertainment in the home. But other leisure interests such as motoring, sport, travel, food and drink, recorded and live music all offered their own attractions. The cinema started to slip from the dominant position it had held for some thirty years. In 1951 box-office admissions in the United Kingdom exceeded 1,300 million seats, meaning that an average member of the public went to the cinema 27 times during those twelve months. Ten years later, despite the blandishments of colour, wide-screen, multi-channel sound and higher technical quality in every field, attendances had fallen by two-thirds. By the mid-1970s admissions were less than one-tenth of the 1951 level (despite a larger total population) representing only two visits per person during the year. This pattern of decline in movie-going was repeated in the United States and throughout Western Europe. For example, in both the US and

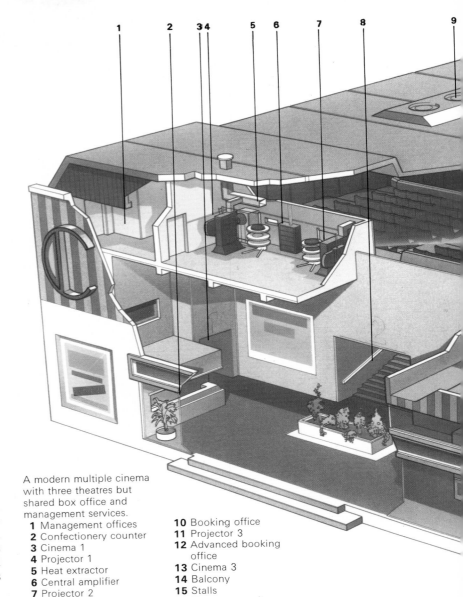

A modern multiple cinema with three theatres but shared box office and management services.

1 Management offices
2 Confectionery counter
3 Cinema 1
4 Projector 1
5 Heat extractor
6 Central amplifier
7 Projector 2
8 Cinema 2
9 Airconditioning ducts
10 Booking office
11 Projector 3
12 Advanced booking office
13 Cinema 3
14 Balcony
15 Stalls
16 Emergency exit
17 Curved widescreen

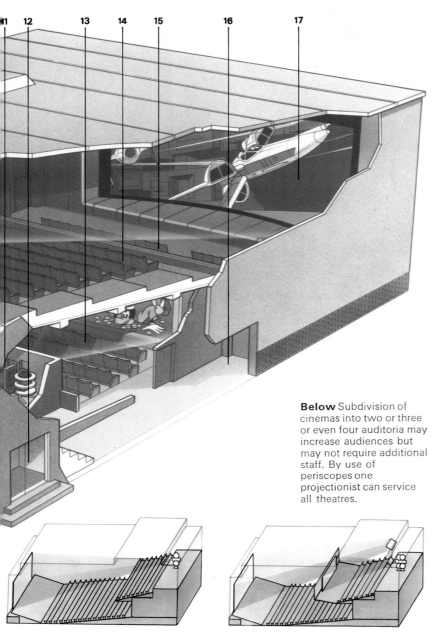

Labels: 11 12 13 14 15 16 17

Below Subdivision of cinemas into two or three or even four auditoria may increase audiences but may not require additional staff. By use of periscopes one projectionist can service all theatres.

During the 1920s and 1930s many large cinemas of strikingly modernistic design sprang up, particularly in Europe and the US. Art Deco, Neo-Egyptian and neo-Classical styles proliferated. Seen here are **Left** the Leicester Odeon in the UK, **Right** the San Francisco Granada, and **Far Right** the Gambetta Cinema in Paris.

Germany attendances fell by two-thirds over the fifteen years after 1961.

By the 1960s it had become clear that this decline was not going to be reversed. The industry would have to re-shape its way of life and recognize that a sparsely attended performance in a large theatre positively deters the pleasure seeker. The typical movie palace was no longer a viable business, except perhaps in the entertainment centres of a few capital cities. In both town and suburb, cinemas were closed down – often the largest and most spectacular first – and their sites redeveloped, sometimes to include a small theatre as part of the plan. Between 1961 and 1976 the number of cinemas in the United Kingdom dropped from over 4,500 to little over 1,500. The average seating capacity in each cinema fell from about 1,800 to less than 550, emphasizing the marked trend to smaller units.

Later in the 1960s an interesting development occurred, with the conversion of large older cinemas into multiples. They housed two, three or even more separate cinemas under the same roof, sharing common box-office and management services, and often operated from a single projection room. A typical conversion might provide one fairly large unit seating up to 500, and two others for audiences of 200–250 and 100–150. All would be equipped for the various forms of widescreen presentation, but only rarely with multi-channel sound.

In Britain the number of such multiple complexes grew from seventeen in 1969 to 271 in 1976, totalling 739 separate cinemas, practically half of all those in the country. The yearly box-office takings at these multiple centres now considerably exceed those for single halls. The variety of theatre size allows popular and more specialized programmes to be presented at the same location and allows plans to be altered to meet changing demand. For an outstanding popular success all units can show the same programme.

Projection by computer

At the same time automatic long-playing projection equipment has been developed so that the number of operators required to run multiple shows could be reduced. For many years the maximum length of a reel of 35mm film as

Shaping the Modern Cinema 2

Above In the 1930s cinemas became elaborate 'shrines' for the dream industry. They were built and decorated in a bewildering and extravagant variety of exotic styles. The interior of the Astoria Cinema, situated in Brixton, London, boasted this chocolate-box Mediterranean style.

projected was 600m (2000 ft). The operator had to change over from one projector to another every twenty minutes or so throughout the show. Now the use of reels up to 1800m (6000 ft) is common, and a full length feature lasting over two hours can be run with only one reel change.

With more sophisticated long-play facilities a continuous show lasting up to four hours can now be run without a break, so that a complete performance can be given from a single projector without further attention. Some projectors even re-wind the film automatically so that the whole programme can be repeated immediately. Automation in the projection room can also extend to switching the auditorium lighting, opening and closing the curtains in front of the screen, starting and stopping the projector and playing intermission music, all carried out to a pre-set time-table without the constant attendance of an operator. By such devices the multi-cinema complexes are cutting back operating costs.

In the United States, and some other countries where the climate is suitable and the car dominates the way of life, the open air drive-in cinema became popular. This allowed a family to drive from their home, view a movie programme and return without ever leaving their car. Drive-in theatres have to occupy a large landscaped space to allow cars to be manoeuvred and parked with a clear view of the picture, so the screen must be very large and the projection light powerful. Sound is reproduced from local speakers located by each parking position. Although successful in such territories as California and Southern Italy, the adverse winter weather conditions and long summer evenings in Britain and Northern Europe has weighed heavily against open air performance.

It is not easy to forecast the future pattern for the cinema theatre in the West. Certainly the weekly visit to the movies in company with a thousand others will never return. Nowadays more people than ever before are watching films – but not in the cinema! For instance, in Britain alone on the three available television channels nearly 1,000 feature films are broadcast every year. And new methods of distribution, such as the video-cassette, and in due course the video-disc, can further extend the programmes available for the home viewer. Nevertheless the cinema theatre, at its best, offers a form of entertainment which cannot be experienced in the living room – not only because of the technical qualities of the big screen in colour and sound, but also the excitement added by the presence of an audience.

FILM MAKING TODAY

Cinema is based on illusion. Its technology depends on visual trickery. Its effect is frequently escapist or visionary. Yet behind the mystery and effects lie a series of technical inventions, a tightly organised industry, a complex series of precise skills and processes.

Cinema depends on the professional expertise of a remarkably wide range of people: accountants, artists, sound-engineers, electricians, chemists, carpenters, photographers, musicians, writers, actors and dozens more. It uses a series of vital pieces of specialist equipment: the movie camera, the projector, the contact printer and lighting units. In the following section some of the equipment basic to the industry is examined in greater detail: How does it work? How has it evolved? After that, each stage of making a feature film is described, from its first conception to its final release.

How the Camera Works

Above The earliest movie cameras were cranked by hand. They ran at 16 frames per second. Peter Bogdanovich's nostalgia movie *Nickelodeon* re-created the atmosphere of the early cinema.

Below Electronic Monitoring enables several people to view the scene simultaneously. In affect the television view-finder replaces the camera man's eye with a tiny TV camera.

Far left The Panaflex 35mm camera is now widely used for feature films. In 1977 it was employed in filming eighty-two per cent of the major Hollywood movies.

Left The modern portable camera facilitates filming in a wide variety of situations. Here the cameraman for *Isadora* (*The Loves of Isadora* in US) – 1968 crouches at the water's edge.

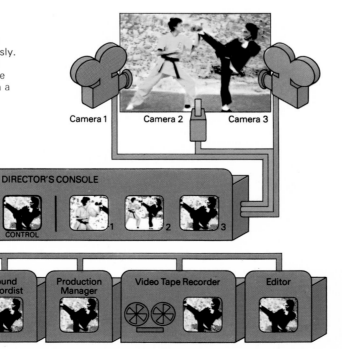

Camera 1   Camera 2   Camera 3

DIRECTOR'S CONSOLE

CONTROL

Continuity Girl | Sound Recordist | Production Manager | Video Tape Recorder | Editor

All the essential features of the modern motion picture camera can be found in the earliest inventions of the pioneers working in the last decade of the nineteenth century. So in the cameras of both 1898 and 1978 there must be: **1.** A lens to form an image of the scene on the film. **2.** An intermittent movement mechanism to hold the film in position while each picture is exposed, and then to move it the distance required to bring the next unexposed area into position. **3.** A shutter to prevent light from the lens reaching the film while it is being moved between successive exposures. **4.** A container (the magazine) from which new film can be fed into the camera mechanism and into which it can be taken up after exposure. **5.** A viewfinder to help aim the lens accurately at the scene so that the chosen area is recorded on the film.

The early inventors applied their greatest ingenuity to the design of the intermittent mechanism. The movement had to be rapid – producing sixteen exposures every second; precise – since quiet small irregularities would show as an unsteady picture when projected; and uniform with each exposure of exactly the same duration otherwise the picture would flicker. Edison's use of a strip with precisely perforated holes down each edge provided a fundamental technique, since the film could be located by a pin engaging in one of these holes during exposure and moved as a whole by a toothed wheel known as a sprocket.

Originally, the drive for the mechanism was provided by the cameraman himself turning a crank-handle. Later, motor drives were introduced, initially clockwork and subsequently electric, which gave exact control of speed.

With the introduction of sound films, from 1927, the rate of exposure was increased to twenty-four pictures per second. A new demand was also imposed on the mechanism – it had to be quiet enough not to be picked up by the microphone recording the actors' voices. For many years the only answer was to suppress the sound – first by enclosing the whole camera and its operator in a sound-proof room (with severe limitations on the ability of the camera to follow the action) and later by enclosing only the camera and its motor in a sound-absorbing box called a 'blimp'. Only in recent years have improved designs begun to meet the high standards of noiselessness demanded.

Varieties of lens

Lenses for cine cameras have followed all the improvements of optical technology. Unlike the still photographer, the cine cameraman has a rigidly fixed exposure-time, normally about 1/50th of a second. To increase illumination in the studio is expensive in lighting equipment, power and labour. Instead the industry has constantly demanded faster and faster lenses with high performance at full aperture, eventually doubling the amount of light reaching the film.

The angle of view of a lens critically affects the composition of a scene. When working in the studio with a large and heavy 'blimped' camera, it is inconvenient to move the camera to cover various angles. Therefore studio cameras are supplied with an extensive range of interchangeable lenses of different focal lengths.

Working under studio conditions, with appreciable breaks between shots, the time taken to change a lens is a minor problem. But on location a

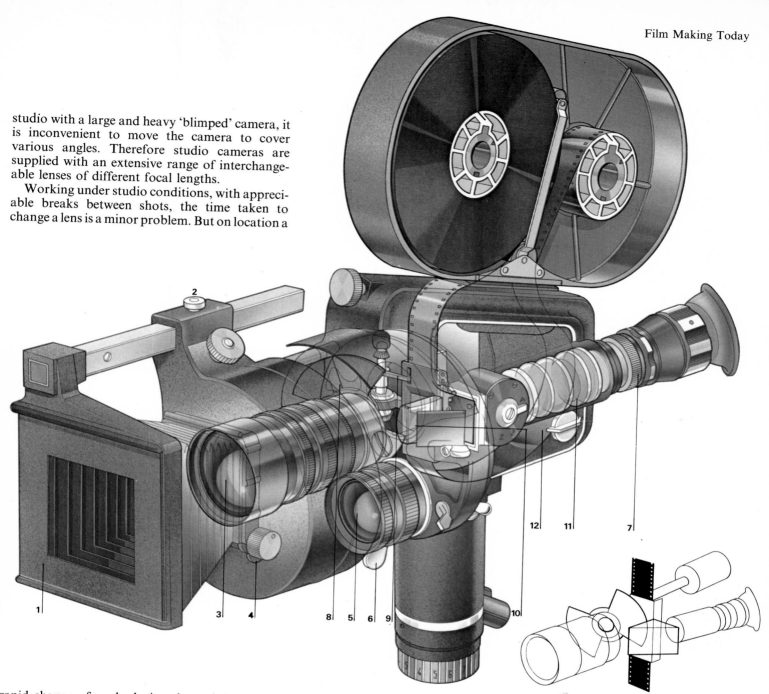

rapid change of angle during the action is vital. For such shooting many cameras used to be fitted with turrets, which mounted three or even four different lenses which could be swung speedily into position. These have been almost entirely superseded by the zoom lens. This allows the effective focal length, and hence angle of view, to be continuously varied. Modern zoom lenses span a range of focal lengths. With the trend to more fluid camera viewpoints during the action and the need for flexibility of angle, the zoom lens has become an important tool.

The development of widescreen systems in the 1950s introduced a new set of camera problems. The first anamorphic processes used optical attachments to existing lenses, often very bulky and limiting the light transmitted and the range of focus adjustment, and sometimes severely distorting close-up shots. But the modern anamorphic lens is a complete unit, little larger than a normal lens, available with large aperture over a long range of focal lengths and free from distortion. Even anamorphic zoom lenses are now produced.

The viewfinder has been greatly developed over the years, to give the cameraman a better presentation of the scene being photographed, and to help him compose the shot. On early cameras, the finder was merely a peep-hole with a wire frame. But subsequent optical finders gave a bright image either viewed directly or formed on a small ground-glass screen.

The accuracy of the limits shown in the viewfinder was always a problem in such systems. Unless the finder lens and the camera lens were exactly aligned, the edges of the picture viewed would not coincide with the picture photographed. For precise composition many of the older studio cameras had a 'rack-over', which allowed the camera body containing the film to be slid to one side, allowing the cameraman to examine on a separate ground-glass screen the image actually formed by the main camera lens. The problem of limits was not entirely solved until the invention of the 'through-the-lens' reflex finder, in which the camera lens simultaneously forms the images for both viewfinder and film.

Above The Arriflex, a light, portable camera, was introduced in the late 1950s and made hand-held filming techniques possible.

1 Matte box
2 Front adjustment
3 Front and rear filter racks
4 Lens
5 Alternative lens and mount
6 Focusing levers
7 Viewfinder focus
8 Mirror shutter
9 Intermittent film claw
10 Prism and ground glass screen
11 Viewfinder optics
12 Film

How the Projector Works

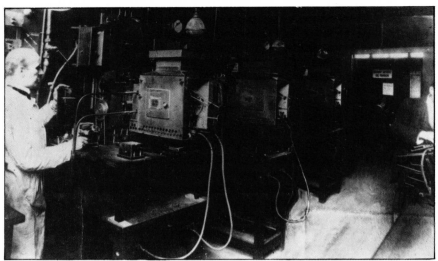

Above The projection room of the Gaumont Palace in Paris, 1909. A battery of projectors is set up to screen a succession of short films.

Projection is an essential step in the sequence which links the creative ideas of the director to the entertainment of the eventual audience, providing the final presentation of picture and sound from the reel of printed film.

Essentially, the mechanism of the projector parallels that of the camera. The film is moved one frame at a time, each separate picture being illuminated from a light source and imaged by a lens on to the screen. The rapid succession of these images, 24 times a second, produces the appearance of movement by the persistence of vision of the viewer's eye. The fundamental feature of a projector is therefore an intermittent drive to move the film past an aperture or 'gate'. The 'still' period should be long and the moving time as short as possible. Many mechanical designs have been tried but the most successful is still the

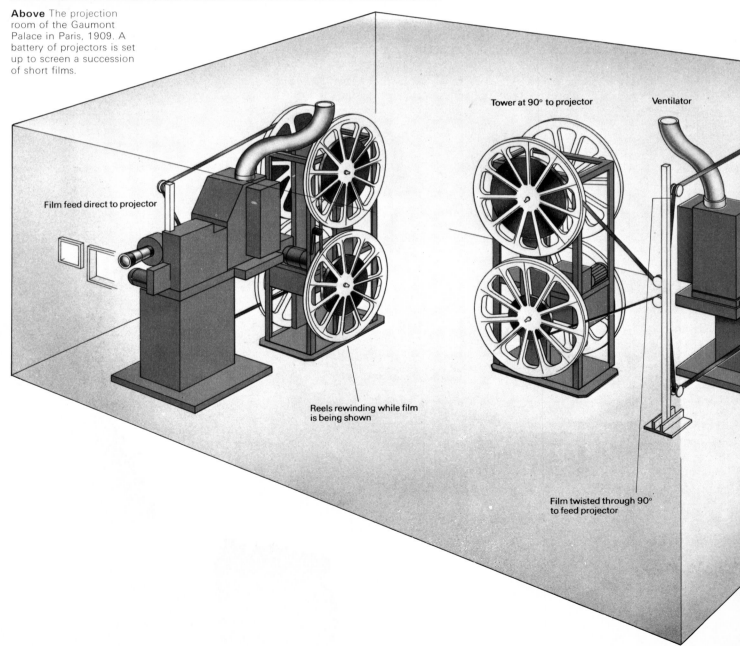

Film feed direct to projector

Tower at 90° to projector

Ventilator

Reels rewinding while film is being shown

Film twisted through 90° to feed projector

Maltese Cross or Geneva intermittent. This rotates a toothed sprocket below the gate, and moves the film in one-third of the time that it remains still.

Shutters and lenses

Like a camera, a projector has a shutter synchronized with the drive mechanism, so that no picture is projected during the short period while the film is being moved. This blanking-off takes place 24 times a second – but at this frequency an irritating amount of flicker would be visible. An additional sector is therefore fitted to the shutter giving another cut-off while the film is held in the gate. This increases the interruptions to 48 per second, too fast to be seen as a flicker.

In cinema theatres, projectors taking 35mm film are normal but the use of 70mm film for special showings must be catered for. There are now dual gauge machines which allow both sizes to be run on the same machine, with very few adjustments.

Again as in a camera, the projector must have a lens. But unlike the camera lens, the projector lens is designed for maximum light transmission at all times, so no diaphragm control is fitted. The focal length required depends on the size of screen in the theatre and its distance from the projector. Just as cameras are sometimes used with special anamorphic lenses for wide-screen photography, it must be possible to fit a corresponding anamorphic projection lens to show such films in their correct proportions. Projection lenses are therefore easily interchangeable by the operator. For convenience two or three different types may be mounted on a rotating turret so that the change-over from one to another can be done in a moment.

The enlargement from the film frame to the cinema screen is very great – 500,000 times the area in a large theatre. A very powerful light source is therefore necessary to get a sufficiently bright picture. For many years the only lamps strong enough were high intensity carbon arcs with large spherical mirrors, and these are still preferred in very large cinemas. But a more convenient alternative became available – the xenon lamp. This provides a steady and consistent light output over a long period, without the need for the continuous attention to the carbon feed of the older type of arc. It is now used in all small and medium-size cinemas.

Reproducing the sound track

In addition to showing the picture, the projector must also reproduce the sound track printed on the film. There are two types of track currently in use – photographic (optical) and magnetic – so many projectors are fitted with two types of sound head. At the picture gate the film is moved intermittently, frame by frame, but at the sound head it must move continuously and smoothly. The sound head must therefore be separated from the picture gate far enough to allow the change of movement. By tradition the optical sound pick-up is located after the picture gate. The position of the

magnetic head, on the other hand, is always ahead of the picture gate. These separations mean that the point on the sound track corresponding to a given picture frame must be printed appropriately displaced for reproduction of synchronized picture and sound. On 35mm copies the photographic sound must be 20 frames ahead of the picture, while the magnetic sound must be 28 frames behind. 70mm prints are made only with magnetic tracks, which are 24 frames behind.

The electrical signal picked up at the sound head is amplified and fed to the loudspeaker system of the theatre, installed behind the screen on which the picture is projected. The optical track of a 35mm print feeds a single speaker system. But magnetic prints allow multi-channel stereophonic sound from three speakers behind the screen, right, left and centre, and a fourth series of speakers in the auditorium for an 'all-around' effect. 70mm prints provide six channels, five behind the screen and one in the auditorium.

Film must of course be continuously fed to the mechanism during projection. For many years, only twenty minutes of 35mm film could be run at a time, from spools holding 2000 feet, so that two projectors had to be used alternately to provide a continuous show. But now large spools holding 14,000 feet can be fed from a separate tower mounting, giving an uninterrupted performance of more than two and a half hours from a single machine.

Right An early silent projector. the GB Kalee 6, dating from the early 1920s

Capturing Colour

From the first achievement of a moving picture it had always been a target to add both colour and sound. In the event it was the coming of sound which transformed cinema more radically. The silent film disappeared soon after 1930. But, despite the availability of numerous colour systems, black-and-white pictures were still made in the 1970s.

In the very early days colour had been added to black-and-white images by applying an overall tint or tone, or by hand-colouring, using stencils. But true colour cinematography required the camera to record the colour components of the original scene and then reproduce them on the cinema screen.

The first commercially successful solution of the problem was Kinemacolor, shown in England in 1908 and in the United States in the following year. The Kinemacolor camera ran at twice the normal speed, and photographed the scene on black-and-white film through a rotating shutter with alternating red-orange and blue-green filters. Thus alternate black-and-white negative frames contained different colour information. When a black-and-white print from this negative film was projected through a similar rotating filter, the eye merged the alternating images on the screen (as a result of persistence of vision) to give the appearance of a colour picture. Since this process depends on adding together two images, it is known as an additive method.

The next twenty-five years saw many attempts in all parts of the world to improve colour cinematography. But methods using additive colour principles generally required special projectors and optical systems.

Subtractive methods, in which coloured transparent images were actually printed on the film, were much more convenient. In the 1920s most methods used red-orange and blue-green components in a two-colour process. Of these the Technicolor process became the best known. Technicolor prints were made by the dye-transfer method. A relief image, known as a matrix, was used as a kind of printing plate to transfer the image in transparent dye onto the gelatine-coated film. This dye-transfer process was used for such famous silent films as Douglas Fairbanks' *The Black Pirate* – 1926.

Below White light is split into seven different colours when passed through a prism: red, orange, yellow, green, blue, indigo and violet.

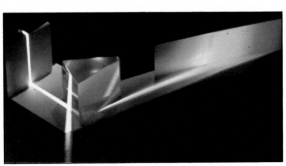

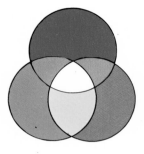

Above The basis of the additive colour system. Beams of projected red, green and blue light give cyan, magenta and yellow where they overlap one other beam; where all three overlap the screen appears black.

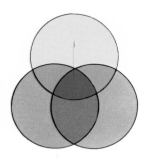

Above The basis of the subtractive colour system. A beam of white light projected through cyan, magenta and yellow filters produces red, green or blue where they overlap one other filter; black where they all overlap.

The three-colour system

But any two-colour system is extremely restricted in the range of colours it can reproduce. It was again Technicolor that developed a practical and commercial three-colour system, and as a result dominated colour motion pictures for more than twenty years from the mid-1930s. Three-colour reproduction needs a print in which the blue, red and green parts of the original scene are recorded in their respective complementary hues: yellow, blue-green (cyan) and red-purple (magenta).

The first short film shot with the Technicolor three-strip camera system was Walt Disney's

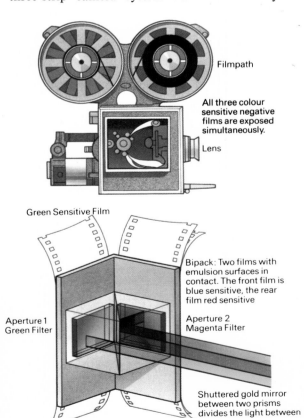

Filmpath

All three colour sensitive negative films are exposed simultaneously.

Lens

Green Sensitive Film

Bipack: Two films with emulsion surfaces in contact. The front film is blue sensitive, the rear film red sensitive

Aperture 1 Green Filter

Aperture 2 Magenta Filter

Shuttered gold mirror between two prisms divides the light between the two apertures

Right In the Tripak or multi-layer system, the blue, red and green aspects of the original scene are recorded as separate layers on one strip of film. The negative film is coated with three layers of emulsion, separated by filters. The top emulsion is exposed only by blue light, the middle by green, and the bottom layer by red light. During development an image in the complementary colour is formed in each layer: yellow in the top layer, magenta in the middle, and cyan (blue) in the bottom. The colour negative has an orange overall appearance, since it is dye-masked to aid reproduction.

Colour negative can be printed direct onto positive film, which again has three layers of sensitized emulsion. During printing the negative images form corresponding positive images on the print film. The superimposed images in yellow, cyan and magenta combine to reproduce the colours of the original scene.

Right The Technicolor system produced a three-colour print by developing a special camera in which three separate strips of black-and-white negative were exposed simultaneously through the same lens. An optical prism split the light beam so that one film recorded only the blue light, a second only the red, and a third strip only the green. From these three black-and-white negatives, three relief-image matrices were printed. These matrices were used to transfer in turn yellow, cyan and magenta dyes onto a strip of blank film, which had previously been printed with the sound-track in black-and-white.

Above left The Technicolor camera requires a complex film-feed system.

Left The Technicolor three-colour camera uses three strips of negative film.

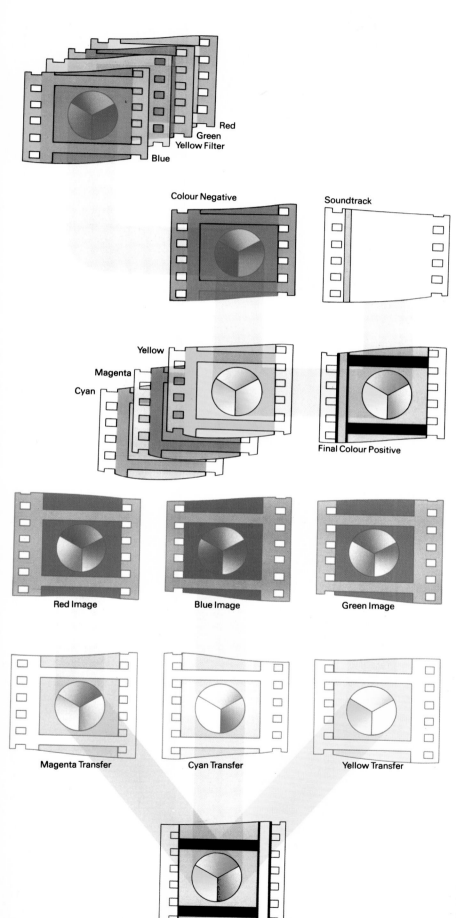

Red
Green
Yellow Filter
Blue

Colour Negative

Soundtrack

Yellow
Magenta
Cyan

Final Colour Positive

Red Image

Blue Image

Green Image

Magenta Transfer

Cyan Transfer

Yellow Transfer

Final Colour Positive

Flowers and Trees – 1932 and the first feature film *Becky Sharp* – 1935. From then on until well into the 1950s most major colour film productions were processed by Technicolor. One of the outstanding reasons for Technicolor's commercial success was that large numbers of copies could be made for general distribution to cinemas throughout the world. Once a set of matrices had been prepared, they could be used over and over again, to complete many hundreds of prints. For foreign language versions only the films sound track had to be altered.

Colour negative comes

Although the Technicolor camera was an outstanding piece of optical design and precision engineering, it was large and heavy in operation. The rate of work was slowed down by its use of three separate rolls of film. Much attention was therefore given to developing a single film system, which could be used in an ordinary black-and-white camera to record the three colour components of a scene. For the amateur cine photographer using 16mm film such a material had in fact been available since 1936 in the form of Kodachrome. During and after World War II, a number of documentary films shot in 16mm on Kodachrome were enlarged to make 35mm three-strip negatives and printed by the Technicolor process. In Germany between 1939 and 1945 Agfa developed a 35mm colour negative film. From 1950 the Eastman Kodak Company introduced the material which rapidly became the standard for motion picture colour photography: Eastman Color Negative.

Film technology advances

These single-strip films record as separate images the blue, red and green aspects of the original scene, but in three layers on one strip; hence the system is termed multi-layer or tri-pack. The commercial availability of these multi-layer materials rapidly changed the whole basis of colour cinematography by upsetting the effective monopoly of Technicolor. Ordinary black-and-white cameras could now be used in the studio and colour prints could be made by any processing laboratory equipped to handle the new materials. The three-strip camera immediately became obsolescent and was not used after 1955.

At the present time all colour motion picture photography and printing uses the multi-layer tripack film. Although for many years the products of Eastman Kodak dominated the market, competitive materials are now produced by several manufacturers in western Europe, eastern Europe and Japan. While the basic principles have remained unchanged, technical improvements have produced greater sensitivity. Less light is necessary in shooting, more faithful colour reproduction is achieved, and finer grain is the norm. Production using the smaller 16mm negative is now frequent, while more rapid processing has increased laboratory productivity.

Film Magic:
Special Effects

The range of 'trick shots' – special effects – which may be needed in a major feature film is almost limitless, but several basic techniques are common. Some are derived from the illusions of the live theatre: a capsule of red dye under a uniform is punctured to represent a wound; small explosives buried under plaster are fired electrically to represent striking bullets; larger charges buried in the ground, set off by remote control, provide a rain of shell-fire on the battle-field.

Models and miniatures

Models are used where life-size structures would be impossibly expensive. A vaulted cathedral roof or skyline of a futuristic city can be a scale model built to exact perspective and supported in front of the camera as a 'hanging miniature'. Seen through the lens it matches up precisely with the full-size structure at ground level, where the action takes place. An alternative, less-expensive, method is the glass shot. Here the missing parts of the scene are painted on a large sheet of glass mounted in front of the camera. The outline of the painting is accurately lined up with the details of the actual set, which the camera views directly through the clear areas of the glass.

Moving models must often be used – collapsing or burning buildings, sinking ships, crashing cars or planes, and flying saucers. Here a special technique of photography must be used to slow down the model action and avoid a toy-like effect. The camera must be run faster than normal, so that when the picture is projected at the usual speed the time taken is expanded. The smaller the scale of the model, the faster the camera must run. In practice, extremely small-scale models are never very satisfactory, except for brief glimpses.

Slow-motion photography is often used with normal live action for dramatic effect, or to allow the action of an athlete or an animal to be studied in detail. Here a time exaggeration of two to four times is usually sufficient. Alternatively, time may be apparently speeded up by running the camera more slowly than normal. This also can be used for dramatic emphasis, for instance in the hair-breadth near-misses of a car chase – performed slowly and carefully while shooting and speeded up on projection. By taking only one frame every few minutes, or even hours, movements occurring over several days take place on the screen in seconds. This is time-lapse photography, familiar from many films in which the growth of a plant or the blossoming of a flower takes place in a few moments. The same principle is used in animation shooting; a cartoon or a puppet is photographed one frame at a time, with small changes to the drawing or figure being made between each frame. When eventually projected, the action appears to be continuous.

Back projection

Many special effects are concerned with changes in space. A frequent requirement is to show actors performing in a location which they have never

Top The set is prepared for front projection shooting. Both the camera and the projector which throws the background image are mounted on the trolley. A half-silvered mirror allows the projector to throw the image along the same line as the camera.

Bottom The front-projected scene as viewed through the camera. Since camera and projector are aligned on the same axis, the camera does not pick up the shadows thrown by the player and set. The set lights are adjusted to 'wash out' the background image projected onto the actors.

isited. One way of achieving this was discovered
arly in film history: back projection. Here the
ction is played in front of a large translucent
creen, on to which a picture of the exotic
ackground is projected from behind. For a static
etting a still projector with slides can be used. But
o show movement, as in a sea-scape or the view
hrough a car window, a film projector is used,
arefully synchronized with the shutter of the cine
amera.

ront projection
Vhen very large moving backgrounds are re-
uired it is difficult to get a bright enough picture
ehind the actors using back projection. In recent
ears the translucent screen has often been
eplaced by the more efficient front reflex-
rojection system. Here the actors work in front of
. highly reflective surface covered with minute
lass beads on to which the background picture is
rojected. The projector is mounted close to the
amera, and a semi-transparent mirror in front of
oth allows the projected beam to be lined up with
he centre of the camera lens. The beaded screen
eflects the background picture through the mirror
lirectly back into the camera lens, which is
hotographing the actors at the same time. The
amera sees a very bright background scene, and
ny projector light falling on the actors in the
oreground is negligible.

Travelling mattes
3ut both these systems require a print of the
ackground scene to be available before the
oreground action is shot. This is not always
ossible, and an alternative method of composite
photography is the travelling matte shot. For this,
the foreground is photographed against a uni-
formly illuminated bright blue background surface. Printing operations in the laboratory then
produce a pair of black-and-white silhouette
masks, or 'mattes', from this negative. In one of
these the foreground action is reproduced in solid
black on a clear surround, while in the other the
foreground is clear on an opaque ground. The first
matte is used when making a print from the
background scene, to keep an unexposed area in
each frame; the foreground picture is then printed
into this space, using the second matte to protect
the background area.

Cartoon plus actor
Similar 'travelling matte' processes are used when
cartoon figures appear with live actors. The real
action is photographed first, and the cartoon
movement drawn to match. If the live actor is to
appear against a cartoon background, he is shot as
the foreground against a blue-backing. However,
if the cartoon figure is to be part of a real scene, the
animated drawings are photographed on colour
negative. By additional black-and-white shooting,
the pair of silhouette mattes are obtained from the
same drawings. The live action scene is then used
as the background, and the cartoon figure as the
foreground, in composite printing using the
mattes.

Special effects formed an essential part of
Stanley Kubricks *2001: A Space Odyssey* – 1968.
They included back projection, front projection,
models, travelling matte, multiple printing, animation and many others all taken to a particularly
advanced degree.

Stretching the Image
The Widescreen Scene

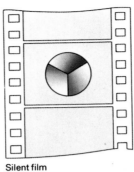

Black and white projection

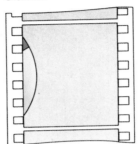

Silent film

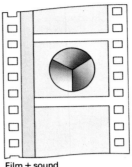

Film + sound

Parts of a standard early 35mm film system: **far left** The screen for silent movies had a width-to-height ratio of 1.33:1. **centre** The frame size of early black-and-white silent films was similarly of a 1.33:1 ratio **right** The aperture on early sound films was reduced to 1.2:1 to allow the sound-track to run down one side of the film.

The pioneer inventors of cinematography had used many different sizes of film in their equipment. But the commercial success of Edison's system soon brought some standardization. By the early years of this century the 35mm gauge was well established. The space for the picture was approximately 24 × 18mm. When projected, the image on the screen had a proportion of width to height ('aspect ratio') of 4:3 or 1.33:1, which became standard for silent motion pictures. With the introduction of sound-on-film in 1927, space had to be made for the printed sound-track; the picture area was correspondingly reduced. But the proportion of 1.33:1 was maintained for all general cinema presentations.

Special shows occasionally used wider film or unusual projection systems for dramatic effect. One of the most spectacular of these, 'Vitarama', was seen at the 1939 New York World's Fair. Eleven projectors were linked to throw a composite picture onto a huge curved screen. In 1952 a somewhat simplified version, Cinerama, was launched and achieved immediate acclaim. The films, photographed in a triple-lensed camera, were projected from three projectors, and together covered a screen more than 16 metres (50 feet) wide and 8 metres (25 feet) high. The frame on each film was more than twice the normal area, giving outstanding brightness and clarity.

Cinerama was much too complex to install in the average cinema. But its success made a great impression on the film industry, which at that time in the United States was feeling the first impact of the competition of television entertainment. Stimulated by this, in 1953 Twentieth Century-Fox took the bold step of introducing Cinema-Scope, the first of the modern wide-screen systems, with their feature *The Robe*.

The outstanding public interest aroused by the CinemaScope format led to the development of a number of rival wide-screen systems. Some of these used alternative types of anamorphic optics. Others believed a similar effect could be obtained in normal 35mm photography merely by reducing the height of the frame and projecting with greater enlargement in the theatre. This gave rise to the practice of cropping ten per cent or more from the top and bottom of the frame, and composing the picture within the smaller height.

Unfortunately the use of a smaller frame area to fill a bigger screen magnified the problems of film grain, poor definition and inadequate brightness.

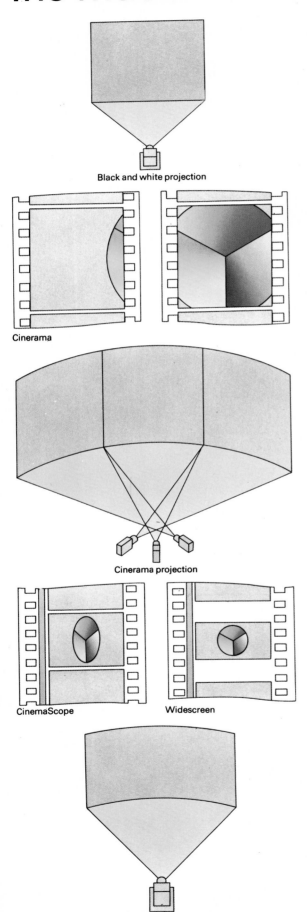

Cinerama

Cinerama projection

CinemaScope

Widescreen

Widescreen projection

Left For Cinerama, three separate cameras are used simultaneously to film the spectacularly wide view. Similarly, three projectors are needed to project the three films. The multi-track sound is recorded on a further film. The screen is curved to accommodate the wide image.

Far left In CinemaScope, the image is recorded on standard 35mm film, but is compressed sideways (anamorphosed) by means of a spherical lens. The image is projected through another special lens to unsqueeze it, and give a widescreen effect.

Left Another method of obtaining a wide-screen effect is by using a lower aperture on standard width film. American standard widescreen aspect ratio is 1.85:1; European standard widescreen aspect ratio is 1.66:1. In both cases the screen itself must be curved to take the wide image.

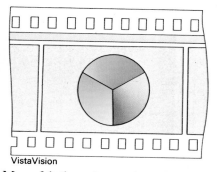

VistaVision

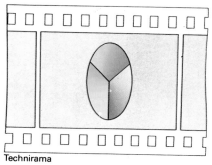

Technirama

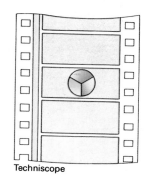

Techniscope

Far left In the VistaVision technique, the film runs horizontally past the camera aperture. Each frame is the size of two normal frames. **Centre** Technirama similarly runs the film horizontally, but also uses an anamorphic process to stretch the image. **Right** Techniscope runs 35mm film vertically through the camera, as normal, but the aperture is half the normal height ('half-frame') giving a widescreen effect.

Many felt that a larger size of film was necessary to produce satisfactory results. One such system was VistaVision, which used a special camera in which the film ran horizontally, exposing a frame twice the normal size. This gave a bright and clear picture on a very large screen. But the special equipment required was not popular with theatre owners, and for general distribution most features shot in VistaVision were optically reduced to make ordinary 35mm prints.

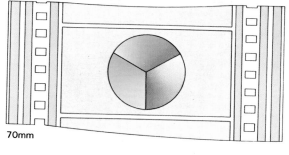

70mm

The widescreen scene

Another large film-system was Todd-AO, which revived the hitherto experimental use of cameras taking film 65mm wide with a frame aspect ratio of 2.21:1. Prints were made on 70mm film to give room for six magnetic sound stripes. Although special projection equipment was required, the quality of picture and sound which could be obtained in the largest theatres was superb. Todd-AO was launched in 1955 with *Oklahoma!* and this was followed in 1956 by *Around the World in 80 Days*. Shortly afterwards the similar large film Panavision was brought into use by MGM and others, and in due course manufacturers introduced dual gauge projectors which could show both 70mm and 35mm prints. In the USSR, too, 70mm was adopted for both camera and projector as the best large-film system for major cinema productions.

At the same time Fox experimented with anamorphic photography for a short period in 1955, using a film 55mm wide. Meanwhile Technirama photographed a partially squeezed image onto a double frame area on 35mm. This was then used as a source for making all types of optical print: 70mm, 35mm anamorphic and 35mm flat. This system was extensively used in Europe between 1956 and 1968. But in the 1960s, the grain and resolution of colour film improved, gradually removing the need for large-area negatives. In fact in 1963 a smaller frame system was introduced as a more economical method of photography for anamorphic release prints: this was Techniscope.

Recently most large systems of photography have disappeared. Feature production is normally on 35mm, using either anamorphic lenses and the picture composed in the aspect ratio 2.35:1, or normal lenses for 'flat' wide-screen composition with a frame 1.66:1 or 1.75:1. Cinemas project respectively anamorphic or flat from 35mm prints.

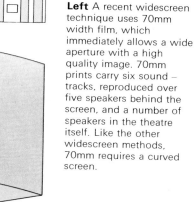

70mm projection

Left A recent widescreen technique uses 70mm width film, which immediately allows a wide aperture with a high quality image. 70mm prints carry six sound tracks, reproduced over five speakers behind the screen, and a number of speakers in the theatre itself. Like the other widescreen methods, 70mm requires a curved screen.

Below The aspect ratio of the widescreen film does not fit the TV screen. If the full width of the frame is included, black areas will remain at the top and bottom of the TV screen. If the picture is made to fill the TV screen from top to bottom, part of the image will be lost on each side.

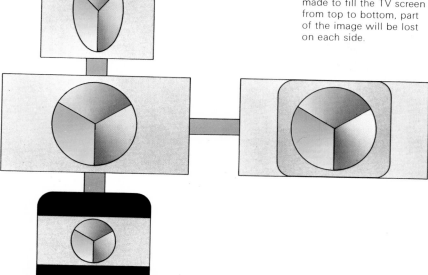

TV transfer

Ways of Using Sound 1

'The cinema is a visual medium' was the protesting cry of those who tried to bar the way to the coming of sound. The film soundtrack, comprising dialogue, music and sound-effect, had arrived and is here to stay. But the cinema engaged in many heart-searchings before it accepted and successfully integrated the new dimension of sound into its products.

Using dialogue

The biggest problems, both technically and artistically, came with spoken dialogue. Anyone who has seen *Singin' in the Rain* will have got some idea – glamorized but not inaccurate – of how in the early years of sound Hollywood tried to cope, with sound-proof booths, microphones in vases of flowers, and the innumerable safeguards taken against offset noises such as passing cars or planes. The dialogue recordist's job was a logistical nightmare. The greatest directors overcame such practical problems.

Artistically, the problems were no less daunting. First there was the dilemma of the successful star of the silent era who could not make the transition to sound because of a weak or unattractive voice. Then there was the more fundamental problem of how dialogue could be used 'cinematically'. Many early dialogue films simply used cinema to record on film stage plays.

It has only been by analyzing and refining the role of human speech in movies that dialogue has been successfully integrated into the cinema. A purpose had to be found for human speech that did not weaken, or relegate to a secondary role, the power of the image.

The French writer, André Malraux, suggested there are three categories of film dialogue: 'expository' dialogue (which lets the audience in on initial plot details); 'mood' dialogue (which gives clues to a character's personality and feelings); and 'stage' dialogue (which advances, or forms part of, the narrative flow). Mood dialogue is the type most at home in the cinema. Here what counts is the tone and inflection of the voice as much as the meaning of the words. The camera lens and the tape recorder magnify and pick out such details and make them far more revealing on the screen than they would be on the stage. Vocal quirks form a vital part of the film actor's personality, making the cinema the great arena for impressionists. It emphasizes identifying tics and mannerisms, such as Bogart's lisp, James Stewart's drawl and Cagney's nasal rasp, that would be lost in the theatre.

The great screenwriters have tended to be the least florid and verbose, the most conscious of the supremacy of the visual image, and the most sensitive to the importance of vocal texture as well as verbal meaning in dialogue. This was true of the great early Hollywood scenarists – Ben Hecht, Jules Furthman, Herman Mankiewicz, Billy Wilder and Preston Sturges – and of contemporary writers such as Robert Benton and David Newman in *Bonnie and Clyde* – 1967,

Robert Towne in *Chinatown* – 1974 and *The Last Detail* – 1973, and Joan Tewkesbury in Robert Altman's *Nashville* – 1975.

The films of Altman, the greatest modern innovator in the field of dialogue, have revolutionized audience expectations. In films such as *M*A*S*H* – 1970, *McCabe and Mrs Miller* – 1971 and *The Long Goodbye* – 1973 and above all in *Nashville* – 1975, Altman has experimented with overlapping dialogue and fluctuating sound levels to a remarkable extent. He is trying to wean the filmgoer from his dependence on catching the precise meaning of dialogue rather than its emotional drift or texture. The scant, impromptu vitality of Altman's approach to dialogue is already affecting other film-makers – especially in

he US – and opens up fascinating possibilities for
he future of screen dialogue.

Music and the screen

n the days before synchronized sound, virtually
very public screening of a film was accompanied
y music or some other form of aural embel-
shment. The history of music in the cinema
egins with the birth of the cinema itself.

The simplest principle in musical accompani-
nent is 'let the music suit the mood'. The movie
ianist knew what music to provide at each stage
n the action: rumbling bass notes for thunder or
nelodrama, fast rhythm for riders on horseback,
uting high notes for love scenes.

Certain silent directors arranged or com-
nissioned their own orchestral scores and had
ney played during the film. Griffith, Lang, Von
troheim and Eisenstein were among the leading
xponents of this practice.

The first film to use synchronized speech and
nusic recorded on disc was *The Jazz Singer* –
927. But the synchronization difficulties were far
reater, and permitted far less precision, than did
ne later fixed sound track.

The most concentrated mixture of music and
lm was to be found, of course, in the musical.
ound, so often considered a constraint on the
inema, was here a liberator. The coming of music
> movies produced one of the most free-flowing
nd inventive genres in the cinema's history.

Once film-makers could join the musical score
> the film itself, the possibilities for subtleties of
nusical expression multiplied. In the 1930s René
lair, Jean Vigo, Ernst Lubitsch, Rouben
1amoulian, G. W. Pabst and Carl Dreyer were
mong the directors who used music (the first two
ften by French composer Maurice Jaubert) not
nerely to apply a general atmosphere but to pick
ut and point up details that the filmgoer might
ot otherwise readily catch.

Many film directors worked closely with well-
nown composers. Abel Gance and Arthur
lonegger, Grigori Kozintsev and Dmitri
hostakovitch, Laurence Olivier and William
Valton, Benjamin Britten and the Grierson
ocumentary team in England are four outstand-
1g examples of such partnerships. In Russia,
ergei Prokofiev's scores for *Alexander Nevsky* –
938, and *Ivan the Terrible* – 1943/6 written in
lose association with Eisenstein, are among the
rime elements in the films' impact. Some film-
nakers have even written their own musical scores
- for example Charles Chaplin and Satyajit Ray.

Despite the considerable musical talent avail-
ble to American movies, music often tended to
ecome merely another ingredient: one thrown
nto the mixture at the last moment, when the film
vas a finished product so far as its director was
oncerned. Frequently music so composed simply
pelt out what was already amply clear in the film.

But some composers did retain their in-
ividuality even in movie-land: for instance Erich
Volfgang Korngold, Alfred Newman and

Above Benjamin Britten
(1913–1976) composed
notable music for such
films as *Night Mail* –
1936, and *Instruments of
the Orchestra* – 1946, for
which he wrote
'Variations and Fugue on
a Theme of Purcell'.

Left Dmitri Shostakovich
(1906–75), the Russian
composer, wrote a
number of film scores in
the 1930s – for Yutkevich,
Ermler, Kozintsev and
Trauberg. He later wrote
the scores for Kozintsev's
Hamlet – 1964 and *King
Lear* – 1971.

Ways of Using Sound 2

Bernard Herrmann. Herrmann's film music, ranging in time and cinematic style from *Citizen Kane* – 1941 to *Taxi Driver* – 1976 via a host of marvellous scores for Hitchcock's films (notably *Psycho* – 1960), is among the best ever written. Virgil Thomson and Hanns Eisler wrote some memorable music for documentaries.

In Europe, film-makers have tended to be more spare and discriminating in their use of music. Frequently, they judiciously used music already written and familiar to the audience: from classical composers such as Bach and Mozart to modern folk, jazz or pop. In *A Clockwork Orange* – 1975 Stanley Kubrick culled music from sources as diverse as Beethoven's Ninth Symphony and *Singin' in the Rain*. In *Hour of the Wolf* – 1968 Ingmar Bergman drew a whole pattern of motifs and references from Mozart's opera *The Magic Flute* (which he later filmed).

Music has changed very little in the commercial cinema since the 1930s. New possibilities for the use of music are found in the films of independent directors in countries such as Italy and Germany – such as *Padre Padrone* by the Taviani brothers, or in Herzog's *Aguirre, Wrath of God* – 1973.

Aural signposts

Sound effects, like words, can advance or signpost a film's narrative (the knock on the door, the crack of a pistol shot). Like music, they can be used to create a mood or an atmosphere (the creaking timbers of a ship at sea, the twittering of birds on a summer day). But in using sound effects, should the film-maker aim to accompany and reinforce the visual image – or to evoke the unseen, providing information omitted by the pictures on the cinema screen?

Hitchcock's *Blackmail* – 1929 was the first British sound film and remains a classic demonstration of how sound effects can be used to create a world beyond the visible. Even some of the dialogue in this film is used expressionistically – as in the nightmare repetition of the word 'knife' in the mind of the terrified heroine.

The 1930s set some remarkable precedents for the use of the sound effect. In Britain, the group of documentary film-makers spearheaded by John Grierson battled against primitive recording equipment to create intriguing experiments in sound. They used everyday industrial noises – the roar of machinery, the rumble of traffic, the hubbub of a crowd, cries from a busy street – and orchestrated them in sound-tracks with an almost musical rhythm and expressiveness, with scores by the young Benjamin Britten.

The secret of a successful use of sound lies as much in knowing what to leave out as what to put in. A cinema audience wants noises pre-selected, or it will be confused by the cacophony, however 'realistic' it may be.

Some noises cannot easily be left out. It strains an audience's belief, for example, to see a man dive into a pool without an audible splash, or to see a car drive off without the engine's sound. But other everyday noises are not needed on the sound-track unless they serve a particular expressive purpose. The ticking of a clock, for example, is superfluous unless the film-maker wishes to convey a sense of waiting, or suspense, or simply the tedious passage of hours.

It is curious how few directors have extended the use of sound effects beyond the believable and 'realistic'. Those movie genres that are less shackled to realism – horror and science fiction employ a far freer range of sound effects.

Above Mike Wadleigh's *Woodstock* – 1970, a documentary record of the four-day rock festival. It captured live sound – not necessarily technically perfect, but with all the atmosphere of the occasion. The guitarist is Alvin Lee.

How a Film is Made

The prospect of visiting a set during the production of a feature film promises to be both exciting and revealing. In the event the reverse can be true. Anything from a few dozen to several hundred people are engaged in what appears to be utter confusion. There is a sudden shout to 'Clear the set' by somebody with the voice of a sergeant major. Gradually the babble and activity subsides.

The scene is to feature a couple of stars; but the two people standing on the set are not the stars. Looking through the camera is the director, giving instructions to the performers. He asks for some objects to be moved. Several other people also look through the viewfinder. Finally the director seems satisfied. There are further instructions, and chaos returns.

Eventually everything is ready and the actual stars come on to the set. Again the set is cleared and the actors rehearse their dialogue and action. When the director and actors are ready, they repeat the action for the camera and sound departments. Further adjustments are made. The final checks on wardrobe, make-up and continuity are made, and at last everything seems ready.

The final countdown begins. 'Clear the set.' 'Everybody quiet; we're going for a take.' 'Turn over.' 'Turning.' 'Mark it.' 'Slate 143, take 1.' 'Action.' The actors now perform what they have rehearsed. The director calls 'Cut'; he is not happy. He asks the camera and sound crew for comments, and makes appropriate changes. The scene is filmed repeatedly until everybody is satisfied. Then the process begins again for the next 'set-up'.

All this may have taken a couple of hours; in the finished film, if used, it may last about twenty seconds. It has probably already taken about a year from somebody having the idea for the film, to the actual scene being filmed; and it will probably be another year before the finished film is screened. The scene filmed seems to have little impact and the whole process appears disorganized and inefficient. Yet in the finished film the 'shot' being filmed appears totally convincing and completely necessary.

Costing the Film

Scott Fitzgerald summed up the shooting of a film as '...the net results of months of buying, planning, writing and rewriting, casting, constructing, lighting, rehearsing and shooting – the fruit of brilliant hunches or of counsels of despair, of lethargy, conspiracy and sweat . . .'

Yet the making of a film is based on a budget. A balance sheet is drawn up in the same way as for any other commercial or industrial process. It is worked out in terms of personnel, equipment, material and supplies, and of time and quantity.

The balance sheet

A budget is prepared after the script has been completed. It is broken down under various headings: preparations and tests, locations, main shooting, music, dubbing and post–syncing and finishing costs. Usually the budget is prepared in terms of 'above the line' and 'below the line' costs. 'Below the line' costs are calculated for a 'tight', 'average' or 'generous' scheduling of time, studio/location usage and other costs. Once the scale of the film has been fixed, 'below the line' costs would be roughly similar whoever made the estimates.

'Above the line' costs vary, since the amount of money spent on the story and script, and the fees negotiated by the producer, director and principal artists all vary. The latter change according to the reputation, experience and current commercial reputation of the person involved. Sometimes such people accept part of their payment as a fee, the rest being paid from the income of the film, with a share of any profits. 'Below the line' costs can be reduced by using a shorter shooting schedule, but this demands constant overtime work.

One British post-war survey gave the following breakdown of a budget:

Production staff (includes producer, director, script, technical grades)	18·5
Actors and musicians (all persons photographed)	18
Other staff (craftsmen and general labour)	14
	50·5%
Materials and services	15·5
Stage rents and equipment hire	14·5
Overheads	10·5
Other costs (purchase of property, publicity, insurance and sundries)	9
	100%

One of the film industry's favourite myths is that only two out of ten films make money. This is true, but misleading. In fact, while two in ten films make a great deal and two in ten films lose, the remaining six neither make nor lose great sums.

The key to current film financing is the distributor, not the producer. The producer, if he uses his own money at all, buys options on and develops the 'property'. He then tries to get an agreement from a distributor promising to distribute the finished film and to pay him a sum of money after the film has been released – normally about eighteen months later. To cover production costs the producer, or the distributor on his behalf, borrows money from a bank using the distribution guarantee as security. The producer may also be required to obtain a completion guarantee, a kind of insurance policy against going over budget,

Left *Cleopatra* – 1963, one of the most extravagantly-made films. It was originally budgeted for 3 million dollars, and was to be made in England, starring Peter Finch as Caesar. It eventually took four years to film, and cost roughly 40 million dollars. But by 1968 it had already earned 26 million dollars. The film's spiralling costs almost ruined Twentieth Century-Fox. Here director Joseph L. Mankiewicz rehearses a scene with its stars Elizabeth Taylor and Richard Burton.

Right How film production is organized. Film production must be carefully planned in advance since it involves a number of complex and interrelated processes.

which will cost him five per cent of the budget.

Since film production is a highly speculative investment, the producer will have to pay high interest on his loan. He may also have to mortgage his share of the film's returns to a number of people. Usually at least the main actors and the director will get a share of the producer's profits. Some of those involved may have deferred their fees, and must be paid before the producer takes any profits. The distributor too will get up to fifty per cent of any profits.

Spreading the risk

If, as is likely, the producer is unable to find one hundred per cent financing from one source, he will have to spread the risk by pre-selling the film in several markets, and perhaps to television companies, a lengthy and involved process. His major problem after he has completed the film is to get his share of the money. Normally the distributor has to recover all his costs before the producer receives a penny.

However the producer is covered against loss by the distributor. He normally receives a substantial fee for producing the film, and his overheads are generously included in the budget as indirect costs. The risk is taken by the distributor, who handles more than one film, and who in any case has his distribution fee to console him. The power of the distributor today is due primarily to his financing ability, not to his marketing function.

Right Cecil B. DeMille, the Hollywood producer-director who specialized in epic productions. At first an independent producer, he later worked for Paramount, to film the spectacles inseparably connected with his name.

How film production is organized

Music

Sound effects

Sound editing

Magnetic tape

Magnetic film

Dubbing

Exposed picture negative

Shooting in studio

Editing

Work print

Optical transfer

Sound track negative

Rushes

Shooting on location

Process laboratory

Production planning

Special effects

Answer print: 1st copy of picture & sound

Written By...

One day by a brilliant sleight-of-hand somebody transformed the nebulous literary source for a film into a thing of substance by calling it *'the property'*. It could now be bought, borrowed against, developed, built upon, traded and sold. This is the business side of the beginnings of a film. Money is required before the creative work can be started.

As long as a work is in copyright, nobody can start using it as the basis of a film until they have secured the film rights. These can either be purchased outright for an agreed amount, or an 'option' can be bought – usually a percentage of the eventual purchase price – allowing the buyer to 'develop the property' for a limited period, At the end of this period the purchaser may be able to renew the option for another period, on payment of a further fee. If the film is made under an option agreement, then the full purchase price will be 'payable on the first day of principal photography'. The owner of the copyright may also receive a share of any profits made by the film.

Early in 1978 the film rights for the American smash-hit musical *Annie* were sold for a record $9.8 million. The purchaser cannot release the film until sometime in the 1980s, when it is thought that the life of the stage musical will be exhausted.

Book into film

The novel is probably the most popular film script source. It vividly portrays characters, plot and atmosphere in a narrative that potential purchasers of film rights can respond to. 'Best sellers' are expensive, but no guarantee of a film's box office success. Many literary masterpieces and fine novels cannot be adapted for film, while a poor novel or even pulp fiction can be the basis of a first-rate film.

Other film sources include short stories, newspaper stories, magazine articles, biographies, books on historical or current events, characters in a TV series, or even an LP record. Ken Russell's financial success *Tommy* – 1975 was based on the record by the rock group The Who. Once a work is out of copyright, or 'in the public domain', anybody is free to use it as the basis of a film. The Bible has been the source of numerous films.

The original screenplay

For some purists, the original screenplay is the only proper source for a film, since from its conception it is developed in cinematic rather than literary terms. Two recent box office successes, *The Godfather* – 1972 and *Love Story* – 1970 were conceived as films, but first published as best-selling novels. The circle is finally completed when an original screenplay becomes a successful film, and is 'novelized' into a book which becomes a 'best-seller'.

The finance to employ a writer or writers to work on the script will come from a production company, studio or individual. It is rare for a writer to create an original screenplay or adaptation merely in the hope of selling it after completion. But a writer may work on the synopsis of a film idea on which finance can be raised to write a script. The synopsis will give an outline of the story in a few pages. A longer version – the treatment – will give a fuller account of the narrative, plot and characters.

Who wrote it?

Films sometimes have a number of writers named on the credits, either because different writers worked on different versions of the scripts, or because the script was co-written by two or more writers. Sometimes the director himself writes, or co-writes, the script of his movie. But normally the director collaborates with the writer. Sometimes the script will have been written under the guidance of the producer, who obtained the film rights and finance.

Below Many films are based on novels or short stories. *Sadie Thompson –* 1928 was based on Somerset Maugham's short story 'Rain'. Gloria Swanson starred in the name part.

Left The Bible has always provided an attractive source for film producers – not least because no copyright is involved. A monumental Charlton Heston poses here as Moses with the two tablets of stone in Cecil B. DeMille's 1956 re-make of *The Ten Commandments*.

Above A poster for the box-office success *Airport* – 1970 publicizes the fact that it is based on a best-selling book. The film was noted for Helen Hayes' memorable acting as a seventy-year-old stowaway.

If the script is based on an existing work, two main problems have to be resolved. Firstly, what narrative form best translates the original work into cinematic form? Secondly, what has to be cut, condensed, dropped, enlarged or developed from the original both to assist the translation into cinema and to fit the running time of a film?

For example: How can a state of mind described at great length by the author be shown visually, verbally and economically by scenes that do not appear in the original? How can the previous history of characters arise naturally from the narrative or dialogue, to replace a description lasting several pages in the original? How can a relationship which takes up a considerable length of the original be condensed, but retain equal weight in the film? Can dialogue be translated into a visual, non-verbal form?

A small number of scripts are written in a frenzy of activity and inspiration over a brief period. But most take anything from a couple of months to over a year to reach the final 'shooting script'. In the process writers, conception, characters and plot can have changed so greatly that the 'shooting script' bears almost no relationship to the original 'property'. This change may be due to creative necessity – or gross ineptitude.

Left Ben Hecht (1894–1964) made his name as a scriptwriter with such films as *Scarface* – 1932, *The Scoundrel* – 1935 and *Nothing Sacred* – 1937. He had been a journalist, and wrote the stage play *The Front Page* – 1928 with Charles MacArthur. As a team they produced scripts noted for their naturalistic dialogue, acid wit and black humour.

115

The Producer

It has been said that 'a producer is someone who calls himself one, and people believe him.' The producer need have no formal qualifications, no previous experience of producing – or even making – a film. All an aspiring producer needs is credibility. This has been true since the days of the silent cinema, when the enormous sums of money now required to produce a film were not necessary. The first film producers were often salesmen or exhibitors of the primitive movies. They went into film production to feed a growing market and hungry audiences.

The early producers frequently formed partnerships with directors and players, offering to handle the business side, leaving the 'artists' free to create. Sooner or later the director discovered he no longer had control over what he could make or how he could spend the money. Directors claimed they did not receive their proper share of the profits. Meanwhile the producers had become studio owners.

In the modern film industry there are two kinds of producer: the 'independent' and the 'line producer'. The independents form a majority. Each time they make a film they have to raise their own finance. The line producer is put on a film by a studio or production company solely as a manager. He is not expected to make a significant creative contribution. A producer sometimes employs a line producer to manage the day-to-day making of a film; he is then called the film's 'associate producer'.

Setting up the film

The producer creates the framework within which a film is made. First he has to choose which film to make. He may be swayed by a multitude of factors, from a personal obsession to the recognition that an idea or work will provide the basis for an easily financed film.

Then the producer has to select his personnel. He must use his previous experience and working relationships, knowledge of people's skills and strengths, financial judgement and 'hunches'. Unless the producer has unique authority and easy access to finance, a series of considerations of what must be fulfilled before money will be advanced take control. Too often these tend to keep new talent or innovation out of film-making.

Assembling the package

The producer has to ask himself: Is the subject commercial? (Is it one of the types of film that is making money at the moment?) But spy films were not commercially successful until the first Bond film. Mafia films were not commercially viable until *The Godfather* – 1972. The producer also needs to be convinced from reading the script that it will make money.

Next the producer finds he has to suggest writers, directors and stars who are 'bankable'. Have they made recent films that are commercially successful? Are they reliable? Are they rumoured to be flooded with work? If the producer owns a

'hot property', or has interested a 'hot' director, writer, or star, he can use this to attract other people in what becomes known as 'the package'. The producer knows he has succeeded when he receives the finance and go-ahead to make the film, possibly announced to the press as 'a major motion picture'.

The producer collaborates, supports, interferes or stays away during the making of the film according to his personality. If he expects a share of the profits, he gets involved in the publicity and promotion of the film during its initial distribution and exhibition.

The good producer brings together a variety of different talents, enabling them to collaborate on a film with all the support they need. The bad producer can, by interfering, prevent the talent he has assembled from making a good film. Both new and experienced producers can break every rule of the 'package' requirements and produce a film that is unexpectedly a commercial and artistic success. The previous unknowns, without a 'track record', become the new 'hot' names!

The producer's team

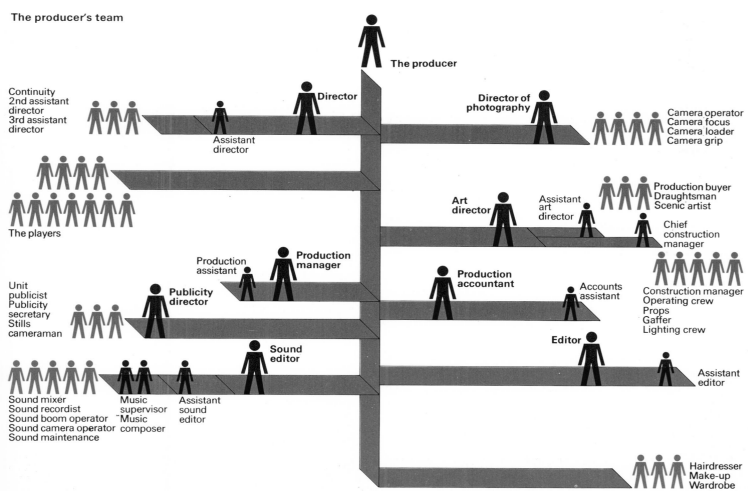

The Director

Directors can now receive as much publicity in the media as the 'stars' of their films. Yet to most cinemagoers the name of the director of the film is unimportant. The millions of people who went to see a Chaplin movie because they loved 'the little tramp' could not have told you that he also directed, wrote and produced the film, as well as composed the music.

Directors receive relatively little public recognition as 'authors' because of the collaborative nature of film. When films are created along industrial mass production lines it is more difficult for the director to make an individual contribution. Moreover the director often has limited authority and control. He cannot insist on the credit due to him in a business which benefits from his vulnerable position, and knows that, unlike the stars, the name of a director will not sell an appreciable number of extra tickets at the box office.

The ideal director

It is the director's role to coordinate and orchestrate the talents of writers, actors, photographers, art-directors, editors, composers and innumerable other crafts and skills. Ideally, the director works on an idea from the beginning, encouraging and stimulating the writer with suggestions and ideas. He will contribute his own interests, passions, preoccupations, experience and originality in such a way that the writer can apply or transform them with his own talent, without feeling a mere hack writer. If the director uses a completed script, he reworks it or develops it along different lines, possibly changing the story, the characters or the emphasis.

The director may also write new scenes or dialogue himself, without necessarily getting credit. For a variety of reasons a script can still be being written or re-written while a film is in production. Nobody likes this – even if it is a temperamental necessity for the director.

The director will know exactly what he must get from each scene, since he has written it in collaboration with the writer. Some directors know this, but do not decide exactly how to construct and film the scene until they are actually on the set with the crew, equipment and cast. Others decide exactly, shot by shot, how to shoot the scene well in advance; others film the scene

Above Alfred Hitchcock directs on location in Covent Garden, London, for his thriller *Frenzy* – 1972.

Below *Day for Night* – 1973 was François Truffaut's homage to cinema. It features film-making within a film, and shows many of the technical and dramatic aspects involved.

Right François Truffaut
in dynamic action filming
Bed and Board – 1970,
which concerns the
character Antoine Doinel,
first featured in *Les
Quatre Cents Coups* –
1959. The complex
camera-head mechanism
is also clearly visible.

Far right Veteran
American professional
William Wyler directs on
set. His successes
included *The Little Foxes*
– 1941, *The Best Years of
our Lives* – 1946 and
Roman Holiday – 1953.

Below right Andy
Warhol, perhaps the best-
known of the
'underground' film-makers
who sprang up in the
1960s. His films have
tended to reflect his work
as a graphic artist, and
have been detached from
developments in
'mainstream' cinema.

from numerous angles and set-ups so they can
make a choice in editing. Hitchcock claims that his
work is over when the shooting script is ready – the
rest is mere mechanics!

Trust the cameraman
A director with a highly-developed visual sense
needs to work with a director of photography who
can capture on film the director's precise vision of
the style for the film. This requires close collaboration, trust and a camera crew capable of
realising the director of photography's instructions. A director may have as much camera
knowledge and experience as the cameraman, but
during filming he has neither the time nor the
attention to do the job himself.

The great directors of photography light and
shoot each film according to its director's vision,
even adding to that vision rather than merely
mechanically carrying out instructions. Cameramen have different qualities and talents. A director
will try to choose the cameraman with the same
care as the writer or cast. During filming there is no
time to re-shoot any but a bare minimum of
footage; the director must have total confidence in
the abilities and judgement of his director of
photography.

However large and expensive a film may be,
every director has to work within a budget that is
ultimately limited. At planning stage he must
decide on the allocation of time, money and
resources according to the importance of a scene
or sequence in the film. Everything has to be
considered and requested so that it is there when
required for filming. During filming and editing
the director must both think of the film as a whole,
and concentrate on all its detail. If that balance is
lost the film will probably fail.

The Actors

For the audience (and financier) the stars are a film's major attraction. In choosing his actors, the director has to try to balance between the requirement for stars, his own preferences and the 'weight' of different characters that the script requires. He has to resist the wrong actor being forced on him at the insistence of the source of finance, or alternatively persuade them to allow him to cast an actor who is believed to lack box office attraction.

Casting is a major task for the director. He may know the actor he wants to cast, but has to discover if that actor is free and willing to do it. The director may cast an actor of known ability, thinking him right for the part, only to find that he is a disaster.

Casting the film

Directors and producers often work with casting directors. The casting director, having read the script, discusses the parts with the director, picking up specific ideas or qualities the director is looking for. The casting director sees a large number of applicants for the smaller parts, and provides a shortlist for the director to interview. This economizes on the director's time, and also gives him the benefit of the casting director's knowledge of thousands of actors. Ultimately casting is a personal choice which only seems obvious or inspired when it is right.

The director and actor must trust one another. When discussing a part with a star, the director explains what he hopes to achieve with the film, and how he conceives the role. The star may have doubts about the script or the director, and need reassuring, and perhaps persuading, before accepting the part. The director has to guess the kind of working relationship they will have if he casts the actor, and try to decide on the actor's suitability for the part.

With supporting or lesser known actors, the director has discussions and possibly a 'reading'. In a reading the actor reads aloud the dialogue from a scene for the part for which he is being considered.

The screen-test also helps indicate an actor's suitability for a role. It may take the form of acting a scene, improvising or simply acting out a situation from the film. People can appear and sound very different on film from how they are in everyday life. Sometimes a director watches the

Above Alain Resnais' *Providence* – 1977 has a particularly strong cast. Among its actors are (left to right) David Warner, Ellen Burstyn, Sir John Gielgud and Dirk Bogarde, all of whom contribute intelligent and accomplished performances.

Left *Riot* – 1969, set in a US jail, used both prisoners and professional actors in its cast. Here they run through the script with director Buzz Kulik. The actor Gene Hackman, No. 21310, is in the centre.

performance of an actor in a previous film to help him decide.

Preparing to film

Once cast, the actor must be available for costume fittings, selection of a wardrobe, wigs (if necessary) and possibly make-up tests for technical or appearance purposes.

Before filming begins, a period of rehearsal may be needed for the director and actors to discover and develop a role, or work out complicated sequences. Some actors like to meet and study people whose lives are similar to the role they are playing, to help them build up the part. Others rely on their own resources or the guidance of the film's director.

During filming the actor must arrive on the set having learnt the dialogue for the scene being filmed, and having given some thought and preparation to the part. But he must be flexible, since dialogue, characterization and action may all have to be changed on the set.

The actor new to films has to learn the different characteristics and needs of film acting. He must learn that the camera exaggerates gestures and performances. He has to adjust to what may seem underplaying or even non-acting. The art of film acting is to interiorize a role, and transmit it by the subtlest actions, gestures, looks and inflections of the voice. The director has to guide his actors by ideas and suggestions.

Directors have different ways of working. Some, such as Vincente Minnelli and Ernst Lubitsch, act out and impose a performance on an actor by showing how to do everything, right down to the last detail. Other directors build on, or amend, a basic performance given by the actor. Ideally the director should be flexible, able to vary his approach according to the part and the actor.

Directing the actor

Michelangelo Antonioni is reported by actors to give them no help at all. He says: 'I prefer to get results by the hidden method; that is, to stimulate in the actor certain of his innate qualities of whose existence he is himself unaware – to excite not his intelligence but his instinct – to give not justifications but illuminations. One can almost trick an actor by demanding one thing and obtaining another. The director must know how to distinguish what is good and bad, useful and superfluous, in everything the actor offers.'

The film actor also has to learn to perform, while remembering to 'hit the mark' so that the camera and sound can move with him. If the actor makes a mistake, then focus, camera movement and sound will also probably go wrong. Actors are legendary for being wildly temperamental. Total professionalism is easier for the director. In any event the director has to possess infinite patience, or go to extreme lengths, to get the best out of the actor.

Once 'action' has been called, the actors are on their own. They need the ability to repeat subtle or intense actions time and time again, with a consistent performance. It is frequently hot, uncomfortable, tiring, repetitive and tedious. It is popularly regarded as glamorous.

Set versus Location

Movies are made in studios or on location. A location is a site outside a studio used for filming. It can be anything from a telephone kiosk to the Taj Mahal. Similar appearances can be obtained by using a set, model, process work or a combination of these (special effects) in the studio. In deciding which method to use, cost, convenience, control, practicality, effectiveness and the director's preference must all be considered.

Freedom and realism

Sometimes a movie is promoted as more 'realistic' because it was filmed entirely on location. The director and actors may feel they responded differently in the actual location than they would have done in a studio, and this is reflected in the film. Or they may feel they are breaking away from some of the artificiality of a studio production. But a studio can be either suffocating or liberating, depending on circumstances.

It is sometimes claimed that filming in a studio is more expensive than filming on location, because the studio is run on a strictly commercial basis, with as many costs as it can charge plus an overhead. This can be true, but is not a general rule. For instance, a location (a short shop scene for example) may be available for a nominal fee, or free – while to build such a set in the studio would cost several thousand pounds. But when the costs of transport, support and supply for the location unit are added up, it may work out cheaper to build the set, and film in the studio.

A bonus offered on location is the possibility of the unexpected. Ingmar Bergman tells of the making of one famous shot in *The Seventh Seal* – 1957. 'You know the scene where they dance along the horizon? We'd packed up for the evening and were just about to go off home. It was raining. Suddenly I saw a cloud; and Gunnar Fischer swung his camera up. Several of the actors had already gone home, so at a moment's notice some of the grips had to stand in, get some costumes on and dance along up there. The whole thing was improvised in about ten minutes flat.'

Hitchcock as technician

Alfred Hitchcock is both a great director and a master technician. There are many instances of the way the master uses the facilities and resources of a studio to achieve his aims. Hitchcock revealed that for *North by Northwest* – 1959 he had an exact copy made up of the United Nations lobby. Somebody had used that setting for a previous film, after which Secretary General Dag Hammarskjold

Below Preparations for filming in Pinewood Studios' open-air tank – the largest in Europe. Among the other facilities at this British studio are thirteen stages, including the new '007' stage (the world's largest), a special effects stage, and a studio lot of roughly seventy-two acres.

prohibited any shooting of fiction films on the premises. Hitchcock did shoot one scene of Cary Grant going into the building, by using a concealed camera. He used colour stills to reconstitute the settings in the studios.

For *The Birds* – 1963, to get the characters right Hitchcock had every inhabitant of Bodega Bay – man, woman, and child – photographed for the costume department. The restaurant is an exact copy of the one there. The house of the farmer who is killed by the birds is an exact replica of an existing farm: the same entrance, halls, rooms and kitchen. Even the mountain scenery outside the window of the corridor is completely accurate.

Studio techniques

Filming in a small, cramped setting can be more interesting visually in a studio, because a wall can be removed (or 'flown') to give director and cameraman more space for their picture composition or camera movement.

Stanley Cortez, the cameraman on Orson Welles' *The Magnificent Ambersons* – 1942 describes a scene which was only possible because of the ability to 'fly' a wall in a studio. 'In another shot we went through 6 or 7 rooms . . . Every time the camera went through a room, we saw four

walls and a ceiling! Walls moved on cue, (were flown) and in went a light on a predetermined line, all while the camera was moving. It was a symphony of movement, noise notwithstanding!'

One director may never leave the studio; another may never enter a studio. They make different kinds of film. Script, subject, budget and preferred ways of working are the main factors in deciding whether a film is made in studio, on location, or both.

Left One of the magnificent desert scenes for *Lawrence of Arabia* – 1962, filmed amidst the heat and sand. The camera is set up for a 'tracking' shot, on a wooden 'railway'. The film featured Peter O'Toole, Alec Guinness and Omar Sharif, and was typical of its director, David Lean, in its care, skill and attention to detail. It also featured the outstanding photography of Freddie Young.

Left This studio set, built around a 50,000-gallon water tank, was used in filming Red Skelton's comedy *Whistling in Dixie* —1942. Right to left the actors are: Ann Rutherford, Rags Ragland, Red Skelton, George Bancroft and Diana Lewis.

The Production Unit

'What do all these people do?' 'Why are there so many people standing around doing nothing?' These are the inevitable questions asked when people see a movie being made.

People with a wide variety of different talents and skills, belonging to different craft and labour unions, are all involved. The small, flexible, non-union film crew is only possible on low-budget films, which account for only a small percentage of annual production. People stand around part of the time apparently doing nothing, because different processes happen at different times, and people must be available to work when needed.

A varied team

The production unit is the part of the crew which looks after planning and organisation. Directly responsible to the producer is an associate producer or production supervisor, then the production manager and location manager and their assistants and secretaries. Their actual titles vary according to authority and previous experience. The size and nature of the film determines how many of these positions are filled and how far responsibilities are shared. This part of the unit is employed from pre-production. They negotiate fees and hire other members of the unit, prepare a production schedule and breakdown requirements for pre-production, filming and post-production stages, in consultation with the producer and director.

Organizing to film

During filming three assistant directors are responsible for controlling, coordinating, and servicing the director and unit. They do anything from organizing and instructing the 'extras' or 'crowd' players in large sequences, to calling for 'quiet' or informing other departments, not present during filming, of sudden or future requirements of the director.

The camera, sound, art and editing departments are serviced by the production unit, but remain responsible to the director and producer.

The script supervisor (or continuity clerk) makes sure that details of one shot (the placing of objects, clothes worn, hand and body positions and so forth) match details in another shot filmed later. She also keeps a record of the numbered takes for each shot, describing the action and actors involved. Such a record is essential for editing, so that film and sound takes can be identified and located.

A stills cameraman is present during filming to take the publicity photographs used for promoting the film.

Right A large production team filming a scene for Frank Capra's *Meet John Doe* – 1941. The camera is mounted on a crane, microphones are suspended strategically over the crowd of extras. A large team of technicians is necessary to operate the rain machine, lighting, sound and camera. The film features a typical Capra hero: Gary Cooper plays this figure, who fights the threat of Fascism.

Below An extraordinarily elaborate studio set for *Lydia* – 1941. Julien Duvivier, a French director, made this film, which starred Merle Oberon, in Britain. The lighting, wind-machine, sound apparatus and set are all clearly visible.

A wardrobe designer is responsible for designing or selecting the clothes worn by the cast. Costumes are often hired from companies with large stocks for every conceivable period or situation. During filming the wardrobe staff supply and maintain the costumes and dress the actors when elaborate costumes are involved. Make-up and hairdressing staff, responsible to a chief, ensure that artistes are ready when required for filming, and that continuity is maintained.

Carpenters, stagehands, riggers, painters, property staff, electricians, special effects men, stunt people and technical advisors all belong to the production unit. Their labour and expertise is called on whether in studio or on location.

The second unit

On some films, on large and complex scenes, a second unit covers part of the action from a different position to the main unit. The second unit may be used in a battle, for instance, or in parts of the filming where the principal actors are not involved (or 'stand-ins' can be used) to get additional or linking material.

A production unit is large, but not necessarily cumbersome. In shooting a film, a large, efficient and hardworking crew can give the director great freedom to achieve his vision.

The Art Department

In Scott Fitzgerald's novel about Hollywood, *The Last Tycoon*, there is a passage in the projection room. The tycoon, Monroe Stahr, studio head of production, is viewing the result of the previous day's filming, and addresses the art director.

"'There's something the matter with the set.'' There were little glances exchanged all over the room. ''What is it, Monroe?'' ''You tell *me*,'' said Stahr. ''It's crowded. It doesn't carry your eye out. It looks cheap.'' ''It wasn't.'' ''I know it wasn't. There's not much the matter, but there's something. Go over and take a look tonight. It may be too much furniture – or the wrong kind. Perhaps a window would help. Couldn't you force the perspective in the hall a little more.'' ''I'll see what I can do . . . I'll have to get at it right away . . . I'll work tonight and we'll put it up in the morning.'''

It is easy to imagine an art director designing a set for a film, or choosing and adapting a location in consultation with a director. But these comments reveal some of the problems with a set design when it has been filmed and appears on the cinema screen.

The Last Tycoon is set in pre-war Hollywood, when the studio production head reigned supreme. The director rarely saw the screening of the first prints. The system has changed, and today the director is always present at the screening of the first prints or 'rushes', and he or the producer may make this kind of comment.

The contribution of the art director or production designer may be spectacular or unobtrusive, but he largely determines the visual quality of the film. The director makes suggestions, provides reference photographs or reproductions of what he is after, and makes choices and objections. But normally he relies on the art director to visualize the imaginative possibilities of a film script.

The art director's team

The art director has a team working under him. One or more assistant art directors design smaller sets, details and props, while the art director works on the larger aspects. Draughtsmen translate the designs into working drawings from which the construction manager and crew build. Scenic artists paint the sets or backcloths, and sometimes a sign writer too is employed. The property buyer hires or purchases all the props not made by the art department. During shooting a set dresser has the job of placing props in position, and moving them as required, helped by other 'props' personnel.

The art director either works closely with the wardrobe designer, or designs the wardrobe himself. Specialists in building and using models,

Below left A design by John Box for David Lean's *Lawrence of Arabia* – 1962.

Bottom left The train explosion scene in *Lawrence of Arabia;* the careful composition becomes evident when this still from the film is compared with the storyboard drawings opposite.

Below Designer Hein Heckroth at work with a model set for *Red Shoes* – 1948. Michael Powell, its British director, attempted to combine music, ballet, film and painting in what was a considerable achievement of technique.

ecial effects and process work collaborate with
e art director, according to the film's subject.

The director's role

here are times when the director is happy neither
th the work of the art department nor with
ture! When Vincente Minnelli was filming a
make of *The Four Horsemen of the Apocalypse* –
62, he had to shoot in the Bois de Boulogne in
ris in November. Minnelli thought the leaves
uld stay on the trees, as they do in California.
hen they fell off, he started nailing leaves on; but
e authorities would not allow that, so he glued

them. It was raining. Then he disliked the leaves
they bought, so he had them painted.

Such actions may seem capricious , but they are
usually done for a reason. The director Rouben
Mamoulian explained that colour cinematography tends to brighten and cheapen natural
colour. He believed that colour in films was near to
painting. He devised what came to be known as
the 'Mamoulian palette'. Beside him on the set he
had a huge box of scraps of material – scarves and
handkerchiefs in all colours – so that if a costume
or a set needed a bit more of a particular colour he
put it in himself.

Below Part of the storyboard for *Lawrence of
Arabia.* The train of events
can be followed clearly.
The care put into the
accurate storyboard
treatment is reflected in
the beauty and precision
of the finished film.

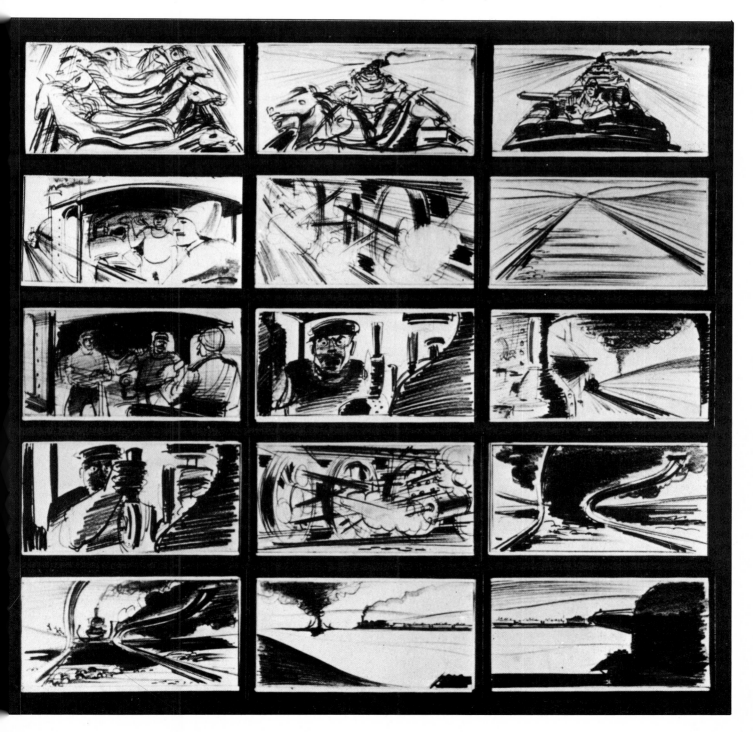

Lighting:
The Cameraman/Cinematographer

Photographic techniques in film production have always centred on two vital areas: lighting the scene, and mounting and moving the camera. In the very early days, the camera position was fixed and the lighting was daylight, even for interior scenes, which were set in glass-roofed studios. But it was not long before the need for consistent results at all times of day and seasons of the year led to the building of enclosed studio stages and the use of artificial lighting for all except genuine outdoor scenes requiring daylight.

Lighting the set
Initially even black-and-white negative was not very light-sensitive and the only light source powerful enough for the large indoor stages was the arc lamp. Still pictures of 1920s production studios often feature enormous Klieg lamps which created great heat and fumes as well as light. As improved black-and-white film stocks were produced, less light was necessary and large incandescent tungsten filament lamps provided a much more convenient form of studio lighting. It was not until the early 1950s, with the arrival of the single-strip colour negative, that the arc light started to disappear from the studio.

About 1965 a greatly improved light-source became available – the tungsten-halogen, or quartz-iodine, lamp. The halogen (iodine) vapour it contained ensured that the light output remained high and consistent in colour throughout its working-life. The smaller bulb size also allowed much more compact mountings (luminaires). The work of the cameraman is well described by the title director of lighting. It is by distributing light and shade creatively within the scene to be photographed that his effects are achieved. At one time studio lighting required an army of workmen to rig, position, direct and operate a vast number of separate lamps, standing on the stage floor and hanging in cradles from the studio roof. The arc lamps had to have their carbons replaced every forty minutes or so.

In modern studios everything is much more mechanized. The overhead lighting units are suspended on adjustable stalks or pantographs, sometimes from a roof grid, and the height and angle can be set by remote control. Luminaire switching, location and distribution can be set from a central console, and the exact conditions decided by the lighting director during rehearsal can be recorded and automatically reproduced whenever required during the actual shooting of the scene.

Location work
Outdoor photography on location cannot rely solely on natural daylight. Harsh, direct sun must be softened by gauze diffusion screens, while deep shadow areas must be illuminated by strategically placed reflectors. Sometimes available light must be supplemented by artificial lighting powered by a mobile generator, filtered to match the daylight colour. For location work, a wide range of mobile trucks have been developed to provide everything needed for lighting units, power supplies, picture and sound equipment and even facilities for make-up, dressing rooms, and canteen services.

Below The 10K Fresnel is one of the two main incandescent lights used in filming today. It functions as a key-light.

Below Preparing to film the departure from Istanbul for Sidney Lumet's *Murder on the Orient Express* – 1974. Stand-in actors are used while the camera crew work out correct focus and exposure readings. The film featured Albert Finney, Lauren Bacall, Ingrid Bergman and Sir John Gielgud among a strong cast.

Over the years cameramen and directors have demanded greater and greater freedom in viewpoint. In very early story-films, the still photographer's practice was followed and the camera located on a fixed tripod, remaining there throughout the action on the set, which would be seen from a single viewpoint. Somewhat later the camera was mounted on a movable tripod head, which could be rotated about a vertical axis to follow the action. This 'panorama head' allowed 'panning'. A further freedom was soon added: rotation horizontally, to tilt the camera up and down. These two movements have remained basic to camera mountings ever since. Modern types of pan and tilt mount include the friction head, which allows rapid but rather imprecise movements; the fluid head, in which the rotation is smoothed by a viscous liquid; and the geared head, which offers the smoothest and most accurate movement, but calls for considerable skill in operation.

The moving camera

To provide a fully mobile viewpoint, the camera is mounted on a movable platform (or 'dolly') and provided with a hydraulic arm or column for adjusting the height. There are usually seats on the dolly for the camera operator and assistant, and the whole unit is manoeuvred by other members of the crew. Castor-mounted trolley wheels allow movement sideways ('crabbing', hence 'crab-dolly') as well as forwards and back. On rough surfaces and out-of-doors it may be necessary to lay a track for the wheels – hence the term 'tracking shot' for any scene that is photographed from a moving viewpoint.

The maximum rise available from a dolly-mounting is usually about two metres from the floor. For greater heights a camera crane is used. A power-operated boom-arm carries a platform for the director, camera operator and assistant, with the camera on its pan and tilt head, and allows the viewpoint to move spectacularly in all three dimensions.

Hand-held camera

The most mobile viewpoint of all is provided by the hand-held camera. Cameras were designed with shoulder supports and well-balanced weight to meet the demand for flexibility. But it was practically impossible for a walking cameraman to take a shot in which irregular unsteadiness was not immediately obvious.

This problem was solved in the mid-1970s by the development of various types of stabilized camera harness in which a light-weight counter-balanced camera was supported by a linkage of spring-loaded arms attached to the camera operator's body. A television viewfinder was incorporated so that it was unnecessary for the operator to keep his eye to an eyepiece on the camera itself. The mobile operator could concentrate solely on controlling the camera viewpoint and position, and an assistant set lens focus and diaphragm by remote control. It is now possible to achieve results from a mobile hand-held camera which are as smooth in action as the best results from a tracked dolly, under conditions where the latter would be completely unusable.

Below The 5K Sky Pan is the second main incandescent light in use today. It functions as a general flood.

Below This modern sound stage at Pinewood Studios, England, is equipped for both film and television use. A full range of lighting equipment is displayed together with a crane-mounted camera.

Capturing Sound

Some directors treat the sound department as the poor relation in making a movie. It is the last to receive attention, and is then expected to cause no trouble and fit in with everybody's demands. Others have the highest regard and respect for the talents of the sound recordist.

Choosing the sound
In England and America it is normal practice to use when possible 'sync sound', recorded at the time of the take. By contrast in mainland Europe and elsewhere sound is normally 'post-synchronized': the actors' voices are recorded while viewing the film, so that the dialogue fits the actors' lip movements.

Sync shooting takes longer, and often requires more takes, to get something satisfactory for both camera and sound. The microphone must be as close to the actor speaking as possible, to give a clear recording and minimize background noise. On static set-ups the microphones can sometimes be hidden behind props, but on wide, tracking or panning shots the microphones will need to be on a 'boom' that can move according to the actors' movements. When the set-up has been decided, the actors' movements worked out, the set dressed, and the lighting set, the sound recordist is in a position to see the problems; he must try to get the cooperation of the camera and other departments to solve them. He needs the support of the director to resist the pressures to 'get on and make do'.

The sound recordist has a variety of microphones with different responses to choose from. After the recordist has heard a rehearsal, he may alter his choice, causing further delays. Other problems arise through actors having to project their voices louder that they would prefer to achieve a satisfactory recording level. Finally good takes can be made unusable because of unexpected background noises during shooting.

A director who is not prepared to go to this trouble, or who prefers to instruct the actors during a take, will ask the recordist to get the sound for use in post-syncing, or make do with merely adequate sound.

Pre-recorded and post-sync sound
Other normal sound techniques include the use of pre-recorded sound and music in musicals or dance sequences. The actors mime or sing to a playback of the recording during the take. Western or action films, usually shot on location, use a formal, almost stylized, form of dialogue, particularly suited to post-sync sound. The

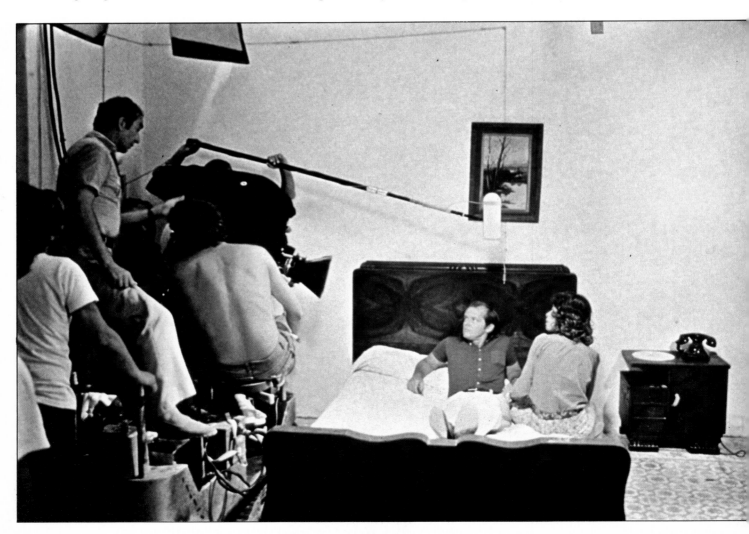

Below Shooting Antonioni's *The Passenger* – 1975. Sync sound is recorded from the microphone suspended by a hand-held boom over the actor's heads. For such intimate scenes, the sound recordist must work carefully to achieve realistic effects.

director who regularly uses post-syncing does so because it is cheaper, or because he believes he can get a better performance from the actor when free from the pressures of a shooting schedule. Post-syncing also allows an actor's voice that is found unsuitable to be completely replaced by an alternative voice. Also, dialogue can be completely changed and yet still fit the lip movements.

Post-syncing often has a 'dead' effect, lacking sound perspective, and fails to fit the lip movements, as in many Italian films. But an audience that is only used to this poor quality will accept it and not find it disconcerting.

Sync or direct sound recording is, at its best, an art. The master recordist will be able to record sound that has a subtlety, vitality, tone and perspective that contributes an additional dimension to the film.

Technical advances

During recent years technical developments have extended the resources of the sound recordist. For instance the radio microphone with its own radio transmitter, worn by the actor, can be used in situations where it would be impossible to use a conventional microphone because of distance from the camera, background noise, the number of actors, or wide shots on a large set. Most recordists only use a radio microphone as a last resort, because the quality is cruder, it lacks sound perspective and it can be sensitive to interference.

Stereo recording has also made the recordist's job easier and more flexible. Before stereo, the recordist had to balance the volume from the different microphones on a single sound track, which presented limitations. Stereo allows the use

of at least two tracks, which are then transferred separately for editing. These can cope with different and unexpected volume changes from the individual microphones during a take and add for the overall breadth of sound.

The American director Robert Altman makes films which are distinctive for their dense and complex sound tracks. He apparently uses eight-track recorders, originally developed for music recording, together with individual radio microphones on each actor. He gains a freedom which allows the actors to improvise, overlap dialogue (with two people speaking simultaneously) or record several different conversations within one shot, without the sound being unusable.

For post-syncing, the actor sits or stands in a recording booth watching the piece of film to be synced projected in a loop. He wears earphones, through which the 'guide track' is played on a loop. The take is recorded repeatedly until both performance and lip movements match.

The Editors

The editor is responsible for joining a film together into its final form. Unless the director has a distinctive editing style, or the working relationship between the director and editor is known, it is impossible to tell from seeing a film what contribution the editor made.

Directors have different approaches and abilities during editing. Some stand over the editor fussing over every cut. Others lack any sense for the rhythm of editing a sequence or for the development and construction of narrative. There are also directors with complete mastery of the editing process.

There is no standard method of working. If working collaboratively, the editor and director look at the various takes for a sequence, select preferred takes and discuss the construction and editing of a scene. When the editor has assembled the sequence, they view the result together. Further changes are made for practical and artistic reasons, until both are satisfied with the result.

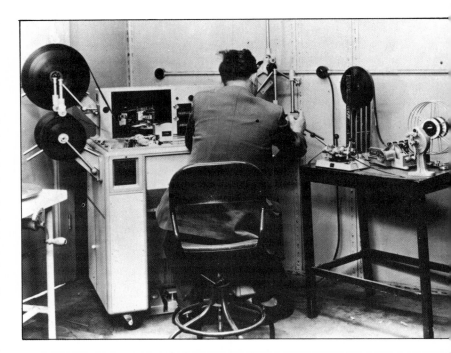

Cutting to size

Sometimes an editor assembles the film in a rough order during filming ('assembly') so that the director can decide if a sequence is likely to work, or judge how an actor's performance will work when edited. The first cut, called the 'rough cut', normally contains all the sequences filmed. Over several months the film is worked on, refined and changed, until it is finally finished. At this stage it is known as the 'fine cut'.

The film changes constantly during editing. Sequences may be completely altered and the running order rearranged so that the emphasis and importance of characters are changed. Sequences may be constructed that were not even filmed as such, but created in the editing out of the material shot for a different purpose.

The importance, meaning and effectiveness of a sequence can be radically altered by placing it in a different order or context than scripted. The director Billy Wilder gives an example of this from the opening of *Some Like It Hot* – 1959, a close-up of Jack Lemmon and Tony Curtis wobbling along on high heels. He found that preview audiences howled so much that he went back and added all the footage shot from every angle. In fact they walk past the same railroad car six times.

Capturing the rhythm

Editing consists of finding the best way of joining individual shots together to give them meaning, and indicating spatial, reactive, dramatic and narrative relationships, then locating these shots within a sequence which reinforces these effects. The process continues as the sequence is located within the film's structure. With some films the structure is only built during the editing. Editing, then, is a process of making connections and refining, until the film has a rhythm, and all the different elements balance.

During editing, differences of opinion may occur. But a scene can be edited different ways

Left A film editor at work. A frame from the piece of film he is working on is displayed on his console.

Below left Sergei Eisenstein, the great Russian director, was noted for his innovatory and creative approach to editing. It was clearly evident in *The Battleship Potemkin* – 1925.

Below Frank Sullivan, one of MGM's veteran film-editors, at work on 35mm film.

before a final decision is made. Ultimately the director's views must prevail.

The mechanical operations performed in the cutting room are relatively simple. The positive prints of the previous day's shooting are generally called the 'rushes'. The sound is recorded on a quarter-inch magnetic tape and transferred to magnetic sprocketed film of a similar gauge to that of the film being used – 16, 35 or 70mm. The first job is to synchronize the sound track with the picture. The clapper board used at the beginning of a take, showing the scene and/or shot number and take, records the precise moment of contact between the clapper and board. The moment of contact on the sound track and picture are matched; when run together the sound and picture will continue in sync.

The various takes are held together by a 'tape joiner', which grips the film sprockets so that the picture or sound can be cut by the guillotine blade. Picture and sound are gradually built up into separate reels of workable length, then passed through a machine that prints numbers at 30cm

(one-foot) intervals along the edge of the film. These numbers and the corresponding takes are logged so that during editing any piece of picture or sound can be identified.

Next the director and editor view the complete reels in a projection theatre to decide which takes to use in cutting. The editor next views the film on an editing machine, usually known by its trade name—'Steenbeck', 'Moviola' or 'Editola' for example. The editing machine has a separate sound and picture head so that sound and picture can be run simultaneously at different speeds, for close examination and selection. When the editor has decided where he wants to cut, he marks the appropriate frame with a wax pencil and cuts the film with the joiner. The editor can work with precision since there are twenty-four individual frames of picture or sound for each second of running time. This means that, if required, 1/24th of a second of picture or sound can be added or subtracted until the effect is achieved. It is the precision and power of editing that appeals to many directors.

The Laboratory

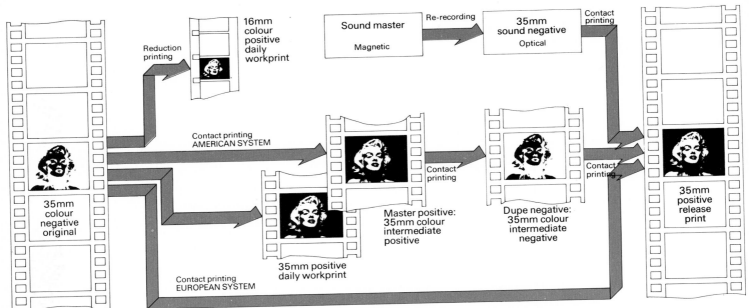

16mm colour positive daily workprint

Sound master Magnetic

Re-recording

35mm sound negative Optical

Contact printing

Reduction printing

Contact printing AMERICAN SYSTEM

35mm colour negative original

Contact printing EUROPEAN SYSTEM

35mm positive daily workprint

Contact printing

Master positive: 35mm colour intermediate positive

Contact printing

Dupe negative: 35mm colour intermediate negative

Contact printing

35mm positive release print

The often-forgotten film processing laboratory provides a number of important technical links in the chain stretching from the creative artist in the studio to the final public presentation on the screen. The laboratory's services may be divided into three: first, the functions carried out day by day during the initial shooting period; second, the wide range of activities on both picture and sound records in preparing the first show print; and third, the manufacture of all the further release copies for general distribution to cinemas throughout the world.

Front end work
In the first two stages, together termed 'front end work', the laboratory must keep closely in touch with the production company, working in personal contact with the director, cameraman and editor. However in supplying release prints the laboratory operates almost as a mass-production factory, turning out repeated prints of consistent quality at high speed. Although the same basic processes – printing and developing rolls of film – are involved at each stage, the equipment and organization reflect the differing demands.

When the original film exposed in the camera is received by the laboratory, it is first developed. This involves passing the film through a series of chemical baths to change the latent and invisible image into one of black-and-white or colour. After drying, it can be examined and used to make a print for projection. The original negative is extremely valuable – it may be the only record of a day's work costing tens of thousands of pounds. So negative developing machines are designed to handle the film with great care and uniformity.

The roll of film from the camera will contain some scenes in which the action has met the director's requirements, and some which are not usable. After developing, the unusable must be removed, in a 'break-down', and the correct shots joined together again. From these a contact print

is made by exposing a suitable colour positive stock through the negative. This print is developed on another type of developing machine, and inspected by projection on a screen in a review theatre, before delivery to the editor at the production studio cutting rooms.

Up to this stage the laboratory is concerned with the picture film only. The corresponding sound is recorded on magnetic tape and sent direct to the editor for synchronizing with the picture print. In film production, time is money. These laboratory processes are generally all carried out overnight, after the day's shooting, so that the first prints can be in the editor's hands early next morning. These silent ('mute') prints are thus known as 'daily rush prints' ('dailies' or 'rushes' for short).

This regular service of negative developing and rush print delivery continues throughout the period of shooting. The laboratory often stores the chosen negative takes, while the editor builds up the rushes into his work-print, as the director requires. As the work-print is assembled, the laboratory may be asked to prepare some special effects scenes which were not originally photographed in their final form.

At the editor's cutting rooms the picture rush prints and their matching sound tracks are assembled into the sequence eventually approved by the director, until the final cutting copy has been agreed and a magnetic sound record mixed to combine all the dialogue recordings, music and effects. At this point the laboratory comes into action again. The selected takes of the original picture negative are matched to the editor's cutting copy, cut to length and joined in the required order. Meanwhile the completed mixed magnetic track is transferred to produce a black-and-white photographic sound negative, which is then developed and synchronized with the corresponding cut reel of picture negative. Now the first 'married' print, in which picture and sound appear

Above How film is processed. The successive processing stages necessary between exposing the film and arriving at a release print.

Above right Some of the special effects that can be obtained by using an optical printer.

1 The original action as photographed.

2 Skip-frame: every other frame is printed. The action will appear twice as fast when projected.

3 Stretch-frame: each frame is printed twice. The action takes twice as long when projected.

4 Hold-frame: the same frame is repeated for as long as required, giving a still image. (Also known as stop-frame or freeze-frame.)

5 Blow-up: part of the original scene is enlarged to take up the whole frame.

6 Reverse action: the frames are printed in reverse order from shooting. The action appears to go backward.

7 Flop over: the action is reversed from right to left. It appears as a mirror image of the original action.

8 Zoom: each frame is printed slightly more magnified. It appears that the image is moving towards the camera.

9 Fade: the scene darkens to black.

10 Wipe: a boundary moves across the frame, gradually replacing one scene with another.

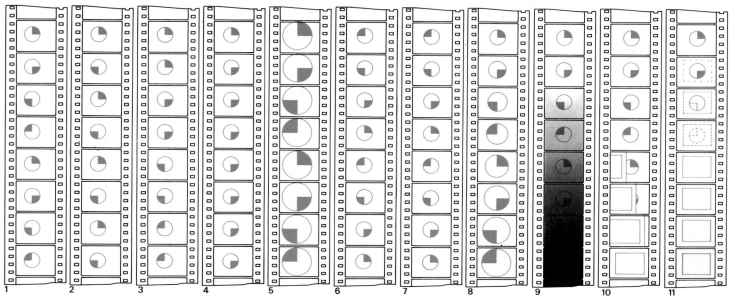

on the same strip of film, can be made.

Laboratory and production staff must co-operate closely in the important function known as 'grading': the assessment of how to print each separate scene of the reel to get the visual result required by the director and cameraman. A single reel, lasting some twenty minutes, may contain 200 or more scenes, while a modern colour film printing machine provides a range of fifty different steps of intensity, known as 'points', for each of the three colours, red, green and blue. For grading, the light from the printer lamp is divided into three separate beams of red, green and blue, by means of dichroic reflectors, which transmit only one colour and reflect the remainder. The intensity of each beam is controlled by a light valve which can be opened and closed by very precise amounts. The three beams are combined together again by dichroic mirrors after passing their valves. Thus the film at the printing aperture is exposed to light containing exactly controlled amounts of red, green and blue.

To choose the best combination of light for each scene requires skilled judgement. Most laboratories now use an electronic colour analyzer to help. Although the colour analyzer takes much of

the guess-work out of grading, it is still an operation which requires experienced judgement, and an understanding of the cameraman's intentions. In practice, two or three prints with further small corrections are made before the production team is satisfied with the laboratory's work. Then all the final details of printing are recorded for use in making further copies.

Prints for release

Once the grading has been approved, the laboratory is instructed to make additional prints for general distribution. The first few of these may be made from the cut reels of original negative. But when large numbers are needed, often in different parts of the world, it is usual to prepare one or more full-length duplicate negatives, so that the original can be kept safely. Modern duplicating materials, known as colour reversal intermediates (CRIs), allow a copy negative to be made directly from the original with little or no loss of quality, and are now widely used for release printing. They can be made to incorporate the grading corrections needed for the original. Thus they require no variations of printing scene-by-scene and can be run on much faster printing machines.

The equipment used for release printing is designed for high rates of printing and developing – an understandable requirement when it is realized that one copy of a two-hour feature film represents about 3,500 metres (11,000 feet) of 35mm film. In the United States for example several hundred copies will be needed for the general release of a successful film. Modern machines provide continuous output of completed prints at 200 to 300 metres (600 to 800 feet) a minute – for the latest installations 1,000 feet a minute is reported. At these high rates very precise control of all stages is necessary to ensure a uniform process. Much use is now being made of computers to check and correct both printing and developing conditions.

Adding Music and Dialogue

When the director and editor are satisfied with the rhythm, timing and pace of the film as a whole (after the fine cut), the music for the film is composed or selected. However, for a musical, the film is shot to a pre-recorded score on a 'playback system', with which the actors can sing and dance. The film is then edited to the same music.

For some sequences the director may want to use existing music, either for its effect, or because the sequence has been conceived in terms of image and music. On low budget films, music from recorded music libraries is sometimes used. They hold extensive selections specially recorded for film use. This music covers the whole range of requirements: themes, moods, categories, tempos, orchestrations and timings. The music may last from a few seconds – to emphasize off-set or link images – to several minutes – for carrying a whole sequence. A royalty fee is paid on the music used, according to its length and the type of exhibition for which it is required.

New music

It is more complex and expensive, but potentially more rewarding artistically, for the director to work with a composer who will compose and arrange a score to meet the film's needs and the director's conceptions. The director may play the composer existing music, or even use it during editing to show what he wants. The director, editor and composer view the film on an editing machine, discuss needs and possibilities in detail, and note the timings needed to fit the music within and between individual shots, as well as fit the complete sequence.

The composer agrees with the producer the number of musicians and range of instruments, and then composes the score according to the time schedule. The editors meanwhile break down the film into separate sections or sequences in preparation for the recording session.

The music is recorded in a special studio where the conductor and musicians can watch the film while they play the music. The different instruments are recorded on separate tracks and mixed to achieve the required balance. Both director and editor are present at the recording in case changes are needed to the score when heard against the picture and dialogue. The orchestration can be changed, tempo and key altered, or cuts and extensions effected. The composer or conductor can play a score differently to fit the precise timings demanded.

The Russian director Sergei Eisenstein worked with the composer Sergei Prokofiev, and the musical result of their collaboration has entered the classical music repertoire. In *Alexander Nevsky* – 1938, for some sequences the shots were cut to a previously recorded music track; for others the entire piece of music was written to a final cutting of the picture; other sequences contain both approaches.

Dubbing is the final creative stage in making a film. First sound editors break down the dialogue

Top The orchestra records the music for Olivier's *Hamlet* – 1948. Composing and scoring for film is a precise art, requiring exact synchronization with the screen image. To aid simultaneity, the film is projected as the orchestra records the score.

Above This sound recording studio theatre at Pinewood Studios, England, is equipped for both mono and stereo recording, and dubbing for film sound-tracks. Three people are required to operate the elaborate console.

sound into at least two tracks, so that different volume, perspective and overlap can be utilized in the dubbing. There are one or two music tracks, and anything up to several dozen effect tracks, depending on the complexity of sound required. These tracks, interspersed with blank film, are assembled on reels.

The dubbing, or re-recording, of the sound is carried out in a dubbing theatre, where the picture is projected and the sound tracks are played in synchronization with it. The equipment allows the volume of each separate sound track to be varied and its quality altered. First a pre-mix of the effects tracks is made into one or more tracks, to balance the effects with each other. This process is repeated with the other tracks, reducing the sound eventually to a single track. A good dub is achieved when the sound is imaginatively and skilfully recorded to give a new dimension to the film.

For foreign versions of a film a 'music and effects track' is recorded for use with other languages. The foreign dialogue must be a translation of the original meaning, but also use words that fit the lip movements of the original actors. 'Dubbing' is also the term used for recording actors' voices in a foreign version. The mechanical process is the same as in post-syncing.

Sub-titled

Sub-titling presents a similar challenge. Methods of adding the written sub-titles to the picture differ according to the country, tradition and economics involved as well as the number of release prints required for showing in the cinemas. For a small number of prints, the sub-titles are done individually on each release print by etching or printing. For a large number of prints the sub-titles will be added to a 'dupe negative' from which multiple copies can be made.

In some countries films which can expect a small audience are sometimes shot in one language, dubbed into another, and have two further languages sub-titled on the same print.

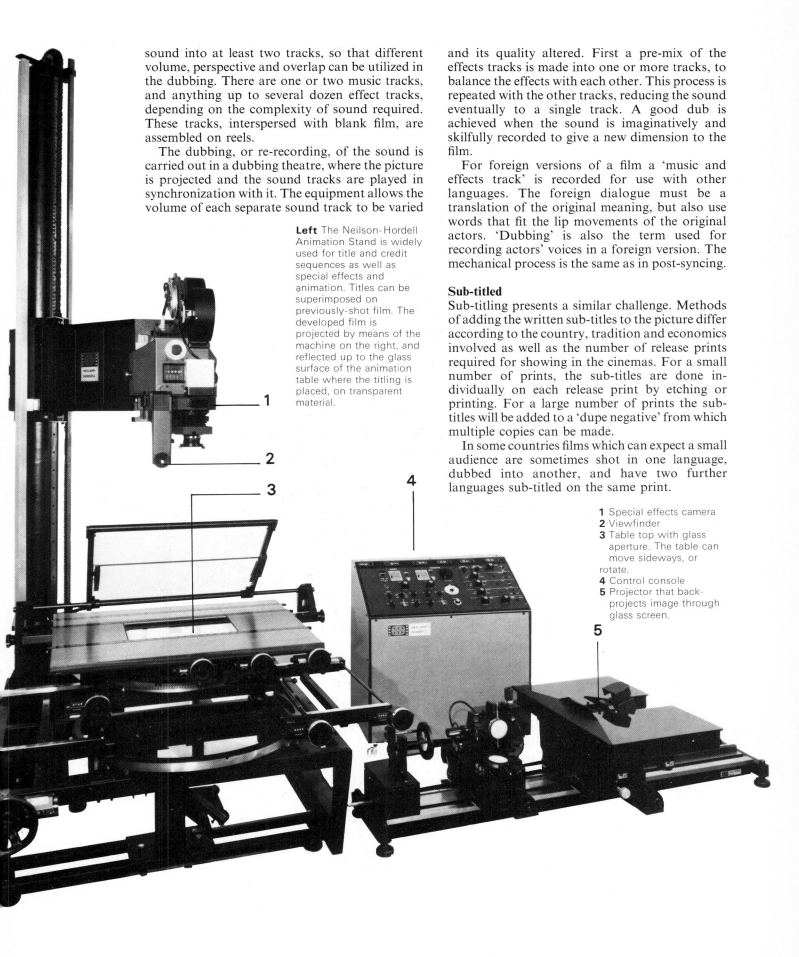

Left The Neilson-Hordell Animation Stand is widely used for title and credit sequences as well as special effects and animation. Titles can be superimposed on previously-shot film. The developed film is projected by means of the machine on the right, and reflected up to the glass surface of the animation table where the titling is placed, on transparent material.

1 Special effects camera
2 Viewfinder
3 Table top with glass aperture. The table can move sideways, or rotate.
4 Control console
5 Projector that back-projects image through glass screen.

Selling Movies:
Publicity and Advertising

Joseph E. Levine, head of the distribution company Avco-Embassy, sums up his approach to film publicity: 'Get the picture into as many cinemas as possible in as short a time as possible, and spend as much money as possible in as many advertising media as possible.'

But it is not quite as simple as that. If it were, then all a producer would have to do is spend, spend, spend. The public seems able to make up its own mind whether or not to see a particular film. A publicity campaign can help to get an initial audience to a cinema, and then encourage the public to continue going once a film has caught on. But it cannot persuade a mass audience to go to a film once a negative reaction has got around. For example the remake of *King Kong* – 1977 had a prodigious publicity and advertising campaign, and opened to record-claiming box office receipts – but never sustained that initial success. The public was unenthusiastic.

The best publicity for a film is its own unexpected success. This happens when a studio or distribution company see no real potential for a film, open it modestly, only to discover it is a runaway winner. Word-of-mouth, press reviews and television coverage report how the film is being received. They carry articles on the director or stars, copy the fashions featured, play the sound track or music from the film, until eventually the publicity for the film is based on its box office and public success!

The publicity campaign

Every film has a publicity campaign – even if it consists of *no* publicity and a closed set. The campaign may start when the property is acquired, at which point the purchase price is presented as a news item. Another news item comes with the signing of the stars. During production a unit publicist and a stills photographer take publicity shots for press and publicity use.

A public relations company may be employed to create the publicity campaign during the filming and promotion periods. The PR firm will liaise with the press, arrange interviews and feature articles and issue press releases giving background

Below An extravagant sales conference organized by MGM. The flamboyant setting, with its giant back-cloth, orchestra and star-shaped dining table, reflects dreamland Hollywood.

information and suggesting angles for the press to follow up. If the film includes shooting on a foreign location, a special trip is often arranged for a group of journalists, which can result in extensive press coverage. The overall aim is to prepare public interest and anticipation for the film's release.

The star publicity system has become an industry in itself. During previous decades as many as 500 correspondents were assigned to Hollywood to feed the world news and gossip about the stars. It is estimated that they sent 100,000 words from Hollywood every day. Today although television has reduced the mass influence of the movies, the myths and legends established during the golden years have survived and continue to influence the movie-going public – and the avid readers of film books and magazines.

When the movie is completed an advertising

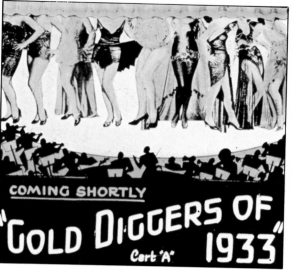

Left What people expect of a film depends heavily on its publicity. Film posters are a crucial part of the publicity. A cinema foyer card for *Golddiggers of 1933*.

Below left Charles Chaplin's characteristic features – the moustache and bowler – were employed to construct a strong public image for the star.

Below A bold and charming poster for an early Paris cinema – the Parisiana.

campaign is devised. This is based on one or more aspects of the movie that can be encapsulated to attract an audience. It is adapted to the requirements of the various media – newspapers, magazines, television, radio and posters. The advertising campaign itself is handled by a department within the distribution company. The producer and director may be consulted at this stage, depending upon their interest, involvement and contractual relationship. Similarly the number, placing and size of the credits is agreed under contract. It is regarded as extremely important within the film industry, as reputations are thought to be made and lost on the basis of previous and current credits.

An important aspect of publicity, of which the public is largely unaware, is carried by the trade publications. They cover every aspect of the business: the purchase of properties, signings of writers, directors, producers and cast, the making of deals, progress during production, post-production developments, distribution deals, exhibition policy, box office returns, the rise and fall of personnel within companies, formation of companies, mergers, take-over bids, profits, bankruptcies, litigation, births, marriages, divorces and deaths. All this, presented with suitably sensational headlines and frozen smiles, captured by the popping flashguns.

Release:
Promotion and Distribution

The distributor obtains a film from its maker and negotiates its rental for exhibition to the cinema owner in return for a share of box-office receipts, or an agreed hire fee. In the early years distributors found that insufficient new films were being produced to satisfy demand and therefore became involved in film production. They supplied the finance and dictated the kind of films and stars they wanted, according to their knowledge of public demand.

In the US the film distribution headquarters were based in New York, and the production centre in Hollywood, in the West. Some distribution companies owned their own cinema chains, while others had agreements to distribute their films exclusively to cinema chains. In time there grew up independent owners of individual cinemas and small chains of cinemas which book films from various distributors.

Distributors and major cinema owners exercise a 'barring policy', under which an independent cinema may not book a film either while it is being screened by a major chain, or within a stated distance. Independent owners obviously dislike this practice, and constantly try to declare it contrary to free trade practice.

Getting films seen

Distributors also try to persuade cinema owners to take their less successful films, by offering them packages of the good with the poor. Promotion is intended to inform the public of a film's existence, and to persuade cinema owners to book it and the public to see it. Specialized promotion appears in the form of advertisements in the various film trade publications.

Distributors employ salesmen to promote and sell films to cinema owners. For a distributor's major film the salesmen view the film and are guided on promoting and selling it at a sales conference. Decisions have to be made on how much to spend on promotion and advertising, policy precedents, and how, where and when to open the film.

By-products of film

Another important aspect of promotion is merchandising. This aims to make the public intensely aware of a film's existence, creating a wish by everybody to see the film. It probably started with the distribution of handbills. Then the name of the film and possibly its stars began to appear on T-shirts or other novelty items such as photographs, pens and matches. Next came the idea of selling these items, and extending them to games, toys, clothing and stationery. Finally merchandising became an industry in itself, whereby the film is promoted and vast sums of money are earned. It is said that a significant part of the finance for the massively successful *Star Wars* was raised by pre-selling merchandising rights to manufacturers throughout the world.

Promotion also makes advertising tie-ins with other products featuring the stars of a film –

Left A spectacular cinema display in America draws attention to the current screening: Douglas Fairbanks' *The Black Pirate* – 1926.

Below *Star Wars* – 1977 spawned a bewildering variety of spin-off products – from toys and food to games and books. This reporter has gathered a selection of the merchandise available.

usually on the film set – such as milk, cosmetics, automobiles, sports equipment and watches.

A series of special screenings is normally arranged for the press prior to the film's release, so that magazines and newspapers can include reviews and feature articles which are simultaneous with the films release. Feature writers will be given background information for writing articles about the film and its stars without actually reviewing or passing critical judgment.

Distributors wield tremendous power which is based on their financial resources. They take many of the important decisions in the making of a film, as well as having the power to decide whether to distribute a film made with independent finance. They then decide how much to put into promoting it. There are many sad stories of a distributor killing a film by wrongly deciding it has no potential.

Left An early Warner cinema in the US: The Cascade in 1903. Admission to the continuous performance was a mere five cents.

Below A glittering floodlit first night at Grauman's Chinese cinema, Los Angeles. The event was to celebrate the film premiere of the first American collaboration between Marlene Dietrich and Josef von Sternberg: *Morocco* – 1930.

Censorship 1

The vividness and power of the screen image and the wide popular access to the cinema made authorities aware of the 'dangers' of cinema from an early stage. The type of risk they fear varies according to place and time: sex, violence, crime, politics or even style have been among the targets of the censor.

Belgium alone has never operated pre-censorship of films; Denmark, Uruguay and Holland have recently abandoned it. Everywhere except in the US, Britain, Japan and Germany the censor is a state official; in these four countries the film industry itself operates the censorship system.

In addition to official censorship, the film industry has always reacted to prevailing currents of opinion and attitudes. In wartime, or other crises, films, like other media, reflect changes in public opinion. For example the British film industry rallied to national sentiment during World War II; and the films of many socialist countries are noted for their unity of tone, largely reflecting their sense of being embattled societies.

In USSR and other socialist countries, the nationalized film industry operates its own form of control. The topic and approach are examined before starting, and production itself is scrutinized. The extent and nature of control vary according to prevailing political realities. For example, for a few years after the 1917 Revolution, revolutionary themes predominated in Russia – and there was almost no restriction on style.

Censorship in Britain
Film censorship arrived in Britain somewhat surreptitiously. Concern about theatre fires (about 200 were recorded in various parts of the world between 1887 and 1896 alone) reached a head with a fatal blaze at the Grand Charity Bazaar in Paris in 1897. In Britain local authorities zealously enforced fire regulations in places of entertainment. In 1909 the Cinematograph Act strengthened their powers to license the new, purpose-built picture palaces that were springing up, rapidly extending these powers to control the content of the entertainment too.

The film trade soon realized that the only way to avoid confusion, with hundreds of local censors, was to set up a central censorship body, whose rulings the local authorities would confidently accept. In 1912 the British Board of Film Censors was set up as an independent body financed by the film trade. From January 1913 every film shown in Britain bore the Board's certificate, accepted by the local authorities as evidence that films conformed to their licensing requirements regarding morality and propriety. They interpreted the Board's classification of films as 'suitable for universal exhibition' ('U') or 'more suitable for adult audiences' ('A') by ruling that unaccompanied children should not be admitted to 'A' films.

This system, with various modifications, has survived to the present. In the earlier days the BBFC applied the narrowest and most paternalist standards in granting permission. Crime was not to be needlessly or approvingly depicted; explicitly sexual behaviour was virtually prohibited; and films likely 'to foment social unrest and discontent', (open to very wide interpretation) were not allowed. As films made elsewhere in Europe became more adult and sophisticated, fewer and fewer foreign films appeared on British screens. One film historian has suggested that 'To some extent the very poverty of imagination in British film production, and the early contempt in which it was held, may have been due to the fact that

Right Stanley Kubrick's *A Clockwork Orange* – 1971 used stylized brutality to communicate its violent story. In Britain the film was released during a reaction against the loosening of film censorship, and met divided audience reactions.

Left Brutal sexual intimacy was explicitly portrayed in Bertolucci's *Last Tango in Paris* – 1972. The film became the centre of the contemporary argument over censorship and the dangers of screening overt sex. In the UK a private citizen tried unsuccessfully to prosecute the exhibitors under the Obscene Publications Act.

Right In the US Erich von Stroheim's *Foolish Wives* – 1921 stimulated an early controversy over sexual explicitness. The censor cut several sections after the film had already been edited by its producer. Stroheim himself played the amoral and cynical Count Karamzin.

people simply did not know what could be done, and in fact was being done abroad, with the film medium.'

Only after World War II and the Cinematograph Act (1952) did more liberal policies appear. The Board introduced a new 'X' category for films restricted to those over sixteen. This permitted a considerably wider range of film content. Throughout the 1960s the BBFC Secretary, John Trevelyan, showed great skill in keeping the Board's rulings in line with rapidly changing public attitudes in taste and morals.

After 1970, influenced by puritan pressure groups, local authorities began to use their powers more energetically to reverse the Board's decisions. A number of legal actions brought against films, including Bertolucci's *Last Tango in Paris* – 1972 and the Swedish *Language of Love*, mainly showed up the abnormal situation of film in the eyes of the law. However, in 1977, a new Act established that the Obscene Publications Act of 1959, with its provision for the defence of 'public good', should also apply to films.

Hollywood and the Hays Code

In the United States, censorship of a sort existed as early as 1907, but it was not fully organized until the 1920s. Hollywood's moral reputation fell after a series of much publicized scandals in the late 1920s. The comedian Fatty Arbuckle was put on trial after a young girl died at one of his parties. Wallace Reid, regarded as the ideal of young American manhood, died of drug addiction. To counter the delighted public's image of Hollywood as Sodom and Gomorrah, the industry founded the Motion Picture Producers and Distributors of America Inc., under the presidency of Will Hays, a former Postmaster General. In 1930 a production

Censorship 2

censor

Mrs. Grundy

code was drafted, significantly guided by representatives of the Catholic Church. From the mid-1930s the film industry agreed to distribute solely films which had the seal of approval of the Production Code Administration.

For the next two decades the somewhat narrow provisions of the Code regulated what was shown on American screens, though in the early 1950s it was questioned whether such limitation was in fact constitutional. By the 1970s the Code as a form of pre-censorship had disappeared. It was replaced by a system of advisory classification mainly devised to exclude under-17s from cinemas showing 'X'-rated films. In the climate of the 1970s this seems the most satisfactory way of reconciling freedom of communication with the need to protect certain sections of society from films which (it is assumed in the absence of hard evidence) might in some way harm them.

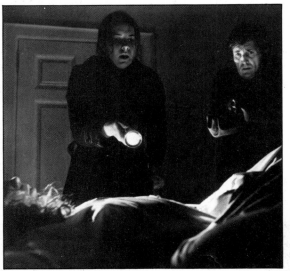

Above D. W. Griffith was stimulated to write a pamphlet linking censorship with intolerance when liberal Americans tried to ban screenings of his *The Birth of a Nation* – 1915. The film was notorious for its prejudice against blacks. An illustration from Griffith's pamphlet.

Left William Friedkin's *The Exorcist* – 1973 stimulated debate about the propriety of showing the macabre and demonic on the screen. The film was promoted as producing extreme revulsion in audiences.

WAYS OF LOOKING AT FILM

Like any other art, film deals with mysteries. It wants to describe and illuminate things that are difficult to put into words. Film reaches for an understanding just beyond the surface of consciousness. It is metaphorical: it looks beyond its own images and sounds to create new meaning.

At the same time, unlike other arts, film often seems to capture reality. It appears to reproduce the sights and sounds of everyday life in an objective way. Turn the camera on, start the tape-recorder and machines without cultural prejudices take over. They etch as perfect a lasting record as we can expect of the event.

So film both deals with mysteries – and captures reality. Its nature and significance in human affairs have been investigated during the past seventy-five years by philosophers, sociologists, psychologists, anthropologists, technologists, economists, humanists, theologians and poets. The cinematic experience cannot be easily summed up. But theories drawn from almost any system of belief will reveal some truths about it and these intersect and react with each other to suggest new truths. Combined, they bring us as close as possible to a fully rounded view of the movies.

In the following pages we look at the nature of film from four basic viewpoints. 'Film and Society' investigates cinema in its economic and social context. Second, 'The Genre Approach' describes some of the common classifications into which most movies fall. Third, 'The Director as Auteur', discusses several film-makers in the light of the theories and developments consistently seen in their work. Finally two of the most exciting contemporary approaches to film theory are outlined.

Appreciation through Understanding

The French film critic Christian Metz once wrote that 'a film is difficult to explain because it is easy to understand.' There is no greater truth about cinema. With language we have to learn how to speak, then how to read, before we can understand what is going on in print. But children watch films (or television, at least) almost from birth. Film is very much like reality.

Yet for that very reason real effort is needed to comprehend how a film means what it means, and to explain it. In a sense we do 'read' a film. In the first place the process of viewing a film involves active participation, even when we are not aware of it. We cannot see the entire cinema screen at one time. We choose where to look, and our eyes 'read' the image like a painting or a photograph. There is drama and a sense of time and narrative even in the single image. The same is true for sounds. We hear them all, all at once; but unconsciously we choose which to emphasize and which to ignore.

We have learned this physiological/psychological participation in the process of cinema through cultural influences. A citizen of, say, Nigeria, brought up in a quite different culture from ours, sees the images of a film differently from the way we do. Similarly, a man of eighty, who remembers a world without movies, responds to a film in a different way from a girl of six, to whom movies, television, transistor radios and cassette recorders are as natural as grass, sky, trees and buildings. Similarly a woman who has spent ten years in the feminist movement reacts to a Marilyn Monroe picture quite differently from the average western male. In the same way somebody who has studied eighteenth-century literature and painting is going to find a great deal more in Stanley Kubrick's *Barry Lyndon* – 1975 than people for whom that film is the first experience of that period.

How do we see films?

Clearly each of us sees his own film. We see the film that we want to see; and we see the film that we are culturally, emotionally and intellectually equipped to see. The same is true for most of the other arts, no doubt.

Film, however, presents special problems. In the first place, although 'it is easy to understand', we do need special knowledge to enjoy and comprehend it. A film by Jean-Luc Godard or Jean-Marie Straub, for example, probably makes no sense at all to viewers who know nothing of their cinematic theories. We may at a simple level comprehend the images and sounds. But we do not know what they mean in the complex worlds these film-makers have created.

Film is now at the point where it has developed a rich fabric of its own traditions and an extensive history. A great many films now made depend to a

Above In *Some Like It Hot* Marilyn Monroe painted a diverting naivety but the cost in studio time and nerve was considerable. The blatant and classic female sex appeal of Monroe may be viewed in different ways.

Left First impressions would suggest that film is easily understood and taken in. Certainly it is a medium which is accessible to large numbers of people; but the process of 'reading' a film is complex. This massive movie audience is at the huge Radio City Music Hall in New York City.

certain extent on our familiarity with this histori-cal film culture.

Secondly, film (and television) holds a special position among the arts: it can include all of them – literature, poetry, drama, painting, architecture, music, photography and recording. This makes film a complex medium. Ideally, it demands a familiarity with the history, tradition, aesthetics and practice of all of these older arts.

Talking about film

Film theorists have been struggling with these problems since the earliest days of movies. Vachel Lindsay, the American poet, was one of the first serious film theorists. He pointed out as early as 1915 that the observer had to be considered an active participant in the process of film. Hugo Münsterberg, a psychologist, pointed out only a year later the similarity of films to dreams. He re-emphasized the importance of the observer's mental activity in the cinema experience. Recently critics have returned to the dream function of movies first briefly suggested by such early writers as Lindsay and Münsterberg.

Many of the major film theorists from the 1920s to the 1960s described not what film *was*, but what they felt it *should be*. A number of writers, such as

Rudolf Arnheim, emphasized that film-makers could manipulate reality in an expressionist or formalist manner. Others, such as Siegfried Kracauer, tended to emphasize that cinema can capture the world with precise realism.

Meanwhile, film-maker/theorists such as Eisenstein and later Godard focused on the practical work of movies. They were especially concerned with the relationship between illusion and reality represented by montage and *mise en scène*. Montage (editing, cutting) is the major trick film plays on reality; *Mise en scène* (essentially the concept of staging) seemed to represent cinema's commitment to the reality which is its subject.

Eisenstein once used a helpful metaphor for various types of film theory. In his 1945 essay 'A Close-Up View', he described film theory which deals with film in its political, historical and social context as 'long shot'. 'Medium shot' film criticism focuses on the human scale and emotions of the film. 'Close-up' theory considers the construction of and their constituent elements. Each approach aims to increase film viewers' abilities to appreciate and therefore understand a particular movie. As participants in this process, we can re-create movies by appreciating them. 'To ap-preciate', after all, means 'to increase in value'.

Above With some films the viewer's appreciation depends greatly on his previous knowledge. For example, Stanley Kubrick's *Barry Lyndon* – 1975 drew extensively on the visual and aesthetic values of eighteenth-century European literature and painting. Film-goers familiar with such traditions find the pace, style and content of the film more readily comprehensible.

Film Criticism and the Audience

How much power do film critics exert? Nobody really knows. Theatre critics in New York can sound the death knell for a production. But with films, there is no direct link between the critics' approval and eventual success at the box office.

Most film producers and distributors admit that glowingly positive reviews can be a useful selling tool for a particular film. But while they obviously do not enjoy seeing their films savagely attacked, even if the critics come out unanimously against a film this is usually only a minor annoyance.

In effect film critics and reviewers simply provide publicity through the mass media. The first objective in the release of a film is simply to let the public know it exists. Reviews are one way among many. A film made from a popular novel – such as *Love Story* – 1970, *The Other Side of Midnight* – 1977 or *The Betsy* – 1978 – is hardly affected by critical reviews, even when they are almost unanimous. People who have bought, read and enjoyed the book will often go to see the movie, no matter what critics say about it.

Countering the critics

A producer or distributor can try to critic-proof what he expects may be a 'difficult' movie by holding preview screenings for audiences who have not yet been influenced by reviews. They hope that the audience will recommend it to their friends and colleagues. If all else fails, even reviewers' attacks can be useful. The distributor simply constructs an advertising campaign with a 'controversial' theme such as: 'You may love it, or you may hate it! But you *must see it!*'

Of course most review quotations are positive and reviewers are well aware of that state of affairs. A quote emblazoned on a hoarding or a newspaper ad advertises the critic as well as the film. Some budding film reviewers have even built careers for themselves by getting themselves continually quoted.

Critic as celebrity

American film critics in the 1970s have become celebrities in their own right. They are taste-makers, as they always were, but they are now also colourful personalities. Andrew Sarris began writing in the early 1960s for the then underground publication *Village Voice*. Unlike most previous American or English critics, he had a particular stance: auteurism, borrowed from the French *Cahiers du Cinéma* in the 1950s. His work

Right A genre which has almost escaped the critics' attention, possibly because it is beneath their contempt, is the popular horror film. *The Legend of the Seven Golden Vampires* – 1973.

Below right The British-made *Carry On* series, now numbering more than twenty-six films, has a long history of box-office success in spite of critical disdain. Kenneth Williams in *Carry On Cleo* – 1965.

Below Certain films gain a wide popularity despite savaging by the critics. One example is *Love Story* – 1970, with its story of modern young lovers parted by premature death.

attracted little attention until other critics, equally unkown, began attacking him and his position. For example, Pauline Kael did so in the small journal *Film Quarterly* – and was soon writing for major national publications.

John Simon, the third major contemporary American critic, wrote for small-circulation journals for more than ten years before he broke through to magazines with wider readership. Part of his success must be ascribed to the image he created during those years, of the uncompromising, often outright nasty, 'critic you love to hate'. Sarris, Kael and Simon regularly attacked each other in print, but Simon's move to theatre criticism disturbed the cozy round of backbiting. All three were intelligent, perceptive observers of film, but found it necessary to establish strong public images to call attention to their work. However the critic as celebrity seems to be a solely American phenomenon.

Meanwhile the general level of film criticism has risen quite significantly during the last fifteen or twenty years. Once television had freed cinema of its obligations as the primary mass medium of entertainment and information, film was accepted as 'high culture'. Now in the 1970s it is a subject of serious study at colleges and universities in the US and elsewhere.

Review or criticism?

The job of the daily film reviewer may still be to report on the substance of a film and then give a short evaluation. But film critics, at their best, are writers with a variety of interests, worth reading for more than their evaluations. In addition to Sarris, Kael and Simon such reviewers include Molly Haskell (the leading feminist critic in the US), Richard Roud (longtime contributor to *The Guardian*), Penelope Gilliatt (*The New Yorker*), John Russell Taylor, and a new breed of younger critics including David Robinson, Richard Corliss and Jan Dawson. All have helped to raise the level of discussion about movies in the last few years. Finally a group of scholar/critics such as Raymond Durgnat and David Thomson devote their main energies to books.

Much of the best writing about film today takes place in specialist journals devoted to film, television and popular culture. Prominent among these are *American Film*, *Sight and Sound*, *Take One*, *Film Comment*, *Cinéaste*, *Jump Cut* and *Movietone News*. More academic journals include *Screen* and *Film Quarterly*.

Except for the academic journals (the number of which is rapidly multiplying) most of the writing in these magazines is in the practical English and American tradition of film criticism, established in earlier years by such writers as Harry Potamkin, Otis Ferguson, James Agee and Robert Warshow. Meanwhile a movement is growing to examine movies with a greater awareness of their political and economic contexts. It is concerned with how the business of movies influences, controls, even dominates the art of film.

1 FILM AND SOCIETY

All arts work to reflect and shape social values. But film, much more than any previous art, is related intimately and vitally with the broad range of culture. It is surrounded by it, feeds on it, reflects it and often affects it.

This is because film is the first great democratic art. For centuries paintings were seen only by a chosen elite. Even in mid-nineteenth century England and America novels were largely an exclusively middle class form of expression. Until the twentieth century most people were familiar only with folk music; art-music, like painting, was a privilege of class.

Film changed all this. Enrichment came easily through eye and ear. Sensually, film provides a universal language and a common bond of experience across the classes, and occasionally even between nationalities and ethnic groups. While the great mass newspapers and magazines were moving in this democratic direction at the end of the nineteenth century, print culture still reflected divisions in society.

But film tended to unify its audience. Only when television began to take over the function of movies as the major mass medium did film start to develop more separate approaches to various segments of society. The clearest example of this was the growth in the 1950s and 1960s of 'art films' and their accompanying film culture, which had to be learned before some of the films could be intelligently appreciated.

It seems to make less sense each year to try to separate film's social impact from the other audiovisual media, or even from the print media. Movies owe more and more to audio recordings and to popular fiction and non-fiction. Film has been involved in a love/hate relationship with television since its inception. Now it looks as if the development of cheap video cassettes and discs will further blur the borders between the two media.

Film among the media

The various media are also linked industrially. Film companies own record companies (Warner Bros. makes more from discs than from movies). Record people produce films (pre-eminently Robert Stigwood). The old Hollywood studios manufacture much of the prime time television material, and some of them also own publishers.

The media are also merging in aesthetic and technological terms. The technique of multitrack mixing, perfected in the recording industry, has affected film sound significantly. The novelist who writes today without a constant eye on the visual possibilities of his 'property' is rather short-sighted. For economic reasons, movies must be shot with the requirements of the TV screen in mind.

Clearly, film's own relationship with society is inextricably intertwined with the relationships of the other contemporary media. Why then does

Right The featuring of black actors in film reflects, and can enhance, the image blacks hold in society. *Rocky* – 1976.

Below right Documentary film is intended to reflect society as it is. *Nanook of the North* – 1922 was made by Robert Flaherty, who spent sixteen months among the Eskimos trying to film their vanishing way of life.

Below far right *Housing Problems,* a documentary on British working-class housing made in the 1930s, reflected contemporary society, but was also intended to alert the public to the slum problem.

Below The decline of the cinema. In many western countries the number of commercial cinemas fell noticeably between 1955 and 1975.

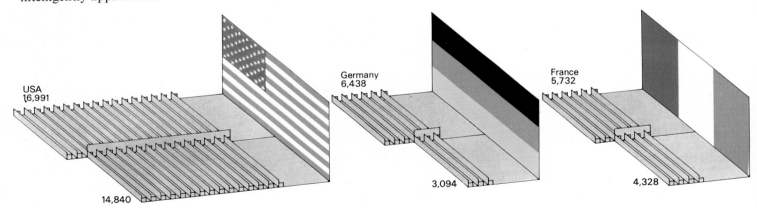

USA 16,991
14,840

Germany 6,438
3,094

France 5,732
4,328

Cinemas – decline in numbers 1955 and 1975

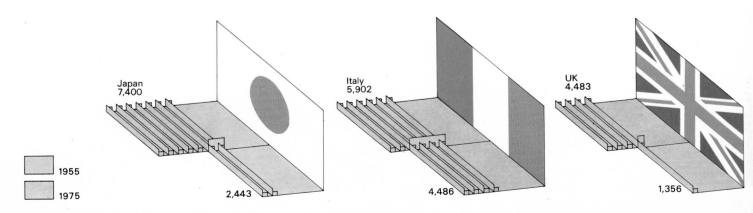

1955
1975

Japan 7,400
2,443

Italy 5,902
4,486

UK 4,483
1,356

film seem to rank as more important? Partly because more of our audiovisual heritage still resides in movies than in television. Partly because films, unlike television programmes, are individual works that can be discussed separately.

Global culture

In addition movies have formed the strongest bond between differing societies. The 'global village' which Marshall McLuhan wrote about may reach perfection with satellite-broadcast television, but it began with silent film. Television is still more limited than film by national boundaries, despite American dominance. Recorded music is probably more widely dispersed throughout the world than films, but probably sight-and-sound carries more cultural information than sound alone.

The effects of this global media culture can be measured in several ways. Film in general, and particular films, influence individuals within society. They transmit values. They also express ideas and feelings of a whole society or group. So it is clear that they have a psychological effect on the individual, and a social impact on the group. Whether we are talking about who makes films or who sees them, what their influence is, or how they themselves are influenced, it is important to distinguish between film as an individual experience (psychological) and film as a collective social undertaking.

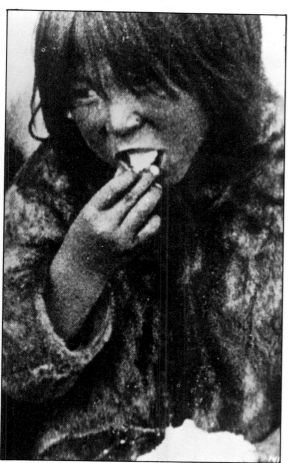

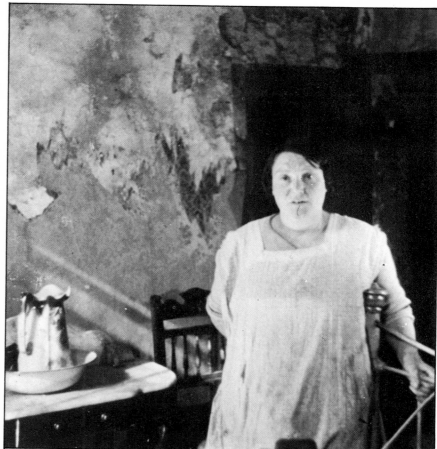

Who Makes Films and Why

People make films for a number of reasons. One of these is economic. While other arts often make profits, film almost has a duty to make money since it is by far the most expensive of all the arts. People can write novels without investing any cash except in paper and a few pens. But even the cheapest 16mm film costs thousands. And a 35mm film for theatrical release will have a budget measured in millions of dollars.

So a film is not just an artistic gamble, it is always a sizeable financial wager too. The budget for an average Hollywood feature – a 'small' film – would provide average advances for at least two hundred novelists.

This presents an interesting paradox. Film is clearly a democratic art as regards its form (you need not even be able to read to watch a movie). But it is the most inaccessible of arts in terms of its production. Without considerable amounts of money it is impossible to make movies at all, except on the smallest of scales. The more democratic the art form the greater means, apparently, necessary to produce it.

However, film production has become more democratic. Feature films may cost more, both relatively and absolutely, than they did thirty years ago. But the development of effective 16mm equipment and the proliferation of advanced super-8 cameras and projectors, which can record sound direct, have opened up filming to large numbers of people in recent years. It remains more expensive to make your own film than to write your own novel, but at least you can now consider the possibility of film-making.

Who distributes movies?

Although film production is open to ever larger numbers of potential film-makers, film distribution remains tightly controlled. In the 1970s the Hollywood 'studios' concentrated on distribution. This gave them effective control of production at one end and exhibition at the other, without the bother of having to tie up substantial sums of capital in those aspects.

So to some extent the question now is not: Who makes movies? but: Who *distributes* movies? Who decides which films we may have a chance to see? In the US: Universal, United Artists, Warner Bros, Twentieth Century-Fox, Columbia Pictures and Paramount, together with several successful minor distributors such as Walt Disney's Buena Vista and Allied Artists. They also dominate the business in Britain.

So far no company has successfully challenged the six remaining traditional Hollywood 'studios'. Both ABC and CBS, not lacking in economic resources or business expertise, failed quickly when they tried to compete in the late 1960s and early 1970s. Perhaps the mystique of Hollywood gives the major distributors such unchallenged positions.

A joint undertaking

But if we ask 'Who makes films?' in the creative

Above Akira Kurosawa, the well-known Japanese director, started making films in 1943, but became known in the West when his film *Rashomon* – 1950 won a prize at the Venice Film Festival in 1951. He emphasizes the importance of the script. Several of his costume-dramas have inspired western remakes.

Left Clint Eastwood began his career as a Hollywood actor, making his name in westerns. He then appeared in several of Sergio Leone's Italian 'spaghetti westerns', such as *For a Fistful of Dollars*. (A *Fistful of Dollars* in US). In 1971 he made his first film as director, *Play Misty for Me*. He has gone on to make further films as director/leading actor.

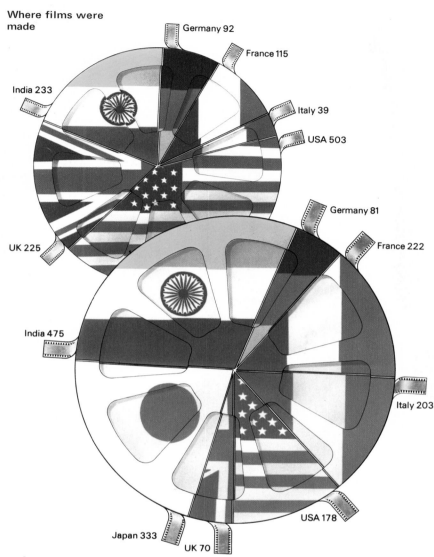

Where films were
made

Germany 92

France 115

India 233

Italy 39

USA 503

UK 225

Germany 81

France 222

India 475

Italy 203

USA 178

Japan 333

UK 70

sense, the answer is different. Any film is made by large numbers of people, in a highly collaborative enterprise.

In the 1930s, as discussed previously, films were identified mainly by their stars and their studios. The director or producer was mentioned only occasionally. Few people knew what a cinematographer or film editor did, and writers were noteworthy only when they were famous novelists, 'slumming' in Hollywood. The rest of the technicians were faceless.

The director's role
In the 1950s, this attitude began to change. The European art films of directors such as Fellini and Bergman attracted some attention. The auteur theory strongly emphasized the director's importance. But the theory was modified by experience. François Truffaut as a critic championed the auteur theory. But when he actually directed a trilogy of films, his conception of their central character Antoine Doinel, changed radically when he began to work with the actor playing the role, Jean-Pierre Léaud. The character was the result of the true collaboration of the director and actor.

Today most critics realize that the strengths and weaknesses of a particular film can be credited to a number of members of cast and crew. Film specialists can discern the contributions made by such technicians as Douglas Trumbull (special effects), Haskell Wexler (cinematographer), Verna Fields (editor) or Robert Evans (producer). Even the general public is aware of the particular styles and personal concerns of the directors and writers who largely brought about the 'Hollywood Renaissance' of the 1970s, and who attract similar attention to stars in newspaper and magazine reviews.

The diverse origins of film present knotty problems to the critic or scholar, who wants to categorize and order the art. But since films usually represent the end products of numerous sensibilities, this means that they reveal a common consciousness. A whole range of factors comes into play to influence and affect the making of a film: social, political, economic, cultural, psychological and aesthetic. A particular film results from the unique mix of talents and traditions involved: director and screenwriter, studio style and economic resources.

Above left Satyajit Ray is the best-known Indian director outside his own country. He started film-making in the early 1950s, with the *Pather Panchali* trilogy.

Above Where films were made. The top film can shows the number of feature-length films produced by some major countries in 1935. (Figures for Japan are not available for that year.) The bottom film can shows the number of films produced in 1975.

153

Who Sees Films and Why

Movies are seen, at one time or another, in one way or another, by almost everybody. They are distributed to cinemas and by television, on videotape and soon by videodisc too. They convey drama and news, information and entertainment, art and advertising.

But more narrowly, film as a narrative entertainment exhibited primarily in cinemas has an increasingly precise audience. Forty years ago, the audience at which a particular film was directed was a massive cross-section of society, although more women than men might see a particular movie. Some films were made expressly for children, and a few critics suggested that they were aimed at an elite, highly educated public.

Since the coming of television this situation has changed. Like most other media, films are now marketed with sophisticated techniques. Today's film producer is well advised to work out in advance what his potential audience may be and to design his film with it in mind.

This adoption of market research has helped stem the long-term downward trend in film viewing in the US. Hollywood films broke their attendance records in 1946, just after World War II. For the next 25 years movie audiences decreased at a fairly steady rate of six per cent per year. By 1971 yearly audiences were only a quarter of the size they were in 1946.

But in the 1970s the trend reversed. US cinema admissions have increased at a rate of more than four per cent each year (though these figures do not take into account the general population increase). Nevertheless, it is clear that the industry is more than holding its own in the 1970s.

Selling the cinema

The main reason for this increase has been the new marketing techniques. In the late 1960s, the film companies realized that young people in their late teens and twenties formed the core of filmgoers. They had both the time and the freedom to go to the cinema. As films were made to speak more directly to the concerns of the younger generation, their popularity increased.

At the same time, the film industry stopped trying to fight television. The eventual sale to television became an important element in a film's budget. Television advertising campaigns for cinema programmes, once extremely rare, began to yield returns.

By the mid-1970s, the strategy of the blockbuster ruled. A handful of films on release at any particular time took the majority of ticket sales. Single films such as *Jaws* – 1975, *Star Wars* – 1977 or *Saturday Night Fever* – 1977 could account for twenty per cent or more of weekly box-office income.

The studios learned to guarantee the success of a film by carefully exploiting it in hard-cover books, mass-market paperbacks, television spinoffs, records and the rest. One result was that small films were squeezed out. While the size of audiences was gradually increasing in the 1970s,

Above Johnny Weissmuller as Tarzan, the character created by writer Edgar Rice Burroughs. The Tarzan sound films of the 1930s reflected a kind of romantic noble-savage; they appealed to audiences for their escapism and excitement but lacked real menace. Weissmuller was partnered by Maureen O'Sullivan as Jane.

Left Total enthralment. Children's attention and imagination is completely captured by film. A Saturday matinee for children at a British cinema.

the number of films produced each year dropped. Clearly, the studios had learned how to earn more money with fewer films.

Films for minorities

On the fringes of the industry, a number of companies made remarkable profits by catering for minority audiences. Using market research techniques, these companies identified target audiences – generally low-income families who had previously seen perhaps only one or two movies a year. They made surveys to discover what kinds of films such people wanted to see (outdoor adventure, family stories, mock-scientific pseudo-documentaries) and proceeded to design the movies to fit. The technique worked very well – the fact that the movies were sloppily made, crudely plotted and without stars seemed to make little difference.

At the same time a more sophisticated film culture was spreading. The core of the movie-goers, people between the ages of 18 and 34, brought with them a greater knowledge of film art and technique than ever before. Directors had become celebrities, interviewed on TV talk shows about their aims and methods.

In the US college film courses blossomed in the 1970s, and newspapers and magazines began to devote more and more space to the movies. For the first time, a director could expect a large audience to come to a popular film with a reasonable knowledge of the traditions of the art. Mel Brooks, for example, has made a number of highly successful movies parodying classic genres

and directors, depending for their effect on familiarity with old movies and film history.

Ironically, television contributed to the development of this new film culture. From the late 1950s literally hundreds of old films were shown on TV, ensuring them of massive exposure. From the hardcore film freaks who see ten or twenty films each week, to the low-income parents who cannot afford to go more than three or four times a year, the range of moviegoers today is ever widening.

Film-goers are attracted for the same reasons as ever: entertainment, thrills, laughter and escape. But more often than we realize people now go to the movies because they want to see a work of art or because they expect a film to give a better reflection of society and its problems than television provides. Television has changed rather than stopped the movie-going habit.

Cinema attendances – 1955 and 1975

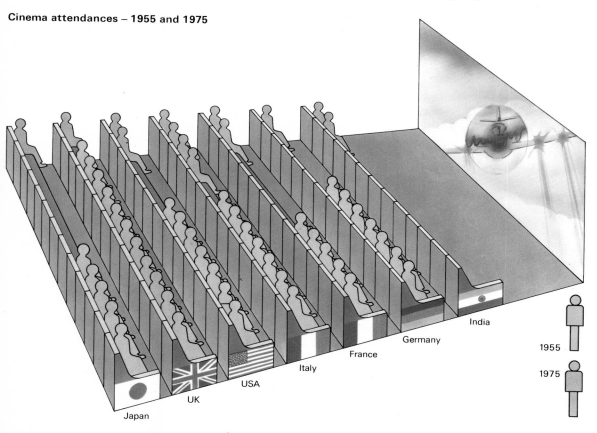

Left Who goes to the cinema. Average annual per capital cinema attendance figures for 1955 and 1975. Each seated human represents two attendances. No attendance figures for India were available for 1955. The fall in cinema-going in the West is immediately apparent.

Japan
UK
USA
Italy
France
Germany
India
1955
1975

Film Reflects Society

One of the oldest arguments in film theory concerns how far film influences society – and vice versa. We naturally expect film to reflect reality. On the other hand many movies are made up of fantasy and dreams since film gives a unique reality to fantasy.

Then, too, because the movies (and television) are so powerful and widespread, we expect them to influence society directly. Can a violent film, for example, inspire violent behaviour? Could a film spark a revolution? We used to ask these questions of literature. We have stopped, not because literature is less powerful than it once was, but because movies have so clearly taken over from books as a dominant cultural force.

But we must remember that film, like all other arts, is not separate from society, but an integral part of it. In one way, since film, with print, provides the major record of history, it *is* society. For example, unless we have lived through the 1920s, the main way we come to know that period is through the film and print record of it which has passed down to us. We can examine only the evidence that survives. This is one major reason for demanding realism in certain types of film: the record is going to last and it will become increasingly difficult to correct distortions.

A distorting mirror?

Although film is technically the most exact medium yet invented for capturing a true image, in practice the reality it captures is often distorted. First, since films are made by people with their own prejudices, concerns and idiosyncracies, what we see on film is what its authors want us to see. This is especially important to bear in mind in

Below Jimmy Cliff as Ivan in *The Harder They Come* – 1972. This was the first Jamaican film to achieve wide release. Its story reflects contemporary Jamaican life. Jimmy Cliff plays a country boy who comes to the capital, Kingston, becomes a pop star, but is forced into crime. The fact that the film achieved considerable popularity on its release indicates its reflection of public attitudes.

evaluating the truth of documentaries which can be used as convincing propaganda.

Second, numerous artistic conventions operate, especially in fiction films, which prevent film from precisely reflecting reality. Films are basically dramas, depending on neatly constructed conflict for their vitality and attractiveness. Real life simply does not happen this way. Clearly a commercial fiction film will distort its material. For instance the editors are very likely to snip out the 'dead times', when nothing particularly 'interesting' happens. Then, too, the film is probably brought to a pointed conclusion: the story will finish – whereas stories in real life normally dribble to an indeterminate conclusion.

These major distortions are echoed in literally thousands of minor variations. Film is an art form, and our expectations of what a film should be are relatively rigid. Within those expectations, the film-makers further modify what reality remains. We expect this in fiction films, where the author creates part of the truth conveyed. But we do not expect it in documentaries, which are supposed to emphasize the reality in front of the camera, not the idiosyncracies of the artist behind it.

Documentary truth

In the early 1960s, for example, the narrator was removed from the documentary in the techniques of Direct Cinema (sometimes called *cinéma vérité*). The film's images and sounds were supposed to speak for themselves, without commentary. On the surface, this seemed a more accurate approach to reality. Yet whether they speak or not, films always have authors, and whether they want to or not, authors always modify their subjects. We are more likely to remember that what we see and hear has been filtered through the author if we hear a spoken narration.

Because film is a vivid record of experience it also confirms values in real life. For example, black people comprise twenty percent of the population of the United States. If only one per cent or less of film actors and characters are black, that disparity, which lasted for more than fifty years in film and has only recently improved, works to invalidate black experience. Similarly, if women are shown in movies only as helpmates, sidekicks and sex objects, it makes it less likely that a young girl will realize she could become a lawyer or a doctor, an active rather than a passive member of society. Most social critics agree that women have been portrayed negatively in films and on television since 1950. This must affect men's and women's consciousness.

So film distorts as it reflects society. Yet the distortions themselves are important, for they give us a picture not of what is true, but of what we wish were true, at least as it is filtered through the perceptions of the people who control movies and therefore decide in large part what we see. If movies are not reality, they are certainly very close to our myths and dreams.

Left War films such as Richard Attenborough's *A Bridge Too Far* – 1977 seem to gain much of their popularity from their nostalgic re-enactment of crucial events. They allow audiences to relive the excitement safely.

Below Lewis Milestone's *All Quiet on the Western Front* – 1930 caught up and expressed the revulsion against war in the West in the late 1920s. Based on Erich Maria Remarque's best-selling novel, it explores the disillusion of seven German schoolboy recruits in World War I.

Film Affects Society

Film should, in theory, have a direct, immediate and measurable influence on society. It is, after all, a much more powerful medium than print. To read a book is an act of will, imagination and literacy. To watch a film calls for only consciousness and open eyes. The psychological power of films can be demonstrated: even a simple pattern of black-and-white frames creating a stroboscopic effect can induce epileptic seizures.

In fact film's influence on the way we live and the political and cultural decisions we make is not at all clear, at least in the short run. There are few occasions indeed where a particular film began a revolution, changed the course of history, or even caused a law to be passed.

Leni Riefenstahl is often cited by historians as a film-maker of extraordinary power who did much to celebrate the Nazi psychopathology. But Riefenstahl followed respectfully in Hitler's wake. If Hitler's *Mein Kampf* provided the ideas behind Nazism, the film disseminated those ideas more widely. The film undoubtedly influenced more people. The fact is that we still turn to print for the expression of ideas, and for the most part it is ideas that have political effect.

The CBS television documentary *Hunger in America* is often given as a more recent example of a film with a direct political effect; but it came six years after Michael Harrington's book *The Other America*. Film's main function seems to be to expand and document ideas that have first been expressed in print, and to expose those ideas to a much wider audience. There are exceptions, of course. In the 1960s, Jean-Luc Godard produced film essays that were equal in intellectual complexity to the best work being done in print at that time. But his interesting theories had a minimal effect on society.

Nevertheless films do have a measurable and wide-ranging influence on attitudes and life-styles. Since the early 1920s (when Douglas Fairbanks made the suntan socially desirable) we have looked to movies (and television) as a guide to fashion, hairstyles, and fashionable attitudes.

Media personalities

This curious influence is as much due to the celebrities the media create as to film and television themselves. In the early twentieth century, film made it possible for the first time for society at large to participate in selected private lives. Previously, we had admired certain individuals at a distance for what they did: these were heroes. Now we shower great affection on people who are well-known mainly for their 'well-knownness'. These celebrities comprise a sort of abstract and brief summary of our ideal of society. We attribute to celebrities, the people who live out their lives in the media world, a special power that we do not claim for ourselves. Their opinions have more weight, their faces seem more real we mimic them.

The media present us with models for our behaviour. Usually, the effect is general and pervasive. For example, the Civil Rights movement in the US in the 1960s forced television

advertisers to use black people regularly in commercials. Many observers believe that change did more to lessen racism in the country than any number of laws. For the first time, white audiences saw black faces and personalities daily in situations which they recognized as similar to their own. Whether this was a conscious or an unconscious recognition, the effect was the same.

Films and violence

On the other hand, a number of commentators believe that the irresponsible attitude towards violence in both commercial film and television has helped convince a generation that disregard for the effects of violence is normal. But the *form* of film is influential too. The media theorist Walter Benjamin explained how film's unique ability to multiply itself and to meet audiences on their home ground 'shattered tradition', and was hence profoundly revolutionary.

In the 1960s and early 1970s, Jean-Luc Godard made a number of films that tried to discover a radical form for radical content. He called this quest 'making political films politically'. In the last few years, a number of critics have argued that television powerfully moulds children's minds. They believe that TV has created a generation that is both passive and impatient: passive, because they become receptors only; impatient, because the only real power the viewer has is to switch to another station.

The debate on the influence of film on society has just begun.

Screen Sex and Violence

Sex and violence are exploited in a wide variety of ways in the movies. There is the direct approach of pornography and kung fu, genres which are both designed to stimulate audiences to the maximum amount with a minimum of distracting plot and character. On the other hand there is the more subtle style of genres such as the romance and the western, which translate the blunt physical expression of these emotions into more socially acceptable forms.

Sex and violence are very important to the film business. A quick look at the film advertisements in any newspaper reveals this. What is for sale? Entertainment and excitement, more often than not connected with sex and violence. People go to the movies for a wide variety of reasons. But very often a major reason, whether conscious or not, is to satisfy repressed desires. Many passions drive screen drama, but eroticism and physical aggression are clearly primary.

Recent changes in attitudes toward public morality – the so-called sexual revolution of the 1960s – now permit film-makers to exploit sex and violence more directly and openly. But they have

featured in film ever since its beginnings. As early as 1896, Edison's Kinetoscope loop *The Kiss* resulted in an outpouring of moralistic fury. Ever since, the movie business has periodically had to respond either formally or informally to repeated calls for censorship.

The Hays Code
American (and foreign) audiences were exposed to an unnaturally puritanical world in the movies after 1934, when Joseph Breen joined the 'Hays Office' of the Motion Picture Producers of America (responsible for enforcing the MPPA 'Code'). Not till the late 1950s did this highly effective effort at self-censorship in the industry die out in the face of the challenge from television.

The code made absurd demands on film-makers. Not only were explicit acts of sex and violence strictly prohibited, but so were double beds – even for married couples. Such mild expletives as 'hell', 'damn' and 'nuts' were forbidden. In fact the silent movies of the 1920s were often as explicit and mature about sex and violence as films in the 1970s. The MPPA code

Below Bruce Lee's martial arts ('kung fu') movies offer one popular form of screen violence. The stylized oriental brutality somehow distances the audience from the violence. A scene from *The Way of the Dragon*.

produced a distorted picture of American society during the 1930s and 1940s and this, in turn, influenced British and American culture.

In most countries, censorship is mainly a matter of politics. In the western liberal tradition, however, political content of films is controlled more subtly by social and cultural pressure, which makes the direct censorship of sex and violence even more remarkable. During the late 1960s, libertarians gained considerable ground in their continuing battle against the censors. By 1973, hard-core pornographic films such as *Deep Throat* and *The Devil in Miss Jones* were being discussed openly on TV and reviewed by newspaper critics. Pornography had become chic.

No easy answers

But at the same time, led by feminist critics, film commentators were beginning to develop a more sophisticated attitude toward sex and violence. They began to recognize that there were real social problems involved in depicting physical passions on the screen. The critics have tried to assess the impact of film sex and violence on society and politics. In general, the two problems are seen as separate issues. Groups that oppose the depiction of sexual activity on screen on moralistic grounds (much less powerful than they once were) tend to be more tolerant towards violence. By contrast those groups, mainly liberal, who campaign against violence on film (and especially in television) often contrast it directly with sex.

Indeed sex is often seen as the active expression of the life force and violence as the active expression of the death force. The argument then runs: the more sex on screen, the better, the less violence, the better. But this ignores the actual practice of film in the 1970s. As it happens, hard-core sex in movies is almost always sadistic. Most feminists, in addition, feel that porn is sexist and exploitative – it is directed almost entirely to male audiences.

It is never clear how the influence of film on society and its reflection of society are related, least so with regard to sex and violence. Recently the sexual exploitation of children has become chic, though few critics take a purely laissez-faire attitude so far as children are concerned. Somewhere the line must be drawn: if not at the age of twenty-one or eighteen, then at twelve or nine or six.

What *is* pornographic and clearly obscene is the crude expression of the death force to titillate, shock and thrill audiences for profit. This often happens in 'X-rated' hard-core porn. But it also occurs in what passes for ordinary entertainment: films that are increasingly violent, sado-masochistic, sexist and exploitative of children. Clearly pornography is not merely strong language and erotic realism. It also includes the marketing of the death force in various guises by film-makers intent on exploiting the latent psychopathology of audiences for whom they show only contempt.

Left Sam Peckinpah's *The Wild Bunch* – 1969 became notorious for its violence and carnage. It is set in the 1914 Mexican revolution, and examines the wayward lives of a band of outlaws.

Left Cartoons often feature exaggerated violence. Popeye, the sea-captain animated by Dave Fleischer, (seen here in *A Dream Waking*) appeared in countless violent encounters with his arch-enemy Bluto. He could always rely on a tin of spinach to restore his flagging energy.

Below Emmanuelle and numerous follow-ups and imitations epitomised the soft-porn, mass market releases of the 1970's.

FILM GENRES

Genres in the cinema are easier to recognize than to define. One obvious genre is the western. A traditional definition might suggest that it is essentially a matter of cowboys and Indians. Yet there are many westerns featuring neither cowboys nor Indians. Alternatively it might be claimed that the western deals with some more or less historical aspect from America's pioneer past. Yet westerns have borrowed themes from as far and wide as Shakespeare and classical tragedy. They have been used to comment exclusively on current affairs. They have even incorporated such non-pioneer elements as the automobile and the aeroplane.

What the audience expects

What we can say, however, is that each genre has over the years built up a number of instantly recognizable conventions. A film belongs to a genre if it adopts those conventions (or in certain cases reacts against them). For example, John Ford's western *Stagecoach* – 1939 is based on Maupassant's novella *Boule de Suif* – and it could equally well have been adapted as a historical costume adventure. There is nothing specifically American or frontier about the theme. But Ford and scriptwriter Dudley Nichols turn it into an archetypal western. They had the stagecoach pursued by Indians (complete with traditional cavalry charge to the rescue) instead of Prussian soldiers. They peopled it with characters conventional to the western, instantly recognizable in manner, costume and situation: The lone gunslinger wandering the desert, the prostitute run out of town by righteous ladies, the drunken doctor, the frock-coated Mississippi gambler and the bowler-hatted travelling salesman.

The genre conventions were in a sense de-

veloped to tell the audience what to expect. The first musicals, devised to capitalize on the coming of sound, were little more than a string of revue sketches and songs performed on a real stage. Often each item was introduced by a presenter. As the genre developed, by way of putting-on-a-show plots, and then romantic adventures interspersed with musical numbers, certain 'signals' had to be provided to orientate the audience. Dance numbers, for instance, would begin on a recognizable stage, before spilling over on to elaborate and more expansive studio sets. As a young couple murmured soft endearments to each other in the moonlight, a few chords from an off-screen orchestra would gently herald the switch from dialogue into song.

Such devices of course became unnecessary as

showing he is not so fast on the draw as he claims.

The measure of a good genre film is the skill with which these time-honoured characters and situations are either used in fresh, unexpected patterns, or turned upside-down to provide new insights. In each case the audience finds pleasure primarily in *recognition*.

Using the genre

It is important to be aware of genre, especially in dealing with the American cinema. First, it is a useful corrective to 'auteur' criticism, which seeks to deal with films as the creative expression of one person, usually the director. Under Hollywood's mass production system, many first-rate films owed their excellence less to any particular creativity in the director than to the ready-made patterns which could be subtly varied. Genre conventions can be a creative force in their own right. They can govern not only character and situation but plot, structure and photographic style.

Second, awareness of genres is necessary to appreciate the skill with which film-makers working within a genre may not only use the conventions in entirely different ways, but also overturn them or direct them to entirely new ends. A classic example is the opening sequence of Sam Peckinpah's *Guns in the Afternoon* – 1962. What appears at first to be a familiar western street scene suddenly becomes unfamiliar, as we notice a policeman, a race between a horse and a camel, and Buffalo Bill doing a sideshow act. The disorientation is deliberate: Peckinpah is chronicling the death of the old West. He introduces us to a world in which the old heroes, left high and dry by the passing of tradition, no longer find it easy to be heroes.

the genre developed. Finally musical numbers were integrated with the plot, with the seams hardly showing. The signals became clichés to be satirized. In more than one 'Road' film, Bob Hope commented cynically on the unseen orchestra tuning up as Bing Crosby prepared to croon over Dorothy Lamour in the jungle.

In the more elaborate genres, such as the western and the gangster film, however, the conventions became an essential part of the game. Expectations here count for everything. If a rattletrap car speeds down a dark, rain-glistening street past a plush restaurant, gangster tommy guns will inevitably spray the diners with lead in a vengeful gang war. If a lone gunslinger enters a western saloon, somebody will inevitably crowd him at the bar, hoping to provoke him into

The Western

The oldest and most home-grown American movie genre is the western. The western is about the West, and the West is uniquely North American.

The western is about the West specifically during the second half of the nineteenth century. At that time the North American states were in the process of coming together, and a wild, fragmented continent was searching for peace, growth and unity. The men opening up the West rode roughshod over the territorial rights of the Red Indians, much as the movies later rode roughshod over the moral issues posed by the Indians and other persecuted minorities. Recent cinema has tried to redress the balance with a dose of 'liberal' films such as *Little Big Man*–1970 and *Soldier Blue* – 1970. Ironically these did not appear until the western was virtually on its death-bed.

The first cowboy films came soon after the turn of the century – from such directors as Edwin S. Porter, D. W. Griffith and Thomas H. Ince. It was indeed a western, Cecil B. DeMille's *The Squaw Man* – 1913, that came to be regarded as the foundation-stone of Hollywood itself. But the range and evolution of the genre over its seventy-year history is astonishing, following the cinema's advance from the primitive to the sophisticated. The genre spans the whole history of the movies, unlike the gangster film, the horror film or the musical. It is a uniquely flexible form, capable of taking in comedy, suspense, adventure and romance.

It is also a genre carrying all the moral issues of which 'great drama' consists: right and wrong, order and anarchy, and the individual versus the mob. The primitive kingdoms to which Shakespeare reached back for some of his greatest tragedies, such as *King Lear* and *Macbeth*, are remarkably similar to the moral wilderness in which the western hero has to carve out his own ethics and ideals.

The early heroes
Broncho Billy Anderson, William S. Hart and Tom Mix were the great cowboy heroes of the pre-sound cinema. Westerns then were little more than trials of courage and shooting skill between the good guys and the bad guys. In the 1920s the pioneer western came into fashion with James Cruze's *The Covered Wagon* – 1923 and John Ford's *The Iron Horse* – 1924. Both films opened up the cinema screen much as their heroes were opening up the West itself.

In the 1930s Ford's work took on a new distinction and a new poetry. Ford had been making westerns since 1914, but the coming of sound seemed to transform his work. It now had a lazy rhythm, spaciousness and nostalgia that had been missing in the silent period. Ford's golden year was 1939, when he gave us *Drums Along The Mohawk*, *Young Mr Lincoln* and *Stagecoach*.

Stagecoach is the enduring classic of the West. It is the story of a motley cross-section of frontier society in peril from the marauding Indians and the unconquered wilderness. The film gave John Wayne his first starring role after *The Big Trail*–1930. It was also the first to feature the unmistakable towering buttes of Monument Valley, and *Stagecoach* has remained a popular masterpiece. In his later movies – *Rio Grande* – 1950, *The Searchers* – 1956 and *Cheyenne Autumn* – 1964 – Ford was foremost among Hollywood film-makers in showing that the western could be more than a rough-and-tumble celebration of male machismo; it could also reflect the hopes and dreams of a society in transition.

The TV Western
The success of the cinema cowboy was reflected in the television western of the mid-fifties. This took the form of series, which originated from second features produced for the movie houses in the 1930s and 1940s. Among the defectors from the large to the small screen were the Lone Ranger, Hopalong Cassidy and Roy Rogers, with his incomparable wonder-horse, Trigger. Later popular series included *Gunsmoke*, *Wyatt Earp*, *Bonanza* and *The Virginian*. The TV western boom left its mark on the cinema; the small screen allowed the audience access to the man behind the hero.

Late masters
Among the greatest western directors half a dozen other names loom large: Howard Hawks (*Red River* – 1948, *Rio Bravo* – 1959), Anthony Mann (*Winchester 73* – 1950, *Bend of the River* – 1951), Delmer Daves (*3.10 to Yuma* – 1957), Budd Boetticher (*The Tall T* – 1957), Sam Peckinpah (*Guns in the Afternoon* – 1962, *The Wild Bunch* – 1969) and the Italian Sergio Leone.

Leone's 'spaghetti westerns', with Clint Eastwood, revitalized the genre in the late 1960s, when it appeared to be breathing its last. He brought out the dramatic and dance-like qualities basic to the western. In America during the same period the 'autumnal' western abounded, for instance *True Grit* – 1969 and *The Culpepper Cattle Company* – 1972. The western stars themselves were growing old in the saddle.

In many ways the western's middle period is its most fascinating. In the years after *Stagecoach* and before *For a Fistful of Dollars* – 1964 (*A Fistful of Dollars* in US), the genre gathered to itself moral and psychological shadings undreamt of in the era of Tom Mix and William S. Hart. Daves, Mann and Boetticher applied mid-tones to a canvas hitherto strictly divided between white and black. In the 1960s Sam Peckinpah used the cinema's equivalent of a spray-gun to turn the old-master compositions of the West into powerful and ferocious action-paintings.

Peckinpah's *The Wild Bunch* paved the way for the urban crime thriller, the genre that has usurped the western in the 1970s. The cinema no longer has to reach back into frontier history to find anarchy. Anarchy is alive and well and living on the city streets of the modern United States.

Opposite Justice reigns. The villain bites the dust in a classic western climax.

Some Great Westerns

Destry Rides Again – 1939; dir. George Marshall; James Stewart, Marlene Dietrich, Brian Donlevy.

Stagecoach – 1939; dir. John Ford; Claire Trevor, John Wayne, Thomas Mitchell.

My Darling Clementine – 1946; dir. John Ford; Henry Fonda, Linda Darnell, Victor Mature.

High Noon – 1952;dir. Fred Zinnemann; Gary Cooper, Grace Kelly.

Shane – 1953; dir, George Stevens; Alan Ladd, Jean Arthur, Van Heflin, Brandon de Wilde, Jack Palance.

The Searchers – 1956; dir. John Ford; John Wayne, Jeffrey Hunter, Natalie Wood, Ward Bond.

Gunfight at the OK Corral – 1957; dir. John Sturges; Burt Lancaster, Kirk Douglas, Rhonda Fleming.

3.10 to Yuma – 1957; dir. Delmer Daves; Glenn Ford, Van Heflin, Felicia Ferr.

The Magnificent Seven – 1960; dir. John Sturges; Yul Brynner, Eli Wallach, Steve McQueen, Horst Buchholz, Robert Vaughn, James Coburn, Charles Bronson.

The Wild Bunch – 1969; dir. Sam Peckinpah; William Holden, Ernest Borgnine, Robert Ryan.

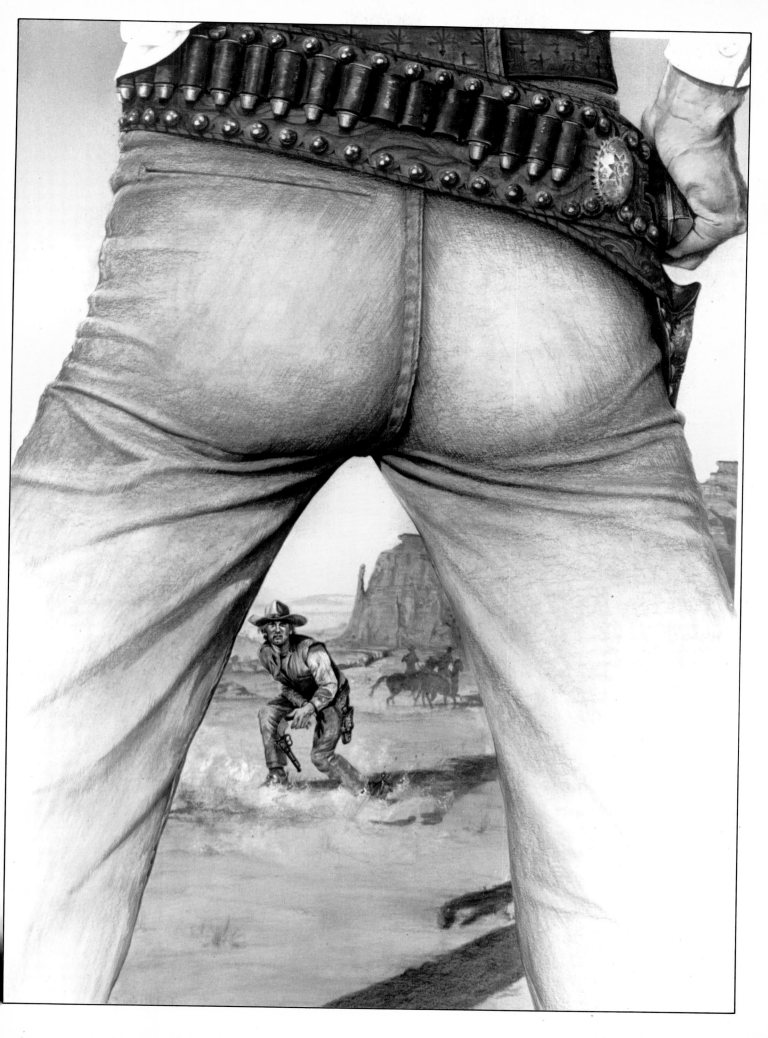

The Comedy

Comedy was the stuff of movies from the beginning. The cinema's earliest film with a story-line, the Lumière brothers' *Watering the Gardener*, was a comedy. A naughty boy treads on the garden hose. The gardener peers down the nozzle and is soaked when the boy takes his foot away.

The earliest film comedies were made up of slapstick incidents – soakings, chases, practical jokes, accidents, slipping on banana skins and falling off ladders. Quickly, though, it became clear that they derived additional humour from the person involved. The comedian was as important as the joke.

The first group of cinema comedians emerged in France in the years when she dominated the world's cinema industry. The first true clown was André Deed, recruited from the theatre by the Pathé studios in 1906. A series of one-reel comedies in which Deed played 'Boireau' brought him world fame.

But all were eclipsed by a young comedian who took over from Deed at Pathé. Max Linder brought a new quality and subtlety to clowning. The comedy arose from the contrast between his own smoothness and restraint and the absurd chaos around him. He was prodigiously inventive: to this day almost every visual gag can be traced back to his films. The peak of Max's career and world fame was between 1909 and 1914. World War I however brought about his personal eclipse, with the decline of the French cinema industry. After an unsuccessful attempt to launch a new career in the US, he died in a suicide pact with his young wife in a Paris hotel room in 1925.

Now American cinema dominated the world film industry. American comedy began to appear as a distinctive genre around 1910. The first comic star to win universal popularity was the fat, cheerful and put-upon John Bunny. But in 1912 Mack Sennett, who had learned the craft of cinema at Biograph alongside D. W. Griffith, founded the Keystone Studios. With Sennett as their inspired producer-in-chief, Keystone developed a whole style of American slapstick comedy and enriched folklore with a host of absurd characters.

For Keystone no extravagance was too great and no feat too dangerous, difficult or daft for the comedians to attempt. They would cheerfully throw themselves out of cars, under trains, into rivers, or off roof-tops, so long as it won a laugh. The watchword was improvisation, and a single prop could provide endless comic variations.

Sennett's Keystone was peopled with larger-than-life eccentrics such as Fatty Arbuckle, cross-eyed Ben Turpin, whiskery Mack Swain, Chester Conklin and Billy Bevan, and the Keystone Kops, who upturned all law and order. The studio was an unrivalled school of comedy, where directors learned new, fluid camera and editing techniques.

An age of giants

Three great giants of American silent film comedy spent some time at the Sennett Studios. Charles Chaplin was recruited to Keystone from the English variety act, Fred Karno's Sketch Company. Harold Lloyd, with his hornrimmed spectacles and an enthusiasm for perilous feats on the sides of skyscrapers, spent some time with Sennett. Harry Langdon, the moon-faced elderly baby, met his best director, Frank Capra, when they were both working at Keystone.

Buster Keaton came into films at the age of 21 as a vaudeville veteran. He started in films as partner to a former Keystone star, Fatty Arbuckle. Plot and gag construction and Keaton's own performance made masterpieces such as *Our Hospitality* – 1923, *The General* – 1926 and *The Navigator* – 1924.

With these four giants, as well as a whole generation of less well-remembered stars such as Larry Semon and Raymond Griffith, silent comedy reached a peak of artistry which, for economic and historical reasons, has never been equalled. The coming of sound made film production costlier and more complex, and coincided with the consolidation of the giant film companies. The rise of the supervising producer also took away much flexibility and freedom. Apart from Chaplin, the old star comedians no longer enjoyed independence of creation in their own studios. A new generation of comedians now arrived; men such as Jack Benny, who had achieved fame through sound radio. From the early 1930s, comedy took on more and more of the design and calculation of a radio script. But there still remained stars recruited from vaudeville and musical comedy, such as the Marx Brothers, Eddie Cantor, Joe E. Brown, Mae West and incomparable W. C. Fields. Laurel and Hardy teamed up in the last days of silent films and found their complementary characters improved by the subtle use of dialogue.

In Britain too the music halls provided star comedians. Their modest comic films have often lasted well. The most consistently successful stars were Gracie Fields, George Formby, Arthur Askey and the delightful Will Hay, who personified doubtful authority.

Since World War II, the traditions of silent cinema, variety and vaudeville have vanished. Comedy has become a matter of comic actors in comic scenarios. Abbott and Costello were a pale shadow of the old slapstick comedy teams; Danny Kaye and Red Skelton had comedy vehicles built around their talents in the 1940s. Jerry Lewis outlasted his partnership with Dean Martin to make a brave attempt at reviving older styles of slapstick star comedy in films such as *Ladies' Man* – 1961 and *The Errand Boy* – 1962. In Britain successive stars of television comedy series have been thrust into films. Peter Sellers alone has the status of a star comedian, notably in the ever-declining *Pink Panther* series.

France seems once more to have taken the comic initiative, with popular star comedians such as Louis de Funès and Bourvil and one comic genius, Jacques Tati.

Opposite Laurel and Hardy, the inseparable duo, walk into trouble under the zany gaze of Ben Turpin.

Some Great Comedies

The Gold Rush – 1925; dir. Charles Chaplin; Charles Chaplin, Mack Swain, Tom Murray.

Exit Smiling – 1926; dir. Sam Taylor; Bea Lillie.

The General – 1926; dir. Buster Keaton; Buster Keaton.

Monkey Business – 1931; dir. Norman McLeod; Marx Brothers.

Way Out West – 1936; dir. James W. Horne; Stan Laurel, Oliver Hardy.

His Girl Friday – 1940; dir. Howard Hawks; Cary Grant, Rosalind Russell.

Hellzapoppin! – 1941; dir. Henry C. Potter; Ole Olsen, Chic Johnson, Mischa Auer, Martha Raye.

Monsieur Hulot's Holiday – 1951; dir. Jacques Tati; Jacques Tati, Nathalie Pascaud, Michele Rolla.

Some Like It Hot – 1959; dir. Billy Wilder; Tony Curtis, Marilyn Monroe, Jack Lemmon, Joe E. Brown, George Raft, Pat O'Brien.

Annie Hall – 1977; dir. Woody Allen; Woody Allen, Diane Keaton, Shelley Duvall.

The Romance

'A fictitious narrative of which the scene and incidents are very remote from ordinary life' is how a dictionary defines 'romance'. But it does not quite pinpoint the popular idea of movie romance. The scene and incidents of *Frankenstein* – 1932 are remote from ordinary life, but it is not a romance. The scene and incidents of *Love Story* – 1970 are *not* very remote from ordinary life, but it *is* a romance. The item missing from the dictionary definition is, of course, love. Romance in the movies is about unrequited love; or love that goes through many a disappointment before it is requited; or love that is no sooner requited than it is stolen away again by death or separation.

Romance is as much a quality in the cinema as a genre. It is adoration of the unattainable. One single image embodies it: the glittering, soft-focus close-up on the giant movie screen in front of which a thousand filmgoers sit gazing in awe. A book can be picked up and put down; a painting can be contemplated with detachment; a play is always at arm's length. But a film hovers over the spectator, scattering its magic in the silvery projector beam.

The beginnings of romance

Romance came into existence the first time that a movie audience tremblingly identified with a character–male or female–caught up in the throes of love. Indeed the object of that love was usually attracting double devotion: one from his or her romantic co-star, one from the movie-going public. Many of film's romantic liaisons are notably one-sided in glamour. In Garbo's and Dietrich's films, the on-screen male admirer is little more than a handsome symbol: a personality to be occupied by the filmgoer while the film lasts, and through whose eyes he may adore the heroine more closely.

Romance has a double, and sometimes conflicting, function. On the one hand it sets out to introduce filmgoers to a dream world to which they can never aspire: the baronial splendours of *Rebecca* – 1940, the magnificence and high-tone spirituality of *Queen Christina* – 1933. On the other hand, it consoles the audience by assuring them that the dream world is always flawed, short-lived, or in some way imperfect. Manderley burns down in *Rebecca*, *Queen Christina* ends by her losing both throne and lover. The audience can enjoy its secret yearning – and at the same time rationally assure itself it is happier than the suffering stars up there on the screen.

Romance and the stars

Romance is most mystical and religious when set in the remote past, most immediate and involving when set in the present. The great Hollywood stars could even be divided between those whose beauty and magnetism seems always to demand the pedestal of a period setting, and those whose simpler girl- (or boy-)next-door appeal suits modern subjects. Garbo and Dietrich are goddesses in a truer sense than that overused word often implies. They simply *are*: a radiant, unattainable (often teasing) icon for filmgoers to worship. By contrast such stars as Greer Garson, Jane Wyman, Jean Arthur and Joan Fontaine move in the real world (or Hollywood's approximation to it) and show that Great Love can sometimes descend upon poor twentieth century mortals.

Potential of the romance

What, if anything, can an intelligent director do with such a highly sentimental genre? It seems to rule out the use of wit, ferocity, realism or any hard, unglamorized look at human relationships. The greatest of the directors to have taken movie romance (almost) on its own terms are Frank Borzage and Max Ophuls. Borzage's films – for example *Seventh Heaven* – 1927, *Three Comrades* – 1938 and *The Mortal Storm* – 1939, have an unrivalled magic and simplicity. For his characters, who are usually caught up in social crisis or war, love is a shield against the harshness of the world at large. Similarly the heroines of Max Ophuls (Joan Fontaine in *Letter From an Unknown Woman* – 1948, Danielle Darrieux in *Madame de . . .* – 1953) are soulful creatures pursuing their obsessive loves amidst a hostile society.

The beloved woman

Other directors tackled romance effectively by adding a satirical element, a touch of distance and wry distortion to toughen their material. Von Sternberg's films treat love-sickness almost as authentic madness. The beloved woman (usually Marlene Dietrich) is so glorified as scarcely to be a recognizable human being at all. She is a divine mystery, draped in veils, patterned by shadows and shielded by half-closed eyes.

Similarly, the 1950s Hollywood director Douglas Sirk inflated the tear-jerking exaggerations of the 'woman's picture' almost to bursting point. In films such as *Magnificent Obsession* – 1953 and *Imitation of Life* – 1959 he called forth a world of rich Technicolor heartache that hovers on the brink of parody. Sirk managed the remarkable feat of giving his customers what they wanted at the same time as mischievously rebuking them for their maudlin tastes.

In the 1970s the romance tended to fight a losing battle with sexual freedom. When the physical conquests of love are easier, the emotional rewards are less (at least in the simple arithmetic of popular cinema). One exception, that seems to have dampened many handkerchiefs is *Love Story* – 1970 ('Love means never having to say you're sorry'). Ryan O'Neal and Ali McGraw lose little time in going to bed together. But the 1970s have invented another made-to-be flaunted taboo just as powerful, and just as darkly romantic, as sex— early death. With the heroine's untimely end from leukaemia, longing and fulfilment are once again separated. Romance blossoms in the space in between.

The War Film

Modern warfare and the cinema both came of age at roughly the same date – 1914. As early as the Boer War the value of film as propaganda had been recognized. The primitive newsreels and dramatizations of 1900-1902 invariably expressed jingoistic sentiments. War movies have ever since tended to reflect not merely contemporary attitudes, but official ones. During World War II, no British or American film was released that was not solidly behind the war effort.

Expressions of regret for the young men being led to the slaughter were permitted, but only if they did not hint at needless waste. John Huston's documentary *The Battle of San Pietro* – 1944 ran into all sorts of trouble because its commentary suggested that: 'These lives were valuable. Valuable to their loved ones, to their country, and to the men themselves.' Not until *A Walk in the Sun* – 1945 could a feature film venture to imply, even covertly, that a soldier's prime concern in war might be personal survival.

Action-packed and flag-waving war films could be made with discretion, for instance, William Wellman's *The Story of GI Joe* – 1945; with decency, for instance, Anthony Asquith's *A Way the Stars* – 1945; or with sentimental condescension, for instance, Noël Coward and David Lean's *In Which We Serve* – 1942. But all of them carefully avoided deeper issues, such as the causes and conduct of the war, or troublesome issues, such as racial prejudice, class conflict or conscientious objection to conscription.

British films tended to feature the stiff upper lip, American ones the free-and-easy swashbuckler. But both followed the pattern laid down by Stephen Crane in his novel *The Red Badge of Courage*, where he labelled his characters as 'The Youth', 'The Tall Soldier', 'The Loud Soldier' and so on. An action, naval, military or air, must be accomplished no matter what the cost. The seasoned leader fusses over his brood, the tired veterans loudly complain, the timid recruits wonder where they will find the courage (that never fails), the rest quietly do their duty. Win or lose, the flag is kept flying.

Pacifist films

After World War I, a spate of anti-war films culminated in Lewis Milestone's *All Quiet on the Western Front* – 1930, Anthony Asquith's *Tell England* – 1931 and G. W. Pabst's *Westfront 1918* – 1930. Sincere and moving in their protest, they make little attempt to analyze war, contenting themselves with voicing a cry of outrage at the pity and the waste of it all.

A rather subtler, and ultimately more effective, form of protest emerged during the same period in films such as Howard Hawks' *The Dawn Patrol* – 1930 and William Dieterle's *The Last Flight* – 1932. *The Dawn Patrol* wastes no effort in registering pacifist sentiments with which no sane person would disagree (in peacetime, at least). It anticipates Joseph Heller's *Catch 22* – 1970 in chronicling the spiralling sense of fear and futility

beneath the devil-may-care exploits of a Royal Flying Corps squadron. Even more telling in its understatement, *The Last Flight* traces the fall to earth of war's 'spent bullets', a group of shattered aviators. They aimlessly drink their way to self-destruction in post-war Paris, with the bleakly gay abandon of Scott Fitzgerald's lost generation.

Five years later Jean Renoir's *La Grande Illusion* – 1936, spoke the last word on the absurdity of the war. Set in a German prison camp, it demonstrated the futility of conflict in a world where national boundaries mean less than class allegiances. It is one of the few films to attempt to analyze the social structures and significance of war.

After World War II

After World War II few anti-war films appeared. This was probably because prompt circulation of the Nazi atrocity pictures left little room for doubt that this had been a just war. Britain contented itself with a flood of films nostalgically celebrating the days of heroism (most profitably in a series of prison camp escapes).

The US, as always more prepared to wash dirty linen in public, made well-meaning but naive attempts to tackle some of war's less palatable aspects. These included the problem of paraplegics in *The Men* – 1950 and racial prejudice in *Home of the Brave* – 1949. Stanley Kubrick's *Paths of Glory* – 1957 was a scathing indictment of militarism and its conduct of war. Such attitudes became enormously influential in the growing cynical disillusionment of the 1960s and 1970s. Kubrick uses a true incident from World War I that offers astonishingly prophetic parallels with Vietnam. He demonstrates with devastating logic that the ordinary soldier is simply a pawn in the game of private power politics.

Spies, hitherto glamorously exotic, like Garbo in *Mata Hari* – 1931, or sleekly sinister, like Conrad Veidt in *Dark Journey*, came down to earth in World War II. Ordinary men and women found themselves spirited into foreign territory, heroically ferreting out secrets on behalf of the war effort. They were safe from the shame that had formerly been connected with the profession. But their adventures, though set in a wartime context, still really belonged to the thriller genre, with dark streets, pursuit and mystery.

The cold war made traditional spies big business again as Hollywood frantically hunted for the red menace under the bed. The increasingly complicated exploits of secret agents escalated into the absurdities of James Bond. But the Korean War and the Communist brain-washing techniques also gave spies a new military role. Brainwashing featured in a number of Hollywood films, reaching a peak in John Frankenheimer's brilliant fantasy *The Manchurian Candidate* – 1962. In this film an American war hero captured by Communists in Korea is primed to kill the US President when he receives a certain stimulus. The spy here is turned, literally, into a ticking bomb.

The Epic

Epics are the cinema's homage to the proverb 'biggest is best'. Most of a film's main ingredients – from the cast and the settings to the time-span and the moral and dramatic issues – are inflated well beyond their normal size. The epic aims at grandeur and spectacle and hopes to arouse awe and wonder in its audience.

For the Greeks, the epic was a poetic form in which the hero's moral development was emphasized. For the Romans, the epic had connotations of national glory, achieved through struggle and pre-ordained greatness. Hollywood chose the Roman style, with its easier parallels with US history.

Epics are as old as the cinema itself. The 'cast of thousands' is an institution that goes back at least as far as Enrico Guazzoni's *Quo Vadis?* – 1913 in Italy and D.W. Griffith's *Intolerance* – 1916 in America. The Italians were the first into the epic field. The visual extravagance of films made by Guazzoni, Mario Caserini and Giovanni Pastrone are a revelation to audiences brought up to believe that size, spectacle and glitter belong solely to Hollywood.

The Italian epic
The most famous Italian epic is Pastrone's *Cabiria* – 1916, set in ancient Carthage and introducing the soon-to-be-legendary Italian he-man Maciste. Italy's flair for historical epics continued into the 1920s, with Guazzoni especially active. Although the Fascist government curbed invention during the late 1920s and the 1930s, there was a late flourish from Carmine Gallone with *Scipione L'Africano* – 1937.

Meanwhile, Hollywood was busy making the genre its own. Griffith's two most famous films, *The Birth of a Nation* – 1915 and *Intolerance*, started it all. The Babylonian sets for *Intolerance* are still the standard by which all cinema extravagance is finally measured. Griffith's mantle soon passed to Cecil B. DeMille, who made a series of epics each more overdressed (or, when the censorship codes permitted, underdressed) than the last. *The Ten Commandments* – 1924, with its famous parting of the Red Sea, was followed by *King of Kings* – 1927, *Sign of the Cross* – 1932 and *Cleopatra* – 1934. After that his epic output was fitful, but notable landmarks were *Samson and Delilah* – 1949 and *The Ten Commandments* number two – 1956.

The coming of the wide screen
Once it had discovered the wide screen in the early 1950s, there was no holding Hollywood. The first CinemaScope film was *The Robe* – 1953, in which Jean Simmons, Richard Burton and Victor Mature grappled with the mysteries of the Resurrection. Thereafter there was *Ben-Hur* – 1959, *Solomon and Sheba* – 1959, *Spartacus* – 1960, *El Cid* – 1961, *King of Kings* – 1961, *Barabbas* – 1961, *The Fall of the Roman Empire* – 1963, *Cleopatra* – 1963, *Sodom and Gomorrah* – 1963, *The Greatest Story Ever Told* – 1964 and many more tributes to the Bible, or to the glories that were Greece or Rome.

The word 'epic' tends to be applied only to films set well back in history – preferably ancient history. For example, *Gone With The Wind* – 1939 and Vidor's *War and Peace* – 1956 are both epic in their panoramic spheres of action and their casts of thousands, but they do not quite qualify for the genre.

The epic has also tended to attract all that is most absurd in Hollywood film-making: the glamour, the size, the showy eroticism, and the careless anachronisms alongside the too-careful attempts at 'period' language and manners. Yet there *is* a curious grandeur about the epic. Many westerners today, when they wander around the ruins of Delphi, Olympia or ancient Rome, see them with eyes influenced by Hollywood's epic pictures.

The Biblical epic
The Bible has inspired many epics. Such films have been based on both Testaments. But there are problems about portraying Christ. Until recently he was not usually directly depicted: he would be represented by a hand, a voice or a misty figure. Cecil B. DeMille would not even allow the actors playing Christ and his disciples in *King of Kings* – 1927 to drink or swear on set.

The epic has always been handicapped by its expense and the sheer logistical nightmare of actually staging it. With so much money involved, and so many vested interests pulling in different directions, the resulting film tends to be either a weak compromise or a mish-mash of wildly conflicting elements. The director often becomes a kind of traffic policeman, telling which army to march in which direction, or which group of dancing girls to enter at which point in the banquet. Even talented directors such as Nicholas Ray (*King of Kings* – 1961), Stanley Kubrick (*Spartacus* – 1960) and Anthony Mann (*The Fall of The Roman Empire* – 1964) tend to find themselves faced with a new set of problems when put in charge of an epic.

Epic appeal
One fascination of the epic lies in the idea that the Graeco-Roman era (or, going further back, the Egyptian) was a great watershed in human history. It marked a transition when the primitive and mythic heroism of pre-history first glimpsed 'civilization'. Strength and beauty, grandeur and refinement existed together in a brief, miraculous Golden Age.

One almost unvarying feature of the epic is the contrast between the muscle-bound machismo of the men (from Victor Mature to Charlton Heston to Kirk Douglas) and the swooning femininity of the women (from Claudette Colbert to Jean Simmons). That fact, in addition to suggesting that the epic is Hollywood's oldest source of sexist stereotypes, pinpoints its unique attraction: as an arena for larger-than-life contrasts and conflicts.

Opposite Echoes of the famous chariot race from *Ben Hur*.

Some Great Epics

Intolerance – 1916; dir. D. W. Griffith; Robert Harron, Mae Marsh, Miriam Cooper, Walter Long, Howard Gaye, Erich von Stroheim, Margery Wilson, Spottiswoode Aitken, Tully Marshall, Elmer Clifton, Alfred Paget, Lillian Gish.

Napoleon – 1927; dir. Abel Gance; Albert Dieudonné, Abel Gance, Antonin Artaud, Gina Manes.

Alexander Nevsky – 1938; dir. Sergei M. Eisenstein; Nikolai Cherkassov, Nikolai Okhlopov, Alexander Abrikosov, Dmitri Orlov, Vasili Novikov.

The Robe – 1953; dir. Henry Koster; Richard Burton, Jean Simmons, Victor Mature, Michael Rennie, Richard Boone.

The Ten Commandments – 1956; dir. Cecil B. De Mille; Charlton Heston, Yul Brynner, Edward G. Robinson, Anne Baxter, Cedric Hardwicke.

Ben Hur – 1959; dir. William Wyler; Charlton Heston, Stephen Boyd, Jack Hawkins.

El Cid – 1961; dir. Anthony Mann; Charlton Heston, Sophia Loren.

King of Kings – 1962; dir. Nicholas Ray; Jeffrey Hunter, Robert Ryan, Siobhan McKenna, Viveca Lindfors.

War and Peace – 1963–68; dir. Sergei Bondarchuk; Ludmila Savelyeva, Sergei Bondarchuk, Vyacheslav Tikhonov, Anastasia Vertinskaya, Vasily Lanovoi, Irina Skobtseva, Kira Ivanov-Golokov, Boris Zakhava, Vladislav Strzhelchik.

172

The Musical

The musical, one of the cinema's most distinctive genres, paradoxically had its roots deep in traditions of the stage – in operetta and musical comedy. The operetta leaned towards the romantic. The musical comedy, particularly in the 1920s and in the work of the Gershwins, Irving Berlin, Jerome Kern, Cole Porter and Rodgers and Hart, was more inclined to be flip and funny, cynical and contemporary. The last years of the silent pictures coincided with a peculiarly rich crop of stage shows of both types.

The first singing picture

Small wonder that the first talking picture (using discs) was actually a *singing* picture – *The Jazz Singer* – 1927. But the first musical sound films tended to be stage-bound adaptations of operettas, such as *The New Moon* and *The Vagabond King* or musical comedy successes, such as *No, No, Nanette* with Joan Crawford – but with the songs removed! Finally there were rapidly-strung-together film 'revues', used to try out the vocal talents of the studios' contract artists – *Hollywood Revue*, *Paramount on Parade*, *Happy Days* and similar films.

As the initial technical problems of sound recording were overcome, the film musical proper began to take shape – or rather a variety of shapes. In France René Clair's scintillating and supremely musical *Sous Les Toits de Paris* – 1930 and *Le Million* – 1932 seem to have had no successors. But Germany, with her advanced technical expertise in camerawork and recording, embarked on a series of film operettas which reached an early peak in the Lilian Harvey vehicles *Drei von der Tankstelle* – 1930 and *Congress Dances* – 1931. The series continued throughout the 1930s and the first years of the Third Reich.

Ernst Lubitsch's silent films always had the atmosphere of operetta. He created a totally new and delightful genre with the witty *The Love Parade* – 1929, *Monte Carlo* – 1930 and *One Hour With You* – 1932. Lubitsch's most glittering musical stars, Maurice Chevalier and Jeanette MacDonald, appeared together in one of the most sparkling and original film operettas of the period, Rouben Mamoulian's *Love Me Tonight* – 1932.

Meanwhile *Broadway Melody* – 1929, deriving more from vaudeville, was the first of many backstage musicals. Among the Broadway stars attracted to Hollywood was Eddie Cantor. For Cantor's first sound film, *Whoopee* – 1930, Busby Berkeley came from Broadway to direct the dance sequences. He stayed on to create a wholly original and distinctive film musical style, using show girls as the plastic material for extraordinary abstract screen compositions. The enormous success of his dance designs for *Forty-Second Street* – 1933, *Footlight Parade* and *Gold Diggers of 1933* – 1933 lifted the musical from a slump into which it had fallen, after the public had tired of the initial novelty of sound and of the very first, limited musical films.

The 1930s and early 1940s were an era of musical stars of outstanding, or at least eccentric, talents. The dancing of Fred Astaire and Ginger Rogers expressed dynamically art deco style. They added distinction to all their films, whether directed by Mark Sandrich, William A. Seiter or George Stevens, and whether with music by Berlin, Kern or Porter. Jeanette MacDonald and Nelson Eddy warbled their way – she with a nice wit, he an amiable blankness – through romantic operettas. Stars included the infant (Shirley Temple), and the juvenile (Deanna Durbin, Mickey Rooney, the young Judy Garland), a skater (Sonja Henie), and a swimmer (Esther Williams), and troupers such as Alice Faye, Betty Grable, Eleanor Powell and Bing Crosby.

Freed's revolution

Revolution came at MGM in the 1940s. Arthur Freed (who had arrived in Hollywood to write the score for *Broadway Melody* in 1929) promoted a new musical form in which the musical elements of the film, the song and dance were an integral part of the story. Freed also promoted singular talents such as the directors Vincente Minnelli and Stanley Donen, and the accomplished dancer-director Gene Kelly.

Minnelli was to direct, under Freed's guiding hand, *Cabin in the Sky* – 1942, *The Ziegfeld Follies* – 1946, *Meet Me in St Louis* – 1944, *Yolanda and the Thief* – 1945, *The Pirate* – 1948 and *An American in Paris* – 1951. Donen directed the dance in *Cover Girl* – 1944, *Anchors Aweigh* – 1944 and *Take Me Out to the Ball Game* – 1948, and made a memorable debut as director with Kelly in *On The Town* – 1949, and then the scintillating *Singin' in the Rain* – 1952.

Minnelli and Kelly directed two of the best musicals of later years – respectively *On A Clear Day You Can See Forever* – 1960 and *Hello, Dolly!* – 1969. But the musical could never again be the same after the fall of the old studio system. The work of such men as Freed, Berkeley or Astaire, or a team such as MacDonald and Eddy, depended on the economic stability of a studio to keep together their carefully orchestrated set-up.

After the fall of the studios, it became vastly expensive and risky to produce a musical. Producers have played for safety by falling back on the old practice of adapting Broadway successes. Sometimes they were artistically satisfying – *A Star is Born* – 1954, *Funny Face* – 1956, Rouben Mamoulian's *Silk Stockings* – 1956 and *Thoroughly Modern Millie* – 1967; sometimes financially profitable – Robert Wise's *West Side Story* – 1961 and *Sound of Music* – 1965, and Joshua Logan's *South Pacific* – 1958.

Younger directors such as Peter Bogdanovich – *At Long Last Love* – 1975, and Martin Scorsese – *New York, New York* – 1977, have, with varying success, attempted nostalgic recreations of 1930s musical traditions. Robert Altman used a new style of music to give a true musical structure to *Nashville* – 1975 which was based on country and western music.

The Thriller

Dark streets and lurid neon signs, lush penthouse suites and seedy rooming-houses, garish night-clubs and sleazy bars: all call up a nightmarish world where any attempt to move from darkness to light invites death and destruction, or at best disillusion. This is the urban underworld of the gangster-thriller – 'not the real city, but the dangerous and sad city of the imagination'.

The first inhabitants of this world were the bootleg racketeers of the Prohibition era played by Edward G. Robinson in *Little Caesar* – 1930, James Cagney in *Public Enemy* – 1931 and Paul Muni in *Scarface* – 1932. These three films attracted enormous box office success through their vitality and violence. They largely laid down the ground-rules for the genre.

There had, of course, been gangster films before this; but they were basically romances in a criminal setting. The gangsters in Sternberg's *Underworld* – 1927, for instance, had a certain quaintness in dress and behaviour. Their leader, Bull Weed, ox-like but chivalrous, bows out gallantly when he finds himself at the wrong corner of a romantic triangle. Rouben Mamoulian's *City Streets* – 1931 and Tay Garnett's *Bad Company* – 1931 are concerned primarily with the trials of a pair of young lovers getting themselves out of a gang. *City Streets* is said to have been Al Capone's favourite movie, because all its killings happened discreetly off-screen. Both films anticipate *The Godfather* – 1972, a subtler 1970s development of the genre, in portraying the gangster as a respectable tycoon with hirelings to do the dirty work behind the scenes.

Compulsive violence

These Prohibition racketeers, however, lived and died in violence. They revelled in the rattle of machine gun fire within a closed society that largely excluded tenderness. They nursed a grudge against society for the privileges it had denied them. Innocent bystanders did not get involved. Their compulsive, almost all-American, quest for success was doomed to end in bloody failure.

The gangster movie was given a new lease of life by nostalgic films such as Arthur Penn's *Bonnie and Clyde* – 1967, Roger Corman's *Bloody Mama* – 1969 and John Milius' *Dillinger* – 1973. Two new features appeared. One was the emphasis on open country and placid rural landscapes, which brought the films closer to the western than the gangster movie. The other new feature was that the gangsters, still unmistakeably psychotic, were now portrayed as eccentric and endearing charmers.

Robinson, Cagney and Muni, the prototype gangsters, were hardly charming. Loud-mouthed, brutal and entirely egocentric, they imposed themselves as heroes mainly through their vitality, their soaring ambition and their ruthless contempt for authority. They inhabited an ugly world where love and friendship inevitably meant double-cross, and where dark streets and shiny limousines heralded death. Even the weapons – the sawn-off shotgun, the snub-nosed automatic and the tommy gun – had none of the leisurely grace of the Winchester, the Colt or the bow-and-arrow of the western. In this ugliness lurked a thrill of fear. Something was lost from the genre when its world of darkness and light was ousted by colour in the 1960s and 1970s.

In 1934 the Legion of Decency was formed in the US, and the Production Code more toughly applied. The next year William Keighley's *G-Men* heralded a series of films to counter the accusation that Hollywood had been glorifying the gangster. A G-Man hero usually infiltrated the gang and worked undercover. But nothing else changed; the films remained indistinguishable from the earlier ones in themes and images. After the repeal of Prohibition in December 1933, public interest in gangster exploits slackened.

The rise of the thriller

At almost the same time the hard-boiled detective of the pulp magazines was beginning to appear in books by Dashiell Hammett, and later by Raymond Chandler. Traditional detective mysteries had of course existed almost as long as the cinema. The first movie adaptations of Hammett tended to stress either the wisecracking detective (for example *The Thin Man* – 1934) or the gangster elements (for example *The Glass Key* – 1935). But gradually the hard-boiled detective began to venture into the gangster's 'dangerous and sad city of the imagination'. By 1941, with *The Maltese Falcon*, the genres had met.

In the thriller, unlike the detective story, the 'whodunnit' aspect is relatively unimportant. And unlike the gangster film, the innocent bystander all too frequently gets involved. In gangster movies, the threat was always recognizable: an ambitious colleague or underling, the police or a rival gang. In the thriller the menace is more abstract (a reflection of the anxiety created by the war). The city becomes a shadowy, menacing jungle. Nobody should be trusted, even love is probably a betrayal. The only certainty – as Sam Spade notes in *The Maltese Falcon* – is that 'everyone has something to conceal'.

The principle, as Chandler himself remarked, was that when in doubt what to do next, you opened a door on a man with a gun. That man could be your best friend, your lover, your mortal enemy, or – most likely – a total stranger. Themes varied from crooked boxing promotions (*The Set Up* – 1949) and violent anti-Semitism (*Crossfire* – 1947) to monopolies and terrorism in the whole-sale fruit trade (*Thieves' Highway* – 1949). The hero might be a world-weary private eye (*The Big Sleep* – 1946), a solitary hired killer (*This Gun for Hire* – 1942) or a law-abiding citizen suddenly without explanation finding himself on the run (*The Woman in the Window* – 1944). Always nightmare circumstances created a dark, endless tunnel from which the only possible exit seemed to be menaced by murder and sudden death, keeping the audience on the edge of their seats.

The Animated Film

Animation, obviously, brings movement to inanimate objects. Devices exploiting the phenomenon of persistence of vision for this purpose appeared early in the nineteenth century.

Animation only became linked to the infant cinema industry in about 1900 when J. S. Blackton, co-founder of the Vitagraph Company, discovered stop-motion photography accidentally. Blackton found he could make objects and people appear and disappear at will by simply stopping the hand-cranked camera and making the change. But his *Humorous Phases of Funny Faces* – 1906, generally accepted as the first cartoon animated in this way, is of technical interest only.

It was Emile Cohl in France who developed animated cartoons as an art. In his *Fantasmagorie* and *Cauchemar de Fantoche* – 1908, Cohl metamorphoses matchstick characters with masterly comic inventiveness.

The early American animation was largely based on comic strips, since the newspaper syndicates financed the expensive animation process, and were normally commercial in outlook. Winsor McCay went on tour in vaudeville with his *Gertie the Dinosaur* – 1910, giving live instructions to which the animated dinosaur responded.

But in Europe animation was from the beginning valued more for its artistic potential. In Russia, Ladislas Starevitch exploited Blackton's techniques using animated model insects, with fables of human folly. The first German cartoons, in the 1910s and 1920s, were abstract art brought to life, by the painters Pinschewer, Eggeling, Richter, Finschinger and Ruttman. Lotte Reiniger animated legendary characters in cut out and jointed paper silhouettes, notably in *The Adventures of Prince Achmed* – 1926. In France the team of Hoppin and Gross took up this lyrical tradition with their lively cartoon ballet *Joie de Vivre* – 1934.

In the US the commercial tradition continued. Animators were organized into vast studios to mass-produce cartoon series. One of the most successful studios belonged to the Fleischer brothers. Betty Boop, the cartoon vamp, made the studio's name, and Popeye, appearing in 1933, confirmed it.

The Disney treatment

Walt Disney's gift for creating series characters was revealed with the first Mickey Mouse film, *Plane Crazy* – 1928. But Disney's genius was also financial; his studio was the first to invest in synchronized sound (*Steamboat Willie* – 1928) in colour (*Flowers and Trees* – 1932) and in devices such as the multiplane camera, seen to its fullest effect in *Pinocchio* – 1939. He also risked massive investment in features – at the right moment.

The great classics amongst the Disney features, *Snow White* – 1938, *Pinocchio* and *Fantasia* – 1941, *Dumbo* – 1941 and *Bambi* – 1942 have largely eclipsed many miniature masterpieces. These include *The Three Little Pigs* – 1933, appearing at the depth of the Depression to become a national clarion call.

The late 1930s and 1940s were the Golden Age of Hollywood cartoon comedy. Chuck Jones, Friz Freleng and Bob Clampett at Warners created Bugs Bunny and Daffy Duck, while at MGM William Hanna and Joe Barbera created Tom and Jerry. Tex Avery produced a batch of the most violent, vulgar and hilarious cartoons ever.

The mass-production system operating in the US affected the rest of the world. In Britain in the 1930s Anson Dyer established the Disney System and to a certain extent imitated his style, turning out the most polished cinema commercials. Germany, unable to import Disney films during the war, set up its own mass-production studios.

But some Europeans resisted the Disney formula. In Britain, the government-financed GPO film unit could afford to do so. Norman McLaren began here, and developed camera-less animation techniques, notably in *Love on the Wing* – 1938, which is painted direct onto film. In 1939 McLaren left for Canada, where he has become an experimental wizard, animating anything from pastel chalks to still photographs to mathematical representations of sound.

The 1950s saw a turning against the Disney approach all over the world. Labour was becoming more expensive and cinema attendances were declining. The style now was sparser design and limited animation.

In the US this trend was spearheaded by the UPA studio. Their work was determinedly two-dimensional, angular and crude. Successes included Robert Cannon's *Gerald McBoing Boing* – 1950 and John Hubley's *Rooty Toot Toot* – 1952, a version of the Frankie and Johnnie story.

Richard Williams, George Dunning and Bob Godfrey pushed Britain into the limelight during this period, mainly with similarly pared-down design, first seen in Williams' *The Little Island* – 1958.

But the most exciting developments in the 1950s took place in Eastern Europe, where government funds were available for normally unprofitable short films. Yugoslav artists in Zagreb first came to world attention in 1957 with Vukotic's parody western *Cowboy Jimmie*. The Zagreb animators Vukotic, Mimica, Marks, Grgic, Dragic and others using reduced animation walked off with most of the festival prizes for the following decade.

Czechoslovakia's animating tradition went back to the 1920s. Traditional puppet animation techniques blossomed immediately after World War II. The great artist Jiří Trnka's best work came in films such as *The Czech Year* – 1947 and *The Song of the Prairie* – 1949, probably the model for *Cowboy Jimmie*. Trnka's technique and artistry were inherited by Bretislav Pojar. But it was Karel Zeman who brought Czech animation to the West in the 1950s with features combining live action with animation, notably *Journey Into Prehistory* – 1955 and *Baron Munchausen* – 1961.

Opposite Mickey Mouse, the world-famous Disney cartoon figure. He first appeared as Mortimer Mouse in 1927. He was always drawn by Disney's artist Ub Iwerks, and appeared in a galaxy of roles from explorer to Arab, from convict to clock-cleaner.

Some Great Animated Films

Snow White and the Seven Dwarfs – 1937; prod. Walt Disney.

Fantasia – 1940; prod. Walt Disney.

Pinocchio – 1940; prod. Walt Disney.

Animal Farm – 1954; prod. John Halas, Joy Batchelor.

The Little Island – 1958; prod. Richard Williams.

Labyrinth – 1962; prod. Jan Lenica.

Yellow Submarine – 1968; dir. George Dunning.

Fritz the Cat – 1971; dir. Ralph Bakshi.

Fantastic Planet – 1973; dir. Reni Laloux.

Allegro non Troppo – 1976; dir. Bruno Bozzetto.

Horror and Science Fiction

In one nicely horrific moment in Méliès' otherwise quaintly charming fantasy *The Conquest of the Pole* – 1912 the Abominable Giant of the Snows gobbles up an unfortunate polar explorer. Earlier still, shortened versions of classic books such as *Dr Jekyll and Mr Hyde* – 1908 and *Frankenstein* – 1910 had been produced. The pre-war German cinema had already prepared the way for its later Expressionist era with films such as *The Student of Prague* – 1913 and Paul Wegener's *The Golem* – 1914.

But it was *The Cabinet of Dr Caligari* – 1919 that established a virtual blueprint for cinema horror. Cesare the sleepwalker is set by the evil Dr Caligari to murder those who mock his work. He glimpses the pretty heroine at the fairground where he is exhibited in a coffin. When he is sent to murder her in her bedroom, the sinister Cesare, clothed in black, gathers her up in his arms instead. Trailing white draperies in a sequence of nightmarishly weird beauty, he steals away with her over the rooftops into the night. These three characters – the mad doctor, the monster he has created, and the girl who is terrorized by their evil intentions – became an essential part of the horror film genre. Even today sophisticated audiences sucumb to the titillation of innocence at the mercy of evil.

The roots of horror

By coincidence, *Caligari* and the other great German Expressionist fantasies came to Hollywood's attention just as Broadway was enjoying a profitable fashion for spoof horrors and haunted houses. As a result Paul Leni (imported from Germany) and Benjamin Christensen (from Denmark) had to direct their skills to playing horror for laughs in Hollywood films such as *The Cat and The Canary* – 1927, *Seven Footprints to Satan* – 1929, and *The Last Performance* – 1929.

Dracula and *Frankenstein* both met with extraordinary and unexpected success in 1931. Both films featured oppressed white-robed heroines, madmen and monsters – though Dracula was both madman and monster. Soon mad geniuses were everywhere, busily creating human waxworks (*The Mystery of the Wax Museum* – 1933), man-beasts (*Island of Lost Souls* – 1932) and animated manikins (*The Bride of Frankenstein* – 1936). Meanwhile a bizarre assortment of beasts, from Frankenstein's monster to King Kong himself, forlornly pursued their beauties in a hopeless quest for love.

Dr. Caligari

In *The Cabinet of Dr Caligari*, Dr Caligari is revealed to be the sinister but benevolent director of a lunatic asylum, where all the other characters are confined. One of its scriptwriters, Carl Mayer, had brushed with an army psychiatrist who diagnosed his rebelliousness towards authority as mental instability. The other scriptwriter, Hans Janowitz, was obsessed with the belief that thousands of undetected and unrepentant murderers were roaming the streets.

Part of the strength of the horror genre lies in its reflection of a world of dictatorial authority in which anybody who diverges from the norm is not tolerated. All such deviants are monsters to be rejected in disgust and ruthlessly exterminated. Dr Frankenstein's creature, when newly born, ecstatically raises his hands and face to the warmth of the sun. It is only after meeting his fellow-beings' implacable hostility and incomprehension that he becomes a monster. King Kong is hunted down and killed by an outraged society when he dares to aspire to love and beauty. In the great horror movies the monster is the hero: misbegotten and misjudged.

Fighting for sanity

A few classic horror films escape the madman-monster-maiden pattern. But they also get their power from a vision of the world as a lunatic asylum, in which a tiny haven of sanity and innocence must be fought for and preserved. Count Zaroff in *The Most Dangerous Game* – 1932, who sadistically titillates his hunting dog's appetite by pursuing human prey, can be seen as a Führer figure. And Edgar Ulmer's *The Black Cat* – 1934 weaves a web of anguish out of its sense of all-embracing evil. Two men, Boris Karloff and Bela Lugosi, left morally dead by their wartime experiences, duel to the death over an innocent soul. This is surely one of the bleakest judgments on war and its spiritual results to come out of any cinema studio.

Science fiction

Science fiction has been around the cinema as long as horror. But its record in treating space travel and futurist visions is not impressive. Early efforts such as Fritz Lang's *Metropolis* – 1926 and William Cameron Menzies' *Things To Come* – 1936 were striking to look at, but naive in thier ideas.

The spate of space operas launched from the 1950s onwards were mostly tatty, repetitive and idiotic. A notable exception was *Forbidden Planet* – 1956, based on Shakespeare's *The Tempest*, from which it borrowed a pleasing level of myth and magic. More recently, Stanley Kubrick's *2001: A Space Odyssey* – 1968 and Steven Spielberg's *Close Encounters of the Third Kind* – 1977 have restored the visual splendour and added both breadth and ideas. But they have also tended to tumble into pomposity and pretension by determinedly chasing greatness.

The wit, poetry and imaginative subtlety of the best science fiction novelists – such as Alfred Bester, Fredric Brown and Henry Kuttner – remains totally untapped by the cinema. Meanwhile, the best science fiction films remain those that might equally well be called genre horror movies: *The Thing from Another World* – 1951, Don Siegel's *Invasion of the Body Snatchers* – 1956 and Jack Arnold's *The Incredible Shrinking Man* – 1957.

Opposite Some classic horror film ingredients: a Transylvanian castle, barren windswept landscape, a brooding presence, vampire bats . . .

Some Great Horror and Science Fiction Films

The Cabinet of Dr Caligari – 1919; dir. Robert Wiene; Werner Krauss, Conrâd Veidt, Lil Dagover, Friedrich Feher.

Metropolis – 1927; dir. Fritz Lang; Brigitte Helm, Gustav Froehlich, Alfred Abel.

Frankenstein – 1931; dir. James Whale; Boris Karloff, Colin Clive.

King Kong – 1933; dir. Merian C. Cooper; Ernest Schoedsack, Fay Wray, Robert Armstrong, Bruce Cabot.

The Invisible Man – 1933; dir. James Whale; Claude Rains, Henry Travers.

Forbidden Planet – 1956; dir. Fred McLeod Wilcox; Walter Pidgeon, Anne Francis, Leslie Nielson.

The Incredible Shrinking Man – 1957; dir. Jack Arnold; Grant Williams, Randy Stuart.

2001: A Space Odyssey – 1968; dir. Stanley Kubrick; Keir Dullea, Gary Lockwood.

The Exorcist – 1973; dir. William Friedkin; Ellen Burstyn, Max von Sydow, Lee J. Cobb, Jason Miller, Linda Blair.

Close Encounters of the Third Kind – 1977; dir. Steven Spielberg; Richard Dreyfuss, François Truffaut, Teri Garr, Melinda Dillon.

The Documentary

A documentary film can include one or more of a varied list of qualities. It can treat 'reality' either by means of direct recording or indirectly by reconstructing what happened – or by a combination of the two. It can concern itself with social problems, often out of a desire to change things. Recently, it has made much use of the hand-held camera and direct 'on-the-spot' interviews.

The 'factual' film can trace its roots back to Lumière and his recordings of everyday events in front of his fixed camera – for example, *Workers leaving the Lumière Factory*. The tradition was continued in America by Edison with films such as *Chinese Laundry* – 1894 and *President McKinley's Inauguration* – 1898. Together Lumière and Edison can be credited with laying the foundations for the modern newsreel.

Film truth

The next major step in the evolution of the documentary was taken by Dziga Vertov in Russia during and after the 1917 Revolution. He edited actuality into newsreels in an attempt to educate and indoctrinate the people about the revolution. The most famous was *Kino Pravda* – Film-Truth.

In América Robert Flaherty emerged as the major chronicler of man's relationship with his environment. *Nanook of the North* – 1922 was part-observation and part-reconstruction of Eskimo life in Canada. He followed this with *Moana* – 1926, *Man of Aran* – 1934 and *Louisiana Story* – 1948. In Europe such key figures as Alberto Cavalcanti with *Rien que les Heures* – 1926 and the Dutchman Joris Ivens with *The Bridge* – 1928 and *Rain* – 1929 produced 'realistic' impressions of city life.

The birth of the British documentary movement, fathered by John Grierson, marked the early maturing of the genre. *The Drifters* – 1929, about herring fishermen on the North Sea, was the only film he actually directed. But Grierson wielded enormous influence as leader of the British Empire Marketing Board Film Unit, set up in 1929. The Unit continued after 1933 under the direction of the General Post Office, and was renamed the Crown Film Unit in 1940.

The Unit worked together to educate and inform the public and propagate the ideals of liberalism and social democracy in the class-bound Britain of the 1930s. Edgar Anstey, Alberto Cavalcanti, Arthur Elton, Humphrey Jennings, Stuart Legg, Paul Rotha, Harry Watt, Basil Wright and others produced a large number of films on social problems in Britain, all sharing a concern for reform. Give the people the facts, and they will know what to do.

Meanwhile in the US Time-Life's *The March of Time* brought to the screen from 1935 onwards a series of dramatized reconstructions and staged interviews interspersed with actuality. These films *were* documentary for most Americans at the time. Pare Lorentz showed how far America was ahead of Britain in producing technically sophisticated government-sponsored films, with *The Plow that Broke The Plains* – 1936 and *The River* – 1937.

World War II saw the greatest flowering of the documentary-propaganda film. All the countries involved made films to train and boost the morale of their armed forces, to uplift and inform the general public, and to win the support of other nations. In the mid-1930s came the Nazi propaganda films of Leni Riefenstahl, *Triumph of the Will* – 1934 and *Olympia* – 1938.

The British documentarists harnessed their principles in support of the war effort in films such as Humphrey Jennings' *Listen to Britain* – 1942 and Harry Watt's *Target for Tonight* – 1941. In America the chauvinism of *The March of Time* was joined by the indoctrination of Frank Capra's *Why We Fight* series.

After the war fewer documentaries appeared, as sponsorship declined and television appeared on the scene. In Italy the neo-realist films of Visconti, Rossellini and De Sica, emphasizing social themes and using non-actors and real settings to recreate actual events, continued the realistic-documentary tradition, as did the National Film Board of Canada under Grierson. In Britain in the 1950s came the Free Cinema movement, led by Lindsay Anderson and Karel Reisz. Their films showed the working classes in a broader social context, contrasting with the 1930s emphasis on their working lives.

'Direct Cinema' and *cinema vérité* developed very rapidly in the late 1950s and 1960s. The terms are used to emphasize the attempt to get close to events. Sync-sound interviews replace the all-knowing narrator, individuals, often in a crisis, are recorded direct. The editing is claimed to be non-manipulative.

Direct cinema

Pioneers in direct cinema included D. A. Pennebaker and Richard Leacock in the early 1960s (*Primary* – 1960, *David, Jane, Crisis* – 1963). Pennebaker alone made *Don't Look Back* – 1966, *Monterey Pop* – 1968 and *Sweet Toronto* – 1970. Albert and David Maysles, who made *Gimme Shelter* – 1970, claimed 'Our films are spontaneous eruptions that we find ourselves catching with our cameras.' Frederick Wiseman made such films as *Titicutt Follies* – 1967 and *High School* – 1968. This new kind of cinema depended on the greater mobility offered by the 16mm camera and transistorized sound equipment.

Since the 1960s, television's docudramas have been the main source of new techniques. TV tends to use *cinéma vérité* techniques but with a 'voice-of-God' narrator. The major British documentary makers have all done some work in television docudrama. Peter Watkins made *Culloden* – 1964, and *The War Game* – 1966; Tony Garnett and Ken Loach *Cathy Come Home* – 1966, *Poor Cow* – 1967 and *Days of Hope* – 1976. Ken Russell, Dennis Mitchell, Norman Swallow and Roger Graef are some of the others. The American line-up is equally impressive.

Opposite *Olympia*, a record of the Berlin Olympic Games held in 1936, made by Leni Riefenstahl, was claimed to be apolitical but the parallels with the heroic Nazi image are obvious. This shot is from the opening sequence which is set in Ancient Greece glorifying not only the human form but also the architecture.

Some Great Documentaries

Nanook of the North – 1922; dir. Robert J. Flaherty.

Drifters – 1929; dir. John Grierson.

Night Mail – 1936; dir. Basil Wright; Harry Wyatt.

The Plow that broke the Plains – 1936; dir. Pare Lorentz.

Olympia – 1938; dir. Leni Riefenstahl.

A Diary for Timothy – 1945; dir. Humphrey Jennings.

Nuit et brouillard – 1955; dir. Alain Resnais.

Warrendale – 1967; dir. Allan King.

The Sorrow and the Pity – 1970; dir. Marcel Ophuls; Pierre Mendes-France, Louis Grave, Albert Speer, George Bidault, Jacques Duclos, Sir Anthony Eden.

Woodstock – 1970; dir. Michael Wadleigh.

The Political Film

The simplest kind of political film is the propaganda film. Such a movie celebrates a particular ideology and aims to coerce the audience to believe in it. As it happens, propaganda is most often seen by people who already believe in the ideology the films express. Examples include Leni Riefenstahl's films for the Nazis before and during World War II, and Frank Capra's 'Why We Fight' series made for the Allies during the same war. Such movies reinforce peoples' ideas. They convince few people to switch sides.

In the broadest sense, film is inherently political, because movies most often centre on dramatic conflicts. The 'political film' *may* deal with obvious ideological questions, such as elections, international relations and economics. But it can include a wide variety of approaches in style. No one thinks of Griffith's *The Birth of a Nation* – 1915 as a political film, yet it helped to confirm the ideology of the Ku Klux Klan in the 1920s and its effect was felt for years after. Often the most effective films in political terms do not state their ideological basis, but rather pretend to be horror movies, westerns, adventures or romances.

Varieties of political film

Basically every movie has a potential political effect, because films give social acceptability to certain kinds of experience. Films project our idea of society and therefore help to define our view of what is possible politically. The underlying spirit of rebellion caught so subtly in Sidney Lumet's *Dog Day Afternoon* – 1975 is one example of the 'mythic' political power of film. The story-line of George Lucas' *Star Wars* – 1977, which ranges from childish fantasy to latent fascism, is another. Nobody would argue that films such as these have direct and measurable political consequences. But they contribute to the ideological climate in which we make our choices. Television is clearly most important in this respect because it reaches so many people and repeats its messages weekly. Children use television characters to model their own personalities.

Secondly films that tell stories about political situations are consciously and intentionally political. Such films can range from highly ideological cinema, such as Eisenstein's *Battleship Potemkin* – 1925, to broadly populist movies such as Frank Capra's *It's A Wonderful Life* – 1946 or Michael Ritchie's *The Candidate* – 1972. This category of narrative films includes those intend to stimulate political awareness, such as Costa Gavras' *Z* – 1968, *The Confession* – 1970 and *State of Siege* – 1973, and Rosi's *Salvatore Giuliano* – 1962 and *The Mattei Affair* – 1972.

But the narrative films of Costa Gavras or Alain Tanner, for example, often verge on the next category: the revolutionary film. Whether narrative in style or not, the revolutionary film aims at revolutionary action. It is most often found where people have already been highly politicized. Examples include the Soviet films of the 1920s and many Third World films such as *The Hour of the Furnaces* – 1968, and *The Battle of Chile*. Revolutionary cinema clearly has a much narrower focus than narrative political cinema, and therefore directs itself to limited audiences.

During the last ten years, a number of film-makers concerned with the links between politics and cinema have become deeply involved in trying to revolutionize or politicize film form as well as content. This category, structural and analytical film, marks the final break with conventional forms of narrative. Jean-Luc Godard described it as an attempt to make 'political films politically'. This is the most avant-garde political cinema and so has the most limited audience. Its value is theoretical rather than practical. Interestingly, this fourth category of political film reaches back to the first. Structural and analytical film concerns itself greatly with how political films of the first category create myth.

Making an impact

Film makers who want to make a political impact are most likely to produce films that fit into the second category of narrative movies. Narrative, popular political films strongly want to make a measurable effect on their audiences, and therefore face film makers with some basic structural problems. George Bernard Shaw thought it was necessary to 'sugar the pill'. The danger here is that the audience will very happily suck off the sugar and spit out the 'pill'.

Bertolt Brecht, still the most influential writer on how politics and drama relate, suggested a more complex approach. Brecht wanted to distance his audience from the logic of his dramas. In this way they could analyse the politics of the situation from their own points of view. This sophisticated approach avoids talking down to the audience since it allows them a full measure of participation. Yet the danger is that the audience will be alienated by being distanced from the action.

Propaganda uses the power of the movie medium to affect the emotions of its audiences. It may be the most obvious political use of cinema, but it doesn't necessarily lead to the strongest politics. Real political change depends on intellectual conviction as well as emotion. Political film-makers who are not propagandists must understand that it is the audience's right to choose whether to act. The film-maker can only point the way. Some political narrative films fail simply because they pay no attention to this delicate balance between film-maker and audience.

For example, if the ideology of the film is put over in simple melodrama, the hero's fate presents a dilemma. If the hero wins against the forces of evil, the audience is likely to conclude that that particular piece of political business has been taken care of. If the hero loses, on the other hand, the audience feels oppressed and passive. Somehow, the film-maker must strike a balance that makes it clear to audiences that the task is theirs, it has yet to be done, and success is possible.

3 THE DIRECTOR AS AUTEUR

Towards the end of the silent period, when the cinema came of age, Hollywood came under fire from the critics. They claimed that it could not hope to rival the Russians, the German Expressionists, or the French avant-garde in matters of art since it was dominated by profit motives and masterminded by illiterate moguls.

There was a good deal of truth behind their claims. Often potentially subversive scripts were toned down by cohorts of rewrite artists. The film-makers themselves were rarely permitted to nurse along an idea of their own, and were often assigned to projects with which they had little or no sympathy.

So the idea grew up that you generally looked to the European cinema for art although Hollywood could occasionally throw up serious and good films amid its welter of entertainments. The result can be neatly illustrated by comparing the reputations of Marcel Carné (working in France) and John Ford (in Hollywood) just before World War II. Carné was enthusiastically hailed as a major artist for the doom-laden poetic realism of *Quai des brumes* – 1938, *Hotel du Nord* – 1938 and *Le Jour se lève* – 1939. Ford was rated almost as highly for *The Informer* – 1935, which was awarded four oscars, *Stagecoach* – 1939 and *Drums Along the Mohawk* – 1939. But the critics felt that he blotted his copybook in between by producing lightweight entertainments such as the Will Rogers comedy *Steamboat Round the Bend* – 1935, the historical melodrama *Mary of Scotland* – 1936, and the Shirley Temple vehicle *Wee Willie Winkie* – 1937.

Reputations overturned

The critics' judgements have since been turned upside-down. On the one hand, Carné's reputation has dwindled to almost nothing. His later films went from bad to worse. The lion's share of the praise for *Quai des brumes*, *Hotel du Nord* and *Le Jour se lève* has been more correctly credited to Jacques Prevert's magnificent scripts. On the other, John Ford's reputation has soared, ironically for reasons that have much to do with the whimsically nostalgic, rustic Americana of *Steamboat Round the Bend*.

The chief move to reassess Hollywood movies in general came during the early and mid-1950s. In 1948, the French critic and film-maker Alexandre Astruc argued that certain directors – Jean Renoir, Orson Welles and Robert Bresson – were now using the camera much as a writer uses a pen. A few years later this notion was taken up by the French film magazine *Cahiers du Cinéma* and expanded into 'the auteur theory'.

Film-makers such as Renoir, Welles and Bresson either wrote or actively collaborated on their own scripts. They could therefore be described as 'authors' of their films in the way a novelist is of his book. But many Hollywood directors started their work only after the script had been more or less completed. Could they also be described as 'auteurs'?

Above Alfred Hitchcock (1899–   ), the British director whose name is synonymous with a certain brand of suspense film. His movies also display a characteristic sly humour and sense for visual drama and film technique.

Left Howard Hawks (1896–1977), US director who has made films in a wide range of different genres. His films display his assured grasp of dramatic pace.

186

The *Cahiers* critics (who included future film-makers such as Godard, Truffaut, Rivette, Rohmer and Chabrol) closely analyzed various Hollywood film-makers who had worked exclusively within the studio system. They demonstrated how a creative personality could surface even through seemingly unpromising material. A gifted director could shape characters, situations

Above Orson Welles (1915–), US director and actor, whose *Citizen Kane* – 1941 is one of the most impressive first films made by any director. His subsequent career as a director has been both brilliant and erratic.

Above right John Ford (1895–1975), US director who made his first film in 1917. He caught the American Frontier experience more effectively than any other film-maker. He was a master story-teller and a great image-maker.

and attitudes, add his personal preoccupations, impose a distinctive personal and visual style, and finally transform alien material into his own.

The method was open to abuse since bad artists can have just as many personal quirks and just as distinctive a style as good ones. For a time it seemed that every French film critic was busy discovering as an 'auteur' some half-forgotten minor director making second-rate films. Nevertheless the *Cahiers* critics added immensely to the appreciation already paid to well-known film-makers such as Hitchcock and Hawks. They also drew attention to hitherto totally neglected film-makers such as Samuel Fuller, Don Siegel, Anthony Mann, Jacques Tourneur and Budd Boetticher. Their 'auteur' method is now fairly generally used as a yardstick for assessing films.

One of the most fruitful aspects of the auteur theory is that it insists that each film should be considered not in isolation, but in relation to the director's total output – or at least those films with which it may be linked in style or theme. From this approach the director's personality will emerge after a viewing of his work as a whole.

Limits of the theory

But the exaggerated use of the auteur theory has led to many abuses. Some enthusiasts tend to hail in advance any film by an established 'name' director, simply because it bears his signature. In addition, auteur critics may judge a film less by their reactions to it than by their appreciation of the inner world and personal idiosyncrasies of the director. This results in some directors becoming 'cult' figures. Films have often been rescued from deserved obscurity merely because an *auteur* critic has discovered in them some personal, stylistic quirk, which was evident in a 'masterpiece' by the same director.

The auteur theory often tends to minimize or disregard the contributions of all the other people who worked on the film. Certainly a film *may* be shaped essentially by the artistic vision of one man. But the director's role in a particular film need not always be supreme.

Opponents of the theory have highlighted crucial contributions of people other than the director. Some films are dominated by an actor's performance. For example it can be argued that Greta Garbo's contribution to *Ninotchka* – 1939 is at least as important as the director's (Ernst Lubitsch). The American critic Pauline Kael maintained that the film *Citizen Kane* – 1941 owes as much to Herman Mankiewicz's original draft scenario as to Orson Welles' direction and performance. But if so, why is it that Mankiewicz's other scripts do not look and sound like *Citizen Kane?* Obviously film-making is a collective activity. Anyone who was not present during the making of a film finds it difficult to assess the relative importance of the many contributors or to decide who was responsible for what.

John Ford and Howard Hawks

Both John Ford and Howard Hawks were superb storytellers. They sketched their plots swiftly and sparingly, leaving themselves plenty of time to explore mood and character. They both almost always chose an eye-level, head-on stance for the camera. Both shot scenes in such a way as to ensure a smooth flow to the story. The editing rarely drew attention to itself for purposes of shock, show or comment. They were, in fact, excellent examples of the 'invisible' director, beloved by the major studios, who never intruded artistic yearnings into the entertainment.

Neither Ford nor Hawks was particularly showy in style. They both belong to the D. W. Griffith tradition – the later Griffith of *Broken Blossoms* – 1919, *True Heart Susie* – 1919 and *Isn't Life Wonderful* – 1924, who had mastered film language and was using it subtly and softly.

Versatility

Hawks worked in an extraordinary variety of genres. He covered among others the gangster film (*Scarface* – 1932), musical (*Gentlemen Prefer Blondes* – 1953), thriller (*The Big Sleep* – 1946), screwball comedy (*Bringing Up Baby* – 1938), detective story (*Trent's Last Case* – 1929), war film (*The Dawn Patrol* – 1930), western (*Red River* – 1948, *Rio Bravo* – 1959), historical epic (*Land of the Pharoahs* – 1955), and science fiction (*The Thing From Another World* – 1951).

Ford ranged equally far and wide, though he returned persistently to the western and related subjects (*Young Mr Lincoln* – 1939, the small-town Americana of *The Sun Shines Bright* – 1953 and his three Will Rogers films). His films vary from *Hurricane* – 1937 to *Mary of Scotland* – 1936 by way of his ancestral Irishry (*The Plough and the Stars* – 1936, *The Quiet Man* – 1952, *The Rising of the Moon* – 1957), social documentary (*The Grapes of Wrath* – 1940) and 'art' (Expressionistic conscience-stirrings in *The Informer* – 1935, Eugene O'Neill playlets in *The Long Voyage Home* – 1940, and Graham Greene's tormented whisky-priest in *The Fugitive* – 1947).

Unmistakeable style

Yet Hawks and Ford both managed to make an unmistakable body of work out of this widely differing material. One method by which this is achieved is illustrated by Ford's *The Grapes of Wrath*, hailed by almost everybody at the time as a great social document and a superb adaptation of John Steinbeck's novel. In dealing with his subject – the official abandonment and ensuing ruthless exploitation of the Oklahoma farmers, whose land had been parched by the dustbowl erosions of the early 1930s – Steinbeck took a harshly 'scientific' approach. Ford, on the other hand, is subjective, almost sentimental; his characters glow with human warmth.

Nostalgia is one of Ford's central concerns – for example in his westerns, with the young couple struggling to establish a homestead in the wilderness (*Drums Along the Mohawk* – 1939), the weary

Top John Ford made *How Green Was My Valley* in 1941, basing it on the novel of the same name. The story concerns the life of a mining family in the South Wales valleys.

Bottom A group of gangsters in *Scarface* – 1932, Howard Hawks' archetypal gangster film, based on actual gangland incidents in Chicago during the Prohibition era. The film ran into heavy censorship problems for its alleged condoning of violence.

Mormons gaining their first sight of the Promised Land *(Wagonmaster* – 1950), and the furious race to lay the tracks for the first transcontinental railroad *(The Iron Horse* – 1924). Such themes celebrate the pioneer spirit, but also add up to a glorious record of the old West and its legends.

Ford is recreating a nostalgic memory. He is not so much painting the world as it was, but as it should have been. It is pointless to accuse Ford of racism in *The Sun Shines Bright* – 1953. He portrayed a small Kentucky town still glowing with Southern gallantry years after the end of the Civil War. He incorporated Negro characters who are Uncle Toms – smiling water-melon smiles and breathing dog-like devotion to their white masters. Pointless, too, to complain of militant militarism; in Ford's world a long line of heroes perform their duty without question. The most characteristic image of his films is the sense of proud, sweeping gallantry with which the cavalry ride over the skyline with pennants flying in *She Wore a Yellow Ribbon* – 1949.

Hawks is sustained by professionalism. It is all in the opening scene of *Rio Bravo* – 1959, where sheriff John Wayne enters a saloon just as his alcoholic deputy (Dean Martin) is about to grovel for the price of a drink tossed into a spittoon. A slightly angled shot, with Wayne towering over the crouching Martin, introduces the theme of the film: the long climb facing the fallen man as he fights to win back skill, self-respect and friendship.

Hawks' vision has frequently been described as an 'all-male world'. He is most at ease in situations where expertise and group loyalties are prized – aviators, racing drivers, cowboys, gangsters and big game hunters. Ford's women are often wives and mothers, patiently waiting with shaded eyes for the return of their menfolk. Hawks' women are sirens, waiting equally patiently for their charms to be noticed when the man's work is done. Ford's heroes, guided by tradition and inbred loyalties, belong to a family or group that ultimately suggests the brotherhood of man. Hawks' heroes are essentially loners.

Hawks' hero usually is, or becomes, a member of a group, such as the mail-plane pilots in *Only Angels Have Wings* – 1939 or the rehabilitated deputy in *Rio Bravo*. But within that group, concentrating entirely on the job in hand, each man is still entirely responsible for his own actions. Unlike Ford, Hawks could never be described as a chronicler of legend or a historian. Even when he dealt with the motor torpedo boats newly foisted onto a reluctant navy during World War II in *They Were Expendable* – 1945, Ford shows how the crews sacrificed to tradition in order to create a tradition. Hawks' heroes are self-sufficient and pragmatic, content to let history pass them anonymously by. They rest secure, knowing that they have done their jobs and done them well.

Above *Stagecoach* – 1939: in some people's opinion one of the greatest westerns. It was John Ford's first western for thirteen years, and the first to be shot in Monument Valley, with its memorable scenery. It was also the film which elevated John Wayne from a B movie actor to a leading star. The story follows a group of stagecoach passengers on a dangerous journey through Indian country, and looks at their varying reactions to stress.

Orson Welles and Alfred Hitchcock

There is a famous story about a producer who went on set to complain that John Ford was lagging behind schedule. Ford simply ripped a handful of pages out of the script, declaring that he was now back on target again. With Ford it just might have happened: his films often give the impression of having been improvised on the spot. With Alfred Hitchcock, such a story would be completely unthinkable.

Ford and Hawks were 'invisible' directors in Hollywood's mainstream. Hitchcock, along with Chaplin, is probably the only film-maker whose name is recognized by the general public. His roots are in the equally classical tradition based on Eisenstein's principles of montage. Celebrated as 'The Master of Suspense', Hitchcock delights in engineering nasty shocks and ingenious surprises for his audiences. What better way to make them jump than the sudden cut, the unexpected revelation, the bizarre montage?

Every detail of a Hitchcock film is planned in advance, every effect calculated in terms of spectator reaction. For example in the shower-bath murder in *Psycho*, seventy separate camera set-ups were made for a 45-second scene. Nobody has ever toyed quite so skilfully with audience expectations and feelings. He gleefully blew up an innocent schoolboy in *Sabotage* – 1936 and killed off the heroine in the first third of *Psycho* – 1960. He let the hero of *The Man Who Knew Too Much* – 1934 escape unharmed from his sinisterly vulner-

able position in a dentist's chair with a gas-mask over his face, only to fall prey to a dear old lady in a mission church, who produces a gun from her shopping bag.

The typical Hitchcock trick is to create outlandish terror by having the familiar become unfamiliar. One example is when the plane peacefully crop-dusting in the fields suddenly turns murderously on Cary Grant as he waits by the roadside in *North by Northwest* – 1959. This Hitchcock suspense cannot be imitated in style. His imitators rarely match his wit or elegance; for instance his long, unblinking dolly-shot towards the end of *Young and Innocent* – 1937. The camera moves steadily through a crowded ballroom to discover the man with the nervous eye-twitch for whom we are all looking.

But there is another side to Hitchcock. We become more and more aware of the man who has confessed to a morbid fear of the police, stemming from an incident in his childhood. In the later and greater films, this playful manipulation of fear changes into something deeper and much more disturbing.

Rear Window – 1954, for instance, is about a man confined to a wheelchair who takes to spying on his neighbours. He comes to believe he has witnessed a murder, and becomes involved in a terrifying nightmare. Hitchcock compares the cripple with the filmgoer glued to the screen and suggests that we cannot escape the attack of the

Above The famous scene from Hitchcock's *North by Northwest* – 1959, in which Cary Grant is chased across a barren prairie by a crop-dusting plane. The film is built around Hitchcock's idea of the 'McGuffin' or plot device.

Above right Orson Welles used a comparatively tired plot to make a virtuoso film of *Touch of Evil* – 1958. It can be seen as a parody of 'B' movies, with its complex story of police corruption.

Right *The Magnificent Ambersons* – 1942, portrayed an American upper-class family in decline. Following the scandals of *Citizen Kane*, Welles was strictly supervised. The film was cut from 131 to 88 minutes, and a new ending added. His second film, it reflected his vigorous approach in its camera movements and sound track.

evils we imagine. In *Vertigo* – 1958 and *Psycho* – 1960 heroines who, through their sins, have inadvertently developed insane obsessions, meet retribution. And in *The Birds* – 1965 a world fallen from grace is punished. Here Hitchcock the psychologist and moralist is secretly burrowing away, calling up disturbing echoes of morbid anxieties in the audience.

Revolt into style

Orson Welles, by contrast, belongs to another classical tradition, deriving from the German director F. W. Murnau's use of the ever-moving camera. *Citizen Kane* showed Welles to be somewhat similar to early Hitchcock – for instance in his passion for eccentric angles (including the ceilings, which caused so much comment) and his repeated use of significant close-ups (Kane's hand holding the glass ball, his lips murmuring 'Rosebud').

The Magnificent Ambersons – 1942 made one think instead of the world of John Ford. It nostalgically called up an era of gracious living gently dying under the assaults of industrial progress. The angles, close-ups and deep focus photography no longer suggest sinister plots being hatched in murky depths, but rather remote memories being dredged from forgotten corners.

Actually, Welles' style was unmistakably his own from the outset. It was a mixture of Expressionist extravagance and poetic purity. The keynote of his style is suggested by the truly magical opening sequence of *Citizen Kane*. The camera prowls past a 'No Trespassing' sign and over ornate gates up to Kane's Xanadu, a haunted castle seemingly frozen in time and sternly guarding its mysteries from prying eyes. What memories can be so painful that they are better left to die rather than risk revelation? What monster can have created them, to have so suffered from creating them?

Obsessively, Welles returns again and again to the theme of time and the mystery of the past. Charles Foster Kane amassed power, wealth and the treasures of the world only to find that they will not fill the lonely vastnesses of his Xanadu. He can only shut himself away to brood over Rosebud and the magical moment of lost innocence from his childhood. In his wake, Gregory Arkadin in *Confidential Report* – 1955, Captain Quinlan in *Touch of Evil* – 1958, Falstaff in *Chimes at Midnight* – 1966, Mr Clay in *The Immortal Story* – 1968 all look back from the maze of corruption in which they have lost themselves in their quest for power. They are searching vainly for the thread that will lead them back to their starting point. Welles is continually concerned with masks. It is no coincidence that he described that arch-intriguer, Sir John Falstaff, as the 'most completely good man in all drama'. His characters devote their lives to creating myths in which they themselves become legends. They are revealed as a series of mirror images that shatter one by one, leaving one faced not with *the* truth, but *a* truth.

Ingmar Bergman

The virtually unknown Ingmar Bergman became, overnight, something of a cultural phenomenon, as the art house film-maker whose work simply had to be seen after the revelation of *Smiles of a Summer Night* at the 1956 Cannes Film Festival. He had in fact been making films in Sweden since 1945. For the next few years of Bergmanomania, he seemed inescapable on screens everywhere as a string of dazzling new films – *The Seventh Seal* – 1957, *Wild Strawberries* – 1957, *The Virgin Spring* – 1960 – was accompanied by random unearthings of earlier ones such as *Summer Interlude* – 1950, *Summer with Monika* – 1953, *Sawdust and Tinsel* – 1953 and *A Lesson in Love* – 1956.

The result, apart from the inevitable over-saturation, was an unfortunate misunderstanding. Though glitteringly packaged in a welter of striking imagery, the films invariably deal with spiritual and physical torments, with broken marriages and sexual despairs, with symbolical quests for God and for personal identity. Behind all of them, even the comedies, lurks a sense of unrelieved gloom. Their cumulative effect was to suggest a sort of self-conscious concern with the hand of fate.

Dark themes

The Seventh Seal and *The Virgin Spring*, two of Bergman's most celebrated films, now seem his weakest. Their picturesque medievalism seems to show a deliberate attempt to revive the style and themes of the great days of the silent Swedish cinema when, just after World War I, the films of Sjöström and Stiller had led the world. Death, white-faced and hooded in black as he plays chess for the soul of the Knight in *The Seventh Seal*, might have stepped straight out of one of Sjöström's folklorish mysteries. Just as early Swedish cinema had eventually foundered in ridicule because of its perpetual and self-punishing concern with sin and redemption, so Bergman came to be mocked and parodied for his obsessive stylistic gyrations around a dark night of the Swedish soul.

We can see retrospectively that Bergman himself was always the subject of these films. His obscurely tormented childhood, his succession of unhappy marriages, his self-doubtings as an artist, his gradually waning religious faith and correspondingly mounting social concern, lays a twisted track through his work. As though to counter the misunderstanding, Bergman began a process of purification with *Through a Glass, Darkly* – 1961, *Winter Light* – 1962 and *The Silence* – 1963 – films whose very titles suggest a new asceticism. His style became not simpler but more direct. He turned inwards rather than outwards, and cut away the picturesque trappings with which he had hitherto sought to sugar the pill of his private pilgrimage.

From this point on Bergman revealed a new artistic maturity. He was freed from commercial pressures by his position as the one Swedish film-maker with an unassailable international re-

Above *Persona* – 1966 examines pitilessly the intimate responses of two disturbed women – played by Liv Ullmann and Bibi Andersson. In this film, Bergman also became concerned with the nature of film as a medium: he stipulated that stills from it should be reproduced with sprocket holes to emphasize their origin.

Left Bergman's *Wild Strawberries* – 1957 – a study in man's isolation. It traces an old man's search for self-understanding. Fascinatingly the central role of Professor Borg was played by the veteran Swedish film-maker Victor Sjöström.

Left Ingmar Bergman – born into a strict Lutheran family, his films have been obsessively concerned with private, inner struggles. He began work as a theatre director and still returns to stage directions every winter. His first work in the cinema was as a scriptwriter. His peculiarly close relationship with his players is a key to his achievement.

putation. Bergman's films became less a series of entertainments (serious or otherwise) than a continuing private journal which we are privileged to read. His films remain visually inventive and extremely striking – as the Gothic horror movie imagery of *Hour of the Wolf* – 1968 or the identity changes of *Persona* – 1966 clearly show. But the same characters reappear from one film to another, and the same themes re-emerge from the background into the foreground before fading away again. They represent, essentially, an intimate confession, in which Bergman communicates the brief illuminations that spark out of his obsessive self-exploring.

An inner journey

In 1966, continuing the logical progression, Bergman made a 16mm film about his small son Daniel (included in *Stimulantia*, a joint film with episodes by various directors). He followed this in 1969 with *Farö Document*, a documentary about the island in the Swedish archipelago where he was living and did most of his work. Both of these films are essentially home movies. They are consistent with the impulse which made Bergman cast himself in a small but key role as a priest in *The Rite* - 1969. The film is about a group of artists accused of obscenity; their defence is, in effect, that artistic creation is a kind of religious ritual. Bergman's films, increasingly filled with cross-references and personal footnotes, can no longer be fully understood in isolation from each other.

The actors from his stock company (and the characters from his repertoire) come to each new film trailing associations from their earlier screen appearances.

Bergman's shames

The same thing has always been true to some extent in his remarkably coherent and consistent output. But Bergman has steadfastly repudiated one film, even refusing to allow it to be included in retrospectives of his work. The film is *This Can't Happen Here* – 1950 (also known as *High Tension*) – reputedly a competent and highly enjoyable Hitchcock–style thriller about a Nazi plot to take over Sweden. Detailing some of the difficulties he experienced during shooting, Bergman adds: 'But something much nastier happened, too. I came into contact with some Baltic refugees. To them what we were just *playing* at was grim reality.'

What Bergman is referring to is the post-war shame on Sweden's conscience whereby a number of Baltic refugees were forcibly repatriated – to face almost certain death – by the Swedish government at the insistence of the Russians. Many years later, in *Shame* –1967, a film about the perils of neutrality and the plight of war's victims, Bergman made amends by filming a terrible nightmare vision of a sea filled with the corpses of refugees who never made it in their flight to safety. As a generalized image of the horrors of war, it is powerful enough; understood as a specific memory, it is devastating.

Above The theme of isolation central to *The Silence* – 1963 is reflected in this still from the film. The story concerns a dying woman and her sister, frustrated by unachieved desires, living in isolation in a foreign country. The central roles are played by Ingrid Thulin and Gunnel Lindblom. This is the third film in the trilogy begun by *Through a Glass Darkly* – 1961 and *Winter Light* – 1963.

Jean-Luc Godard

Jean-Luc Godard has probably had a greater influence on the cinema, for both good and ill, than any other contemporary film-maker. His first film, *Breathless* – 1959, was a phenomenal success, with its electrifying use of jump-cuts. Directors everywhere hurriedly removed transitions and continuity shots from their films, hoping to enliven the action. Heroes became insolent, amoral anti-heroes modelled on Jean-Paul Belmondo in *Breathless*. Alienation effects, disruptive switches in mood and tempo; and raw photographic realism all became fashionable musts.

None of these innovations was really new. All Godard had done was to rescue certain film-making attitudes and techniques from disuse and overlays of studio gloss. His real originality lay in his conception of character and in his refusal to prejudge. In *Breathless* the small-time hoodlum, con-man and killer who sees himself as Humphrey Bogart seems beyond defending, morally, socially or sentimentally. Yet in the long, central sequence between him and the girl who ultimately betrays him, Godard gradually switches our sympathies from her to him.

Essentially, Godard is an artist of the moment. He seizes an instant out of the air and sets it down for contemplation. This is why he rarely worked from a completed script. He preferred to rely on improvisation or inspiration to flesh out the bare bones of an outline scenario. This, too, is why his films are studded with quotations, personal reflections and apparent irrelevancies, so that *Made in USA* and *Two or Three Things I Know About Her* – (both 1966) looked almost like collages.

A sense of discovery

Most film-makers aim more or less steadily towards a gesture or a look which they are determined to get from an actor or a setting. With Godard there is a constant sense of surprise at what is revealed, often by chance, by what he has set in motion. It is this sense of discovery that is at the heart of Godard's work: an attempt to *understand* what the camera is looking at and what it means in Godard's scheme of things.

In his second film, *The Little Soldier* – 1960, for instance, Godard tackled a problem which baffled him – 'the problem of war and its moral repercussions'. He restated it through a plot involving the Algerian nationalist struggle against France, and the use of torture in support of political beliefs. He deliberately avoided the ready-made answers of a 'liberal' viewpoint. he characteristically put his hero on the wrong side, as a hired killer for the OAS, while the torturers belong to the Algerian National Front (justified, in 'liberal' eyes by their struggle against oppression). The killer gradually discovers, through his tender involvement with a girl as he does the job he has been paid to do and is tortured for it, that he has no real involvement. 'Perhaps that is what is important,' he comments, 'to learn to recognize one's own voice, one's own face'.

Above Godard's *Two or Three Things I Know About Her* – 1966 concerns a suburban housewife who once a week works as a prostitute in the centre of Paris. Godard is concerned to examine the ways that people prostitute themselves in various ways, in order to live in society today.

Left Jean-Luc Godard first got involved in films as an actor – directed by Jacques Rivette and Eric Rohmer. He later began to write regularly for *Cahiers du Cinema* before making his own films. He has rethought the aims and forms of cinema and is a major influence on many politically motivated directors.

Increasingly, Godard's films showed him trying to master his own voice and to discover his own face. He never fabricated psychological complexities for his characters through his scripts, though he always put them in provocative situations. He drew out the complexities within them by projecting his own doubts, fears and concerns as questions for the actors to try to answer. His marriage to Anna Karina was in the process of breaking up; hence the mounting note of personal distress which progressively darkens the marital bickering of *Contempt* – 1963, the romantic despair of *Bande à part* – 1964 and the bleak nihilism of *Pierrot-le-fou* – 1965. Hence, too, the growing note of concern for the dispossessed of this world, so movingly expressed in *Bande à part* and *Une Femme mariée* – 1964, as his heroines suddenly become aware of their links with those who live in economic misery.

Godard's films are like a series of extracts from a personal diary. They chronicle not only his most intimate concerns but his reactions to events outside (the Vietnam war is casually assaulted several times) and to books, films or ideas that he finds striking. Personal anguish reached a point of no return in *Pierrot-le-fou*. After it social despair begins to filter through like a watermark, grad-

ually blotting out the personal stories. He dissected the French social system in *Two or Three Things I Know About Her*, toyed with the Maoist idea of overturning it in *La Chinoise* – 1967 and left it on the brink of self-destruction (prophetic of May 1968) in *Weekend* – 1967. After this Godard left himself little alternative but to start building again from scratch.

In *Le Gai Savoir* – 1968 he re-examined the whole process of communication, by language and the cinema. In *Un Film comme les autres* – 1968 and his subsequent films he tried to draw up revolutionary principles on which he could build. These later 'political' films are almost unwatchable except as ideological statements or arguments. Godard has deliberately suppressed the visual flair and narrative genius that made his earlier films such electric experiences to watch. Now instead of asking questions, he is tending to supply answers. At the same time these political films are unmistakably the work of the same man, who is passionately devoted to the American cinema. The early Godard systematically destroyed Hollywood's most sacred conventions; the later Godard attempted to destroy cinema itself, since he saw it as an obedient servant of bourgeois society's sacred cows.

Above *Le Gai Savoir* – 1968 was one of Godard's first more overtly political films. It is concerned with how sounds and images are used in communication.

4 FILM LANGUAGE

Opinions vary about the present decade's ranking as a creative era in the history of the cinema. But most people agree that the 1970s are unprecedented as a critical era. Never have so many questions been asked about the nature of the cinema as an art. Never have so many warring factions sprung up to define and defend their different critical viewpoints.

Most of the debates have raged around the question of film as a 'language'. Literature and music each have their own code or language (words in the one case, notation in the other). Cinema seems at first glance to come nearer than any other art to being 'a mirror held up to nature' (a description first given to painting). Film, surely, is immediate and popular because it has no code. It simply reflects what passes in front of it. And unlike the music or literature critics, the film critic surely does not need to bewilder his readers with technical jargon.

But modern writers challenge this view. It is both naive and misleading to treat film merely as a 'slice of life', and the film-maker merely as a recording angel blessed with a machine which miraculously prints reality onto a strip of celluloid. The film artist selects, arranges and 'transforms' reality as much as does the artist in words and music. The means the film artist uses are now called the language of the cinema.

Film punctuation

The most obvious examples of cinema language are the technical devices which work in films as punctuation does in literature. For example the 'lap-dissolve' indicates the passage of time; the 'wipe' carries the story-line across from one scene to the next; the fade-out closes a scene or a film.

But what about the action itself – the clauses between the punctuation? Modern critics suggest that there is a 'code' at work here too. They argue that the signs and meaning of a scene are contained not only in the 'story' it tells, but in such details as the camera angle, camera movement, lighting, colour, even the clothes the characters wear. Some of these 'signs' have become so common as to qualify for the term cliché. For instance, the western villain who always wears black, and the monster whose face is made to look more horrible by low-angle lighting. Other effects have almost become punctuation – for example that time-honoured device where the calendar leaves blow away, to signal the passing of time.

A complex language

But the cinema's sign language is not confined to such easy-to-spot clichés. Recent critics have systematized the study of signs and called it 'semiology'. They have applied some of the principles of linguistic philosophy to film. They examine the subtle ways in which a film's visual messages are made up and put across. They discuss how far those messages improve (or in some cases counterpoint and contradict) the message of the script or story.

Left An evocation of the past and a clever reconstruction of memory from Welles' *Citizen Kane* – 1941. Among other things, the film is full of intense images and visual devices.

Below left Ken Russell's controversial rock-musical *Tommy* – 1975 included some striking visual material. In one scene this Hollywood stereotype of Marilyn Monroe was processed liturgically into a neo-religious ceremony.

Below Lee Van Cleef, with his eagle-like features, has become instantly recognizable as the western villain in over two hundred film and TV appearances. *For a Few Dollars More* – 1965.

This group of critics have busily investigated popular cinema, particularly Hollywood. They believe that in Hollywood there has been a continual battle between imaginative film directors and the conventional or 'limited' scripts they were asked to work with.

Reassessing the film-maker

The work of the auteurist critics has led to important film reassessments. The movies of directors such as John Ford, Howard Hawks and Alfred Hitchcock have been looked at again in the light of their continuity of theme and characteristic features of style. Ford, for example, with wide landscapes and figures silhouetted on the skyline, frames and lights his films in such a way as to emphasize the mythic heroism of his stories. But Hawks favours a rougher, crowded, more spontaneous staging that keeps the action closer and more human. Often the screenplays and stories these two directors work on might be similar. But the way they treat their films visually makes for sharp contrasts in style and attitude.

Many film-lovers have rejected semiological criticism as unnecessarily complicated. Some years ago the American journalist Pauline Kael launched a fierce and famous assault on avant garde criticism. Kael attacked pretentious critics for praising films which 'shove up bits of style through the cracks in the narrative.' She argued that they were deserting films in which script and direction work together for poorer films where they conflict.

Certainly the semiologists have given little attention to European art cinema. Indeed they tend to shy away from films in which the director wrote the script – since such films offer no scope for detective work in sifting the contribution of director from that of scriptwriter. Sometimes such critics give the impression that for them nothing sanctifies a director more than his association with a series of mediocre screenwriters.

But the work of the best writers in this field has broken new ground. Christian Metz, a follower of the French philosopher Roland Barthes, blazed the trail for semiological studies in the cinema. His work is often extremely perceptive, original, challenging and clearly-expressed. In Britain, Peter Wollen's book *Signs and Meaning in the Cinema* has become deservedly the semiologists' Bible. It summarizes and criticizes work in this field, and is the best introduction to the subject.

'Reality' in Film

What is realism in the cinema? No concept has caused more disagreement and confusion among film theorists. Is it a style that a film-maker adopts? Or a goal towards which he aims? And why does the word crop up in cinema criticism more than in any other art?

Before 'story' films were first made, cinema began as a recording technique. It simply and thrillingly presented what was passing before the cameraman's eye more accurately, and with less distortion, than any other means of reproduction. Its early ability to shock and excite stemmed entirely from its 'realism'. Filmgoers leaped from their seats in panic when an express train seemed to be hurtling out of the screen at them. The French film critic Christian Metz has neatly pointed out the uniqueness of cinema: 'The theatre is an art of representation; the cinema is an art of presentation.'

Two traditions

Throughout the cinema's history two film-making traditions have existed. One explores the possibilities of a simple, undistorted realism, and the other favours fantasy and the unreal. The second tradition made use of another of the cinema's special qualities – taking 'real' ingredients and mixing them together in fantastic forms. To the first tradition belong the Lumière brothers, documentary film-makers, the Italian neo-realists, and the underground cinema of Andy Warhol. To the second tradition belong Georges Méliès, German Expressionist cinema, the surrealist films of Buñuel and the underground cinema of Kenneth Anger.

The staunchest champion of realism both as a movie tradition and as a movie philosophy was the French critic André Bazin. His ideals for the cinema were clearness, honesty and 'transparency'. Stroheim in the silent era, Renoir in the 1930s and Rossellini in the 1940s all made films that fitted with Bazin's belief that the audience should almost never be conscious that the camera came between itself and the reality presented on the screen. Renoir, for example, allowed the camera to roam freely through extended, unedited

Right Such was the realism of the first film to be screened in London (in 1896) – the Lumières' *Arrival of a Train at a Country Station* – that it caused a panic among its audience. Their other early films included *Leaving the Factory* – 1895 and *Baby's Meal*.

Below although made entirely in the studio, G. W. Pabst's *Kameradschaft* – 1931 puts across the physical realities of mining with enormous authenticity. The film is based on an actual mine disaster on the Franco-German frontier, when German miners helped rescue their French counterparts.

scenes in his method of *'plan-sequence'*. Rossellini filmed on location for immediacy and handled his narrative in reporter-style.

The truth behind reality

But Bazin's idea of realism was curiously superficial. For him the surface truth of realism was a guarantee of deeper moral and spiritual truth. He had little patience with the idea that artistic truth can sometimes be better achieved by using the language and the artificialities of a medium rather than by pretending that the film-maker is invisible. 'Realism' has been rigorously re-examined particularly by the 'semiological' school of critics. Christian Metz wrote that: 'The filmic fact, even when it is shot in continuity, is still an arranged spectacle, a reinterpretation of the real.' But while no film is wholly realistic, he accepts that some are more realistic than others.

Two other French critics, however, Jean-Louis Comolli and Jean Narboni, pour scorn upon the very idea of realism. 'Realism is nothing but an expression of the prevailing ideology.' This teeters

on the absurd. Since the whole world, and the objects it contains, are material for the movie camera, are we to assume that the whole world (natural as well as man-made) is a 'reflection of the prevailing ideology'? Certainly the very choice of *what* a film-maker should point his camera at (let alone whether he chooses to re-edit or reorganize that reality after filming it) could be considered subjective – and therefore 'ideological'. But so could every other choice he makes – from the food he eats to the clothes he buys.

The simplest and least misleading way to consider film realism is to see film-making as a two-stage process. Stage one is 'the assembly of a series of objects in front of the camera, or, alternatively, the locating of a place where the series of objects can be found.' Stage two is transforming these objects into film language. The realistic film-maker least rearranges the raw material he chooses to place before his camera; and least stylizes, distorts or otherwise transforms that material by cinematic methods – either during shooting or later in the editing room and lab.

Above One of the clearest examples of fantasy in the cinema stems from the lavishly produced musicals of 1930s Hollywood. One example is *Golddiggers of 1933* choreographed by Busby Berkeley, with its violin-wielding chorus-girls creating kaleidescopic patterns.

Above right The theme and style of Robert Bresson's *Mouchette* – 1966 made few concessions to fantasy. The story concerns a young girl's isolation and defiance, and the cruelty which she meets.

Montage Again

At the opposite extreme to Bazin's realism was the montage theory put forward by the early Russian film-makers. For Eisenstein, Pudovkin and Kuleshov, film only became alive and meaningful when its continuity was disrupted and thereby 'improved' by cutting and editing. Kuleshov defined 'montage' as 'the organization of cinematic material'. 'The content of the shots in itself,' he wrote in 1929, 'is not so important as is the joining of two shots of different content and the method of their connection and their alternation.'

It was Kuleshov who proved his theory by the famous experiment in which the same close-up of an actor playing a prisoner is linked to two different shots representing what he 'sees': first a bowl of soup, then the open door of freedom. Audiences were convinced that the expression on the man's face was different in each instance, but it was not. The suggestive power of montage was proved beyond doubt.

Kuleshov and Pudovkin were both primarily interested in montage as a means of making the story itself more vivid and powerful as a tool of narrative. But Eisenstein saw from the first its symbolic possibilities. In his early films *Strike* – 1925 and *October* – 1928 he used shot juxtapositions in much the same way as a writer uses metaphors or similes. In *October*, for example, a shot of the Russian premier Kerensky is cross-cut with a shot of a peacock, to suggest strutting self-importance.

In other films Eisenstein rejected this over-literal and over-literary symbolism and tried to combine intellectual suggestion with emotional force. He even worked out elaborate and mathematically timed rhythms of cutting and montage, for instance in the Odessa Steps sequence in *Battleship Potemkin* – 1925. He was convinced that the film-maker could shape the reactions of his audience almost as precisely as he could shape his own films.

Eisenstein's theory
Eisenstein's theory, which he called the 'montage of attractions', had links with the philosophical system of dialectic. This system suggests that a thesis and its antithesis come together to form a synthesis. Eisenstein argued that two dissimilar shots combine to produce a third and wholly new impression. If a film showed a shot of fire, for example, and followed it with a shot of water, the audience would make the mental bridge between the two, and call to mind the extinguishing of the fire or the combining of the two elements in steam.

Other film-makers similarly moved away from the symbols of the Kerensky-peacock style of montage. Fritz Lang in *Fury* – 1936, his first American film, followed a shot of women gossiping with a shot of hens clucking. The comparison is neat but too obvious (Lang himself has since regretted putting it in). The shot of hens interrupts the otherwise naturalistic story flow.

Modern film theorists favour a more naturalistic use of symbols. Christian Metz argues that

Sergei Eisenstein was one of the most important innovators in film-editing. He suggested that the audience would become more directly involved if contrasting shots followed each other. The audience would have to resolve their apparent divergence in meaning. Eisenstein's *The Battleship Potemkin* – 1925 is probably the film where his ideas are most clearly and completely put into practice. One of the

200

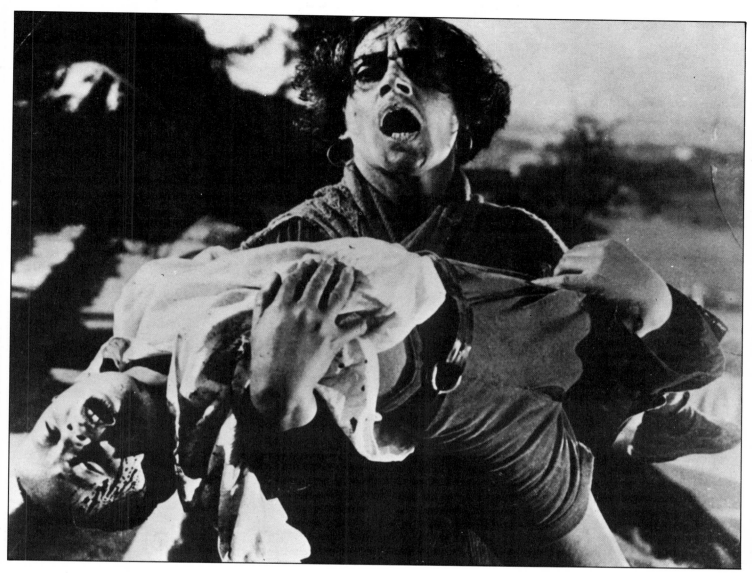

most famous examples of his work is the Odessa Steps sequence. The people of Odessa assemble to congratulate the rebels on the battleship Potemkin, **upper left**, and rush down the steps. Loyal troops appear **centre left** and open fire **left**. A young boy is killed and his mother confronts the soldiers holding her dead son **above**. The crowd panics when the troops fire again **right**.

filmic symbols have to appear 'natural'. They have to give the audience the impression that they are part of the narrative and not artificially inserted by a film-maker.

Montage and realism

Thus even the champions and practitioners of montage cinema relied upon certain basic notions of 'realism'. Kuleshov wrote: 'Before anything else, real things in real surroundings constitute cinematic materials.' For the Russian directors and theorists, the value of montage lay in its intelligent reorganization of the *real* world. The grammar of film language was new, but the individual words and letters must be crystal-clear and recognizable.

Kuleshov insisted that film is a language. It is a set of signs to be 'read' rather than a set of images simply to be seen. This prefigures the recent emergence of 'semiological' criticism. For Eisenstein, Kuleshov and the modern semiological critics, cinema has many expressive devices, conventions and 'codes of meaning'. The film-maker who neglects them is wasting the special

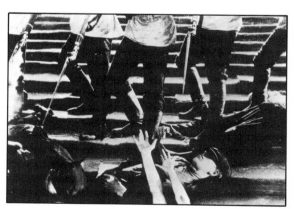

attributes of his craft. Similarly the film critic who neglects them is turning a blind eye to the subtle ways in which film, while appearing to present the simple truth, modifies, selects or stylizes that truth. Montage – at least as Eisenstein intended it – draws the filmgoer's attention to the expressive artifices of what he is seeing. It weans him from a naive belief in its seamless truthfulness and extends the experience.

'Modernity'in Film

A summary of modern trends in the cinema can best be introduced by briefly taking up the theme of montage again. The French film-maker and critic, Jacques Rivette, distinguishes four separate stages in the development of montage. First, its invention by Griffith and Eisenstein. Secondly, the change from a symbolic use of montage to purely dramatic use by Pudovkin, then by Hollywood. Thirdly, the rejection of montage and of the 'manipulative' processes of editing by the neo-realistic directors and by Bazin. Finally, the full-circle return to Eisenstein's ideas of montage in the work of modern film-makers such as Jean-Luc Godard and Alexander Kluge.

Modern critics have given the name 'collage' to this new form of montage. It differs from Eisenstein's montage in the way it flaunts rather then camouflages its disjointedness. It is no orderly process, but rather, 'a terrorist desire . . . for exploding the very notion of an "oeuvre".'

Undoubtedly the most influential modern film-maker has been Jean-Luc Godard. He may have disappeared from the mainstream of European feature film-making, but his spirit and his intelligence still haunt the cinema. They do so because Godard has led the way in three vital areas of change and new thinking in the cinema. Firstly, his use of collage and his delight in drawing on many different cultural sources (theatre, newsreel, books) have destroyed and re-shaped traditional ideas of narrative unity. Secondly, he has helped to carry over into the cinema the ideas of the dramatist Bertolt Brecht, thereby seeding one of the most fertile modern debates about film. Thirdly, he has been in the vanguard of that army of film-makers who could be described as marching under the banner 'All Cinema is Political'.

Awakening the audience

'Collage' can be seen as an attempt to awake audiences from their passivity. Filmgoers weaned on the simplicities of Hollywood expect the film and the film-maker to do the work for them, 'ordering' the experiences of life in a clean, easy, and pleasing narrative. Collage, by contrast, offers us confused, provocative and often random (especially in underground cinema) combinations of ideas and imagery. *We* must do the work in seeing or making links between them. Alexander Kluge's *Occasional Work of a Female Slave* – 1974 for instance, uses oddly-assorted bits and pieces – slogans, captions, still photographs and book illustrations – to build a complex mosaic about woman's place in society.

Some modern film-makers are preoccupied with the theories of Bertolt Brecht. Again, this is from a concern to encourage the film-goer to grow out of his need to get emotionally involved in a film – which makes him an easy prey to the film-maker's propagandizing. They aim to make him trust instead the more discriminating responses of his intellect. The drama is only a drama, Brechtians insist. The actors are only actors, moving with professional agility from one mask to another.

Left The German director Alexander Kluge was one of the leaders of a group protesting against 'Papa's cinema' in 1962. He tries to bring a new reality to film, making a collage of documentary material and acted scenes. *Occasional Work of a Female Slave* was made in 1974.

Below Wim Wenders is another of the new group of German film-makers. He allows human concerns a central place in his films, of which *The American Friend* – 1977 is a recent example.

Brechtian 'alienation' was put into practice in recent films as varied as Lindsay Anderson's *O Lucky Man!* – 1973, Jean-Luc Comolli's *La Cecilia* and Hans-Jurgen Syberberg's *Ludwig: Requiem for a Virgin King*.

The politics of film

The third modern theoretical preoccupation is politics. Political themes dominate the work of many major directors in modern cinema – Fassbinder, Oshima, Straub and the Taviani brothers. At the same time their pen-wielding colleagues the critics are busy discovering political undercurrents in the popular commercial films of today and yesterday.

Film critics have recently spent much time debating how history and the cinema are related. This is yet another attempt to identify and question the ways in which audiences are manipulated by the film-maker. The popular movies have given us emotive, romantic versions of history. A film such as René Allio's influential *Moi, Pierre Rivière*, based on a true nineteenth century murder, lays the facts before us clinically and dispassionately. The films calls upon the audience to examine and judge the evidence for itself. It asks: Is the film's main character a villain or the victim of his times? It does not provide the answer.

Some major directors of our day—Scorsese, Altman, Fassbinder, Herzog, Oshima, Bertolucci and Rosi—similarly require the audience to use its own intelligence in approaching cinema. (Though they do not all share Allio's conscientious cool-headedness.) If life is a jigsaw, it is not the artist's function to fit the pieces together. He should merely suggest different permutations, different emphases, and different lines of approach. In a century in which mankind has suffered more than ever before at the hands of political dictatorship, the conscientious film-maker does not want to occupy a platform from which he will tell other people what to do.

Below Andy Warhol has been an important influence on newer independent film-makers. He has examined the illusion of acting and low-budget film-making. *Lonesome Cowboys* – 1968 parodied the western, exploring intimately the male friendships of the genre.

The Decline of the Narrative

Have the theories and practices of avant garde cinema filtered through yet to commercial film-making? And if so, how do they show themselves? Modern film-makers wish to dismantle the old forms, to reject, or at least to question, the traditional ideas about narrative form and stylistic unity. Possibly the chief victim of this dismantling is the 'story'.

The European novel has a history of 250 years. During that time its form has changed. Once the narrator ordered the events according to his own all-wise vantage point. Today human experience is presented for us in all its raw, fragmented reality.

In the cinema the same process has been taking place. The director has stepped down from the pedestal on which he once stood to orchestrate and moralize about his story. The movie-maker is today as interested in the babble, the confusion, or the mere casual eventlessness of everyday life, as in the strong, clear contours of a well-made story. If we take two American directors of different generations, one up on the pedestal, one down milling with the crowds, we can see how the perspectives of popular cinema have changed.

D. W. Griffith inherited the traditions of the Victorian novel. For him, the artist's function was not simply to 'present' experience. The artist should choreograph life in meaningful, even moralizing, patterns. Both *The Birth of a Nation* – 1915 and *Intolerance* – 1916 give us action stories on a sweeping, panoramic scale. But the action is shaped not by the haphazard course of everyday life, nor even by historians' consensus of what happened. The films are shaped by pre-determined moral patterns imposed by the director.

The story that dictates

Robert Altman is the present-day American director who has perhaps most – and least – in common with Griffith. He works, as Griffith did, in various cinematic genres. Many of his films (*Nashville* – 1975, *Buffalo Bill and the Indians* – 1976) are epic or panoramic in scope. He is fascinated by American history and by the lessons it may teach us. Yet Altman comes half a century later. His creative approach to these areas of common interest could not be more different.

Whereas Griffith's stories are predetermined, Altman's tend to decide their own course. He gives his stories and his characters the gift of life, and sees how they use it. He makes use of improvisation, the confusion of overlapping dialogue, and screenplays that casually string together the plot's events in no fixed or didactic order. The work of Altman proclaims the all-important autonomy of his stories and his people.

The narrative has not, of course, *disappeared* in *Nashville* or *Buffalo Bill*. It has simply become a looser 'envelope' in which events and characters can move about. Nor has narrative disappeared in the films of other modern directors who use improvisation – Michael Ritchie in America, (*Downhill Racer* – 1969 and *Smile* – 1975) or Jacques Rivette in France (*L'Amour fou* – 1968,

Celine and Julie Go Boating – 1974). What have disappeared are the moral certainties that told the director 'this is how the story ought to be'.

People began to question narrative conventions again at the end of the 1950s. American underground cinema and the French New Wave erupted simultaneously. American underground film-makers attacked orthodox narrative forms from two sides. Andy Warhol simply pointed the camera (and left it running) at virtually anything that moved—laissez-faire realism. Kenneth Anger created an anarchic fantasy world in which experience was re-fashioned in whatever perverse, magical and outlandish ways he wanted.

Godard the revolutionary

The French New Wave directors did not depart so radically from narrative traditions. But their influence has been just as far-reaching, possibly more so. In the first wave came Godard's *Breathless* – 1960, Truffaut's *Shoot the Pianist* (*Please Don't Shoot the Piano Player* in US) – 1960

and Resnais' *Last Year in Marienbad* – 1961. In the second wave were Rivette's *L'Amour fou* – 1968 and *Out One: Spectre* – 1973. They showed that it was often fruitful to subvert, and play *against* rules and expectations of the 'story'.

Godard's work, and to a lesser extent that of Truffaut, Resnais and Rivette, revolutionized the narrative film. Those who consider Hollywood to be a bastion of prosperous philistinism might be surprised and interested to know that Godard was asked to direct *Bonnie and Clyde* before the project was offered to Arthur Penn. That coincidence is ironic, for *Bonnie and Clyde* (even without Godard) turned out to be one of the most revolutionary popular films Hollywood has ever produced. It refused to make a judgement about its criminal characters; its inventive and brilliantly free-wheeling story-telling technique broke new frontiers. It gave narrative cinema a new freedom and a new flexibility, and it improved the chances of adventurous young directors getting their films made, shown and widely appreciated.

Future Directions 1

What happens next is anybody's guess. Hollywood, we are told, no longer exists – and this is certainly true so far as the old studio system (and its mass production of films) is concerned. Yet all the warnings of doom, all the forecasts that soon the shrinking market would mean that the only possible way to make films would be in the home-movie manner of *cinéma-vérité* or the underground, seem premature with 'traditional' films such as *The Godfather* – 1972, *Jaws* – 1975, *Star Wars* – 1977 and *Close Encounters of the Third Kind* – 1977 still triumphantly breaking cinema box-office records.

There is still money in movies, even though it is more difficult to earn. This fact in itself is probably enough to guarantee the continuance of cinema in more or less the form that we know it. There are other reasons – the most significant from a practical point of view being television's inability to press its advantage and make cinema entirely obsolete.

The TV challenge

In theory, television is an immediate medium – of people in close-up talking directly from the screen into the home. In practice, now that virtually all programmes are filmed, and movies are being made directly for television, there is (in theory)

nothing the cinema could do that television cannot. Yet in TV movies, plays and drama serials television tends to look like the cinema's poor and shabby relation, doing its best to dress up for the occasion. In its lighting and camera movements, for instance, the BBC's much-vaunted *Forsythe Saga* – 1967 would hardly have passed muster in the great days of the Hollywood studios. Compared with the dazzling elegance and subtlety of films by great visual stylists such as von Sternberg, it hardly gets off the ground.

Part of the reason for this may lie in a vague idea, (deriving from endless debates about the nature of television) that 'immediacy' is more important than 'visual style'. When directors trained in television come to the cinema, they almost always overplay the close-up. However Bernardo Bertolucci, for one, has avoided this trait: for example his *The Spider's Strategem* – 1970 was made for Italian television; when shown on the big screen it is, if anything, even subtler and more sophisticated visually than his work for the cinema. Bertolucci, however, conceived, prepared and shot *The Spider's Strategem* not only from a background in cinema, but with cinema screenings in mind. The style of Fassbinder, too, is apparently unaffected when employed in strictly TV productions. But innumerable Hollywood film tech-

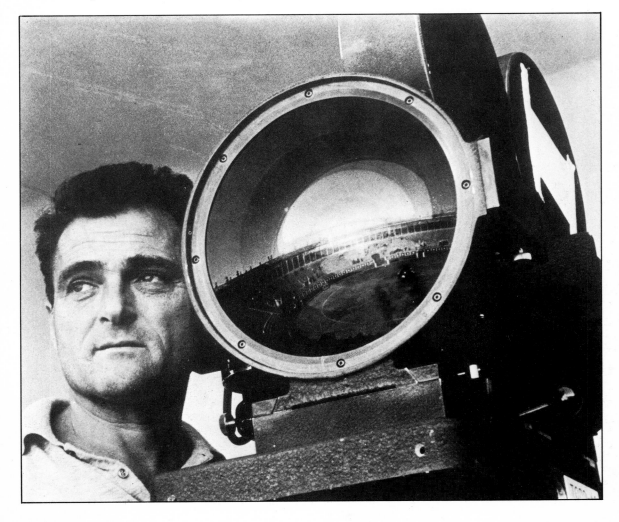

Left During the 1950s many attempts were made to apply new technology to cinema to meet the challenge of television. Todd-AO was developed by the American Optical Co. for Mike Todd, the US film producer, who is seen here with the special camera required. The process produced a widescreen image, and was used for such successful films as *Oklahoma!* – 1955 and *Around the World in Eighty Days* – 1956.

nicians complained, after moving into television, that their perfectionist skills had to be left behind.

Rapidly developing every corner- and cost-cutting technique imaginable, television swiftly became a cut-price version of the cinema. It pioneered, notably, the use of multiple cameras in filming, a technique which saves time and money (the choice of views and angles means that there is a better chance of a usable take), but also lowers visual standards. (Sternberg's systematic use of shadows, of the play between darkness and light, would have been impossible if his cameraman had had to generalize his lighting, so that a scene could be covered from several angles.) On the small screen subtle visual effects tend to be obscured anyway by the squeezing of the image; this technical simplification is not necessarily seen as a deficiency at all.

Cinema's superiority

Basically it is this technical wizardry which lures audiences away from their television sets to films such as *Close Encounters* and *Star Wars*. Hollywood recognized this fact during its panic-stricken campaign of the 1950s to counter the threat of television – but mistakenly saw it purely in terms of size. Fumbling, awkward, often embarrassingly inadequate, the new techniques

(or rather, abandonment of mastered ones) necessitated by the escalation of screen sizes from CinemaScope to Cinerama, did as much as television to endanger the cinema's existence until many directors gave it an artistic raison d'être in the 1950s and 1960s. Now that cinema screens and images have settled down again to a more modest size, the cinema has regained its edge. It does things that television cannot do.

At the same time watching movie re-runs on television leads to the conclusion that good films do not necessarily look good on television. Comedies mysteriously lose much of their precise timing. Westerns lose their 'great open spaces', so that the first appearance of the Indians in *Stagecoach* – 1939, or of the train looming inevitably out of the distance at the beginning of *Bad day at Black Rock* – 1954, go for practically nothing. This is largely because the viewer dominates the television set, but is dominated by the cinema screen.

This all suggests that if the cinema is to survive as both entertainment and art form, it must do so in cinemas rather than by way of television re-runs or television movies. The cinema *is* likely to survive; witness the extraordinary growth of interest in its past, present and future in recent years.

Below Cinerama represented another attempt to extend the visual impact of film, by using a much wider screen than normal. The original system used three projectors and three curved screens, involving the audience intensely in the action. *This is Cinerama* – 1952 was a successful demonstration of the possibilities of the system.

Future Directions 2

Cinema becomes respectable

Even as recently as 1950, mention of cinema in academic circles was usually met by raised eyebrows and a smile: 'Yes, I used to like the pictures too when I was a kid'. Today, university film departments are commonplace. Archives busily unearth and restore lost prints. More and more specialist cinemas ensure that film history is living rather than dead. Innumerable books are published, and research undertaken, attempting to unravel the facts of the past. The *nature* of the cinema is eagerly and exhaustively examined – not only its achievements and its possibilities, but its historical, sociological, aesthetic and cultural implications. It becomes increasingly clear that it has finally been accepted as an art form in its own right.

Given the cinema's strong dependence on finance, it is naturally possible to foresee a time when even the most enlightened backers might find the risks too discouraging. Film-makers would then find it increasingly difficult to finance even the most modest project. Faced by such a situation, most of the great masters from cinema history would probably have been upset but not

entirely disoriented. Great filmmakers such as Hawks and Ford always claimed that they were just 'hard-nosed directors' doing a job of work, with no idea that they were creating art. This attitude may stem from a certain coyness in the face of belated praise (until the 1960s, few – if any – film-makers were thought equal to say, Picasso, James Joyce or Richard Strauss). But these veterans worked at a time (the 1920s and 1930s) when the cinema was creating internationally a new order of artistic modes and practices.

After 1960, and the French *New Wave*, the climate was altogether different. This was the first generation of film-makers brought up on cinema, not only eating, sleeping and thinking it, but assuming it to be an art form. Today in both Europe and Hollywood the film-makers doing some of the best (and most profitable) work – such as Martin Scorsese, Francis Ford Coppola, John Carpenter and Steven Spielberg – feel the same way. To them the cinema is not simply an art form but their means of expression. And if an artist wants to express himself, he will find a way, even if it leads through an increasingly tortuous quest for non-existent finance.

Below George Lucas' *Star Wars* – 1977 is a film which uses all the resources of modern cinema for its technically dazzling effects, and is seen to advantage only on the cinema screen as opposed to the small TV screen. It also lined up a starry cast that included Sir Alec Guinness and Peter Cushing.

REFERENCE
SECTION

6

A-Z FILMMAKERS AND ACTORS

These notes give some information about some of the most influential and best known (by no means always the same thing) figures in world cinema, although there is a bias towards current and English-speaking cinema. Any such list is inevitably subjective. Most of the people are directors and actors, with a few influential producers. Dates given for films are release dates in country of production. Book publication details refer to publication in country of origin.

ALDRICH, Robert

(1918–) US director/writer/producer who worked his way up the industry hierarchy in the 1940s. He formed his own production company in 1955, when he produced and directed two of his finest films, *Kiss Me Deadly* – 1955, a bleak psychological thriller, and *The Big Knife* – 1955, about corruption in the movie business. His anarchistic attitude towards the system is often reflected in his work. Always seeking independence, he bought his own studio in 1968. After several failures, including *The Killing of Sister George* – 1968, he sold the studio and returned to the open market. Aldrich is probably best known for his recent work with Burt Reynolds in the 'action' genre, for example *The Mean Machine* – 1974. He also collaborated earlier with radical figures such as Robert Rossen – *Body and Soul*, – 1947, and Abraham Polonsky – *Force of Evil* – 1949, for Enterprise Productions. His essays in the grotesque, such as *Whatever Happened to Baby Jane* – 1962 are also of interest. His work is uneven, as shown by the excesses of *The Choirboys* – 1977.

Other films include:
Vera Cruz – 1954, *The Dirty Dozen* – 1967, *The Legend of Lylah Clare* – 1968, *Twilight's Last Gleaming* – 1977.

Further reading:
Robert Aldrich, ed. Richard Combs, British Film Institute, London, 1978.

ALLEN, Woody

(1935–) US actor/writer/director – small and skinny, with large eyes peering from behind spectacles, and thinning reddish hair. His habitual film personality is insecure, inspired in his attempts to cope with a hostile world (although usually unsuccessful) and randy. After writing extensively for TV comedy series, he scripted and acted in *What's New Pussycat?* – 1968. His first film as director of original material *Take the Money and Run* – 1969, typically rifled film and TV conventions for a series of inventive gags, the whole an uneven, loosely structured, but often very funny film, as were his next four films as director. His films were characterized by his self-critical, mordant, Jewish humour. However, *Annie Hall* – 1977 marked a new coherence, its story apparently based on Allen's private relationship with its star, Diane Keaton. Received with critical enthusiasm, it won four Oscars. With *Interiors* – 1978 Allen took a bold step, with a serious study, apparently heavily influenced by Bergman.

Other films as director include:
Bananas – 1971, *Everything You Always Wanted to Know About Sex but Were Afraid to Ask* – 1972, *Sleeper* – 1973, *Love and Death* – 1975.

Further reading:
On Being Funny: Woody Allen and Comedy Eric Lax. Charterhouse, New York, 1975.

ALTMAN, Robert

(1925–) US director who gained expertise in directing in television before making his first film *The Delinquents* – 1957. His fifth film *M*A*S*H* – 1970, a zany comedy was a box office success. Since then he has consistently used such successes to win freedom to experiment with subject matter and techniques. These have included overlapping dialogue, a very mobile camera and actors' improvisation. His work is not to all critical tastes. But *McCabe and Mrs Miller* – 1971, *The Long Goodbye* – 1973, *California Split* – 1974 and *Nashville* – 1975 have received particular praise from those who point to his attempts to avoid imposing a structure, leaving the spectator a role in constructing the film. Undoubtedly Altman is important as a filmmaker who is willing to take chances. His practice of fully involving his actors, particularly in improvisation, enables them to do some of their best work.

Other films include:
That Cold Day in the Park – 1969, *Brewster McCloud* 1970, *Images* – 1972, *Thieves Like Us* – 1974, *Three Women* – 1977, *A Wedding* – 1978.

ANDERSON, Lindsay

(1923–) British director who, despite a fairly small film output, has been influential in British cinema, both through his criticism, notably in *Sequence* and *Sight & Sound*, and his uncompromising filmmaking practice. His documentaries include *Thursday's Children* – 1953, which won an Oscar, and *O Dreamland!* – 1953 and *Every Day Except Christmas* – 1957, about Covent Garden which formed part of the Free Cinema programmes put on at the National Film Theatre by Karel Reisz. His first feature *This Sporting Life* – 1963, was widely acclaimed as a powerful, emotional study of a rugby footballer and his painful relationship with a lonely widow, told partly through flashbacks. *If . . .* 1968 attacked the English public school system, using it as a metaphor for Western society. *O Lucky Man!* – 1973 used the same rebel-hero, Malcom McDowell. The film is marred by its ill-digested use of styles and techniques borrowed from Godard and Fellini. Since then Anderson has concentrated on the stage, except for a filmed version of his production of David Storey's *In Celebration* – 1974.

Further reading:
Lindsay Anderson Elizabeth Sussex, Studio Vista, London, 1969.

ANDREWS, Julie

(1935–) British singer/actress, who was a child singing star. Her first film, *Mary Poppins* – 1964, cast her well as a no-nonsense, magic-performing nanny. In the enormously popular *The Sound of Music* – 1965, her freshness and slight tartness helped to leaven the sentimentality of the stage original. She has tried to break away from her 'wholesome' image, but audiences seem to have been uneasy with her love scenes in *The Americanization of Emily* – 1964, and *Torn Curtain* – 1966. The delightful *Thoroughly Modern Millie* – 1967 gave her another unsophisticated role. Recent films have been for director husband Blake Edwards, notably *Darling Lili* – 1970. Recently her career has tended to play second place to her family life.

Other films include:
Hawaii – 1966, *Star!* – 1968, *The Tamarind Seed* – 1974.

Further reading:
Julie Andrews: a biography Robert Windeler, W. H. Allen, London, 1970.

ANTONIONI, Michelangelo

(1912–) Italian director/scriptwriter who made several documentaries before directing his first feature *Cronaca di un amore* – 1950. Its story of a fatal love affair drew on the romantic melodrama tradition which feeds much of his work and shows his use of the environment to express human emotions. The bleakness of urban architecture was most striking in *La notte* – 1961. *L'avventura* – 1960 was greeted by catcalls at the Cannes Film Festival. It received widespread admiration for its elegantly photographed portrayal of disillusion and alienation, and its psychological study of character. It also marks the beginning of his partnership with actress Monica Vitti. His career has fluctuated in recent years. Films made in England and America, *Blow-Up* – 1966, and *Zabriskie Point* – 1970, met with very mixed reactions. More recently he has completed a documentary on China, *Chung Kuo* – 1972. *The Passenger* – 1975 marked a return to his concern with the problems of identity and existence in the modern world.

Other films include:
Le amiche – 1955, *L'eclisse* – 1962, *The Red Desert* – 1964.

Further reading:
Antonioni Ian Cameron and Robin Wood, Studio Vista, London, 1968.

ASTAIRE, Fred

(1899–) US dancer/singer/actor whose first starring role, in *Flying Down to Rio* – 1933, teamed him with Ginger Rogers. This marked the beginning of a legendary partnership which included *Top Hat* – 1935 and *Swingtime* – 1936. A brilliant and dedicated dancer, he was the uncredited choreographer of most of his numbers. His grace, style and modest charm have probably been appreciated as much in the 1970s as at any other time in his career. Three of his finest films were made at the end of his screen dancing career – *The Band Wagon* – 1953, *Funny Face* – 1956 and *Silk Stockings* – 1957. His last musical was *Finian's Rainbow* – 1968. Astaire still continues to work as a straight actor and on TV.

Other films include:
Carefree – 1938, *You Were Never Lovelier* – 1942, *Blue Skies* – 1946, *Yolande and the Thief* – 1946, *Easter Parade* – 1948, *The Belle of New York* – 1952, *The Pleasure of His Company* – 1961, *The Towering Inferno* – 1974.

Further reading:
Starring Fred Astaire
Stanley Green and Burt
Goldblatt, Dodd Mead,
New York, 1973.

ATTENBOROUGH, Richard

(1923–) British actor/
producer/director who
spent the first half of his
career as an actor. He was
often cast as the cockney
weakling stereotype of his
first film, *In Which We
Serve* – 1942, and made
several successful films
with the Boulting brothers.
He moved to production
with Bryan Forbes for *The
Angry Silence* – 1960, in
which he played the ostra-
cized blackleg. He gave
one of his best perfor-
mances in Forbes' *Seance
on a Wet Afternoon* – 1964.
His directing career began
with *Oh! What a Lovely
War* – 1969, an uneven
attempt to transfer Joan
Littlewood's brilliant and
moving stage production
to the screen, with a no-
tably starry English cast. He
has established himself as a
reliable, if unexciting, director of big budget pictures
with *The Young Winston* –
1972, and *A Bridge Too Far*
– 1977.

Other films include:
(as actor) *Brighton Rock* –
1947, *Private's Progress* –
1956, *Guns at Batasi* –
1964: as director: *Maggie* –
1979.

BARDOT, Brigitte

(1934–) French actress
whose 'sex-kitten' image is
now legendary. During the
1950s and early 1960s she
became famous in roles
which presented her as a
rebellious, pouting in-
nocent who was sexually
aggressive. This image was
taken up and exploited by
her first husband Roger
Vadim, a director of art-
house erotic films, in *And
God Created Woman* –
1956. In spite of, or be-
cause of, her one-
dimensional quality, 'BB'
aroused the interest of
French radical intellectuals
such as Jean Cocteau,
Simone de Beauvoir and
Jean-Luc Godard (who

used her in his film about
the movie business,
Contempt – 1963). She has
worked with such distin-
guished directors as René
Clair, Henri-Georges
Clouzot and Louis Malle.

Other films include:
Doctor at Sea – 1955,
Masculin-feminin – 1965,
Shalako – 1968, *Et si Don
Juan etait une femme* –
1973.

Further reading:
*Bebe: the films of Brigitte
Bardot* Tony Crawley, LSP
Books, London 1975.

BEATTY, Warren

(1937–) US actor who
reached stardom with his
first film *Splendour in the
Grass* – 1960. His lazy
charm makes him a popular
sex symbol, but he is also
an intelligent and gifted
actor. He has been involved
in some of the most in-
teresting films to have
come out of Hollywood in
the 1960s and 1970s. They
include *Lilith* – 1964,
Robert Rossen's haunting
and complex study of mad-
ness, *Mickey One* – 1965, a
powerfully paranoic film,
and *McCabe and Mrs
Miller* – 1972, Altman's
view of the reality behind
the western myth. He has
also shown sound judge-
ment as a producer with
Bonnie and Clyde – 1967,
and *Shampoo* – 1976, taking a further step forward
with *Heaven Can Wait* –
1978, which he co-wrote
and co-directed as well as
producing and starring in.

Other films include:
All Fall Down – 1962,
Promise Her Anything –
1963, *The Only Game in
Town* – 1969, *The Heist* –
1971.

BERGMAN, Ingmar;
see p.192.

BERGMAN, Ingrid

(1915–) Swedish actress
who captivated audiences
with her freshness and sincerity in her first American
film *Intermezzo* (UK,
Escape to Happiness) –

1940. She continued to
delight them in such films
as *Casablanca* – 1942,
Gaslight (UK, *Murder in
Thornton Square*) – 1944,
which won her an Oscar,
and *Notorious* – 1946. But
the Americans, who had
idolized her, puritanically
rejected her when she give
birth to Rossellini's child
before they were married.
Since then she has worked
in Europe, where films have
included *Viaggio in Italia* –
1953, the best of several
directed by Rossellini, the
enchanting *Elena et les
Hommes* – 1955, *Indiscreet*
– 1958, a romantic comedy
with Cary Grant, and *The
Inn of the Sixth Happiness*
– 1958. She made a tri-
umphant return to
Hollywood for one of her
best roles in *Cactus Flower*
– 1967. In recent years she
has worked mostly on the
stage.

Other films include:
For Whom the Bell Tolls –
1943, *Spellbound* – 1945,
Joan of Arc – 1948,
Anastasia – 1956, *Autumn
Sonata* – 1978.

Further reading:
Ingrid Bergman Curtis F.
Brown, Pyramid, New
York, 1973.

BERKELEY, Busby

(1895–1976) US director
celebrated for his elaborate
and inventive staging as
dance director. Despite his
Broadway origins, he used
a mobile camera. He shot
so that a number's rhythms
and structure emerged at
the editing table rather than
on the studio floor. With
this went the Ziegfeld
tradition of treating women
as objects to be viewed as
decorative pieces of the
pattern. His most lavish
work is in such Warner
Brothers films as *42nd
Street* – 1933, the *Gold
Diggers* films (1933–38)
and *Dames* – 1934. In 1939
he moved to MGM and
directed, among others, the
Judy Garland/Mickey
Rooney musicals such as
Babes in Arms – 1939,
before reverting to dance
direction only.

Other films include:
They Made Me a Criminal –
1939, *For Me and My Gal* –
1942, *The Gang's All Here*
– 1943.

Further reading:
The Busby Berkeley Book,
Tony Thomas and Jim
Terry, New York Graphic
Society, New York 1973.

BERTOLUCCI, Bernardo

(1940–) Italian director
whose first feature film *La
commare secca* – 1962,
based on a treatment by
Pasolini, for whom he had
previously worked as an
assistant director, was a
fascinating exploration of a
prostitute's murder. It was a
remarkable achievement
for a 22-year-old. *Before
the Revolution* – 1964 confirmed his promise. But his
best film is probably *The
Spider's Stratagem* – 1970,
again an investigation of a
murder. This time the
hero's father (played by the
same actor) is the victim.
The audience is skilfully
drawn with him into the
complexities of the past
and its secrets. *The Con-
formist* – 1970, and *1900* –
1976 are both elegant and
beautifully photographed
films, but lack substance
despite their overtly political themes. *Last Tango in
Paris* – 1972, controversial
for its explicit depiction of
sex, explores desolation
and cruelty.

Other films include:
Partner – 1968, *The Moon*
– 1979.

BOGARDE, Dirk

(1921–) Intelligent and
sensitive British actor who
came to the cinema via the
theatre. After two bit parts
he won the leading part in
Esther Waters – 1947. A
long-term contract with
Rank tied him to roles
which offered little scope.
However he took what
chances there were, no-
tably in *The Blue Lamp* –
1950, and *Hunted* – 1952.
He showed courage in
playing a homosexual hero
in *Victim* – 1961, and gave
an unselfish performance
opposite Judy Garland in
her last film *I Could Go On
Singing* – 1963. But his
present high reputation as
an actor was established
through his work with
Joseph Losey in *The
Servant* – 1963, *King and
Country* – 1964 and
Accident – 1966. Visconti
directed his much praised
performance in *Death in
Venice* – 1971, although
some would value more
highly Bogarde's contri-
bution to Resnais'
Providence – 1977.

Other films include:
Doctor in the House –
1954, *The Doctor's
Dilemma* – 1958, *Song*

Without End – 1960, *The
Singer Not the Song* –
1960, *Darling* – 1965, *The
Night Porter* – 1973,
Despair – 1978.

Further reading:
The Films of Dirk Bogarde
Margaret Hinxman and
Susan D'Arcy, Literary
Services and Production,
London, 1974.

BOGART, Humphrey

(1899–1957) US actor,
with a slight lisp, drawling
delivery and bemused
world-weary look. He
made over forty films be-
fore becoming a major star
with *The Maltese Falcon* –
1942, playing Sam Spade a
tough, cynical but honour-
able, private eye. He took a
series of similar roles in
films such as *Casablanca* –
1943, *To Have and Have
Not* – 1944, (in which he
co-starred for the first time
with Lauren Bacall, who
became his wife) and *The
Big Sleep* – 1946. In the
1950s he had a wider range
of parts. He won an Oscar
for *The African Queen* –
1951, and praise for his
performance as the
psychopathic Queeg in *The
Caine Mutiny* – 1954.

Other films include:
High Sierra – 1942, *Dark
Passage* – 1947, *The
Treasure of Sierra Madre* –
1948, *In a Lonely Place* –
1950, *The Barefoot
Contessa* – 1954, *We're No
Angels* – 1954, *The Harder
They Fall* – 1956.

Further reading:
Humphrey Bogart
Nathaniel Benchley, Little
Brown, New York, 1975.

BRANDO, Marlon

(1924–) US actor who
achieved fame in his re-
markable performance in *A
Streetcar Named Desire* –
1951, in which he repeated
his stage role as the crude,
inarticulate Kowalski. His
mumbling delivery became
a byword, despite an articulate performance in
Julius Caesar – 1953. He is
probably at his best in

strong, masculine roles to which he brings a brooding power, in films such as *On the Waterfront* – 1954 (for which he won an Oscar), *One-Eyed Jacks* – 1961, which he produced and directed, and *The Chase* – 1966. The most popular produce of the New York school of 'method' acting, he was a radical influence, setting aside superficial charm in favour of brutal conviction and physical suffering. In recent years he has taken up the cause of racial minorities and had a popular success as *The Godfather* – 1972. In the notorious *Last Tango in Paris* – 1973 he gave a disturbing, introspective performance which seemed uncomfortably close to self-revelation.

Other films include:
Viva Zapata! – 1952, *Mutiny on the Bounty* – 1962, *Reflections in a Golden Eye* – 1967, *Burn!* – 1968, *Apocalypse Now* – 1978.

Further reading:
Brando, David Shipman, Macmillan, London, 1974.

BRESSON, Robert

(1907–) French director whose austere style reflects a bleak world of deprivation and suffering redeemed by the Roman Catholic doctrine of grace. His films provoke extreme reactions: great admiration or total rejection. His *Journal d'un curé de campagne* – 1951, was the film in which he began his practice of using non-actors. It is a deeply moving account of a young priest who is dying, and is perhaps his most accessible film. Some see his work as mannered and boring. Others point to the intensity produced by the sparseness of his treatment. For example in *Au hazard, Balthazar* – 1966 the sufferings of a donkey are both a picaresque device and a parable of the world which he inhabits. The final scene, in which the dying donkey is slowly engulfed by a flock of sheep, is one of the most poignant in cinema.

Other films include:
A Man Escaped – 1956, *Pickpocket* – 1959, *Mouchette* – 1966, *A Gentle Creature* – 1969, *Four Nights of a Dreamer* – 1971, *Lancelot du lac* – 1974, *Le Diable probablement* – 1977.

Further reading:
The films of Robert Bresson Ian Cameron, Studio Vista, London, 1969.

BRYNNER, Yul

(1916–) Russian-born US actor who worked for several years as a television director after his arrival in America in 1940. His trademark has been the bald head which he first displayed as the King of Siam on stage and then on screen in *The King and I* – 1956. His range as an actor is rather limited. He is probably most effective as the enigmatic gunfighter in *The Magnificent Seven* – 1960, and *Invitation to a Gunfighter* – 1964.

Other films include:
Anastasia – 1956, *The Sound and the Fury* – 1959, *Villa Rides* – 1968, *The Madwoman of Chaillot* – 1969, *Westworld* – 1973.

BUNUEL, Luis

(1910–) Spanish-born director whose first films *Un Chien Andalou* – 1929, made with Salvador Dali, and *L'Age d'or* – 1930 were major contributions to the French Surrealist movement. They ferociously attacked bourgeois society and ideas in images designed to shock and amuse. In 1946 Buñuel began directing again, in Mexico, where he made about twenty films. The third, *The Young and the Damned* – 1950, which won a first prize at Cannes, firmly re-established his international reputation. Other titles include the lighthearted *Subida al cielo* – 1951, *El* – 1952, a tale of obsessive jealousy, *The Criminal Life of Archibaldo de la Cruz* – 1955, a black comedy – a favourite style of Buñuel's – the unusually gentle *The Young One* – 1960, and *Nazarin* – 1958, variously interpreted as be-

ing critical of, or sympathetic, to its priest hero. This led to his return to Spain to make *Viridiana* – 1961. Since this unmistakably attacked the Catholic church, controversy resulted. Meanwhile Buñuel had resettled in France, where *Belle de jour* – 1966 was announced as his last film. Happily over ten years later he is still making master works such as *Tristaña* – 1970, and *That Obscure Object of Desire* – 1977, still attacking the establishment, examining sexual repression and slyly playing with the conscience of his audience.

Other films include:
Susana – 1950, *The Exterminating Angel* – 1962, *Simon of the Desert* – 1965, *La voie Lactée* – 1969, *The Discreet Charm of the Bourgeoisie* – 1972, *Le fantôme de la libertée* – 1974.

Further reading:
Luis Buñuel: a Critical Biography, J. Francisco Aranda, Secker & Warburg, London, 1975.

BURTON, Richard

(1925–) Welsh actor who for a time combined a distinguished stage career with films. He made several modest British features before going to Hollywood to star in *My Cousin Rachel* – 1953, and *The Robe* – 1953. *Cleopatra* – 1963, and his meeting with Elizabeth Taylor, made him a household name. He did most of his best film work in the early years of their marriage, opposite her in *Who's Afraid of Virginia Woolf?* – 1966, and *The Taming of the Shrew* – 1967, and with others in *The Night of the Iguana* – 1964, and *The Spy Who Came in from the Cold* – 1965. Sadly today he seems a major talent who has never reached his full potential, perhaps because he can rely too easily on a rich voice and an actor's presence.

Other films include:
The Last Days of Dolwyn – 1948, *Look Back in Anger* – 1959, *Becket* – 1964, *Dr Faustus* – 1967, *Equus* – 1977.

Further reading:
Richard Burton: a biography John Cottrell and Fergus Cashlin, Arthur Barker, London, 1971.

CAGNEY, James

(1899–) US actor who began his career as a song and dance man. He tends to be associated with gangster parts, as in *Public Enemy* – 1931, (in which he caused a stir by pushing a half grapefruit into his girl friend's face), *Angels With Dirty Faces* – 1938 and *White Heat* – 1949. His performances have enormous energy and an edgy abrasive charm. The dancer's skills, which make him quick and agile, were used more directly in *Footlight Parade* – 1933 and *Yankee Doodle Dandy* – 1942, for which he won an Oscar. His energy was displayed to almost exhausting effect in his last film, a Billy Wilder comedy *One, Two, Three* – 1962. He directed *Short Cut to Hell*, a remake of *This Gun for Hire*, in 1957.

Other films include:
The Crowd Roars – 1932, *Jimmy the Gent* – 1934, *A Midsummer Night's Dream* – 1935, *The Strawberry Blonde* – 1941, *Love Me or Leave Me* – 1955, *Tribute to a Bad Man* – 1956.

Further reading:
Cagney: the actor as auteur, Patrick McGilligan, A. S. Barnes, South Brunswick; Tantivy Press, London, 1975.

CAPRA, Frank

(1897–) Hollywood director whose career began with the silent comedies' star Harry Langdon in *The Strong Man* – 1926. In the 1930s he made a string of films which championed the American political movement known as Populism. He utilised plots in which small-town heroes and whimsical minor characters confront villains personifying a heartless free-enterprise spirit. The best examples are *Mr Deeds Goes to Town* – 1936, and *It's a Wonderful Life* – 1946, which used the folksy personas of stars Gary Cooper and James Stewart respectively as John Doe characters. Capra is best known for his untypical *It Happened One Night* – 1934. Its bedroom scene between Clark Gable

and Claudette Colbert effectively challenged the repressive censorship of the Hays Code, and it coincidentally won an Oscar.

Other films include:
Platinum Blonde – 1932, *Lost Horizon* – 1937, *You Can't Take it With You* – 1938, *Mr Smith Goes to Washington* – 1939, *A Pocketful of Miracles* – 1961.

Further reading:
Frank Capra: The Man and His Films: Richard Glatzer and John Raeburn, University of Michigan Press, 1975.

CASSAVETES, John

(1929–) US actor/director whose first film as director, *Shadows* – 1959, influenced a generation of young experimental film-makers by its low-budget production and improvisational style. His next two films made in Hollywood were commercial failures. He could get no backing for projects until *Faces* – 1968. Meanwhile he acted in films such as *The Killers* – 1964 and *Rosemary's Baby* – 1968, investing his roles with a peculiar intensity. Cassavetes works with a repertory of actors which includes his wife, Gena Rowlands, and friends Ben Gazzara and Peter Falk. He employs a relentless *cinema-verite* technique to observe human behaviour. This method can be both painfully revealing and extremely amusing, as in *Husbands* – 1969, in which he also appeared. Continuing to observe people cracking-up under the strain of being human, he directed his wife and Peter Falk in the highly acclaimed *A Woman Under the Influence* – 1974. His development of an 'objective' style of dealing with highly-charged subject matter is very effective in *Opening Night* – 1977.

Other films include:
(as actor) *A Man is Ten Feet Tall* – 1957, *The Dirty Dozen* – 1967; (as director) *Too Late Blues* – 1961, *A Child is Waiting* – 1962.
Further reading:
Hollywood Renaissance Diane Jacobs, Tantivy Press, London, 1977.

CHABROL, Claude
(1930–) French director who came to the cinema via film criticism. He made his first film, *Le beau Serge*, in 1958 and is regarded as a founder member of the French New Wave. A prolific and highly accomplished film-maker (working for TV as well as cinema) he collaborates regularly with the same actors and technicians, notably his actress wife Stephane Audran, and Jean Rabier, Jacques Gaillard and Pierre Jansen who respectively have photographed, edited and composed music for most of his films. Characteristically Chabrol's films tend to use the thriller form to explore and question the mores and morals of the French bourgeoisie. But his career has been interestingly unpredictable. In such assured masterpieces as *La Femme infidèle* – 1968, and *Le Boucher* – 1969 he contrasts ironically a lyrical style with brutal themes.
Other films include:
Les Cousins – 1958, *Les Bonnes Femmes* – 1960, *Les Biches* – 1968, *La Rupture* – 1970, *Les Noces rouges* – 1973, *Nada* – 1974, *Une Partie de plaisir* – 1974, *Violette Nozière* – 1978, *Blood Relatives* – 1978.
Further reading:
Claude Chabrol Robin Wood and Michael Walker, London, 1970.

CHAPLIN, Charles Spencer
(1889–1977) British actor/comedian/director who rose from vaudeville to become perhaps the greatest clown the cinema has yet known. Working for Mack Sennett in the Keystone Comedies, he rocketed to fame in classic silent one-and two- reelers. He developed the comic style which became 'The Tramp' – the little man at odds with a hostile environment – who was to capture the imagination of the world.

He was soon producing and directing his own films. After the coming of sound he extended his comic vision to produce a satire on modern industrial society, *Modern Times* – 1936. The paranoid political climate of the 1940s and 1950s in the USA was unsympathetic to Chaplin's work, and he was exiled after making *Limelight* – 1952. With the change of climate in the 1960s he was able to get American backing for *The Countess from Hong Kong* – 1967. He was greeted by a standing ovation when he returned to the States in 1972 for the Oscar ceremony.
Other films include:
The Immigrant – 1917, *A Woman of Paris* – 1923, *The Gold Rush* – 1925, *The Great Dictator* – 1940, *Monsieur Verdoux* – 1947, *A King in New York* – 1957.
Further reading:
Chaplin's Films Uno Asplund, David and Charles, Newton Abbot, 1973.

CHRISTIE, Julie
(1940–) British actress who attracted attention with her performance as the free-wheeling heroine in *Billy Liar* – 1963. *Darling* – 1965, a second film for Schlesinger especially designed for her, brought her an Oscar and the leading part in *Doctor Zhivago* – 1965, which confirmed her star status. But it was Losey's *The Go-Between* – 1971 which gave her one of her best parts, as the teasing, selfish, unhappy daughter of the house, who dazzles the small boy hero and uses him in her love affair. Her relationship with Warren Beatty led to an excellent performance opposite him as the madam in *McCabe and Mrs Miller* – 1971. She also starred in his *Shampoo* – 1974, after her troubled wife in *Don't Look Now* – 1973, one of

several films in which she offers an engaging mixture of vulnerability and eager friendliness.
Other films include:
Fahrenheit 451 – 1966, *Petulia* – 1968, *Demon Seed* – 1977, *Heaven Can Wait* – 1978.

CONNERY, Sean
(1930–) Scottish actor best known for his portrayal of James Bond in six commercially very successful films beginning with *Dr No* – 1963. Before this his film roles had been rather routine. By contrast his television work had included an excellent performance in *The Crucible*. He has become an international star, working in Hollywood for *Marnie* – 1964 and *The Molly Maguires* – 1970. He has been based in Europe during the 1970s, seeking to break away from the Bond image, notably as an anti-romantic Robin Hood in *Robin and Marian* – 1976, and as the hero who brings about his own destruction in *The Man Who Would Be King* – 1977.
Other films include:
From Russia With Love – 1964, *The Hill* – 1965, *The Anderson Tapes* – 1971, *Zardoz* – 1973, *The Wind and the Lion* – 1975.

COOPER, Gary
(1901–1961) US actor whose apparent naturalness on screen disguised very considerable acting skill. He is particularly associated with westerns. His biggest initial impact was as the laconic, tough, shy hero of *The Virginian* – 1929, and he won an Oscar for his part in *High Noon* – 1952. Tall and lanky, his performances have a sweetness and grace which endeared him to audiences. His wide variety of films included love stories such as the moving *A Farewell to Arms* – 1932, war films such as *Sergeant York* – 1941, for which he won another Oscar, and especially comedies such as *Desire* – 1936, and *Mr Deeds Goes to Town* – 1936. He continued playing starring roles until his death.
Other films include:
Morocco – 1930, *The Lives of a Bengal Lancer* – 1935, *Bluebeard's Eighth Wife* – 1938, *For Whom the Bell*

Tolls – 1943, *The Fountainhead* – 1949, *Friendly Persuasion* – 1956, *Love in the Afternoon* – 1957, *Man of the West* – 1958, *The Hanging Tree* – 1959.
Further reading:
Gary Cooper René Jordan, Pyramid Publications, New York, 1974.

COPPOLA, Francis Ford
(1939–) US director/writer who was given his first chance to direct a feature by Roger Corman with *Dementia 13* – 1963. He has since himself enabled George Lucas to make his first two films through his company, American Zoetrope. His work as a scriptwriter includes joint credit for the intelligent, equivocal, Oscar-winning script for *Patton – Lust for Glory* – 1969. The considerable box office success of *The Godfather* – 1972, which, with *The Godfather Part II* – 1974, has been edited into a nine-hour TV version, enabled him to make *The Conversation* – 1974. This is an acute study of the paranoid world of a private detective, whose own speciality of bugging is apparently turned against him to destroy the precious privacy which he has taken from others. Coppola is also responsible for *Finian's Rainbow* – 1968, which, though uneven, is also one of the few truly cinematic musicals to be produced since the golden days of MGM.
Other films include:
You're a Big Boy Now – 1967, *The Rain People* – 1969, *Apocalypse Now* – 1978.

CORMAN, Roger
(1926–) US producer/director with a shrewd eye for box office success and young talent. He specialized in small-budget,

exploitation films on which directors such as Coppola, Bogdanovich and Scorsese cut their artistic teeth. As a director, he is probably best known for a series of elegant, witty horror films, based on Edgar Allen Poe stories and starring Vincent Price, some made in England in the 1960s. *The Tomb of Ligea* – 1964 is generally the most highly regarded of these. *The Terror* – 1963, shot in three days utilizing the left-over resources of *The Raven* – 1963, stands as a remarkable *tour de force*. Since his return to the States, he has concentrated on production. He has also directed two of his most distinguished films – *The St Valentine's Day Massacre* – 1967 and *Bloody Mama* – 1970 – both gangster films.
Other films include:
Swamp Women – 1956, *Machine Gun Kelly* – 1958, *The Haunted Palace* – 1963, *The Masque of the Red Death* – 1964, *The Trip* – 1967.
Further reading:
Roger Corman David Will and Paul Willemen, Edinburgh Film Festival, 1970.

COSTA-GAVRAS, Costi
(1933–) Director of Russo-Greek ancestry, based in France. His first film was a big-budget, star-studded mystery thriller, *The Sleeping Car Murders* – 1965. It established his concern with complex plots and aesthetic images. Little in his early films prepared critics for *Z* – 1969. This film earned an international reputation for its explicitness on political issues, and was used to attack the Greek Colonels' junta of the time. In subsequent films, *The Confession* – 1970 and *State of Siege* – 1972 especially, he has attempted to develop a militant and political cinema in the thriller form in an attempt to reach popular audiences. The extent to which he has succeeded in this, and the nature of the compromises made on the way, are much debated. It is noteworthy that his films find audiences at all in an extremely conservative industry.
Other films include:
Un Homme de trop – 1967, *Section Speciale* – 1975, *Clair Dessin* – 1978.

CRAWFORD, Joan

(1908–1977) US actress whose large, rather protruding eyes, strong jaw and heavily painted mouth make her instantly recognizable. Her phenomenally long career as a star seems to owe much to toughness and shrewdness. Her eighteen years at MGM, included *Our Dancing Daughters* – 1928, *Grand Hotel* – 1932, and a successful teaming with Clark Gable, notably in their eighth and last film together, *Strange Cargo* – 1940. She is best known for a series of films made at Warners. This began with *Mildred Pierce* – 1945, for which she won an Oscar, and continued with such films as *Humoresque* – 1946 and *Possessed* – 1947. These provided her with roles which combined ruthlessness and self-assurance with self-sacrifice and suffering in varying proportions.

Other films include:
Possessed – 1931, *The Women* – 1939, *A Woman's Face* – 1941, *Harriet Craig* – 1950, *Johnny Guitar* – 1954, *Whatever Happened to Baby Jane* – 1962.
Further reading:
Joan Crawford Stephen Harvey, Pyramid Publications, New York, 1974.

CUKOR, George

(1899–) US director who, since moving from Broadway to Hollywood in 1929, has had a long and continuing career as a highly regarded 'professional' who pays particular attention to design. He is a sympathetic director of actors, and actresses in particular. A successful association with Katharine Hepburn spans eight films, from her first *A Bill of Divorcement* – 1932 to the recent *Love Among the Ruins* – 1975. They include some of Cukor's best work, with the stylish high society comedy *The Philadelphia Story* – 1940 and a series of films with Spencer Tracy, such as *Adam's Rib* – 1949, which also featured Judy Holliday. He also directed Tracy in the enchanting *The Actress* – 1953. In 1954 he turned his hand to musicals with the powerful Judy Garland version of *A Star Is Born* – 1954 and later directed *My Fair Lady* – 1964.
Other films include:
David Copperfield – 1933, *Camille* – 1937, *A Woman's Face* – 1941, *Born Yesterday* – 1950, *Pat and Mike* – 1952, *Let's Make Love* – 1960, *The Blue Bird* – 1976, *The Corn is Green* – 1978.
Further reading:
Cukor, Carlos Clarens, Secker & Warburg, London, 1976.

DAVIS, Bette

(1908–) US actress with a sulky mouth, prominent eyes and distinctive staccato voice, who is one of Hollywood's major stars. Previously dissatisfied with her career at Warners, her fine performance as the wilful Southern belle in *Jezebel* – 1938 gave her the power to choose her own parts. The next few years marked the peak of her career. She shone in dramatic parts in films such as *Dark Victory* – 1939 and *The Old Maid* – 1939 often playing strong women suffering through self-sacrifice. At her peak she could transform a banal script into a moving performance by the intensity of her acting, but later this became increasingly mannered and artificial. She was poor in *Beyond the Forest* – 1949, but at her best as the fading stage star in *All About Eve* – 1950. In 1961 she played the grotesquely ageing child star in *Whatever Happened to Baby Jane?* – 1962. This led to a series of horror films such as *The Nanny* – 1965 and, for television, *The Dark Secret of Harvest Home* – 1978.

Other films include:
Of Human Bondage – 1934, *Now Voyager* – 1942, *A Stolen Life* – 1946.
Further reading:
Mother Goddam Whitney Stine and Bette Davis, Hawthorn Books, New York, 1974.

DAY, Doris

(1924–) US actress/singer/dancer who rose to fame initially through her ability to put over a number with verve. In some of her early musicals she appeared ludicrously naive. Occasionally, as in *Calamity Jane* – 1953, she displayed a control of zany slapstick humour which was to make her the biggest box-office star of the 1960s. Often criticized for the anachronistic puritanism of her image, as the all-American girl-next-door holding on to her virginity in the interests of marriage, she has nevertheless managed to play a wide variety of parts within that stereotype. She even subverted it slightly in the more farcical comedies such as *That Touch of Mink* – 1962 and *Caprice* – 1967. She remained a popular star in the 1970s, working mainly in television from 1968.
Other films include:
The Man Who Knew Too Much – 1955, *Move Over Darling* – 1963, *The Glass Bottom Boat* – 1966.
Further reading:
Doris Day, George Morris, Pyramid, New York, 1976.

DEAN, James

(1931–1955) US actor, whose death in a badly wrecked sports car, immediately after completing his third starring role in *Giant* – 1956, meshed with his screen image in *East of Eden* – 1955 and *Rebel Without a Cause* – 1955 as a misunderstood, unhappy and rebellious teenager, to create an instant myth. He remains a potent figure, the subject of books, articles, films and even a stage musical made in 1977.
Other films include
(bit parts): *Fixed Bayonets* – 1951, *Has Anybody Seen My Gal?* – 1951.
Further reading:
James Dean, John Howlett, Plexus Publishing, London, 1975.

DE HAVILLAND, Olivia

(1916–) US actress who made her screen debut as Hermia in Reinhardt's nightmarish account of *A Midsummer Night's Dream* – 1935. She was unhappy with the undemanding, sweet heroine parts which mainly followed, and which led to her almost automatic casting as Melanie in *Gone With the Wind* – 1939. She won the legal battle Bette Davis had lost, and prevented Warners from adding suspension periods to her seven year contract. As a freelance, she won Oscars for *To Each His Own* – 1946 and *The Heiress* – 1949. She semiretired on her marriage to a Frenchman. Subsequent films have included the underrated *The Light in a Piazza* – 1961 and *Hush, Hush Sweet Charlotte* – 1964, with old friend Bette Davis.
Other films include:
Captain Blood – 1935, *The Adventures of Robin Hood* – 1938, *The Snake Pit* – 1948, *My Cousin Rachel* – 1952, *The Swarm* – 1978.

DEMILLE, Cecil B.

(1881–1959) US producer/director whose name became synonymous with cinema spectacle with such films as *The Ten Commandments* – 1923, his last and seventieth film as director in 1956 – and his own favourite, *King of Kings* – 1927, *Cleopatra* – 1934 and *Samson and Delilah* – 1949. His first film as director, *The Squaw Man* – 1913 was also the first film to be made in Hollywood, and made a lot of money. He soon became established as an independent producer/director. He cleverly exploited contradictory impulses in American society by filming moral tales in which the sinners did quite a bit of lively sinning before properly repenting or coming to a bad end. The titles were appropriate—*Don't Change Your Husband* – 1919, *Why Change Your Wife?* – 1920, both starring Gloria Swanson, *Manslaughter* – 1922, with its Roman orgy, *Feet of Clay* – 1924 and *The Golden Bed* – 1925.
Other films as director include:
The Cheat – 1915, *The Trail of the Lonesome Pine* – 1916, *Joan the Woman* – 1917, *The Sign of the Cross* – 1932, *Union Pacific* – 1939, *The Greatest Show on Earth* – 1952.
Further reading:
The Autobiography of Cecil B. DeMille Donald Haynes, W. H. Allen, London, 1960.

DENEUVE, Catherine

(1943–) French actress; a statuesque, cool blonde. She starred in films for Jacques Demy – *Umbrellas of Cherbourg* – 1964, and Luis Buñuel – *Belle de jour* – 1967 and *Tristana* – 1970. Her one role in a British film, directed by the Polish Roman Polański, was in *Repulsion* – 1965. She played a hallucinating frigid woman, a role typical of her films. Her occasional appearances in American films have not brought her critical or popular acclaim; the most distinctive has been in Robert Aldrich's *Hustle* – 1976.
Other films include:
The Young Girls of Rochefort – 1967, *Mayerling* – 1968, *La Sirène du Mississippi* – 1969, *The Magic Donkey* – 1971.

DE NIRO Robert

(1943–) US actor who began in the theatre. He was given his first film parts by Brian de Palma in *Greetings* – 1969 and *The Wedding Party* – 1969. He is particularly associated with Martin Scorsese – both of them reaching stardom together with *Mean Streets* – 1973. *Taxi Driver* – 1976 is perhaps the most impressive of their collaborations, with De Niro giving a remarkable performance as the hating, vengeful hero. Although capable of gentleness, his performances have a nervous edgy excitement, suggesting somebody it would be

wise not to cross.
Other films include:
Bloody Mama – 1970, *The Godfather Part II* – 1974, *1900* – 1976, *New York, New York* – 1977, *The Deer Hunter* – 1979.

DE PALMA, Brian
(1940–) One of Hollywood's 'new wave' of young directors. His knowledge of film history is reflected in his sophisticated filming vocabulary. The influence of Godard, important for the anarchic *Greetings* – 1968, his first success, gave way to Freud and Hitchcock. *Sisters* – 1972, also made independently, is a parody thriller which 'quotes' from Hitchcock and Polański. *Obsession* – 1976 re-works Hitchcock's rarely-seen *Vertigo* – 1957, taking its Freudian themes of guilt and obsession to bizarre lengths. His latest film *The Fury* – 1978 is a characteristically surreal mixture of espionage and telekinesis. His reputation comes from his awareness of the political possibilities of film-making.
Other films include:
Hi Mom! – 1970, *The Phantom of the Paradise* – 1974, *Carrie* – 1976.
Further reading:
The Film Director as Superstar Joseph Gelmis, Doubleday and Co. Inc., New York, 1970.

DIETRICH, Marlene
(1901–) German-born actress who began working in Hollywood under the direction of Josef von Sternberg. This followed her success as the femme fatale Lola in his *The Blue Angel* – 1930. He helped her to become a major star in such films as *Morocco* – 1930 and *Shanghai Express* – 1932. She appeared to similarly good advantage in Mamoulian's *The Song of Songs* – 1933. Films made after 1936, and her last film with Sternberg, rarely used her blend of sophistication, wit and sexually ambivalent charm to best advantage, although *Angel* – 1937, *Destry Rides Again* – 1939 and *Rancho Notorious* – 1952 were notable exceptions. However she has found an appropriate setting in her more recent and highly successful career as a nightclub singer.

Other films include:
The Devil is a Woman – 1935, *Desire* – 1936, *A Foreign Affair* – 1948, *Touch of Evil* – 1958, *Just a Gigolo* – 1978.
Further reading:
Marlene Dietrich John Kobal, Studio Vista, London, 1968.

DISNEY, Walt
(1901–1966) US animator and legendary overseer of the most successful conglomerate producing films and other entertainment forms for the family market. The full animation and abstract conceptions within the first feature-length animated film, *Snow White and the Seven Dwarfs* – 1937, and titles such as *Bambi* – 1943 and the more up-market *Fantasia* — 1940 have justified critical admiration. Films made since the 1960s, and especially since Disney's death – notably *The Revengers* – 1977 – have relied more on the formula of songs and stories about children and anthropomorphized animals threatened by evil forces. Disney Studios also popularized documentaries, as in *The Living Desert* – 1953, and produced conventional 'live-action' features such as *Treasure Island* – 1950. In later years the studios developed live-action/cartoon features, the best of which is probably *Mary Poppins* – 1964. Disney is immortalized as the creator of Mickey Mouse, a character who represents Americana globally better than coke and Uncle Sam.
Other films include:
Pinocchio – 1939, *Cinderella* – 1950, *One Hundred and One Dalmatians* – 1961, *Robin Hood* – 1973.
Further reading:
The Art of Walt Disney Christopher Finch, Harry N. Abrams, New York, 1973,

New American Library, 1975.

DONEN, Stanley
(1924–) US director and choreographer. Donen's significance largely begins and ends in his collaboration with Gene Kelly on three classic MGM musicals of which *Singin' in The Rain* – 1952 is arguably the best. Outside the musical form, Donen's career is chequered. His wholly untypical musical *The Pajama Game* – 1957 is one of the few fims to support trade unionism. He has directed light thrillers such as the entertaining *Charade* – 1963, and the ponderous *The Grass is Greener* – 1961, both starring Cary Grant, and comedies which have been sophisticated, such as *Two for the Road* – 1967, and madcap, such as, *Bedazzled* – 1967. Without collaborators to provide subjects and scripts, Donen's style tends to be anonymous.
Other films include:
On The Town (co-director) – 1949, *Seven Brides for Seven Brothers* – 1954, *It's Always Fair Weather* (co-director) – 1955, *Funny Face* – 1957, *The Little Prince* – 1973, *Movie, Movie* – 1978

DOUGLAS, Kirk
(1916–) US actor who came into supporting film roles from theatre. His film personality is arrogant and cynical, often with a manic streak. It is well displayed in *Lust for Life* – 1956, in which he played Van Gogh, and in *The Vikings* – 1958. His range is versatile, however, having played a wholly ruthless and unlikable reporter in *Ace in the Hole* – 1951, an anachronistic cowboy in the modern western *Lonely Are The Brave* – 1962 and a likable rogue in the comedy western *The Way West* – 1967. All these qualities are at work in arguably his most impressive performance, as an alienated businessman suffering from the menopause and the ghosts of his past, in Elia Kazan's *The Arrangement* – 1969.
Other films include:
Out of the Past – 1947, *Champion* – 1949, *The Big Sky* – 1952, *The Bad and the Beautiful* – 1952, *Gunfight at the OK Corral* – 1957, *Paths of Glory* – 1957, *Spartacus* – 1960, *A*

Man to Respect – 1972.
Further reading:
Kirk Douglas Joseph McBride, Pyramid, New York, 1976.

DREYER, Carl Theodor
(1889–1968) Danish writer/director who many people regard as one of the great artists of the cinema. He translates his fatalistic view of the human condition into haunting and unforgettable images, with a masterly control of the cinematic medium. Dreyer held artistic control over every aspect of his films with an obstinacy which explains the small number of films he actually made. Characteristically those films reflect a profoundly religious concern with human suffering and frustrated desire. The symptoms of frustration break out in the form of the 'unnatural': witches (*La Passion de Jeanne d'Arc* – 1927, *Day of Wrath* – 1943) or vampires, as in the most compelling and mysterious of his films, *Vampyr* – 1932. Dreyer is remarkable for his portrayal of strong heroines: women who demand too much and are isolated as a consequence, such as the central character in his last film *Gertrud* – 1964, in which the oppressive atmosphere is precisely captured by relentless camera movements and static acting.
Other films include:
Mikaël – 1924, *Master of the House* – 1925, *Ordet* – 1954.
Further reading:
The Cinema of Carl Dreyer Tom Milne, Zwemmer, London; Barnes, New York, 1971.

EASTWOOD, Clint
(1930–) US actor/ director who was pitch-forked to stardom, after some years as an actor, as 'The Man with No Name' in a series of Italian westerns. *Coogan's Bluff* – 1968 the first film to be made by Eastwood's own company, Malpaso, marked the beginning of a felicitous working relationship with director Don Siegel. They

also produced an effective gothic tale, *The Beguiled* – 1971, and the first of three films about a maverick policeman *Dirty Harry* – 1971. His career as a director began with *Play Misty for Me* – 1971, an intelligent and gripping thriller in which he also starred, as he has tended to do in his subsequent films. (*Breezy* – 1973, a delicately handled love story, is an exception.) Eastwood has tended to be underrated both as an actor and as a director. The accomplishment of *The Outlaw Josey Wales* – 1976, with its subversion of 'The Man with No Name' character, and *The Gauntlet* – 1977, which similarly questions Harry Callahan, seem to have marked a turning point in his career.

Other films include:
High Plains Drifter – 1972, *The Eiger Sanction* – 1975, *Every Which Way but Loose* – 1978.
Further reading:
Clint Eastwood: All-American Hero David Downing and Gary Herman, Octopus Press, London, 1977.

FAIRBANKS, Douglas
(1883–1939) US actor who is famed for his swashbuckling heroes in a series of handsomely produced historical adventures including *Robin Hood* – 1922, and *The Thief of Bagdad* – 1924. The healthy body made him an outstanding athlete. It was matched (so far as the American public was concerned apparently) by a healthy mind, and his eight inspirational books were

popular. His marriage to Mary Pickford in 1920 delighted their respective fans. Together they dominated Hollywood society, but *The Taming of the Shrew* – 1929 was their only film together. Their marriage broke down subsequently – a tragedy for both of them. His son, Douglas Fairbanks Jr, has also had a successful acting career.

Other films include:
The Americano – 1916, *A Modern Musketeer* – 1918, *The Three Musketeers* – 1921, *The Black Pirate* – 1926, *The Private Life of Don Juan* – 1934.

Further reading:
Douglas Fairbanks; The making of a screen character Alistair Cooke, Museum of Modern Art, New York, 1940.

FASSBINDER, Rainer Werner
(1946–) German director/writer/actor whose early film work is spare in style (not in quantity, he is notoriously prolific). He uses devices drawn in part from the theatre (where he began and has continued) as in *Pioniere in Ingolstadt* – 1970 – one of six features made in that year. However his films have become increasingly glossy and stylish as he has successfully sought wider audiences for his critiques of capitalism, once neatly described as 'soap operas of everyday fascism'. For many, his most interesting work dates from the early 1970s and includes *The Merchant of the Four Seasons* – 1971, *The Bitter Tears of Petra von Kant* – 1972, *Fear Eats the soul* – 1973, loosely based on *All That Heaven Allows* (Sirk and Hollywood melodrama are acknowledged influences), *Martha* – 1973 and *Effi Briest* – 1974. More recent films such as *Angst vor der Angst* – 1975, *Chinese Roulette* – 1976 and the English-language *Despair* – 1978 are technically superb but arid. Lacking any positive ideas or characters, they suffer from sterile pessimism.

Other films include:
Warnung vor einer heiligen Nutte – 1970, *Fox* (*Fox and his Friends* in US) – 1975.

Further reading:
Fassbinder Tony Rayns,

British Film Institute, London, 1976.

FELLINI, Federico
(1921–) Italian director who worked with Rossellini before directing his first film *The White Sheikh* – 1952. *La strada* – 1955 was a much admired film which starred his wife Giulietta Masina as a kind of holy fool. But it was *La dolce vita* – 1960, with its exposé of decadent Roman society, which consolidated his critical reputation and established him commercially. His next film, *8½* – 1963, marked a distinct shift, with fantasy and reality blended together as in a dream, and an increased emphasis on images from his childhood, which-had already emerged in his earlier work. His status as a star-director is reflected in the title of one of his later films, *Fellini–Satyricon* – 1969. These have tended to become increasingly flamboyant and sensational. However *Amarcord* – 1974, set in the Rimini of Fellini's childhood, struck a quieter, gentler note.

Other films include:
I Vitelloni – 1953, *Juliet of the Spirits* – 1965, *Roma* – 1972, *Casanova* – 1977.

Further reading:
Fellini on Fellini Anna Keel and Christian Strich, Eyre Methuen, London, 1976.

FIELDS, W. C.
(1879–1946) US actor/comedian who began his career as a juggler with vaudeville. He was a successful stage actor before he made his first film in 1915 (*Pool Sharks*). He made his best films in the late 1930s for Universal Studios, when he was allowed to write his own material. Field's comic screen image was based on a profoundly misanthropic view of the world: nobody

could be trusted, least of all women, children, bankers and dogs. He had an unmistakable face – bulbous nose and puffy features – coupled with a nasal delivery, and reinforced by a nervous twitch. These made him the least sympathetic of all Hollywood's comedians, and one of the most successful.

Other films include:
So's Your Old Man – 1926, *David Copperfield* – 1935, *My Little Chickadee* – 1940, *Bank Dick* – 1940.

Further reading:
The Films of W. C. Fields Donald Deschner, Citadel Press, New York, 1966.

FLYNN, Errol
(1909–1959) Irish-born US actor who was Hollywood's most successful and attractive swashbuckler, especially when teamed opposite Olivia de Havilland in *Captain Blood* – 1935, *The Charge of the Light Brigade* – 1936 and *The Adventures of Robin Hood* – 1938. If the charm did not quite conceal a certain air of conceit, much could be forgiven so handsome a hero. His scandalous private life (exploited by himself in his memoirs *My Wicked Wicked Ways*) apparently added spice to his efficient, but rather limited screen performances, before eventually destroying his health and his career.

Other films include:
The Private Lives of Elizabeth and Essex – 1939, *Dodge City* – 1939, *They Died With Their Boots On* – 1941, *Objective, Burma!* – 1945, *Against All Flags* – 1952, *The Roots of Heaven* – 1958, *The Sun Also Rises* – 1957.

Further reading:
Errol Flynn George Morris, Pyramid Publications, New York, 1975.

FONDA, Henry
(1905–) US actor from the stage with one of the most complex screen personas in Hollywood cinema. An honest naivety was established in *You Only Live Once* – 1937, came to the fore in *My Darling Clementine* – 1946, and was still at work as late as *Firecreek* – 1967. He also displays unsympathetic qualities of social disdain and emotional coldness, seen at their best in the roles of the martinet in

Fort Apache – 1948, and the brutal gunfighter in *Once Upon A Time in the West* – 1969. Most of his roles are as representatives of the American liberal conscience, whether in westerns—most often sheriffs, as in *The Tin Star* – 1957 – or in realist dramas such as *Twelve Angry Men* – 1957, and *Fail Safe* – 1964, in which he played the ultimate authority-figure, the President. The range of roles and rich persona is not only a mark of his versatility as an actor, but also his importance.

Other films include:
Jezebel – 1938, *Young Mr Lincoln* – 1939, *The Grapes of Wrath* – 1940, *War and Peace* – 1956, *The Wrong Man* – 1956, *Advise and Consent* – 1961, *Madigan* – 1968.

Further reading:
Henry Fonda Michael Kerbal, Pyramid, New York, 1975.

FONDA, Jane
(1937–) US actress who acquired a 'sex-object' image early in her career. It was reinforced by a period in France in the 1960s, where she married Roger Vadim, who directed her in *Barbarella* – 1968. However, at home she began to produce interesting performances, demonstrating her talent for comedy in *Barefoot In The Park* – 1967. She won an Oscar nomination for *They Shoot Horses Don't They?* – 1969, and began to campaign against the Vietnam War. Influenced by the women's movement, she has continued to develop as an actress: tough yet vulnerable as the prostitute in *Klute* – 1971, and struggling with the problem of an illusory independence in *Julia* – 1977 and *Coming Home* – 1978.

Other films include:
Cat Ballou – 1965, *A Doll's House* – 1973.

Further reading:
Jane Thomas Kiernan, Putnam, New York, 1973.

FORBES, Bryan
(1926) British actor/writer/director/producer, who began as an actor, but soon started scriptwriting. After the success of their first film as producers, *The Angry Silence* – 1960, he and Attenborough set up Beaver Films together. He made his debut as director with *Whistle Down the Wind* – 1961, which managed to avoid the major pitfalls of a tricky subject involving children who believe an escaped prisoner is Christ. Much of his best work as a director was done in the early 1960s, including *The L-Shaped Room* – 1963, *Seance on a Wet Afternoon* – 1964 and *King Rat* – 1965 in Hollywood. From 1969 to 1971 he was a controversial head of production for EMI. He has since returned to writing and direction, notably with an effective re-working of Cinderella – *The Slipper and the Rose* – 1975.

Other films as director include:
The Whisperers – 1966, *The Raging Moon* – 1971, *International Velvet* – 1978.

Further reading:
Notes for a Life Bryan Forbes, Collins, London, 1974.

FORD, John;
see p. 190.

FREED, Arthur
(1894–1973) US producer and songwriter who was the key figure in the production of the great MGM musicals of the 1940s and 1950s. His first film as producer was *The Wizard Of Oz* – 1939, for which he manoeuvred successfully to get Judy Garland, then relatively unknown. From *Meet Me in St Louis* – 1944 onwards he had his own production unit, in which a crucial figure was Roger Edens. The names of some of the people he recruited and supported tell it all: Vincente Minnelli, Gene Kelly, Stanley Donen, Charles Walters, Irene Sharaff, Robert Alton, Busby Berkeley, Cyd Charisse, Fred Astaire, Rouben Mamoulian and Lennie Hayton.

Other films as producer include:

For Me and My Gal – 1942, *Easter Parade* – 1948, *On the Town* – 1949, *An American in Paris* – 1951, *Singin' in the Rain* – 1952, *The Band Wagon* – 1953, *Silk Stockings* – 1957, *Gigi* – 1958.

Further reading:

The World of Entertainment Hugh Fordin, Doubleday, New York, 1975.

GABLE, Clark

(1901–1960) US actor known as 'The King' after the success of *It Happened One Night* – 1934, for which he won an Oscar. It is his role as Rhett Butler in *Gone With the Wind* –1939 which has assured him of a place in the history books. The part seemed tailor-made for his style of easy male arrogance, coupled with a tough directness. This image had been polished over some ten years at MGM, where he co-starred opposite Jean Harlow, notably in *Red Dust* – 1932, Joan Crawford, with whom he made eight films, and Myrna Loy. His last film, *The Misfits* – 1961, gave him one of his most suitable parts, as an ageing, tough cowboy.

Other films include:

A Free Soul – 1931, *Manhattan Melodrama* – 1934, *China Seas* – 1935, *San Francisco* – 1936, *The Hucksters* – 1947, *The Tall Men* – 1955.

Further reading:

Clark Gable René Jordan, Pyramid Publications, New York, 1973.

GARBO, Greta

(1905–) Swedish actress whose great beauty, combined with considerable reserve, and an early retirement, have made her an object of fascination. Typically she plays passionate women suffering for, or destroyed by, their love, as in *Anna Karenina* – 1935, (also made as *Love* – 1928) and *Camille* – 1936. She also played women themselves the cause of destruction for the men who came under their spell,

as in *The Torrent* – 1926 (her first film after she came to Hollywood with Swedish film director Mauritz Stiller), and *Mata Hari* – 1932. Apart from *Camille*, her finest performance is as *Queen Christina* – 1933. Her films, which have always been more popular in Europe than in America, are frequently revived, and show her magic and erotic power to be undimmed.

Other films include:

The Atonement of Gosta Berling – 1924, *Flesh and the Devil* – 1927, *Anna Christie* – 1930, *Ninotchka* – 1939.

Further reading:

Greta Garbo Richard Corliss, Pyramid Publications, New York, 1974.

GARLAND, Judy

(1922–1969) US actress/singer of considerable talent, who sadly found the pressures of fame too much for her. She had a touching gaucheness as a child and adolescent, when she often co-starred with Mickey Rooney. The high point was *The Wizard of Oz* – 1939. She successfully made the transition to adult roles in a series of excellent musicals, notably *Meet Me In St Louis* – 1944 and *The Pirate* – 1948, directed by her second husband, Vincente Minnelli. He also directed her in a touching love story, *The Clock* – 1944. After *Easter Parade* – 1948 her life became an often unsuccessful struggle to overcome recurring breakdowns. A remarkable series of stage concerts brought her back to Hollywood for an unqualified triumph in *A Star Is Born* – 1954, her last musical. She died of an overdose shortly after her fifth marriage.

Other films include:

For Me and My Gal – 1942, *In the Good Old Summertime* – 1949, *Judgement at Nuremberg* – 1961, *I Could Go On Singing* – 1963.

Further reading:

Judy Gerold Frank, Harper & Row, New York, 1975.

GISH, Lillian

(1896–) US actress who was one of D. W. Griffith's working associates. She was the most remarkable of the talented group of actresses who worked for

him. She has a delicate, frail beauty combined with a strength and intensity seen well in the dramas *Broken Blossoms* – 1919, *Way Down East* – 1920. *The Scarlet Letter* – 1926 and *The Wind* – 1928. Her range is wide; one of her most enchanting performances is in the title role of the charming comedy *True Heart Susie* – 1919. With the coming of sound she went back to the stage where she has continued to work with distinction, as she has in television. She returned to Hollywood in the 1940s, since when she has played a variety of roles. These include the prickly almoner in *The Cobweb* – 1958, and the kindly, resourceful Miss Rachel in *The Night of the Hunter* – 1955.

Other films include:

The Birth of a Nation – 1915, *The White Sister* – 1923, *La Bohème* – 1926, *Duel in the Sun* – 1946, *The Unforgiven* – 1960, *The Comedians* – 1967, *A Wedding* – 1978.

Further reading:

The Movies, Mr. Griffith and Me, Lillian Gish and Ann Pinchot, Prentice-Hall, Englewood Cliffs, 1969.

GODARD, Jean-Luc;

see p. 194.

GRABLE, Betty

(1916–1973) US actress who appeared in mainly small parts from 1930 onwards. She replaced Alice Faye in *Down Argentine Way* – 1940 to become 20th Century-Fox's biggest star in a series of rather unenterprising musicals, including *Coney Island* – 1943, *Diamond Horseshoe* – 1945 and *The Dolly Sisters* – 1946. She was particularly popular with US servicemen, her legs being a much publicized best feature. Her singing

and dancing were unexceptional, but she had a likably straightforward personality. Her career began to slip after the war, despite a successful teaming with Dan Dailey, and a good performance in *How to Marry a Millionaire* – 1953. After 1955 she worked in stage musicals.

Other films include:

Moon over Miami – 1941, *Mother Wore Tights* – 1948, *Call Me Mister* – 1951.

Further reading:

The Fox Girls James Robert Parish. Arlington House, New Rochelle, 1971.

GRANT, Cary

(1904–) US actor born in Britain. Hollywood's first freelance star (from 1937), he is chiefly associated with witty comedy in films such as *The Awful Truth* – 1937 and *My Favourite Wife* – 1940, (with Irene Dunne) *Bringing Up Baby* – 1938 and *The Philadelphia Story* – 1940 (with Katharine Hepburn) and *His Girl Friday* – 1939, which, like several of his best films, was directed by Howard Hawks. He was also one of Alfred Hitchcock's favourite actors. Films with him include *Notorious* – 1946, with its Hays Code-evading love scene with Ingrid Bergman, and *North by Northwest* – 1959. He developed a polished, understated style with a marvellous double-take, which he combined with an easy charm and distinctive voice. All of this probably accounts for the number of times that film plots have him actively pursued by his leading lady.

Other films include:

Only Angels Have Wings – 1939, *I Was a Male War Bride* – 1949, *Every Girl Should Be Married* – 1949, *Monkey Business* – 1952, *Charade* – 1963.

Further reading:

The films of Cary Grant Donald Deschner, Citadel Press, Secaucus, 1973.

GRIERSON, John

(1898–1972) Documentary producer whose reputation as 'the father of British documentary' is true only in the entrepreneurial sense. The film units he established and headed in the 1930s attracted a whole generation of otherwise fringe and *avant garde*

film-makers to the production of documentaries in the service of the state. The definition of documentary film owes much to films such as *Industrial Britain* – 1933, directed by Flaherty, and *Coal Face* – 1935, directed by Cavalcanti. In these and other films he brought together diverse styles of filmmaking and different political interests. They formed an effective propaganda force which worked at a time of Depression and war. The nature and scale of his actual contribution to cinema cannot yet be confidently separated from his substantial reputation. He was Canada's Film Commissioner in the early 1940s, and had his own television programme from 1947–1953.

Other films as producer include:

Drifters – 1929, *Song of Ceylon* – 1934, *Night Mail* – 1936.

Further reading:

John Grierson: Film master James Beveridge, Macmillan, New York, 1978.

GRIFFITH, D. W.;

see p. 16.

GUINNESS, Alec

(1914–) English actor, whose first film performance, as Herbert Pocket in *Great Expectations* – 1946, repeated a distinguished stage performance. He has continued working in the theatre. He is essentially a protean actor, his personality submerged in the characters he plays. The quintessential *Kind Hearts and Coronets* – 1948 provided him with no less than eight parts. It marked the beginning of a fruitful association with Ealing Studios, culminating in *The Ladykillers* – 1956. He went to Hollywood for a gentle romance,

The Swan – 1956. But it was his performance as the stiff-upper-lip officer in *Bridge on the River Kwai* – 1957 which him won an Oscar.

Other films include:
The Man in the White Suit – 1951, *The Horse's Mouth* – 1958, *Tunes of Glory* – 1960, *Lawrence of Arabia* – 1962, *Star Wars* – 1977.

Further reading:
Alec Guinness Kenneth Tynan, Rockliff, London, 1953.

HARDY, Oliver
(1892–1957) and
LAUREL, Stanley
(1890–1965) The fat and thin members, respectively, of the greatest comedy duo in cinema history. Their partnership began in 1926, although both appeared in comedy two-reelers for some years before. Most critics date the formation of their distinctive childlike relationship from *Putting Pants on Philip* – 1927. Olly's pompous reactions to Stan's mishandling of the simplest situations was the constant cause of accelerating disaster and audience mirth. This is seen at its best in the shorts *County Hospital* – 1932, *Busybodies* – 1933 and *The Music Box* – 1932, for which they won an Oscar, and the feature, *Way Out West* – 1936. Laurel's direction and scripting of their best work is little recognized. Ill-health bedevilled their late films. In the last, *Atoll K* – 1952, Stan especially was a shadow of his former self.

Other films include:
Big Business – 1929, *Another Fine Mess* – 1930, *Babes in Toyland* – 1934, *Blockheads* – 1938.

Further reading:
Laurel and Hardy Charles Barr, Studio Vista, London, 1967.

HARLOW, Jean
(1911–1937) US actress who rocketed to fame as the 'Platinum Blonde' in 1930s Hollywood. It was an image characterized by provocative sexuality combined with a shrewd working-class toughness and independence. A match for anything that the roughest of Hollywood's male heroes could hand out, *Public Enemy* – 1931 was her first big success. Her roles opposite Clark Gable in films such as *Red Dust* – 1932 and *China Seas* – 1934 indicate her popular appeal as a woman prepared to try anything, from her quick wits to her sexuality, to get what she wants: usually either a man or money. Not entirely mercenary, however, she often displayed virtues such as honesty and loyalty, as in *Dinner at Eight* – 1933.

Other films include:
Hell's Angels – 1930, *Platinum Blonde* – 1931, *Saratoga* – 1937.

Further reading:
Jean Harlow Curtis F. Brown, Pyramid, New York, 1977.

HAWKS, Howard;
see p. 190.

HAYWORTH, Rita
(1918–). US actress/dancer/singer who earned her reputation as one of Hollywood's legendary 'love-goddesses'. She combined her natural elegance with sultry sophistication and more than a little pride, producing smouldering performances in films such as *Gilda* – 1946. Because of her sensual image she is generally remembered for her portrayal of women misjudged and embittered by their experience of a male world. A talented and graceful dancer, she also starred in several successful musicals with Fred Astaire, Gene Kelly and Frank Sinatra. Later in her career she took on more psychologically complex and interesting roles in films such as *They came to Cordura* – 1959 anc *Road to Salina* – 1971.

Other films include:
Only Angels have Wings – 1939, *The Lady from Shanghai* – 1947, *Pal Joey* – 1957.

Further Reading:
The Films of Rita Hayworth Gene Ringgold, Citadel Press, New Jersey, 1974.

HEPBURN, Audrey
(1929–) Belgian-born actress who combines innocence and elegance. She was an instant success in her first Hollywood film *Roman Holiday* – 1953, sweeping up the acting awards as the runaway princess. She was well cast as Natasha in *War and Peace* – 1956. Hepburn drew on her dancer's training for Stanley Donen's delightful *Funny Face* – 1957, demonstrating that she could sing as charmingly as she spoke, although she was dubbed for *My Fair Lady* – 1964. She made two more films for Donen in the mid-1960s: *Charade* – 1963 and *Two for the Road* – 1967. She retired on her second marriage, but emerged for *Robin and Marian* – 1976 to prove that she was as beautiful and accomplished as ever.

Other films include:
Secret People – 1952, *The Nun's Story* – 1959, *Breakfast at Tiffany's* – 1961.

HEPBURN, Katharine
(1909–) US actress equally at home in comedy, to which she brings immaculate timing, and drama (her trembling lower lip and eyes welling up with tears are famous). She is usually identified with the vulnerable, although apparently self-assured, society roles. These she played in several films, notably *Holiday* – 1938 and *The Philadelphia Story* – 1940. She was closely associated with Spencer Tracy, co-starring with him in nine films, including the battle of the sexes comedy *Adam's Rib* – 1949. She continues to work regularly. More recent parts include Queen Eleanor in *The Lion in Winter* – 1967 for which she won an Oscar for the second year running, and *Love Among the Ruins* – 1975, opposite Laurence Olivier.

Other films include:
Bringing Up Baby – 1938, *African Queen* – 1951, *Long Day's Journey into Night* – 1962, *Guess Who's Coming to Dinner* – 1967, *The Corn is Green* (for TV) – 1978.

Further reading:
Katharine Hepburn Alvin H. Marvill, Pyramid, New York, 1972.

HESTON, Charlton
(1923–) US actor whose splendid physique and granite features are particularly associated with epics. It was his casting by DeMille in *The Greatest Show on Earth* – 1952 and as Moses (and God) in *The Ten Commandments* – 1956 which launched his career. He is very much one of Hollywood's public figures, holding office with the Screen Actors' Guild for some years. He has consistently supported directors in whom he believes. This has resulted in some of his best performances: for example Welles – *Touch of Evil* – 1957, Peckinpah – *Major Dundee* – 1965, on which he gave up his salary, Franklin Schaffner – *The War Lord* – 1965, a subtle and historically convincing medieval story, and Tom Gries – *Will Penny* – 1967.

Other films include:
Ruby Gentry – 1952, *Ben Hur* – 1959, *El Cid* – 1961, *The Planet of the Apes* – 1965, *Khartoum* – 1966, *Soylent Green* – 1973.

Further reading:
Charlton Heston Michael B. Druxman, Pyramid, New York, 1976.

HILL, George Roy
(1922–) US director who made a promising transition from theatre and television when he filmed his stage production of *Period of Adjustment* – 1963. This produced some excellent performances from the cast foreshadowing a consistent success in this area. However subsequent films suggested problems in adjusting to the medium. Some of these he seems to have solved by opting for pastiche, as in the delightful 1920s period musical *Thoroughly Modern Millie* – 1967, which used formal devices such as irising, or careful recreation of the past as in *Butch Cassidy and the Sundance Kid* – 1969, an early and very successful 'buddy' movie. The combination with, and of, Redford and Newman proved a happy one. *The Sting* – 1973 rode to success on this and Scott Joplin's music. Only

Redford was available for *The Great Waldo Pepper* – 1975, an attractive homage to the early days of stunt flying, while Newman stars on his own in *Slapshot* – 1977, a brutal comedy about American ice hockey.

Other films include:
Toys in the Attic – 1963, *The World of Henry Orient* – 1964, *Hawaii* – 1969.

HITCHCOCK, Alfred;
see p. 188.

HOFFMAN, Dustin
(1937–) US actor from the stage whose first starring role as *The Graduate* – 1967 established his box office reputation. His careful choice of roles has confirmed his persona as 'uncertain but sincere'. It was used effectively as a crippled tramp in *Midnight Cowboy* – 1969, an American refugee in the English rural setting of *Straw Dogs* – 1971, and the crusading journalist in *All the Presidents' Men* – 1976. His versatility as an actor is best represented in *Little Big Man* – 1970. Here he played the incredible Jack Crabb in all his guises as white man and Indian, gunfighter and greenhorn, and in all his ages, from youth to decrepit old age.

Other films include:
Madigan's Millions – 1969, *John and Mary* – 1969, *Who is Harry Kellerman?* – 1971, *Papillon* – 1973, *Marathon Man* – 1976.

HUDSON, Rock
(1925–) American actor of conventionally rugged appearance who played minor roles in genre films before starring as *Taza, Son of Cochise* – 1953. Perhaps the most interesting period of his career was his role as mediator of family squabbles in a series of melodramas directed by Douglas Sirk, which include *All That Heaven Allows* – 1955 and *Written*

on the Wind – 1956. The best of his later films were *Pillow Talk* – 1959, one of many starring roles opposite Doris Day, and the uncharacteristic *Seconds* – 1966, a bleak science-fiction drama. Shifting between comedy and action roles in 1960s films, he made a successful transfer of his lightweight persona to television in Macmillan anc Wife, a series which began in 1971.

Other films include:
Winchester '73 – 1950, *Magnificent Obsession* – 1954, *Giant* – 1956, *The Tarnished Angels* – 1957, *Imitation of Life* – 1959, *Lover Come Back* – 1961, *Send Me No Flowers* – 1964, *Man's Favourite Sport* – 1964, *Ice Station Zebra* – 1968, *Darling Lili* – 1969.
Further reading:
The All-Americans James Robert Parish and Don E. Stanke, Arlington House, New Rochelle, 1977.

HUSTON, John

(1906–) US director who began his Hollywood career as a scriptwriter, and has also acted from time to time. A number of his early successes were in association with Humphrey Bogart. Among these were his first film as director, the classic film noir thriller *The Maltese Falcon* – 1941, *The Treasure of the Sierra Madre* – 1948, which also featured his father Walter, and for which both Hustons won Oscars, and *The African Queen* – 1952, an adventure story centred on a developing relationship between a spinster missionary, played by Katharine Hepburn, and Bogart's tough ship's captain. Although Huston has been particularly successful in the thriller/adventure genres, for example *The Asphalt Jungle* – 1950 and *The Man Who Would Be King* – 1977, his range of achievement is impressively wide. His films include *Reflections in a Golden Eye* – 1967, a baroque tale of suppressed passion, *The Unforgiven* – 1960, an atmospheric western, *Fat City* – 1972, an acute, low-key study of failure, and *A Walk with Love and Death* – 1969, which relates modern student politics and attitudes to a finely realized medieval world.

Other films as director include:
The Red Badge of Courage – 1951, *Beat the Devil* – 1953, *Moby Dick* – 1956, *The Misfits* – 1961, *Night of the Iguana* – 1964, *Kremlin Letter* – 1970.
Further reading:
The Cinema of John Huston Gerald Pratley, A. S. Barnes, South Brunswick; Tantivy Press, London, 1977.

JACKSON, Glenda

(1936–) English actress whose first film appearance was in a version of Peter Brook's stage production of *Marat/Sade* – 1967. She has continued to keep a foot in both camps, recently filming another stage success, *Stevie* – 1978. Her performance in *Women in Love* – 1969 won her first Oscar. *In Sunday, Bloody Sunday* – 1971 she played a woman finding the strength to break free from a lover who is unfaithful (with another man). A popular series of BBC TV plays about Elizabeth I led to a repeat of the role in *Mary Queen of Scots* – 1972. *A Touch of Class* – 1972, a stylish comedy, proved a greater box office success, and, like *House Calls* – 1978, demonstrated that the abrasiveness and stridency of some of her dramatic work turn to astringency and wit in comedy.

Other films include:
The Music Lovers – 1971, *The Triple Echo* – 1972, *Lost and Found* – 1978.

KAZAN, Elia

(1909–) US writer and director of Turkish descent; also novelist, stage director and actor. Kazan's heroes are liberal underdogs, struggling to survive within and between the contradictions of personal relationships and repressive institutions, such as the law in *Boomerang* – 1947, corrupt unionism in *On The*

Waterfront – 1954 and the family in *East of Eden* – 1955. The Deep South is often the backcloth to sexual antagonisms such as in *A Streetcar Named Desire* – 1951, or inadequacies (at their most extreme in *Baby Doll* – 1956). These stand for more general emotional obstacles to contented partner relationships. Kazan's heroes most often end up compromising; their only answer to their inadequacies in a complex and hostile world. With the exception of the finally affirmative *Wild River* – 1960, however, 'compromise' also describes his films. They demonstrate a sprawling and inconsistent style, reflecting perhaps the confused politics in his artistic sensibility.

Other films include:
Viva Zapata! – 1952, *A Face in the Crowd* – 1957, *The Arrangement* – 1969, *The Last Tycoon* – 1976.
Further reading:
Kazan on Kazan Michael Ciment, Secker and Warburg, London, 1973.

KEATON, Buster

(1895–1966) US comedian/director, for many the most gifted of all the silent comedians, as well as a subtle, inventive (and sometimes uncredited) director. In vaudeville from the age of three, he joined Fatty Arbuckle in 1917. He then became a star in his own right in a

series of marvellous two-reelers, generally written and directed by himself, such as *The Boat* – 1921 and *Cops* – 1922. His first feature was *The Three Ages* – 1923, a parody of Griffith's *Intolerance*. His second, *Our Hospitality* – 1923, was the first of the great masterpieces, which include *The Navigator* – 1924, *The General* – 1926, and *Steamboat Bill Jr* – 1928. Witty and acutely observed, they integrated into the narrative the difficult and dangerous stunts from which he would emerge characteristically unruffled. In the late 1920s he was sold to MGM in a business deal and lost artistic control. He was able to do some good work, such as *Spite Marriage* – 1929, an unusually painful comedy. But career and self-confidence declined, and he became an alcoholic. Happily he recovered in time to enjoy the great revival of interest in his work, and to appear in a few films.

Other films include:
Sherlock Junior – 1924, *Go West* – 1925, *College* – 1927.
Further reading:
Buster Keaton David Robinson, Secker and Warburg, London, 1969.

KELLY, Gene

(1912–) US actor/singer/dancer/director and choreographer. One of the greatest of Hollywood's song-and-dance men, Kelly's highly original style of dancing combined swash-buckling dynamism with physical sensuality. During his years with MGM studios he played a brash but charming hustler in films like *For Me and My Gal* – 1942 and *The Pirate* – 1948. Always interested in the cinematic medium itself, he co-directed with Stanley Donen such energetic masterpieces as *On the Town* – 1949 and *Singin' in the Rain* – 1952. It was the Hollywood musical at its best, paradoxically inventive yet full of self-parody. Kelly's experimental flair was best expressed in his virtuoso performances with dustbin lids and on roller-skates in that oddly pessimistic film *It's Always Fair Weather* – 1955. He now works almost entirely as a director.

Other films include:
An American in Paris – 1951, *Les Demoiselles de Rochefort* – 1968, *That's Entertainment!* – 1974, as director: *Hello. Dolly!* – 1969.
Further reading:
Gene Kelly, Jeanine Basinger, Pyramid, New York, 1976.

KORDA, Alexander

(1893–1956) Hungarian-born producer/director who played a major part in the development of British cinema. After following a directorial career in Hungary, Austria, Germany, France and America, he settled in England in 1932 and set up London Film Productions, with his brothers Zoltan and Vincent in support. The international success of *The Private Life of Henry VIII* – 1933 – Korda's 52nd film as a director – brought financial backing for a series of lavish productions such as *The Rise of Catherine the Great* – 1934, *Rembrandt* – 1936, which he also directed, *Things to Come* – 1936, and *The Four Feathers* – 1939. His last film as a director was *An Ideal Husband* – 1947, which was rather static, like much of his work. But in his continuing role of executive producer he provided work for such directors as Carol Reed, David Lean, Michael Powell, Laurence Olivier, Frank Launder and Sidney Gilliat.

Other films as director include:
The Private Life of Helen of Troy – 1927, *Marius* – 1931, *Lady Hamilton (That Hamilton Woman in US)* – 1941, *Perfect Strangers* – 1945.
Further reading:
Alexander Korda, Karol Kulik, W. H. Allen, London, 1975.

KUBRICK, Stanley

(1928–) US director who began his career as a very successful photographer, and worked as a television director, before establishing himself in the cinema. He moved to Britain after making *Paths of Glory* – 1957 and *Spartacus* – 1960. Both starred Kirk Douglas, and both concerned the individual's struggle against an oppressive society. Kubrick's output is small, presumably because of the total control which he exercises over his projects. He concerns himself with every aspect right through to publicity design. *2001: A Space Odyssey* – 1968, *A Clockwork Orange* – 1971 and *Barry Lyndon* – 1975 have all been made under these conditions. The care and control show in their immaculate technical quality as well as their thematic coherence. They all centre on man's violent tendencies as he operates within an inflexible and complacent society.

Other films include:
Killer's Kiss – 1955, *The Killing* – 1956, *Lolita* – 1962, *Dr Strangelove* – 1964, *The Shining* – 1979.

Further reading:
Stanley Kubrick Directs Alexander Walker Davis-Poynter, London, 1972.

KUROSAWA, Akira

(1910–) The first of the great Japanese directors to establish a reputation in the West, with *Rashomon* – 1950, followed by *The Seven Samurai* – 1954, both of them remade in Hollywood. The samurai were feudal warriors, and the sword-fighting adventures based on their exploits are sometimes described as Japanese westerns. Kurosawa has specialized in these, with the aid of the marvellous Japanese actor Toshiro Mifune. He combines bravura set-piece battles with ironic humour. He was also responsible for a fine version of Dostoevsky's *The Idiot* – 1951, as well as a celebrated version of Macbeth entitled *Throne of Blood* – 1957. Since *Red Beard* – 1965, Kurosawa has worked less intensively. *Dodeska-den* – 1970, an account of the lives of poor people living in a shantytown, was followed by a Sino-Soviet co-production, *Dersu Uzala* – 1976, a sympathetic and, as always, beautifully-shot study of the relationship between an old man and an army officer.

Other films include:
They Who Step on the Tiger's Tail – 1945, *Ikiru* – 1952, *The Hidden Fortress* – 1958, *Yojimbo* – 1961, *Sanjuro* – 1962.

Further reading:
The films of Akira Kurosawa Donald Richie, University of California Press, Berkeley, 1965.

LANCASTER, Burt

(1913–) US actor and former circus acrobat. His first film was a starring role in *The Killers* – 1946, the first of a number of excellent roles. His star persona features two elements: the athletic, extrovert and toothy hero established in action spectacles such as *The Flame and the Arrow* – 1950, *Vera Cruz* – 1954 and *The Kentuckian* – 1955, the first of two films also as director; and the quieter, authoritative man of conscience in more 'serious' films such as *From Here to Eternity* – 1953, *Birdman of Alcatraz* – 1962 and *The Leopard* – 1963. He won an

Academy Award for his performance as a crusading evangelist in Richard Brooks' *Elmer Gantry* – 1960. He is one of the few Hollywood stars to maintain a film career into the television-dominated 1970s. He gave powerful central performances in genre films such as *Valdez is Coming* – 1971 and *Ulzana's Raid* – 1972, as well as in more pretentious roles such as in Bertolucci's *1900* – 1977.

Other films include:
Brute Force – 1947, *The Crimson Pirate* – 1952, *Gunfight at the OK Corral* – 1957, *The Sweet Smell of Success* – 1957, *The Swimmer* – 1967, *Scorpio* – 1973.

Further reading:
Burt Lancaster, Tony Thomas, Pyramid, New York, 1975.

LANG, Fritz

(1890–1976) Austrian-born director who began his film career writing screenplays for German detective films. His interest in the psychology of crime was to remain a primary concern in his work, both in Germany and later in the US. But his early period is probably best typified by such fantastic epics as *Destiny* – 1921, *Die Nibelungen* – 1924 and *Metropolis* – 1927. These are distinguished by their use of the wonderful special effects characteristic of the German film industry at that time. In 1932 *The Last Will of Dr Mabuse* was confiscated by the Third Reich because of its anti-Nazi content. After being offered the post of head of the German film industry by the Nazi Goebbels, Lang fled to Paris, then to America. There he enjoyed a long and prolific career, which included collaboration with Brecht (whom he greatly admired) on *Hangmen Also Die* – 1943. He is one of the few directors who combine a profound humanism with a desire to encourage the audience to think about social injustice, its causes and effects.

Other films include:
(in the US) *Fury* – 1936, *The Woman in the Window* – 1944, *Scarlet Street* – 1945, *Rancho Notorious* – 1952, *The Big Heat* – 1953, *Beyond a Reasonable Doubt* – 1956.

Further reading:
Fritz Lang in America, Peter Bogdanovich, Studio Vista, London, 1967.

LAUGHTON, Charles

(1899–1963) English actor working mainly in Hollywood, but in several key British films, notably *The Private Life of Henry VIII* – 1933, which led to an Oscar. Some of his best Hollywood films were *Ruggles of Red Gap* – 1935 and *Mutiny on the Bounty* – 1935. As an actor he gave great attention to detail, but today his acting style appears exaggerated. One of his most effective roles was his last, as the guileful Southern senator in *Advise and Consent* – 1962. Latterly he returned increasingly to the stage. He also directed the flawed but haunting *The Night of the Hunter* – 1955.

Other films include:
Rembrandt – 1936, *The Canterville Ghost* – 1944, *Witness for the Prosecution* – 1957.

Further reading:
Charles Laughton: an Intimate Biography Charles Higham, Doubleday, New York, 1976.

LAUREL, Stanley; see **HARDY.**

LEAN, David

(1908–) British director who is much admired by his colleagues for the immaculate technical quality of his films. He was a film editor before directing *In Which We Serve* – 1942 with Noël Coward. He subsequently directed three more Coward scripts, notably *Brief Encounter* – 1945, highly regarded as a classic example of British understatement. He had similar critical success with *Great Expectations* – 1946 and *Oliver Twist* – 1948. In recent years he has concentrated on big budget pictures such as *Ryan's Daughter* – 1971. These tend to be visually stunning, but slow and somewhat tedious, although they do well at the box office and have won numerous academy awards.

Other films include:
The Passionate Friends – 1949, *The Bridge on the River Kwai* – 1957, *Lawrence of Arabia* – 1962, *Doctor Zhivago* – 1966.

Further reading:
The Cinema of David Lean Gerald Pratley, Tantivy Press, London, 1974.

LEONE, Sergio

(1921–) Italian director whose 'spaghetti' westerns won popularity, especially those featuring Clint Eastwood as the anonymous hero, as in *For a Fistful of Dollars* (*A Fistful of Dollars* in US) – 1964. His films have been both satiric comments on the form of the American western, especially *The Good, the Bad and the Ugly* – 1967, and ironic analyses of America itself. Both concerns have been bound by the limits of the epic (both in terms of the history the films cover and the viewing time) and exploration of characters with mythic dimensions which are his constant choices of subject. In recent years, with the commercial failure of westerns in the international market, Leone has taken to production, sometimes still of westerns, such as *My Name is Nobody* – 1977. But his most interesting film has been as director: *Once Upon A Time in the West* – 1969.

Other films include:
For a Few Dollars More – 1965.

Further reading:
The Italian Western – The Opera of Violence Laurence Staig and Tony Williams, Lorrimer, London, 1975.

LEWIS, Jerry

(1926–) US comedian/director who began his film career as the naive 'patsy' to Dean Martin's predatory hustler. This comedy partnership produced eighteen films before it broke apart after *Hollywood or Bust* – 1956, which was directed by Frank Tashlin. Tashlin and Lewis went on to make six more films together. They developed Lewis's unique brand of surrealistic humour, taking his crass naiveté and sexual and physical incompetence to such absurd lengths that many critics have seen these films as very subversive. Although Lewis directed himself in his own films from 1960, they never quite matched the hysterical heights of the Tashlin films. He always acknowledged his debt to the great Stan Laurel. He took his name in *The Bellboy* – 1960, in homage to the comedian who provided the inspiration for his most anarchistic gags.

Other films include:
The Nutty Professor – 1963, *The Patsy* – 1964, *The Disorderly Orderly* – 1964.

LLOYD, Harold

(1893–1971) US comedian, one of the great silent clowns. He made hundreds of short films and evolved a character built on a shy college boy, serious in lensless horn-rimmed spectacles, who would never take 'no' for an answer.

The latter led to some of his famous stunts, such as the unfaked scaling of a skyscraper in *Safety Last* – 1923, one of his first features. *The Freshman* – 1925 was one of the most successful silent films ever made. His popularity continued unabated until the coming of sound. He did not like talkies, despite some success in them (*Movie Crazy* – 1932), and retired a very wealthy man. He emerged briefly for *The Sin of Harold Diddlebock* (*Mad Wednesday* in Britain) – 1947, and two popular compilation films.

Other films include:
Grandma's Boy – 1922, *The Kid Brother* – 1927, *The Milky Way* – 1936.

Further reading:
Harold Lloyd: the Shape of Laughter Richard Schickel, New York Graphic Society, Boston, 1974.

LOMBARD, Carole
(1908–1942) US actress, one of Hollywood's finest comediennes, who was tragically killed in an air crash at 33. Apart from performances as a child, she appeared in films from 1925. These included a series of Mack Sennett shorts, and some generally undistinguished feature films. In *Twentieth Century* 1934 the combined talents of director Howard Hawks and her co-star John Barrymore helped to release on screen the witty, uninhibited, screwball personality by which she is remembered in this and other films, such as *My Man Godfrey* – 1936 and *Nothing Sacred* – 1937, and her last film, Lubitsch's satirical attack on the Nazis, *To Be or Not To Be* – 1942.

Other films include:
Made for Each Other – 1933, *Now and Forever* – 1934, *True Confession* – 1937, *Swing High, Swing Low* – 1937.

Further reading:
Screwball: the life of Carole Lombard, William Morrow, New York, 1975.

LOREN, Sophia
(1934–) Italian actress whose passionate and defiant temperament is exemplified in both her indigenous 'art film' roles, especially in *Two Women* – 1961, for which she won an Oscar, and in a string of domestic dramas, such as

Yesterday, Today and Tomorrow – 1963 and *A Special Day* – 1977, and in Hollywood epics such as *The Pride and The Passion* – 1957, and *El Cid* – 1961. Her films express both her personal social climb from the slums of Naples and the stereotype of the Latin sexual fire-bomb. Her most interesting roles however have been untypical: as a western saloon-cat in *Heller in Pink Tights* – 1960; on the receiving end of Peter Sellers' Indian doctor's stethoscope in the British-made *The Millionairess* – 1961; and manipulated into invisibility in Chaplin's final film, *A Countess from Hong Kong* – 1966.

Other films include:
Woman of the River – 1955, *Desire under the Elms* – 1958, *The Fall of the Roman Empire* – 1964, *Judith* – 1965, *Man of La Mancha* – 1972.

Further reading:
The Films of Sophia Loren Tony Crawley, LSP Books, London, 1974.

LOSEY, Joseph
(1909–) US director who went to Hollywood via the stage. He fell victim to the Hollywood Blacklist, worked in England for some twenty years, and then moved to Paris. He has concentrated on the thriller, often using it to explore social and political issues, directly or obliquely, as in his American films *The Prowler* – 1951 and *M* – 1951 and in England *The Criminal* – 1960, and *The Damned* – 1963, a chilling story of secret preparations for the eventuality of nuclear war. More recently *Mr Klein* – 1976, was based on the French wartime persecution of the Jews. His most celebrated work has been with Dirk Bogarde and/or Harold Pinter. *The*

Servant – 1963, was a disturbing story of moral corruption shot in a baroque style, in evidence in several films of this period, notably *Secret Ceremony* – 1968. *Accident* – 1967 was cooler, although again concerned with the interaction of a small group of characters, and, with *The Go-Between* – 1971, one of Losey's finest achievements.

Other films include:
Blind Date – 1959, *Figures in a Landscape* – 1970, *The Assassination of Trotsky* – 1972, *Les Routes du Sud* – 1978.

Further reading:
Losey on Losey, Tom Milne, Secker and Warburg, London, 1967.

LUBITSCH, Ernst
(1892–1947) German-born director who acted with Max Reinhardt and learned the art of the *Kammerspiel*, which he later translated successfully into film. In Germany he directed historical spectaculars, and developed the black comedies which became his trademark. His first major satire, *Die Austernprinzessin* – 1919 lampooned the American Dream. Yet ironically, because of his reputation as a master of comic detail and a director who handled actors well, he was courted by Hollywood and went there in 1922. *The Marriage Circle* – 1924 was the first in a series of malicious sex comedies revealing the darker side of human relationships with a characteristically European intellectual sophistication. They show a concern with the medium of cinema without losing sight of social reality. He directed several witty musical comedies, for example, *The Love Parade* – 1930. He is best known for his political satires, such as *Ninotchka* – 1939 and the anti-Nazi *To Be or Not To Be* – 1942.

Other films include:
(in Germany) *Die Puppe* – 1919, *Die Flamme* – 1921, (in US) *The Student Prince* – 1927, *Angel* – 1937, *Bluebeard's Eighth Wife* – 1938.

Further reading:
The Lubitsch Touch, a critical study, Herman G. Weinberg, Dover Publications Inc., New York, 1977.

LUCAS, George
(1945–) US director who is a film-school graduate. Typical of the new breed of mainstream filmmakers, such as his peers Bogdanovich and Coppola, Lucas freely embraces genre cinema. Unlike those directors, however, Lucas uses references to Hollywood not only as source for ideas and styles but also to show his nostalgia for an innocent America. *THX 1138* – 1971 places a naive hero in an anaesthetized future society. *American Graffiti* – 1973 delights in the teenage 'bobby-sox' relationships of 1950s pop culture. Compared with these, *Star Wars* – 1977 is less interesting, notable mainly for its homage to the film buff's cinema memories and as the most recent box office phenomenon.

Other films include:
Star Wars II – 1979.

LUPINO, Ida
(1918–) British-born actress/writer/producer/director who went to Hollywood in the early 1930s. She is probably best known as an actress, especially for her portrayal of independent women in the 1940s. She formed her own production company in 1949, directing and scripting a series of low-budget feature films. These had a strong documentary flavour, explicitly concerned with social issues, such as *Outrage* – 1952, a study of the psychological effects of rape. She has also acted and directed in television for many years. It is not surprising that with such a record she has aroused the interest of feminists, although she denies any particular feminist content in her work.

Other films include:
(as actress) *High Sierra* – 1941, *Junior Bonner* – 1972, as director: *Hard Fast and Beautiful* – 1951, *The Trouble with Angels* – 1966.

Further reading:
Ida Lupino Jerry Vermilye, Pyramid, New York, 1977.

MacLAINE, Shirley
(1934–) US actress who played a scatty off-beat heroine in her first film *The Trouble with Harry* – 1953. She then became trapped in variations of the same role, frequently in comedies, such as *Ask Any Girl* – 1959. More powerful dramatic roles included the painfully vulnerable 'dumb redhead' in *Some Came Running* – 1958, one of her finest performances, and the would-be suicide in Wilder's *The Apartment* – 1960. The taxi-dancer heroine in *Sweet Charity* – 1968 was one of her few musicals, despite her having been recruited to Hollywood from stage-musicals. Her role as the tragic lesbian in *The Children's Hour* (*The Loudest Whisper* in Britain) – 1961 gave her a rare opportunity to widen her range in a nicely understated performance. Unhappy with her parts, she withdrew from films for several years to concentrate on politics and a very successful nightclub act. She was tempted back for *The Turning Point* – 1978, giving a strong performance as the retired ballet dancer whose daughter's dancing success leads to a re-appraisal of her own life.

Other films include:
Two for the Seesaw – 1962, *Two Mules for Sister Sara* – 1971.

Further reading:
Don't Fall Off the Mountain Shirley MacLaine, W. W. Norton, New York, 1970.

McQUEEN, Steve
(1930–) US actor from theatre and television. A superstar of the 1960s who first gained prominence as the cool and self-sufficient gunfighter in *The Magnificent Seven* – 1960. His screen personality draws from his private life.

His isolation and daredevil stunts with racing machines are promoted in films such as *The Great Escape* – 1963 and *Le Mans* – 1971. His detached air and machismo allow him to play more sinister figures, however, such as the obsessive card-sharp in *The Cincinnati Kid* – 1965, and the cynical soldier in *Hell is for Heroes* – 1961, his most interesting roles. He gave concentrated performances in the big-budget films, *Papillon* – 1973 and *The Towering Inferno* – 1975.

Other films include:
The Blob – 1958, *Love with the Proper Stranger* – 1963, *Bullitt* – 1968, *Junior Bonner* – 1972, *The Getaway* – 1972, *An Enemy of the People* – 1978.

Further reading:
The Films of Steve McQueen Joanna Campbell, Barnden, Castell Williams, London, 1973.

MANN, Anthony

(1906–1967) US director who served his apprenticeship in 1940s 'B' films. These culminated in a series of taut thrillers typified by *Border Incident* – 1949. He then embarked on a distinguished group of westerns, often starring a neurotic hero played by James Stewart, such as in *Winchester 73* – 1950. His last films continued the move towards spectacle, of which the epic *El Cid* – 1961 is a fine example. Mann's films are tragic tales of power struggles within the family, whether cattle-baron as in *The Furies* – 1950, or Imperial Roman as in *The Fall of the Roman Empire* – 1964. His breathtaking use of natural landscapes is complemented by the scale of dramas in which his heroes' constant denials of social responsibility lead inevitably to destruction – often their own. All Mann's films are emotional experiences but *The Man from Laramie* – 1955 and the lesser known *Man of the West* – 1958 are indisputably masterpieces of the decade.

Other films include:
Devil's Doorway – 1950, *Bend of the River* – 1951, *The Glenn Miller Story* – 1954, *The Far Country* – 1955, *Strategic Air Command* – 1955, *Men in War* – 1957, *The Heroes of Telemark* – 1968.

Further reading:
Horizons West Jim Kitses, Thames and Hudson, London, 1969.

MARX, Brothers

– Chico (1891–1961), Harpo (1893–1964), Groucho (1895–1977), and Zeppo (1900–). American vaudeville comedy team who made a string of enormously influential eccentric comedies in the early 1930s, culminating in *Duck Soup* – 1933, arguably the zaniest. Thereafter, following the shedding of Zeppo, and a change of studio, the conventional comic structures of their remaining films constrained their anarchic humour. Typical of films from the late period is *A Night at the Opera* – 1935. With the commercial failure of *Love Happy* – 1950, they returned to Broadway. In the 1960s, Groucho (of the wisecracks, greasepaint moustache and eyebrows, cigar and loping walk) made a solo career as a television raconteur and quiz-master. But it is as a Marx Brother (with Harpo's 'dumb' harpist and Chico's ice-cream Italian) that many of Groucho's wisecracks (such as 'I don't wish to belong to any organization that will accept me as a member') have attained immortality.

Other films include:
The Cocoanuts – 1929, *Animal Crackers* – 1930, *Monkey Business* – 1931, *Horsefeathers* – 1933, *A Day at the Races* – 1937, *A Night in Casablanca* – 1946.

Further reading:
Groucho, Harpo, Chico and sometimes Zeppo Joe Adamson, Simon and Schuster, New York, 1973.

MASON, James

(1909–) Darkly handsome British actor with a mellifluous voice. He achieved international stardom, as well as immense national popularity, in a series of British melodramas in which he played sullen, bullying heroes, initially in *The Man in Grey* – 1943, and perhaps most effectively in *The Seventh Veil* – 1945. *Odd Man Out* – 1947, which cast him as a fatally wounded IRA man on the run, remains one of the triumphs of his career. He was similarly compelling as a loser in *The Reckless Moment* – 1949 and *A Star is Born* – 1954. Unhappily his films have tended to be poorer than his talent. It is a pleasure to see him matched against Cary Grant in Hitchcock's masterly *North by Northwest* – 1959 and as the obsessed hero of *Lolita* – 1962.

Other films include:
The Desert Fox – 1951, *Julius Caesar* – 1953, *Journey to the Centre of the Earth* – 1959, *A Deadly Affair* – 1966, *Autobiography of a Princess* – 1976 *Heaven Can Wait* – 1978,.

Further reading:
The films of James Mason Clive Hirschlorn, LSP Books, London, 1975.

MATTHAU, Walter

(1920 –) US actor who has played a wide variety of roles on stage and screen, but is best known for his comedy roles. These include the shyster lawyer in *The Fortune Cookie* (*Meet Whiplash Willie* in Britain) – 1966; the slobbish half of *The Odd Couple* – 1968, a happy re-teaming with Jack Lemmon; the elegant man-about-town desperately seeking a heiress to maintain his life-style, in *A New Leaf* – 1970; and the courted newly-widowed surgeon in *House Calls* – 1978, which also features his son Charlie. Tall and stooping, his normal expression in comedy is of lugubrious cynicism, but he launches himself into restless movement when riled. Occasional recent non-comedy roles include the hardened small-time crook who inadvertently ends up with Mafia money when he robs a country bank, in *Charley Varrick* – 1973.

Other films include:
Cactus Flower – 1969, *Plaza Suite* – 1969, *The Sunshine Boys* – 1975, *California Suite* – 1979.

MINNELLI, Vincente

(1913–) US director and supreme stylist of classic MGM musicals such as *Meet Me in St Louis* – 1944, *The Pirate* – 1947, and *The Bandwagon* – 1953. Lesser known but equally interesting as director of low-key melodramas such as *The Clock* (*Under the Clock* in Britain) – 1944, *The Cobweb* – 1955 and *Home From the Hill* – 1960. These, together with the musicals, are argued by some critics to subvert both the forms themselves and the American lifestyles enmeshed within them. His films made since the late 1960s have not won commercial popularity. An increasing eclecticism is noticeable in *The Sandpiper* – 1965 and *On a Clear Day You Can See Forever* – 1970. He is best known as father of Liza Minelli and one-time husband of Judy Garland.

Other films include:
Cabin in the Sky – 1943, *Father of the Bride* – 1950, *The Bad and the Beautiful* – 1952, *Lust for Life* – 1956, *Gigi* – 1958, *Some Came Running* – 1958, *The Courtship of Eddie's Father* – 1963.

Further reading:
Vincente Minnelli and the Musical Joseph Andrew Caspar, Thomas Yoseloff, New York, 1977.

MITCHUM, Robert

(1917–) US actor whose relaxed sleepy-eyed style does not entirely mask an intelligent and perceptive actor. Beginning as a bit player, he built a growing reputation in a wide variety of parts, including chillingly psychotic killers in *The Night of the Hunter* – 1955 and *Cape Fear* – 1962, western heroes and ageing anti-heroes in *The Good Guys and the Bad Guys* – 1969 and *El Dorado* – 1967 respectively. A gentle cuckolded schoolmaster, in *Ryan's Daughter* – 1970, marked a departure from the tough sexuality displayed in many of his other films. He has played various thriller heroes, including the narrator hero in one of the finest films noir, *Out of the Past* (*Build My Gallows High* in Britain) – 1947 and Philip Marlowe in two recent Chandler remakes – *Farewell My Lovely* – 1975 and *The Big Sleep* – 1978.

Other films include:
The Story of GI Joe – 1945, *The Red Pony* – 1949, *The River of No Return* – 1954, *Two for the Seesaw* – 1962.

Further reading:
Robert Mitchum John Belton, Pyramid, New York, 1976.

MIZOGUCHI, Kenji

(1898–1956) Japanese director who is widely regarded as one of the world's greatest filmmakers. Until recently comparatively few of his films had been seen in the West. He has been principally associated with the costume pictures, distinguished by long and elegantly-organized takes, made at the end of his career. They include *Ugetsu Monogatari* – 1953, *Sansho Dayu* – 1954 and *The Princess Yang Kwei Fei* – 1955. Unhappily the majority of his films (over 100) are apparently lost, including everything made between 1922 and 1932. Those remaining typically have contemporary or near-contemporary settings. They deal in personal terms with social/political problems, especially the place and role of women, for example *Sisters of the Gion* – 1936, often geishas – *My Love Has Been Burning* – 1949. They use a remarkable series of actresses, notably Kinuyo Tanaka (Japan's first woman director). The most explicitly feminist films were made during the American occupation, for example *The Victory of Women* – 1946. He returned to these concerns with his last film *Street of Shame* – 1956. Performance and the world of the theatre is another continuing interest, exemplified in *White Threads of the Waterfall* – 1933 and *Story of the Late*

Chrysanthemums – 1939.
Other films include:
The Downfall – 1934, *The Loyal 47 Ronin* – 1942, *The Life of O'Haru* – 1952, *Shin Heike Monogatari* – 1955.

MONROE, Marilyn
(1926–1962) US actress who became a legend as a classic victim of the Hollywood star-system. Promoted by the studios as a sex symbol during the 1950s, she constantly struggled to develop the acting potential which became evident as early as 1950 in *The Asphalt Jungle*. Her career reflected the contradiction between her charismatic screen presence and her desire to be more than an object to be looked at. The Monroe myth of the child-woman who sees the truth in a corrupt world was immortalized in *The Misfits* – 1960, her last film before her tragic death. She perhaps should be best remembered for her brilliant comic performances in *Gentlemen Prefer Blondes* – 1953 and *Some Like It Hot* – 1959.
Other films include:
All About Eve – 1950, *Clash by Night* – 1952, *River of No Return* – 1954.
Further reading:
Marilyn Monroe Joan Mellen, Pyramid, New York, 1973.

MOREAU, Jeanne
(1928–) French actress possessed of a weary sensuality. An early and distinguished stage career was not matched by the twenty or so films she made before Malle's *Les Amants* – 1958 put her on the map. She became a major international star. She gave fine performances for a number of major directors such as Peter Brook – *Moderato Cantabile* – 1960, Antonioni – *La Notte* – 1961, Truffaut – *Jules et Jim* – 1961 (perhaps her best-known role as the amoral, fascinating Catherine who is loved by both men), Jacques Demy – *La Baie des Anges* – 1963, in which she was stunning as an obsessive gambler, Buñuel – *Diary of a Chambermaid* – 1964 and Welles – *Histoire Immortelle* – 1968. Her American work includes a telling performance in *Monte Walsh* – 1970. But her best work has been in

France, where in recent years she has turned her hand to direction with *Lumière* – 1976.
Other films include:
Viva Maria! – 1965, *Nathalie Granger* – 1972, *Souvenirs d'en France* – 1974, *The Last Tycoon* – 1976.

MURNAU, Friedrich Wilhelm
(1888–1931) German-born director, considered one of the greatest Expressionist filmmakers. He was one of the earliest exponents of the moving camera in *The Last Laugh* – 1924. He used the distortions characteristic of Expressionism: bizarre camera-angles, contrasting light and shadow, to produce a dream-like atmosphere. This was used to project subjective fantasies on the screen, revealing the workings of the unconscious mind. In *Nosferatu* – 1922, Murnau's command of the visual produced a ghostly masterpiece, horrific and moving in its picture of man's alienation from the real world, symbolized by the evil but tragic vampire. He continued to explore these areas in America. He used his flair for experimental technique and chiaroscuro lighting to lift melodramatic stories to the level of psychological film-poems in *Sunrise* – 1927 and *Our Daily Bread* (*City Girl*) – 1929. His interest in the primitive aspect of man was reflected in *Tabu* – 1929, a story of persecuted innocence on which Robert Flaherty worked with him for a time. Murnau died in a car-crash in 1931.
Other films include:
Phantom – 1922, *Faust* – 1926.
Further reading:
Murnau Lotte Eisner, Secker and Warburg, London, 1973.

NEWMAN, Paul
(1925–) US actor/director/producer who has done much of his best work with his wife, the excellent actress Joanne Woodward. They first co-starred in Martin Ritt's *The Long Hot Summer* – 1958, an effective melodrama. Newman went on to make three

more films with Ritt. Strikingly good-looking, with piercing blue eyes which tend to suggest a mocking amusement, he has been a top box office star for much of his career, in films such as *From the Terrace* – 1960, *Cool Hand Luke* – 1967 and *The Sting* – 1973. He has shown great ability as a director, especially in *Rachel, Rachel* – 1968, a delicate study of a single woman in a small town coming to terms with her life, and *The Effect of Gamma Rays on Man-in-the-Moon Marigolds*, both starring his wife. Both films offer compassionate studies of the way people with limited lives and understanding may cause harm to those around them. Both end on a tentative note of optimism.
Other films include:
Hud – 1963, *The Hustler* – 1967, *Butch Cassidy and the Sundance Kid* – 1969, *Sometimes a Great Notion* (*Never Give an Inch* in Britain) – 1971.
Further reading:
Paul Newman, Michael Kerbel, Pyramid Books, New York, 1973.

NICHOLSON, Jack
(1937–) US actor with a drawling voice and an indolent mocking charm, tending to abrasiveness. He became a star with his role as the small town lawyer in *Easy Rider* – 1969. He began his film career with Roger Corman, initially as an actor, beginning with the lead in *The Cry Baby Killer* – 1958 and including such films as *The Raven* – 1963. He later worked in a variety of capacities, including scripting – *The Trip* – 1967. He starred in and co-produced, with director Monte Hellman, *Ride the Whirlwind* – 1966. *The Shooting* – 1966, which he also scripted, achieved a considerable critical suc-

cess in Europe. He also wrote and produced Bob Rafelson's first film as director, *Head* – 1968. He did some of his most impressive acting work in Rafelson's next two films, *Five Easy Pieces* – 1971 and *The King of Marvin Gardens* – 1972. Nicholson's only film as director, *Drive, He Said* – 1970, had a disappointing reception. He has since concentrated on acting. The freedom to pick and choose has led to interesting results, including *The Last Detail* – 1973 and *Chinatown* – 1974.
Other films include:
Two Lane Blacktop – 1971, *The Passenger* – 1975, *One Flew Over the Cuckoo's Nest* – 1975, *The Shining* – 1979.
Further reading:
Jack Nicholson face to face, Robert David Crane and Christopher Fryer, M. Evans, New York, 1975.

NIVEN, David
(1909–) Dapper, debonair British actor who charmed his way into a Hollywood career after some years in the army. He proved an accomplished comedian in films such as *Bachelor Mother* – 1939, his first starring role, *The Moon Is Blue* – 1953, *Around the World in Eighty Days* – 1956 and *Ask Any Girl* – 1959. He returned to Britain and the army for the War. But he was released to play two of his best dramatic roles as a stereotype, quietly spoken, quietly heroic Englishman, a test pilot in *The First of the Few* – 1942, and an officer in *The Way Ahead* – 1944. After the War he played another pilot in *A Matter of Life and Death* – 1945. He used the officer facade as the pathetic sexual offender in *Separate Tables* – 1958, for which he won an Oscar. He has written two witty and likable volumes of memoirs.
Other films include:
The Dawn Patrol – 1938, *Bonnie Prince Charlie* – 1947, *Carrington V.C.* – 1955, *The Pink Panther* – 1964, *The Statue* – 1970, *Candleshoe* – 1977.
Further reading:
The Moon's a Balloon David Niven, Hamish Hamilton, London, 1971. *Bring on the Empty Horses*, David Niven, Hamish Hamilton, London, 1977.

OLIVIER, Laurence
(1907–) British actor/director who has had a distinguished stage career. His film career falls into three phases. After a faltering start, he became a dashing romantic leading man in Britain in *Fire over England* – 1937 and *Q Planes* – 1939, and in Hollywood in *Wuthering Heights* – 1939 and *Rebecca* – 1940. He returned to Britain for the War. He eventually embarked on his most generally admired film work as actor/director of a succession of Shakespearean films – *Henry V* – 1944, *Hamlet* – 1948 and, the best of them, *Richard III* – 1953. A fine performance of a man disintegrating under adverse circumstances in Wyler's *Carrie* – 1951 marked a shift in his film roles. He went on to include a repeat of his stage role as the fading stand-up comic in *The Entertainer* – 1960, an excellent muted performance as the detective in *Bunny Lake Is Missing* – 1965, but a rather ponderous and charmless one in *The Prince and the Showgirl* – 1958, which he also directed. He has also appeared in three films of productions from the National Theatre, of which he was the first Director, including *Othello* – 1965. Following a major illness he now concentrates on film and TV work.

Other films include:
Pride and Prejudice – 1940, *Lady Hamilton* (*That Hamilton Woman* in US) — 1941, *Term of Trial* – 1962, *Sleuth* – 1972, *Marathon Man* – 1976, *The Boys from Brazil* – 1978.

Further reading:
Laurence Olivier John Cottrell, Weidenfeld and Nicolson, London, 1975.

OPHULS, Max

(1902–1957) German-born director who worked in several countries. His German period includes *Die verkaufte Braut* – 1932, an enchanting, playful account of Smetana's *The Bartered Bride*, and *Liebelei* – 1933, adapted from a Schnitzler play, and typically softening its harsh irony. This was one of several romantic dramas of unfulfilled love, which include *Letter from an Unknown Woman* – 1948 and *Madame de...* – 1953. He made films in France, Holland and Italy before going to America in 1941. There he made two of his finest films, including a melodrama of a middle class American wife (and mother) encountering blackmail and murder in *The Reckless Moment* – 1949. This film like Ophuls' work in general, readily lends itself to psychoanalytic analysis, both in the use of imagery and subject matter, and in the overall patterning with repetition and flowing camera movements. His last film, *Lola Montès* – 1955, is of particular interest, with its complex flashback structure. The heroine is on display in a circus, a spectacle for the voyeuristic gaze of the audience within and without the film.

Other films include:
Caught – 1949, *La ronde* – 1950, *Le plaisir* – 1952.

Further reading:
Max Ophuls Paul Willeman, British Film Institute, London, 1978.

OSHIMA, Nagisa

(1932–) Japanese director, many of whose films have not been seen in the West (although he has been making them since 1959). His work has aroused great interest among film theorists in relation to film structure and narrative. In *Death by Hanging* – 1968 a man convicted of murder fails (or refuses, as the film puts it) to die when hung, provoking the officials to attempt to make him accept guilt via a reconstruction of events. The result is a film which examines the values of Japanese society and its institutions through a series of devices which break audience expectations of narrative continuity. Political analysis of Japan, and a particular concern with the position of national minorities such as Koreans, appear to be continuing themes. *Boy* – 1969, a moving film which shows the inequities of the world through the eyes of a child victim, and *Realm of the Senses* – 1976, a study of an obsessive erotic relationship, are other films which have been widely seen and praised.

Other films include:
Night and Fog in Japan – 1960, *Diary of a Shinjuku Thief* – 1968, *The Man Who Left His Will on Film* – 1970, *The Ceremony* – 1971, *Empire of Passion* – 1978.

Further Reading:
Second Wave Ian Cameron, Studio Vista, London, 1970.

OZU, Yasujiro

(1902–1963) Japanese director who, like his compatriot Mizoguchi, is known in the West mainly by his later work. His earlier films include some delightful Keaton-like comedies of student life, for example, *I Flunked But...* – 1930. They also include the beginnings of his continuing study of parent/child relationships, concentrating on young families and using some marvellous boy actors, as in *I Was Born But...* – 1932 and *Passing Fancy* – 1933. Later his films were concerned with parents and adult children troubled by their conflicting needs, nowhere portrayed more movingly than in his last film *An Autumn Afternoon* – 1962. In this film Chishu Ryu, who appeared in almost all of Ozu's films, gave one of his finest performances. Often described as quintessentially Japanese, Ozu's mature style is spare and elegant. The camera, as an observer sitting Japanese-style on the floor, watches the events clearly placed for the spectator spatially and temporally. His cameraman from 1941 onwards was Yushun Atsuta, and his other close collaborator, the writer Koga Noda.

Other films include:
There Was a Father – 1942, *A Hen in the Wind* – 1948, *Late Spring* – 1949, *Early Summer* – 1951, *Tokyo Story* – 1953.

Further reading:
Ozu Donald Richie, University of California Press, Berkeley, 1974.

PAKULA, Alan J

(1928–) US director/producer who began his Hollywood career in production. He eventually set up a company with Robert Mulligan, to whom he gave his first chance to direct. Together they made an interesting group of six films, which include *Love with the Proper Stranger* – 1963, *Baby the Rain Must Fall* – 1964, and *The Stalking Moon* – 1968. Comparison with Mulligan's other work suggests that Pakula's contribution was crucial. His own directorial career began with *The Sterile Cuckoo (Pookie* in Britain) – 1969. This funny and painful study of a young girl's first affair had Liza Minnelli beautifully cast in her first starring role. Pakula seems drawn to people at the edges of society, often rather insecure like the couple in *Love and Pain and the Whole Damn Thing* – 1972. His films are technically immaculate. Haunting images sum up whole areas of feeling. In *Klute* – 1971, Jane Fonda's prostitute comforts herself by creating a cosy world to shut out the dark night, but is photographed down through the skylight window as perhaps the murderer might view her.

Other films include:
The Parallax View – 1974, *All the President's Men* – 1976, *Comes a Horseman Wild and Free* – 1978.

Further reading:
A Portrait of All the President's Men Jack Hirshberg, Warner Books, New York, 1976.

PASOLINI, Pier Paolo

(1922–1977) Italian director whose early films, especially *Accattone* – 1961 and *The Gospel According to St Matthew* – 1964, were critically received as social and religious explorations. The next cycle of films were more complex in form. Both *Oedipus Rex* – 1967 and *Theorem* – 1968 were concerned with power in relation to the state and the family. This cycle was followed by films concerning sexual relations. Their form was more conventional, and they reached a wider popular audience – especially *The Decameron* – 1970. His last film was *Salo* – 1976, a controversial and explicit account of the links between sexuality, sadism and fascism. The controversy was caused not only by the film itself, but by Pasolini's declaration of his Italian Marxism and homosexuality. It abated when his mutilated body was discovered in a ditch in circumstances inadequately accounted for by the Italian authorities.

Other films include:
Mamma Roma – 1962, *Pigsty* – 1969, *Medea* – 1970.

Further reading:
Pier Paolo Pasolini Paul Willeman, BFI, London, 1977.

PECK, Gregory

(1916–) US actor from the stage. His early films allowed him the opportunity to play an emotional range which included repressed anger, at which he excelled, as in *Spellbound* – 1945 and *Duel in the Sun* – 1946. As his star status increased in the 1950s he played more stolid heroes, as in *The Big Country* – 1958. This made his theatrical Ahab in *Moby Dick* – 1956 seem even more overplayed than it actually is. He excels as a brooding leader in *Captain Horatio Hornblower* – 1951, and a man-with-a-cause, as in his only Oscar-winning role *To Kill a Mockingbird* – 1963. His career recently found a second wind commercially with the popularity of *The Omen* – 1977.

Other films include:
Yellow Sky – 1948, *The Gunfighter* – 1950, *The Bravados* – 1958, *On the Beach* – 1959, *The Guns of Navarone* – 1961, *Cape Fear* – 1962, *The Stalking Moon* – 1968, *Billy Two Hats* – 1973.

Further reading:
Gregory Peck Tony Thomas, Pyramid, New York, 1977.

PECKINPAH, Sam

(1926–) US director whose films are obsessed with the survival consciousness of the frontier. Peckinpah's heroes uphold a rigid moral code, based on male kinship, which is tested by tensions within the group or by elements thrown up by a hostile world. Most of his films are violent expositions of individualism in a changing world. *Major Dundee* – 1965, *The Wild Bunch* – 1969, and *Straw Dogs* – 1972 are examples. But complementary films are more lyrical and subdued: *Ride the High Country* (in Britain *Guns in The Afternoon*) – 1962 and *Junior Bonner* – 1970. Some critics have found a surrealist streak in his films. Certainly his mythic concerns often take the baroque form of a journey into nightmare, as in *Bring Me the Head of Alfredo Garcia* (*Behold the Head of Alfredo Garcia* in Britain) – 1974 and *Cross of Iron* – 1977.

Other films include:
The Deadly Companions – 1961, *The Getaway* – 1972, *Pat Garrett and Billy the Kid* – 1975.

Further reading:
Horizons West Jim Kitses, Thames and Hudson, London, 1969.

PENN, Arthur

(1922–) US director from television and stage. He had an initial Hollywood flirtation, with

The Left-handed Gun – 1958, followed by an estrangement and a foray into 'art' cinema with Mickey One – 1968. Penn then accepted the strengths and constraints of genre cinema to direct a series of commercially successful films, typified by Bonnie and Clyde – 1967. Penn is concerned with myth-making, which he sees as crucial to an understanding of America. Within that process, he focuses on the Freudian reworking of relationships between substitute father and wayward son (the key to understanding The Chase – 1966 and Alice's Restaurant – 1969 especially) and between teacher and taught, most explicitly in The Miracle Worker – 1962. These relationships are marked by spontaneous acts of repulsive violence, which makes films such as The Missouri Breaks – 1976 gruelling audience experiences.

Other films include:
Little Big Man – 1970, Night Moves – 1975.

Further reading:
Arthur Penn Robin Wood, Studio Vista, 1968.

PICKFORD, Mary
(1893-1979) Canadian-born US actress who became known as 'the world's sweetheart' due to her phenomenal success playing ringletted children of amazing goodness and sweetness, partially redeemed by determination and a sense of fun. She came to hate these parts, but her fans loved her in such films as The Poor Little Rich Girl – 1917, Rebecca of Sunnybrook Farm – 1917, Daddy Long Legs – 1919 and Pollyanna – 1920. In 1919 she set up United Artists with Griffith (who had directed her first films), Chaplin and Fairbanks, whom she married the following year. In 1923 she made the first of several attempts to leave 'Little Mary' behind. She brought over Lubitsch to direct her in Rosita – 1923, but with unhappy results. More increasingly inappropriate child roles followed, but she did manage to play a young girl in the charming My Best Girl – 1927, opposite Charles Buddy Rogers, whom she later married. She finally

retired from acting after Secrets – 1933, one of several unsuccessful adult roles in sound films. She continued on the business side of the company.

Other films include:
Little Lord Fauntleroy – 1921, The Taming of the Shrew – 1929.

Further reading:
Sunshine and Shadow, Mary Pickford, Heinemann, London, 1956.

POITIER, Sidney
(1924–) US actor, possibly the only black superstar. His early roles were in films about the race 'problem'. In films such as No Way Out – 1950 and Edge of the City – 1957 he established an honest but defiant persona. Following the critical and box-office success of The Defiant Ones – 1958 he went on to epitomize the liberal negro in the years of the American civil rights movement, especially in In the Heat of the Night – 1967 and Guess Who's Coming to Dinner? – 1967. Since then he has become increasingly politicized and, together with other black actors, especially Harry Belafonte, has made films into the 1970s which specifically aim at black audiences. The most interesting of these is undoubtedly Buck and the Preacher – 1972, which he also directed.

Other films include:
Porgy and Bess – 1959, Duel at Diablo – 1966, To Sir With Love – 1967, A Piece of the Action – 1978.

Further reading:
The Long Journey: A Biography of Sidney Poitier Carolyn H. Ewers, New American Library, New York, 1969.

POLAŃSKI, Roman
(1933–) Polish-born director whose critical reputation was established through his film school work, notably the short

Two Men and a Wardrobe – 1958, and his graduation feature Knife in the Water – 1961. Since then he has become internationally notorious, both for his private life, tragic and dogged by legal troubles, and for the controversial subjects of his films. The most commercial has been Rosemary's Baby – 1968, the first of the 1960s cycle of films about minds possessed by the Devil. All his films concentrate on the psychotic personality tortured by an alienated world. This is expressed in a style full of bizarre images and comic situations; a particular Polish type of surrealism. Among his infrequent films are some in which he has starred himself: as the lost soul in The Fearless Vampire Killers (Dance of the Vampires in Britain) – 1967, a homage to Hammer horror films, and as The Tenant – 1977, in which he commits a fantastic double suicide.

Other films include:
Repulsion – 1965, Cul-de-Sac – 1966, Macbeth – 1971, What? – 1972, Chinatown – 1974.

Further reading:
The Cinema of Roman Polanski Ivan Butler, International Film Guide Series, London, 1970.

POWELL, Michael
(1905–) British director who also scripted films, such as The Man Behind the Mask – 1936, in addition to those which he directed, often in collaboration with Emeric Pressburger. Powell's films flirt with dream worlds – literally, in the fantastic The Thief of Bagdad – 1940, and with the subconscious, as in his masterpiece, Peeping Tom – 1960. They thus often explore Freudian ideas. Above all his films are concerned with the status of art, simply – as with his dance films such as The Red Shoes – 1948 – or more complexly, by examining the role of the artist. This he does in Age of Consent – 1969, and, by extension, through the skills of the wartime bomb-expert in The Small Back Room – 1948. This is one of the few British films to recognize a world outside British shores, in its use of surrealist imagery and existentialist ideas.

Other films include:
The Edge of the World – 1937, The Life and Death of Colonel Blimp – 1943, I Know Where I'm Going – 1945, A Matter of Life and Death – 1946, The Tales of Hoffman – 1951.

Further reading:
Powell, Pressburger and others edited by Ian Christie, BFI, London, 1978.

PREMINGER, Otto
(1906–) Viennese-born US director whose first major film was the classic film noir Laura – 1944. In general he is much more effective with smaller budget, genre films such as Fallen Angel – 1945, Where the Sidewalk Ends – 1950 and Bunny Lake is Missing – 1956 (all detective films) than with the big-budget and/or message pictures such as Exodus – 1960, on the birth of Israel, Hurry Sundown – 1967, on race, or The Man with the Golden Arm – 1955, on drug addiction. These tend to be rather ponderous. Critics point to the skilful organization of the visual elements in his films, and the use of movement and balance within the frame to make the plot and character points. The River of No Return – 1954 has been particularly admired as the first film to make creative use of CinemaScope. Recent films such as Such Good Friends – 1971 have explored areas of 'doubtful taste' (or black comedy) but have not been very well received.

Other films include:
Daisy Kenyon – 1947, Carmen Jones – 1954, Bonjour tristesse – 1958, Anatomy of a Murder – 1959, Advise and Consent – 1961, Rosebud – 1974.

Further reading:
The Cinema of Otto Preminger, Gerald Pratley, Tantivy Press, London.

RAY, Nicholas
(1911–) US director whose turbulent relationship with the Hollywood film industry produced films interesting for their portrayal of the myth of the outsider, rejected by a cynical and corrupt society which will not tolerate criticism. Each of Ray's films combine his flair for experiment (colour and editing in Johnny Guitar – 1954, camera-angles and wide-screen in Rebel Without a Cause – 1955) with an epic sense of man as the victim of society and his own nature (Bigger Than Life – 1956). After the failure of Fifty-five Days at Peking – 1963 he left Hollywood for good. He spent some time in Europe before returning to the US in 1971 to teach at Harpur College, New York. There he collaborated with his students on the politically radical, experimental film We Can't Go Home Again – 1973. Its making was recorded in the documentary I'm a Stranger Here Myself – 1974, in which Ray himself is depicted as the outsider. Recently he has been working at the Strasberg Institute in New York.

Other films include:
They Live by Night – 1947, In a Lonely Place – 1950, Bitter Victory – 1957, (with others) Wet Dreams – 1974.

Further reading:
Underworld USA Colin McArthur, Secker and Warburg, London, 1972.

RAY Satyajit
(1921–) Great Indian director who is also a gifted designer and musician (he composes the music for most of his films, as well as writing the scripts). His first film, Pather Panchali – 1955, became an instant classic. Together with Aparajito – 1957 and Apur Sansar – 1959, it forms a trilogy about a country family and its move to the city. Ray's work is centrally concerned with particular individuals, for example the bored young wife in Charulata – 1964, one of his masterpieces, and the

young wife who searches for work in *Mahanagar* – 1963. Women often serve as critical, realistic observers, as in the delicate, Chekhov-like *Days and Nights in the Forest* – 1970, and the witty, perceptive and finally quietly tragic *Company Limited* – 1971. In recent years Ray's films have become more overtly political. He analyzes critically, compassionately, and more and more bleakly the weaknesses of Indian society, as in *The Middle Man* – 1975. With *The Chess Players* – 1977 he has made his first film in Hindi (he comes from Bengal) successfully bringing him into contact with a mass Indian audience.

Other films include:
The Music Room – 1958, *Devi* – 1960, *Distant Thunder* – 1973, *The Elephant God* – 1978.
Further reading:
Portrait of a Director: Satyajit Ray Marie Seton, Dennis Dobson, London, 1971.

REDFORD, Robert
(1936–) US actor from drama school who has carefully selected his film roles. His film character is that of the loser, full of charm and bravado but, with a twinkle in the eye, always sympathetic. He is equally at home in serious roles, such as the escaped convict in *The Chase* – 1966, and comic parts, such as the newly-married partner in *Barefoot in the Park* – 1967. His star status really came with the popular *Butch Cassidy and the Sundance Kid* – 1969. Since that film, possibly the first of the 'buddy movie' genre, he has become a hot property, in films such as *The Sting* – 1973 and *The Way We Were* – 1973. These have allowed him opportunity to make less commercial films, such as *Jeremiah Johnson* – 1972, without loss of box office appeal, and to produce and star in films about the American political process, such as *The Candidate* – 1972 and *All the President's Men* – 1976.

Other films include:
War Hunt – 1962, *Inside Daisy Clover* – 1966 *Tell Them Willie Boy is Here* – 1969, *Downhill Racer* – 1969, *The Great Gatsby* – 1973.

Further reading:
The Films of Robert Redford James Spada, Citadel Press, Secausus, 1977.

REDGRAVE, Vanessa
(1937–) British actress, daughter of a famous acting family. She was a successful stage actress before making her first film, *Morgan: A Suitable Case for Treatment* – 1966. Few of her films have been commercially successful. She became a star by virtue of her striking good looks and her reputation as a serious actress who chose her roles according to her left-wing views, portraying them with a thoughtfulness which often transcended the film itself. Her political views came to the fore when she produced *The Palestinian* – 1977, a documentary about the plight of Palestinian refugees, in which she also appears. Her acting partnership with Jane Fonda in the enormously successful *Julia* – 1977, earned her an Oscar, amid some controversy.

Other films include:
Blow Up – 1966, *Isadora* (*The Loves of Isadora* in US) – 1969, *The Trojan Women* – 1971, *Agatha* – 1978.

REED, Carol
(1906–1976) director who was an actor and dialogue director before directing the sea adventure *Midshipman Easy* (*Men of the Sea* in US) – 1936. He made eleven more films in the next five years. They are mainly unpretentious comedies and comedy thrillers, skilfully constructed with well-observed detail. They include *Bank Holiday* (*Three on a Weekend* in US) – 1938 and *Night Train to Munich* (*Night Train* in US) – 1940, both featuring Margaret Lockwood, who appeared in eight of his films at this time. The peak of his career is generally felt

to be the immediate post-war period, with *Odd Man Out* – 1947, *The Fallen Idol* – 1948, a child's disturbed view of the break-down of a marriage, and the most famous, *The Third Man* – 1949. This thriller, set in war-shattered occupied Viénna, had haunting zither music and Orson Welles at his best as the corrupt Harry Lime. *Outcast of the Islands* – 1952, based on Joseph Conrad, had production difficulties and is uneven, but contains some unusually powerful scenes of humiliation and degradation. The rest of his career is unhappily one of decline, although *The Man Between* – 1953 and *The Key* – 1958 were praised and *Oliver!* – 1968 brought him an Oscar.

Other films include:
The Stars Look Down – 1940, *The Public Eye* (*Follow Me* in Britain) – 1972.

Further reading:
Carol Reed Brenda Davies, British Film Institute, London, 1978.

RENOIR, Jean
(1894–1979) French director generally acknowledged as one of the supreme figures in world cinema. Some critics tend to emphasize his work in the 1930s, particularly the pacifist *La Grande Illusion* – 1937 and the capricious *La règle du jeu* – 1939, at the expense of his American work. The latter includes *The Southerner* – 1945, a moving study of a poor farmer's struggle to survive, and the disturbing *The Diary of a Chambermaid* – 1946. His last work includes the serene masterpieces *The River* – 1952 and *French Can-Can* – 1955. His films are pervaded by a tolerance and generosity of spirit which is expressed by the space allowed to his actors and the use of deep-focus photography. They are often concerned with an individual's search for happiness and a role in society. The latter may lead to an oppositional way of life, as in *Boudu sauve des eaux* – 1932, or *Le Dejeuner sur l'herbe* – 1961, or a settling for the moments life offers, as in *Une Partie de campagne* – 1936 and most of the post-war films, or defeat, as in

Madame Bovary – 1934 and *La Règle du jeu* – 1939.
Other films include:
Nana – 1926, *La Chienne* – 1931, *Toni* – 1935, *Le Crime de Monsieur Lange* – 1936, *The Golden Coach* – 1953, *Elena et les hommes* – 1956.
Further reading:
My Life and My Films Jean Renoir, Collins, London, 1974.

RESNAIS, Alain
(1922–) French director who, though associated with the New Wave, has been closer in practice to writers from the *nouveau roman* movement, such as Marguerite Duras and Alain Robbe-Grillet. Both wrote scripts for him, and subsequently directed their own films. He began work as a film editor. He then directed a remarkable series of short films, of which *Night and Fog* – 1955, a formal and powerful study of Nazi concentration camps, is probably the best known. His first feature film, *Hiroshima, mon Amour* – 1959, was regarded as revolutionary in its blending of past and present, memory, imagination and actuality, as were *L'Annee Dernière a Marienbad* – 1961 and *Muriel* – 1963. Resnais's films have an elegance and grace which make them enthralling to watch as well as intellectually absorbing. Examples include his latest films *Stavisky* – 1974, about a famous financial swindle with political dimensions, and *Providence* – 1977, largely concerned with an ageing writer's attempt to make sense of his private relationships by mentally re-writing them.
Other films include:
The War is Over – 1966, *Je t'aime, je t'aime* – 1968.
Further reading:
Alain Resnais James Monaco, Oxford University Press, Oxford, 1978.

RITCHIE, Michael
(1936–) US director who worked in television for eight years (and also with the Maysles brothers on their documentaries) before being selected by Robert Redford to direct *Downhill Racer* – 1969. This concerns the behind-the-scenes world of international ski racing. It delicately reveals the compromises, pressures, manoeuvres and distortions involved in reporting sport in the media. *The Candidate* – 1972 looks at political campaigning in a similar way, and how the system takes hold of even the best intentioned. Apart from *Prime Cut* – 1972, which was considerably altered by its producers, all Ritchie's films so far have looked with a cool, but not unkindly, ironic eye at typical aspects of American life and the success ethic: the beauty contest and small town life in *Smile* – 1975, junior league baseball in *The Bad News Bears* – 1976, and self-help therapy in *Semi-Tough* – 1977. Typically they mix fiction and *cinéma verité* (including the actual staging of a whistle-stop tour and a beauty contest). He often uses non-professional actors in supporting roles.

ROBINSON, Edward G.
(1893–1972) Versatile US actor best known for his roles as an ugly gangster, especially in his first starring role in *Little Caesar* – 1930. His long career spanned a greater variety of parts, however. They include notable cameo roles: in *Double Indemnity* – 1944, as boss to Fred MacMurray's insurance agent, and as the card-king in *The Cincinnati Kid* – 1965. In all these roles he played calm, experienced authority-figures. His age and smallness allowed him to play weaker and pitiable characters, often duped by younger women, as in perhaps his best films, *The Woman in the Window* – 1944 and *Scarlet Street* – 1945.

Other films include:
Dr Ehrlich's Magic Bullet – 1940, *The Sea Wolf* – 1941, *Key Largo* – 1948, *Two Weeks in Another Town* – 1962, *Soylent Green* – 1973.

Further reading:
All My Yesterdays Edward G. Robinson with Leonard Spigelgass, Hawthorn Books, New York, 1973.

ROGERS, Ginger

(1911–) US actress who, despite her personal preference for non-musical roles, is best known for the celebrated and enormously successful Astaire/Rogers musicals of the 1930s, including *Top Hat* – 1935 and *Swing Time* – 1937. As has been said: 'He gave her class and she gave him sex appeal.' Despite her Oscar for *Kitty Foyle* – 1940, about a girl who married for money, with unhappy results, she was at her best in wise-cracking comedy, for which she first established her name in films such as *42nd Street* – 1933. This persona was used to good dramatic and humorous effect in *Stage Door* – 1937, in which she clashed splendidly with Katharine Hepburn. Later films include a reunion with Astaire in *The Berkeleys of Broadway* – 1949, *Storm Warning* – 1950, a thriller, and the Hawks comedy *Monkey Business* – 1952. Since then she has concentrated on stage musicals and nightclub work.

Other films include:
Bachelor Mother – 1939, *The Major and the Minor* – 1942, *Lady in the Dark* – 1944.

Further reading:
Ginger Rogers, Patrick McGilligan, Pyramid, New York, 1975.

ROSSELLINI, Roberto

(1906–1977) Italian director and scriptwriter. In a long and productive career Rossellini has worked in realist and comic modes, in costume dramas and contemporary settings, in narrative fiction and documentary, and in cinema and television. Across this vast range, however, his theme has been consistent. He is concerned with change, and the contradictions between the natural world and the social relations we 'choose' to make in it. This is true, whether of the neorealist *Rome – Open City* – 1945 and *Paisà*–1946 or the sophisticated dramas starring Ingrid Bergman, such as *Viaggio in Italia* – 1953, or documentaries such as the episodic *India* – 1958. Above all, however, is a disposition for the epic canvas and the revolutionary time, be it Garibaldi in *Viva L'Italia!* – 1960, the Apostles in the marathon *Atti Degli Apostoli* – 1968, or *Socrate* – 1970. For the majority of critics Rossellini is one of the most important film-makers.

Other films include:
Germany, Year Zero – 1947, *Stromboli* – 1949, *Francesco, Giullare di Dio* – 1950, *Vanina, Vanina* – 1961, *Anno uno* – 1974, *La Prise de pouvoir par Louis XIV* – 1966.

Further reading:
Roberto Rossellini José Luis Guerner (translated by Elizabeth Caméron), Movie, London, 1976.

RUSSELL, Ken

(1927–) British director whose work provokes extreme and varied reactions. He is certainly an original talent. He established a reputation as a director of imaginative BBC TV drama documentaries on composers, *A Song of Summer* – 1968, on Delius, probably being the finest. It was not until his third feature film, *Women in Love* – 1969, that he made his mark in the cinema. The film contains the seeds of his later work in its use of emphatic stylistic devices to express extremes of emotion. These detractors regard as crude and sensational, and admirers praise as imaginative and creative. His style is seen at its most extreme in *The Music Lovers* – 1970, a study of Tchaikovsky, *Mahler* – 1974, and *Tommy* – 1975, a film version of The Who's successful record album. It is fair to say that the subjects of his biographical films would not be entirely happy.

Other feature films include:
The Devils – 1971, *The Boy Friend* – 1971, *Savage Messiah* – 1972, *Valentino* – 1977.

Further reading:
An appalling talent: Ken Russell John Baxter, Michael Joseph, London, 1973.

SCHLESINGER, John

(1926–) British director who works on both sides of the Atlantic. He began in television, then won a prize at Venice with a short film called *Terminus* – 1961. This led to his first feature *A Kind of Loving* – 1962, one of a group of British films of the time about working class life. *Billy Liar* – 1963, based on a successful play about a north country Walter Mitty, contained an attractive performance from Julie Christie. She starred in his next two films: *Darling* – 1965, notable chiefly for Dirk Bogarde's performance, and *Far from the Madding Crowd* – 1967, with its stunning photography by Nicholas Roeg. *Midnight Cowboy* – 1969 won him an Oscar, and *Sunday, Bloody Sunday* – 1971 was well-received.

Other films include:
Marathon Man – 1976, *Yanks* – 1978.

Further reading:
The film careers of Lindsay Anderson and John Schlesinger Loring Silet and Nancy J. Brooker, G. K. Hall, New York, 1978.

SCORSESE, Martin

(1942–) US director who first attracted attention with a black-joke short *The Big Shave* – 1967. He subsequently gained critical praise for the naturalism and strength of *Mean Streets* – 1973, set in New York's Italian district and starring regular collaborator Robert de Niro. *Alice Doesn't Live Here Anymore* – 1975 was his first popular success. It was followed by *Taxi Driver* – 1976, a brilliant and hating picture of the underside of New York, which, disturbingly, can be read as either an indictment or an endorsement of individual violence. *New York, New York* – 1977 is a fascinating evocation of the world of 1940s Hollywood musicals. Individual scenes are staged as musical numbers, and on these rests the main weight of plot development. Scorsese's documentary work includes *The Last Waltz* – 1978, whose subject matter echoes his editing work on such films as *Woodstock* – 1969.

Other films include:
Who's That Knocking on My Door – 1968, *Italianamerican* – 1975.

Further reading:
Movie Brats Michael Pye and Lynda Myles, Holt Reinhart, New York, 1978.

SEGAL, George

(1934–) US actor who has worked his way up to star status via stage, television and a variety of film roles. These include the young dispossessed farmer seeking revenge in *Invitation to a Gunfighter* – 1963, the title role in *King Rat* – 1964, and the embarrassed junior lecturer in *Who's Afraid of Virginia Woolf?* – 1965. In *No Way to Treat a Lady* – 1967 he gave a performance of wry humour, desperation and considerable charm as the detective under pressure from a possessive mother and a psychotic murderer who insists on talking to him alone. Since then he has played some effective variations on the theme in films such as *The Owl and the Pussycat* – 1970, the brilliant black comedy *Where's Poppa?* – 1971, and *A Touch of Class* – 1972. The desperation is uppermost in *Loving* – 1970, a not-so-funny study of marriage in the commuter belt.

Other films include:
The Quiller Memorandum – 1966, *Blume in Love* – 1973, *Rollercoaster* – 1977.

SELLERS, Peter

(1925) British actor from music hall who appeared in a series of short films which grew from the radio comedy show, 'The Goons'. He then went solo as a character actor in features such as *The Ladykillers* – 1955 and *I'm All Right Jack* – 1959. His international reputation was established through his role as the bumbling French detective, Clouseau, in *The Pink Panther* – 1963, a part he has repeated in several sequels, and playing several parts in Kubrick's satire *Dr Strangelove* – 1963. Playing multiple parts is a strategy he has often employed, for instance in *The Mouse that Roared* – 1959, and is suggestive of his strengths as a mimic rather than an actor. His only film as director, *Mr Topaze* – 1961, is slight. But it is sufficiently interesting to make one sad that his disappointing roles in the 1970s were not avoided in favour of more projects as director.

Other films include:
The Smallest Show on Earth – 1957, *Never Let Go* – 1961, *The Millionairess* – 1961, *Only Two Can Play* – 1962, *Lolita* – 1962, *The Party* – 1968, *There's a Girl in My Soup* – 1970, *Revenge of the Pink Panther* – 1978.

Further reading:
Peter Sellers – The Mask Behind the Mask, Peter Evans, Prentice Hall, New York, 1968.

SELZNICK, David O.

(1902–1965) US producer who worked for several major studios, as well as having his own independent film-making company. He is arguably the true 'auteur' of *Gone With the Wind* – 1939, which he closely supervised from start to finish – as he did many of his productions, not least those starring his second wife, Jennifer Jones. He had a shrewd eye for talent and, among others, brought Alfred Hitchcock and Ingrid Bergman to Hollywood.

Other films include:
David Copperfield – 1934, *A Star is Born* – 1937, *Nothing Sacred* – 1937, *Rebecca* – 1940, *Spellbound* – 1945, *Duel in the Sun* – 1946.

Further reading:
Memo from David O. Selznick Rudy Behlmer, Viking Press, New York, 1972.

SHARIF, Omar

(1923–) Egyptian actor who starred in over twenty films in his own country before being cast by Lean in *Lawrence of Arabia* – 1962. This led to several non-Egyptian films. But it was the same director's *Doctor Zhivago* – 1965 which made him a box office star despite a rather wooden performance as the romantic hero. His appeal seems to rest mainly with his large brown eyes and flashing smile, but *Funny Girl* – 1968 and *The Last Valley* – 1971 show that he can offer more in the right parts.

Other films include:
The Night of the Generals – 1966, *Mayerling* – 1968, *Funny Lady* – 1975.
Further reading:
The eternal male: an autobiography, Omar Sharif and Marie Thérèse Guinchard, W. H. Allen, London, 1977.

SIEGEL, Don

(1912–) US director, earlier montage editor on, for example, *The Roaring Twenties* – 1939. Siegel's career falls into three distinct phases. First, his apprenticeship films, characterized by tightly-controlled narratives in which violent heroes are ejected from even more violent societies. These are shown at their best in the low-budget *Riot in Cell Block 11* – 1954, *Invasion of the Body Snatchers* – 1956 and *Baby Face Nelson* – 1957. Second, films of the early 1960s, in which increasingly psychotic heroes are nonetheless treated with tragic sympathy. Typical are *Flaming Star* – 1960, an Elvis Presley vehicle, *Hell is for Heroes* – 1962 and *Madigan* – 1967. Third, films made with Clint Eastwood, in which the heroes are equally isolated but more conservative characters. Typical of these is *Coogan's Bluff* – 1968, and *Dirty Harry* – 1972. Siegel is always full of surprises. After a creative lull typified by *The Black Windmill* – 1974, the appearance of the bizarre *Telefon* – 1978 signals hope for the future.
Other films include:
The Verdict – 1946, *The Line-Up* – 1958, *The Killers* – 1964, *Two Mules for Sister Sara* – 1969, *The Beguiled* – 1971, *Charley Varrick* – 1973, *The Shootist* – 1976.
Further reading:
Don Siegel Alan Lovell, BFI, London, 1977.

SIMMONS, Jean

(1929–) English actress of great beauty and considerable talent. Sadly she has only worked intermittently since her marriage to Richard Brooks, after he directed one of her finest performances in *Elmer Gantry* – 1960. A child actress, she had several film parts before making an impact as the haughty young Estella in *Great Expectations* – 1946, and the pertly seductive Indian girl in *Black Narcissus* – 1947, later stealing some of the notices with her Ophelia in Olivier's *Hamlet* – 1948. Most of her British films were mediocre however, although *Clouded Yellow* – 1950, a good romantic thriller opposite Trevor Howard, was another exception. She was not much happier about parts in Hollywood when her contract was sold to RKO, although she gave a fine performance as the innocent-seeming killer in Preminger's *Angel Face* – 1952. Perhaps her best performance in the 1950s was in *The Actress* – 1953, Cukor's small scale, beautifully acted film about a young girl's stage ambitions. More recent work includes good performances in an initially interesting role in the western *Rough Night in Jericho* – 1967 and Brooks' unimpressive *The Happy Ending* – 1969.
Other films include:
The Robe – 1953, *Guys and Dolls* – 1955, *The Big Country* – 1958, *Divorce American Style* – 1967, *Dominique* – 1978, *Say Hello to Yesterday* – 1970.

SIRK, Douglas

(1900–) Danish-born director who worked in German theatre and cinema before moving to America in 1940. His experience with romantic drama held him in good stead, since he went on to direct a series of melodramas for Universal Studios in the 1950s. An underrated director, possibly because melodrama itself is often dismissed by film critics as sentimental. Melodrama deals with unresolved sexual and emotional problems in the context of family relationships. Sirk exploited the dramatic potential of this apparently routine material to bring out contradictions. Some critics see in his work a radical critique of the bourgeois American family. Essentially studio productions, Sirk's melodramas depend on the stereotypes and images of the genre to produce an unreal effect, encouraging the spectator to think about the spectacle of film itself.
Other films include:
(in Germany) *Schlussakkord* – 1936, *Zu neuen Ufern* – 1937, (in US) *Magnificent Obsession* – 1954, *Written on the Wind* – 1956, *Imitation of Life* – 1959.
Further reading:
Sirk on Sirk Jon Halliday, Secker and Warburg, London, 1971.

SPIELBERG, Steven

(1946–) US director whose brief career includes two of the cinema's biggest box office successes. Some would rate more highly his first two films – *Duel* – 1971, originally made for television, which creates a frightening presence out of a long distance lorry whose driver remains unseen, and *The Sugarland Express* – 1973, his first theatrical film, heavily cut on release. So far Spielberg's career is more one of interest and promise than major achievement, although his technical expertise is apparent. In *Jaws* – 1975 he uses suspenseful editing rather than on-screen horrors, and in *Close Encounters of the Third Kind* – 1977 he uses sound brilliantly to build atmosphere and depict the extra-terrestrials. Once again a large, formidable force lurks and swoops on men and women who are dwarfed and intimidated. But here the force is benevolent and beautiful (the special effects are superb, almost measuring up to a character's description: 'The sun came out last night and it sang to me').
Further reading:
The Jaws Log Carl Gottlieb, Dell, New York, 1975.

STANWYCK, Barbara

(1907–) US actress who has an enviable reputation for professionalism and helpfulness to her colleagues. Her acting is of consistently high quality and characterized by a lucid intelligence. She had a hard early life, but once launched on an acting career rose quickly to starring roles, continuing to play them for over forty years (in recent years mainly on television). She is most at home playing strong independent characters, both sympathetic, as in *The Bitter Tea of General Yen* – 1933 and *Golden Boy* – 1939, and up to no good, as the blonde seductress in *Double Indemnity* – 1944, perhaps her most famous role. Her wide range includes a foolish but finally self-sacrificing mother in *Stella Dallas* – 1937, a sophisticated card-sharper in Sturges' witty *The Lady Eve* – 1941, a gum-chewing showgirl in *Ball of Fire* – 1941, an unfaithful wife in *Clash by Night* – 1952, and the tough cattle-rancher who fights and loves the hero in *Forty Guns* – 1957, one of a number of westerns in the 1950s.
Other films include:
Union Pacific – 1939, *Cry Wolf* – 1947, *The Furies* – 1950, *Executive Suite* – 1954, *A Walk on the Wild Side* – 1962.
Further reading:
Starring Miss Barbara Stanwyck Ella Smith, Crown, New York, 1974.

STEIGER, Rod

(1925–) US actor, trained in the 'method' style, which is the impetus for his mannered and neurotic performances. After a famous performance as Brando's gangster brother in *On the Waterfront* – 1954, he went on to play Dostoevskyan characters in films such as *Oklahoma!* – 1955 and *Run of the Arrow* – 1957. One of his few controlled performances is as *The Pawnbroker* – 1965. Generally he spurns direction and, since the 1970s, has been difficult to cast. He won an Oscar for his performance as the police chief in *In the Heat of the Night* – 1967. He has been better, notably as *Al Capone* – 1958, and even uncharacteristically comic as a psychotic murderer who is a master of disguise in *No Way to Treat a Lady* – 1968.
Other films include:
The Harder they Fall – 1956, *Across the Bridge* – 1957, *Hands over the City* – 1963, *Dr Zhivago* – 1966, *The Illustrated Man* – 1969, *Waterloo* – 1970, *A Fistful of Dynamite* – 1971.

STERNBERG, Josef von

(1894–1969) Austrian-born director who went to the US in 1908. He is best known for his creative association with Marlene Dietrich, whom he took to Hollywood after directing her in *The Blue Angel* – 1930 in Germany. Sternberg's style consisted of a seductive use of light and shadow, luminous photography and bizarre décor employing nets and lace, to create a cinematic fantasy-world charged with eroticism, in which narrative was secondary. This 'modernist' concern with form was criticized by those who wanted his films to deal with political reality. But Sternberg's greatest contribution was to link politics with sexuality, as in *The Scarlet Empress* – 1934. His use of Dietrich as a sexually ambiguous fetish-figure in *Morocco* – 1930 and *Blonde Venus* – 1932 highlighted the exploitation of woman as spectacle, and the voyeuristic position of the spectator on which commercial cinema rests. His later films without Dietrich never captured the same subversive excess.

Other films include:
Dishonored – 1931, *The Devil is a Woman* – 1934, *The Shanghai Gesture* – 1941, (with others) *Macao* – 1952.

Further reading:
The Films of Josef von Sternberg Andrew Sarris, The Museum of Modern Art, New York, 1966.

STEWART, James

(1908–) US actor whose distinctive drawl and relaxed manner have graced many key genre films since the 1930s. The slow, folksy quality of his film presence has often been used to conceal a more wily sophistication, as in *Destry Rides Again* – 1939, and his Oscar-winning role in *The Philadelphia Story* – 1940. That same quality can also conceal an emotional intensity which has jerked tears in the otherwise comic films of Capra, such as *It's a Wonderful Life* – 1946. The inner energy of his character has also been used differently by three directors: bordering on the obsessive for Hitchcock, especially in *Vertigo* – 1958; hysterical for Ford in *The Man Who Shot Liberty Valance* – 1962; and almost pathological for Mann, typically in *The Man from Laramie* – 1955. Stewart has become an actor of greater versatility and skill than popular reputation allows.

Other films include:
Seventh Heaven – 1937, *Mr Smith Goes to Washington* – 1939, *Call Northside 777* – 1947, *Rope* – 1948, *Winchester 73* – 1950, *The Glenn Miller Story* – 1953, *Anatomy of a Murder* – 1959, *Firecreek* – 1967, *Airport 77* – 1977.

Further reading:
James Stewart Howard Thompson, Pyramid, New York, 1974.

STREISAND, Barbra

(1942–) US actress and singer who came to Hollywood to repeat her stage success as Fanny Brice in *Funny Girl* – 1968, and won an Oscar in the process. Following two further musicals she began to concentrate on non-singing roles, most effectively in the comedy *What's Up Doc?* – 1972. An individual and gifted singer,

her screen personality is a strong one, which some find uncomfortably overpowering. Nonetheless she is one of the very few stars whose presence in a film ensures financial backing. This strong position enabled her to set up and control the re-make of *A Star is Born* – 1976, which has proved a major box-office success.

Other films include:
Hello, Dolly! – 1969, *On a Clear Day You Can See Forever* – 1970, *The Owl and the Pussycat* – 1970, *Up the Sandbox* – 1972, *The Way We Were* – 1973, *For Pete's Sake* – 1974, *Funny Lady* – 1975.

Further Reading:
Barbra: The First Decade James Spada, Secausus, New Jersey, 1974.

STROHEIM, Erich von

(1885–1957) Viennese born US actor/director/writer who began (and finished) as an actor, publicized as 'the man you love to hate'. In his first film as director (also writer and designer), *Blind Husbands* – 1919, he played a cynical European bent on seducing a foolish American wife, a situation developed more complexly in *Foolish Wives* – 1922. His films are virtually unique in American cinema: for their atmosphere of decadence and corruption (with Stroheim himself a strutting, sensual figure), their mordantly witty humour and extremes – of violence and tenderness, for example. His style is based on the meticulous accumulation of detail within each scene. The length which this demanded brought him into conflict with producers, notoriously on *Greed* – 1924, which was reduced from 42 to 10 reels to run $2\frac{1}{4}$ hours. Stroheim's own scheme for two-part films was partly carried out with

The Wedding March – 1928, but part two was issued as another film, *The Honeymoon* – 1929, and is now apparently lost.

Other films include:
(as director) *Merry-go-round* – 1923, *The Merry Widow* – 1925, *Queen Kelly* – 1928, as actor: *As You Desire Me* – 1932, *La Grande Illusion* – 1937, *Pieges* – 1939, *Sunset Boulevard* – 1950.

Further reading:
Stroheim: a pictorial record of his nine films Herman G. Weinberg, Dover Publications, New York, 1975.

SUTHERLAND, Donald

(1935–) Canadian actor who began his film career in a British horror film, *Dr Terror's House of Horrors* – 1965. He first attracted major attention as Hawkeye in the anarchic comedy *M*A*S*H* – 1970. His career since has been varied, but his roles invariably have an obsessive quality. This is most effective when partially hidden by a quiet, controlled exterior, for example in *Klute* – 1971, as a detective investigating a friend's murder, and in a similar role in Chabrol's *Blood Relatives* – 1978; and as the architect whose obsession leads to his own death, in Nicolas Roeg's *Don't Look Now* – 1973. Sutherland regards this as a pivotal film for him, since from it dates his decision to trust his directors completely for better or worse – as in *1900* – 1976.

Other films include:
Steelyard Blues – 1973, *The Day of the Locust* – 1975, *Casanova* – 1976.

TATI, Jacques

(1908–) French comedian/director who worked mainly in the music hall and circus before directing the short film *L'École des facteurs* – 1947 which he developed into the widely admired feature *Jour de fête* – 1949. *Les Vacances de Monsieur Hulot* – 1951 introduced the comic character featured in most of his subsequent films: tall, with a jerky, loping walk, his head

peering from side to side, but blithely unconscious of his role in the chaos which inevitably accompanies him. *Playtime* – 1967 followed a ten-year gap. Tati is a perfectionist, taking several years to prepare each film. *Playtime* is regarded as his masterpiece, refining his technique of complex, detailed action shown in long takes. The camera at a distance encourages the interplay which Tati seeks between the film and its audience, the characters seen in relation to and interacting with their environment.

Other films as director include:
Mon Oncle – 1958, *Trafic* – 1971, *Parade* – 1973.

Further reading:
The films of Jacques Tati Brent Maddox, Scarecrow Press, Metuchen, 1977.

TAYLOR, Elizabeth

(1932–) English-born actress whose first screen role in Hollywood was in *Lassie Come Home* – 1942. A marvellously beautiful child star, her acting talent never really came out until *A Place in the Sun* – 1951. Even then she was not taken seriously until *Raintree County* earned her an Oscar nomination in 1957. In 1958 her scandalous private affairs helped to establish her as one of the highest paid stars in Hollywood. Known for her emotional intensity and sultry glamour, her acting potential occasionally broke through the glossy surface of her image, for example in *Giant* – 1956. Her much-publicized marriage and acting partnership with Richard Burton produced big box office films such as *Who's Afraid of Virginia Woolf?* – 1966, in which her portrayal of the destructive, emotionally frustrated wife was impressive.

Other films include:
National Velvet – 1944, *Cat on a Hot Tin Roof* – 1958, *Suddenly Last Summer* – 1960, *Butterfield 8* – 1961, *The Sandpiper* – 1965, *Boom!* – 1968, *Zee and Co* – 1971.

Further reading:
Elizabeth Taylor Foster Hirsch, Pyramid, New York, 1973.

TEMPLE, Shirley

(1928–) Child actress of the 1930s Hollywood vehicles. Her impossibly sugar-sweet film identify spawned hundreds of look-alikes and virtually constructed the child-star stereotype. Performing in short films at the age of three, she went on to sing, dance, crack jokes and weep on demand from her first film, *The Red-Haired Alibi* – 1932, until about the time of *The Little Princess* – 1939. Between those films her popularity was phenomenal and she was Twentieth Century-Fox's most bankable asset. Never an actress but always a performer, she appeared in only one distinguished film: John Ford's *Fort Apache* – 1948. Her film career ended with *A Kiss for Corliss* – 1949 at the age of twenty-one. She later appeared on TV in *The Shirley Temple Storybook*, and in chat shows in the late 1960s, when, as American Ambassador to Ghana, interest in her films was revitalized.

Other films include:
The Littlest Rebel – 1935, *Dimples* – 1936, *Wee Willie Winkie* – 1937, *Heidi* – 1937, *Rebecca of Sunnybrook Farm* – 1938.

Further reading:
Shirley Temple Jeanine Basinger, Pyramid, New York, 1975.

TRACY, Spencer

(1900–1967) US actor who came to Hollywood via the stage. He was one of America's finest screen actors, giving seemingly natural, effortless performances. Early success as the anti-hero in *Quick Millions* – 1931 led to other roles as brash heroes, as in Borzage's beautiful *Man's Castle* – 1933. But he was equally associated with father-figure roles as in *Captains Courageous* – 1937, *Boys' Town* – 1938, *Father of the Bride* – 1950 and *The Actress* – 1953.

Woman of the Year – 1942 was the first of nine films which he made with Katharine Hepburn (with whom he was to have a close relationship for the rest of his life). The best of them was a series of wise-cracking comedies in which they were ideal foils for each other – she quick-witted and elegant, he steady and solid – for example *Adam's Rib* – 1949 and *Pat and Mike* – 1952.

Other films include:
Fury – 1936, *Northwest Passage* – 1940, *The Last Hurrah* – 1958, *Judgement at Nuremburg* – 1961.

Further reading:
Spencer Tracy Larry Swindell, World Publishing, New York, 1969.

TRUFFAUT, François
(1932–) French director who began as a critic and as such was the first to articulate the 'auteur' theory. His love for the cinema is vividly present in *Day for Night* – 1973, in which he plays the director. His first feature, *Les 400 Coups* – 1959, gained him an international reputation. Its sympathetic study of a young boy drifting into crime was partly based on Truffaut's own experience. The central character was the subject of later minor films such as *Stolen Kisses* – 1968, which suffer from sentimentality. Typically his central characters are obsessive and fundamentally cold (even Catherine in *Jules et Jim* – 1961, despite her apparent warmth, is self-centred). They are unable to form full relationships; because the scientific experiment is more important than the child in *L'Enfant sauvage* – 1970; because of commitment to revenge in *The Bride Wore Black* – 1967, and to death in *La Chambre verte* – 1978; or because of

an inability to see women as other than sexual objects in *The Man who Loved Women* – 1977.

Other films include:
Shoot the Pianist (Please Don't Shoot the Piano Player in US) – 1960, *Silken Skin* – 1963, *Fahrenheit 451* – 1966, *The Story of Adèle H* – 1975.

Further reading:
Truffaut Don Allen, Secker and Warburg, London, 1974.

TURNER, Lana
(1921–) US actress, dubbed 'The Sweater Girl' at the height of her fame in the 1940s, after her performance in *Ziegfield Girl* – 1941. She played a seductive *femmes fatale* in probably her best film, *The Postman Always Rings Twice* – 1945, and opposite Gable in *Honky Tonk* – 1941. Her career fluctuated, however, and perhaps depended for its high-spots on numerous public scandals. She was often badly cast in unlikely genres, such as the musical *The Merry Widow* – 1952. She starred in a string of both down-market and sophisticated melodramas, after which her career faded in the middle 1960s. Of these melodramas *Peyton Place* – 1957 is probably best-known, but *Imitation of Life* – 1959, is certainly her most intelligent performance.

Other films include:
Johnny Eager – 1941, *The Bad and the Beautiful* – 1952, *The Rains of Ranchipur* – 1955, *Madame X* – 1966.

Further reading:
The Films of Lana Turner Lou Valentino, Citadel Press, Secausus, New York, 1976.

ULLMAN, Liv
(1938–) Norwegian actress particularly associated with Ingmar Bergman (personally and professionally). This association started with her first Swedish film *Persona* – 1966 in the difficult, virtually non-speaking role of an actress suffering from a mysterious malady, and in-

cluded *Shame* – 1968 and *Scenes from a Marriage* – 1974, a television serial as well as a film. Her success in the earlier Bergman films, to which she brings a warmth and compassion unusual in his work, and in Troell's *The Immigrants* – 1970, led to several American films in the early 1970s, none of which offered worthwhile parts. She returned to her native Scandinavia to give a brilliant performance in Ingmar Bergman's award-winning masterpiece *Face to Face* – 1975.

Other films include:
Hour of the Wolf – 1968, *The Abdication* – 1973, *The Serpent's Egg* – 1977, *Autumn Sonata* – 1978.

Further reading:
Changing Liv Ullman, Weidenfeld & Nicolson, London, 1977.

VALENTINO, Rudolph
(1895–1926) US actor who was an idol of the 1920s. His 'magic' signally fails to come off the screen today. After some rather dubious activities, he came to Hollywood where he made fifteen films before June Mathis (one of several dominating ladies in his life) cast him in *The Four Horsemen of the Apocalypse* – 1921, a powerful war film in which he made his first appearance dancing the tango (rather well), and became an 'overnight sensation'. His most famous role is probably *The Sheikh* – 1921, which cast him typically as an exotic figure who had a masterful way with his women, a formula rather blatantly re-used in his last film *Son of the Sheikh* – 1925. His early

death provoked some amazing scenes among the vast crowds of his mourning fans.

Other films include:
Blood and Sand – 1923, *Monsieur Beaucaire* – 1924, *The Eagle* – 1925.

Further reading:
Rudolph Valentino Alexander Walker, Elm Tree Books/Hamish Hamilton, London, 1976.

VIDOR, King
(1894–) US director with a long and distinguished career spanning early silent two-reelers to 1950s epics such as *War and Peace* – 1959. Whether working on social conscience movies concerning World War I – *The Big Parade* – 1925, or the Depression – *The Crowd* – 1928; or within genre films such as the western *Duel in the Sun* – 1946, and the biblical epic *Solomon and Sheba* – 1959; Vidor's consistent interest was with tempestuous man/woman relationships. He was a master of that critically-despised form the melodrama. It is ironic that it was after his career had finished that first scholars and then the Hollywood establishment recognized the power of his major movies, *Stella Dallas* – 1937, *The Fountainhead* – 1947 and *Ruby Gentry* – 1952.

Other films include:
The Patsy – 1928, *Billy the Kid* – 1930, *The Champ* – 1931, *Our Daily Bread* – 1934, *Northwest Passage* – 1939, *The Man Without a Star* – 1955.

Further reading:
King Vidor John Baxter, Monarch Press, New York, 1976.

VISCONTI, Luchino
(1906–1976) Italian director who combined Marxist sympathies with an aristocratic background. He was originally associated with neo-realism, and directed his first film *Ossessione* – 1942 after working as Renoir's assistant. *La terra trema* – 1947, a study of the plight of Sicilian fishermen, was in the same vein. *Senso* – 1954, an historical subject shot in colour, marked the start of the operatic and lavish style more typically associated with his work. It was used with equal success in *The Leopard* – 1965

and *Of a Thousand Delights*, (*Sandra* in US) – 1965. Some of his later work was marred by an over-baroque style – for example *The Damned* – 1970 and *Death in Venice* – 1971, although the latter was greatly admired by some.

Other films include:
White Nights – 1957, *Rocco and His Brothers* – 1960, *The Innocent*, – 1976.

Further reading:
Luchino Visconti, Geoffrey Nowell-Smith, Secker and Warburg, London, 1973.

WALSH, Raoul
(1892–) US director who began his career in movies as an actor at the Old Biograph Studio. There he became assistant to D. W. Griffith, directing and acting in more than fifty films between 1914 and the coming of sound. He worked for many different studios and in many different genres. His period with Warner Brothers from the late 1930s to 1951, when he directed a series of films combining a masterly control of genre conventions with a 'social message', is especially interesting. Generally thought of as a director of 'masculine' films, strong on action, his work with Errol Flynn, James Cagney and Humphrey Bogart supports this view. Nevertheless, films such as *Manpower* – 1942, with Marlene Dietrich, *The Man I Love* – 1946, with Ida Lupino, and *The Revolt of Mamie Stover* – 1956, with Jane Russell, suggest that Walsh's view of 'masculinity' and what it entails is more complex than it would seem.

Other films include:
Sadie Thompson – 1928, *The Roaring Twenties* – 1940, *They Died With Their Boots On* – 1942, *Gentleman Jim* – 1942, *Objective Burma!* – 1945, *The Tall Men* – 1955, *The Sheriff of Fractured Jaw* – 1958.

Further reading:
Raoul Walsh, Phil Hardy, Edinburgh Film Festival, Edinburgh, 1974.

WAYNE, John

(1907-1979) A giant and largely maligned talent as an American actor, although his box-office appeal is indisputable. He established his tough-guy image in many western programme-fillers in the 1930s, before coming to personify Frontier values in the landmark *Stagecoach* – 1939. The complexity and understatement of his performances are at their best in the films directed by John Ford, such as *She Wore a Yellow Ribbon* – 1949 and *The Searchers* – 1956. In them he plays creators of the settled West who are nonetheless tragic outcasts. Films directed by Howard Hawks, centrally *Red River* – 1948, and *Rio Bravo* – 1959, play ironically with his authority in the all-male group. He won an overdue Oscar for a parody of his persona in *True Grit* – 1969, and attempted to immortalize it in *The Shootist* – 1976.

Other films include:
The Big Trail – 1930, *They Were Expendable* – 1945, *Fort Apache* – 1948, *Sands of Iwo Jima* – 1945, *The Quiet Man* – 1952, *The Alamo* – 1960, *The Man Who Shot Liberty Valance* – 1962, *The Green Berets* – 1968, *McQ* –1974.

Further reading:
John Wayne and the Movies Allen Eyles, Tantivy Press, London, 1976.

WELLES, Orson;
see p. 188.

WEST, Mae

(1893–) US actress famous for her figure and witty sexual innuendo. A sex object who, by mocking her image and its admirers, remains firmly in control. Her drawl makes even the most innocent remark suspect; but as she insisted on writing all her own dialogue that is not

often a problem. Her second film, *She Done Him Wrong* – 1933, is a version of her famous play *Diamond Lil* – 1928, with a leading man of her choice in Cary Grant, a combination repeated in *I'm No Angel* – 1933. The 1934 Hays Code limited her activities. Although she shows great ingenuity in circumventing it in *Goin' to Town* – 1934 and *Klondike Annie* – 1936, she eventually went back to the freer world of the stage and night club. She returned to steal *Myra Breckinridge* – 1970 ·rom its leading lady, and more recently starred in *Sextette* – 1978, still firmly peroxided.

Other films include:
Belle of the Nineties – 1934, *My Little Chickadee* – 1939.

Further reading:
Goodness Had Nothing To Do With It Mae West, W. H. Allen, London, 1960.

WILDER, Billy

(1906–) Austrian-born US director who began as a script writer, first in Germany, then in Hollywood. There he teamed up with Charles Brackett on such films as *Ninotchka* – 1939 and *Ball of Fire* – 1941. The collaboration continued when he turned director with an engaging comedy, which had Ginger Rogers masquerading as a child, *The Major and the Minor* – 1942, and on his best received dramas – *The Lost Weekend* – 1945 and *Sunset Boulevard* – 1950. However Wilder tends to be best associated with the brilliant, wise-cracking, tending-to-black comedies which he wrote with I. A. L. Diamond. These include *Some Like It Hot* – 1959, *The Apartment* – 1960, and *The Fortune Cookie* (*Meet Whiplash Willie* in Britain) – 1966. *The Private Life of Sherlock Holmes* – 1970 and *Avanti* – 1972 marked a shift to a more compassionate comic view, but unhappily they were commercially unsuccessful, and Wilder has drawn the necessary conclusions.

Other films include:
Double Indemnity – 1944, *A Foreign Affair* – 1948, *Ace in the Hole* – 1951, *Kiss Me Stupid* – 1964, *The Front Page* – 1974, *Fedora* – 1978.

Further reading:
A Journey down Sunset Boulevard: Wilder Appraised Neil Sinyard and Adrian Turner, BCW, Ryde, 1979.

WINNER, Michael

(1936–) British director/producer/writer who had his own company at 24. His second real feature *The Cool Mikado* – 1962 was a cheap rip-off of *The Mikado*. But Winner has gone on to success by sheer determination and hard work. An indefatigable publicist, he is also professional in ways which the film industry approves, keeping to schedules and budgets, aware of the market and what will make money. Some patchy years produced *The Jokers* – 1966, an enjoyable caper film; *Lawman* – 1971, a western and his first American film; and *The Nightcomers* – 1971, a sado-masochistic variation on *The Turn of the Screw*.

Now he has teamed up with Charles Bronson in a series of money-making, if crudely directed, films including *Chato's Land* – 1971 and *Death Wish* – 1974.

Other films include:
The System (US *The Girl Getters*) – 1964, *The Big Sleep* – 1978.

Further reading:
The Films of Michael Winner Bill Harding, Frederick Muller, London, 1978.

WISEMAN, Frederick

(1930–) US director who was a law lecturer before turning to film-making in 1967. One of the most important of the new documentary film-makers to emerge in the 1960s as a result of the '16mm revolution' in the States. Wiseman takes the observational aspect of *cinema verite* to its limits, avoiding

the choice of 'crisis-situations' on which it was originally based. He takes the unobtrusive hand-held camera inside institutions to observe the day-to-day struggles of human beings to retain their dignity in the face of the inhumanity inside. The resulting frustration and confusion reveals the most horrific aspects of American society, often with a black and anarchic humour, as in *High School* – 1968 and *Basic Training* – 1971. Wiseman does much to reveal the ways in which individuals relate to the institutions which govern their lives but offers little criticism of the root causes of oppression.

Other films include:
Titticutt Follies – 1967, *Hospital* – 1970, *Welfare* – 1975, *Meat* – 1976, *Canal Zone* – 1977.

Further reading:
Frederick Wiseman, Thomas R. Atkins, Monarch Press, New York, 1976.

WYLER, William

(1902–) German-born director who went to New York in 1920 to try the movie business. He moved to Hollywood in 1922, where he worked as director on 28 westerns before the coming of sound. In 1935 he began his fruitful collaboration with producer Sam Goldwyn, directing a series of classic narrative films including *These Three* – 1936 and *The Little Foxes* – 1941, in which cameraman Gregg Toland's contribution was significant, manifested in the use of long takes and deep-focus shots. One of Hollywood's 'professionals', Wyler directed films in a wide variety of genres and themes, from thrillers (*The Desperate Hours* – 1955), westerns (*The Big Country* – 1958), romantic comedies (*Funny Girl* – 1968) to social drama

(*The Liberation of L. B. Jones* – 1970). Some of his films are interesting for their formal play rather than their classic realism – for example *The Letter* – 1940 and *Detective Story* – 1951.

Other films include:
Jezebel, – 1938, *The Best Years of Our Lives* – 1946, *The Heiress,* – 1949, *The Collector* – 1965.

Further reading:
William Wyler, Axel Madsen, Thomas Y. Crowell Co., New York, 1973.

ZINNEMANN, Fred

(1907–) Viennese-born US director who worked with documentarists Flaherty and Strand, for whom he directed *The Wave* – 1935, before going to MGM in 1937 to make factual and fictional shorts. Several of his early features were compassionately and unsensationally concerned with the plight of Europeans in the aftermath of World War II, as in *The Search* – 1948 and *Teresa* – 1951, which introduced Per Angeli to English-speaking audiences. *High Noon* – 1952, a classic western, was typical of many of Zinnemann's films. It focused on the individual's responsibility for his/her actions and life, even at the cost of breaks with society and friends. Other examples include *The Nun's Story* – 1959 and *A Man for All Seasons* – 1966, which won him a second Oscar. His first was for *From Here to Eternity* – 1953, which boasted some remarkable performances, as have many of Zinnemann's films, and seemed to hit a contemporary nerve. His later work tends to be rather stolid, but *The Day of the Jackal* – 1973 is an effectively taut thriller.

Other films include:
The Seventh Cross – 1944, *The Men* – 1950, *Oklahoma!* – 1955, *Julia* – 1978.

Further reading:
Fred Zinnemann, Richard Griffiths, Museum of Modern Art, New York, 1958.

GLOSSARY OF FILM TERMS

Absolute Film An abstract film that is nonrepresentational, but uses form and design to produce its effect.

Abstract Film A film that presents recognizable images in a way that is more poetic than narrative.

Academy Aperture The standard aspect ratio of width to height of 4:3 or 1.33:1.

Accelerated Montage A sequence edited into progressively shorter shots to create tension and excitement.

Accelerated-Motion Photography Movement on the screen appears to be quicker than it is in reality. Achieved by filming action at a slow speed and then projecting it at normal speed.

Actual Sound Sound from an object or person in the scene.

Anamorphic Lens A lens used to produce a widescreen image.

Animation Ways in which inanimate objects are made to move on the screen, to give the appearance of life. Methods include drawing on the film itself, photographing cells (drawings) one at a time, and pixillation.

Aperture (1) The opening of a lens which controls the amount of light transmitted. (2) The opening in a camera, printer or projector mechanism at which the film image is presented.

Arriflex A lightweight, portable camera introduced in the late 1950s.

Art Film In the mid-1950s, a distinction grew up between the art film with distinct aesthetic pretensions, and the commercial film.

Aspect Ratio The ratio of the width to the height of the film or television image.

Assembly The first stage of editing, when all the shots are arranged in script order.

Asynchronous Sound Sound that does not operate in unison with the image.

Atmosphere People See Extras.

Auteur (1) The prime author of a film. (2) A director with a recognizable style.

Available-light Photography Recent advances in the chemistry of filmstock have produced materials which are more sensitive to light. For available-light photography no artificial light is used.

Avant Garde The work of experimental and usually non-commercial film-makers in France and Germany c.1916–1933, closely associated with Dadaism and Surrealism. Any films of an abstract or experimental nature.

Backlighting The main source of light is behind the subject and directed towards the camera, silhouetting the subject.

Biopic A filmed biography, especially like those produced by Warner Brothers in the 1930s and 1940s.

Bit Player An actor with a very small part, but which usually involves some dialogue or action.

Black Comedy A comedy style popular during the late 1950s and early 1960s that dealt in macabre subjects.

Blockbuster A film that either is highly successful commercially, or has cost so much to make that it must be exceptionally popular in order to make a profit.

Blocking the Scene Setting out the positions and movements of actors and/or camera in a scene.

Blow-up Enlargement of a film frame.

Boom A travelling arm from which a microphone is hung above the actors and outside the frame.

Booster Light Lamp used on outdoor locations for boosting the daylight.

B Picture Quick, cheap movie made to fill out a double bill when double features were normal.

Bridging Shot A shot used to bridge a jump in time or place or other discontinuity. Examples include falling calendar pages, railway wheels, newspaper headlines and seasonal changes.

Broad A large floodlight giving general illumination.

Brute A high-intensity spotlamp.

Butterfly A net stretched over an outdoor scene to soften the sunlight.

Cahiers du Cinéma Film magazine founded by André Bazin, in 1951.

Cameo Performance A prominent actor's performance in a single scene.

Casting Director A studio official in charge of selecting actors for a film production, sometimes responsible for working out details of their contracts.

Cell Each of the thousands of individual drawings used in animation.

Change-over Cue Small dot or other mark in the top right-hand corner of the film frame that signals to the projectionist to change over from one projector to another.

Cheater Cut Footage cut into the beginning of a serial episode to show what happened at the end of the previous episode.

Cheat Shot A shot that cuts out part of a scene, so that the viewer thinks what appears on screen is different from what it really is.

CinemaScope Twentieth Century-Fox's trade name for its anamorphic technique; also anamorphic processes in general.

Cinematographer Also known as director of photography or, 'lighting cameraman'. Responsible for the camera and lighting.

Cinéma Vérité Now often used of any kind of documentary technique. Originally a cinema technique using lightweight equipment, two-person crews (camera and sound), and interviews.

Cinemiracle 'Seamless Cinerama'. A wide-screen system similar to Cinerama but without the drawback of joining lines between the projected images.

Cinerama A wide-screen system using many cameras, a battery of six projectors and a complex screen built up from 1,110 vertical slats.

Cine-structuralism The application of semiology to cinema.

Clapper Board Also clapstick or clapper. Two short boards hinged together and painted to match. When closed sharply, they give an audible and visible cue which is recorded on film and sound tape simultaneously. This helps synchronize the picture film with the magnetic film in editing.

Clip A short piece from a longer film, shown either for its intrinsic interest or to illustrate something else. A piece incorporated into a longer film.

Commentative Sound Sound coming from outside the reality of the scene being shot.

Compilation Film A film made up of shots, scenes, or sequences from other films.

Completed Treatment A late stage in the development of a screenplay. It is the story material as it emerges from several story conferences, incorporating all the changes required at the conferences and by studio executives.

Computer Film A film in which a computer controls the visual information (and sometimes the sound), usually via a cathode ray tube display .

Contact Printer A printing machine in which the printing stock and the film being printed are in contact.

Continuity The script supervisor is in charge of continuity during film production, making sure that details in one shot match details in another, even though filmed weeks apart. The script supervisor also keeps detailed records of takes.

Credits The list of technical personnel, cast and crew of a film.

Creeper-Title or Roll-Up Title A film title or text that appears to move slowly across the screen, vertically or horizontally.

Cross-Cutting Intermixing the shots of two or more scenes to suggest parallel action.

Cut The most abrupt and immediate of transitions from shot to shot. It is made in the laboratory simply by splicing one shot on to another. On screen the second shot immediately obliterates the first.

Cutaway A shot inserted in a scene to show action elsewhere, usually brief. Most often used to cover breaks in the main take, for example in documentary interviews.

Cutter Either editor or the person responsible for the mechanical rather than the creative side of editing.

Cyclorama The curved backdrop used to represent the sky when outdoor scenes are shot in a studio.

Dailies See Rushes.

Day for Night The use of filters to shoot night scenes during the day.

Découpage The design of the film, the arrangement of its shots.

Deep Focus A technique in which objects close to the camera as well as those far away are both in focus at the same time.

Direct Cinema The dominant style of documentary in the US since the early 1960s. Like *cinéma vérité*, it depends on lightweight, mobile equipment. It is noted for avoiding narration.

Director of Photography See cinematographer.

Direct Sound The technique of recording sound simultaneously with image.

Director The person who interprets the screenplay by orchestrating the actors' and technicians' movements while the film is being made. The director is often the most creative force in film-making.

Dissolve A transition between two scenes, with the first merging gradually into the second.

Dolly A mobile, usually wheeled, camera mount, often used to follow action at eye-level in dolly, tracking or 'trucking' shots.

Double The person who temporarily takes the place of a leading player either to undertake a difficult or dangerous action (stunt double) or to stand in for the actor photographically when the latter is not available (photo double).

Dub (1) To re-record dialogue in a language other than the original. (2) To record dialogue in a special studio after the film has been shot.

Dunning Process A technique to combine shots filmed in a studio with background footage shot elsewhere.

Dynamic Frame A technique for masking the projected image size and shape to any ratio that seems appropriate. For example, as an actor passes through a narrow passage, the image narrows; as he emerges into the open it widens.

Eastmancolor The colour filmstock now used almost universally.

Editor Person in charge of splicing the shots of a film together into final form.

Effects Track The soundtrack on which the sound effects are recorded before mixing.

End Title The title that marks the end of a film.

Establishing Shot A shot, usually close to the beginning of a scene, giving the place, time and other important facts about the action.

Exploitation Film A film aimed to profit by meeting a particular need or desire of the audience.

Expressionism A film style allowing free use of technical devices and artistic distortion. The director's personality is always paramount and obvious.

Extras or **Atmosphere People** Actors who do not have a significant role in a film but are present in various scenes. They perform a variety of functions–from making up part of a large crowd to falling on a battlefield.

Fade In A punctuation mark. The screen is black, but gradually the image appears, Brightening to full strength.

Feature (1) The main film of a multi-film programme. (2) Any film considered to be full-length, i.e. 75 minutes or more.

Film Chain The interlock between projector and television camera which translates 24-frame-per-second film into 30-frame-per-second video.

Film d'Art The early movement in French cinema to film more respectable stage productions.

Film Noir A film with a gritty, urban setting that deals mainly with dark or violent passions in a downbeat way. Especially common in American cinema during the late 1940s and early 1950s.

Filmography A listing of films.

Filmstock The raw material of film.

Final Cut The film as it will be released. The guarantee of final cut assures a film-maker that the producer will not be able to revise the film after he has finished it.

Fishpole A long lightweight hand-held rod on which a microphone can be mounted when the use of the boom is not practical.

Flashback A scene or sequence (sometimes an entire film) inserted into a scene in present time, but that deals with the past.

Flash Cutting Film edited into very brief shots that follow each other rapidly.

Flash-forward Scenes or shots of future time.

Flash Frame A shot of only a few frames length – sometimes a single frame – which can barely be perceived by the audience.

Flat A section of a studio set. Constructed on a wooden frame covered with materials such as plywood or fireproof hessian, treated with paint, wallpaper, papier-mâché, fabric or metal.

Flicker In film projection, a fluctuation in the intensity of the light falling on the screen, caused by the shutter passing across the light beam.

Flipover Wipe A startling wipe transition where the first shot or image appears to turn over and show the second one on the back of the first.

Flood A lamp which provides general diffuse lighting on a studio set.

Flop-Over An optical effect where the image is shown reversed from right to left.

Follow Shot Shot where the camera moves to follow the action.

Footage A measurement of the amount of film shot or to be shot.

Format The size or aspect ratio of a film frame.

Frame (1) Any single image on a film. (2) The size and shape of the image on a film, or on the screen when projected.

Free Cinema A movement in the UK in the middle and late 1950s marked by a series of films at the National Film Theatre by directors such as Lindsay Anderson and Tony Richardson.

Freeze Frame A freeze shot achieved by printing a single frame many times over to give the illusion of a still photograph when projected.

Fresnel Lens A type of lens used on spotlights called fresnels.

Front Projection A more precise way of combining images than rear projection. Live action is filmed against a reflective screen. An image is projected on the screen by means of mirrors along the axis of the camera lens so that no visible shadows are cast.

Gaffer The chief electrician on the set, in charge of lighting.

Gate The aperture assembly of a camera, printer or projector at which the film is exposed.

General Release Widespread simultaneous exhibition of a film with as many as 1,500 prints in circulation.

Glass Shot A type of special effect in which part of the scene is painted on a clear glass plate mounted in front of the camera.

Grip Person responsible for maintaining and adjusting equipment and props.

Guide Track A sound track recorded synchronously with the picture in poor acoustic conditions to be used as a guide during post-syncing.

Heavy The villain or evil force in a film.

High-Key A lighting style in which most of the scene is highlighted. Usually heightened by bright costumes and sets.

Highlighting Sometimes pencil-thin beams of light are used to illuminate limited parts of the subject (most often an actress's eyes).

Horse Opera Nickname for a western.

Hue Modulation A system for hi-fi optical soundtracks in which the sound signal is carried by variations in the colour of the track.

Inky-Dink The smallest focusable studio lamp.

Insert Shot A detail shot that gives specific information needed to understand completely the meaning of the scene, for example a letter.

Insert Title A title appearing in the main part of a film to provide information, commentary, summary or dates, or to give the dialogue in a silent film.

Intermittent The mechanism of a camera, printer or projector by which each frame is held still when exposed and then replaced by the next.

Jam, Camera or **Salad** A camera fault when film piles up inside the camera.

Jelly, or **Gel** (for gelatine). A transparent filter put in front of a lamp in studio lighting.

Jump Cut A cut occurring within a scene to shorten the shot.

Key Light The main light on a subject. Usually put at 45° to the camera-subject axis.

Kinescope Recording Technique of recording on film pictures originating in a television camera.

Library Shot A stock shot.

Lighting Cameraman The British term for cinematographer.

Lighting Instruments The film industry's term for lighting sources.

Lip Sync Synchronization between mouth movement and the words on the soundtrack.

Location Any place outside the studio where parts of a movie are filmed.

Logging, Film Entering in a logbook all the printed shots, scene by scene, with number, length, edge numbers and description of the action.

Loop A length of film joined head-to-tail for repeated continuous running.

Looping A method of post-dubbing. The speaker tries to match dialogue to performance while watching a short piece of the scene formed into a loop.

Low-Key Lighting style where most of a scene is scarcely lit. Usually heightened by dark costumes and sets.

MOS Filming without sound (silent). In the early days German technicians in Hollywood spoke of shooting

'mit out sound'.

McGuffin Alfred Hitchcock's term for a device or plot element that catches the viewer's attention or drives the logic of the plot.

Macrocinematography Filming of small objects, often with lens extension bellows or rings.

Made-For-TV Movie A type of filmed television, midway in style and construction between a drama programme and a cinema film.

Mag-Opt A film print with both magnetic and optical soundtrack records.

Mask (1) A shield placed in front of the camera lens to block off part of the image. (2) A shield placed behind the projector lens to obtain the correct aspect ratio.

Master A positive print made specially for duplicating purposes.

Master Shot A long take of an entire scene, generally a relatively long shot, made to help the assembly of closer shots and details.

Match Cut A cut in which the two shots joined are linked by visual, aural or metaphorical similarities.

Materialist Cinema (1) A modern movement, mainly in avant garde cinema, which celebrates the physical fact of film, camera, light, projector. The materials of filming are the main subject matter. (2) The cinema of film-makers such as Jean-Luc Godard and Robert Rossellini, which combines some of the qualities of (1) with a strong belief that political change is rooted in the basic conflicts of economic reality.

Matte Box A combined filter and/or matte holder and sun shade, mounted in front of the camera lens.

Matte Shot A matte is a piece of film that is blank in one area. When printed with a normal shot, it masks part of the image of that shot. Another scene, reversely matted, can be printed in the masked-off area.

Metteur-en-Scène A modest—sometimes derogatory—term for director.

Microcinematography Film photography through a microscope.

Minimal Cinema A type of extreme, simplified realism, such as in the work of Carl Dreyer, Robert Bresson and early Andy Warhol. Marked by minimal dependence on the technical power of cinema.

Mise-en-Scène Used to refer as a whole to the settings and to the movements of the actors in relation to the settings and lighting.

Mise-en-Shot or Mise-en-Cadre The design of an entire shot, in time as well as space.

Mitchell Formerly the most common type of Hollywood camera. A large, complicated machine needing several operators. Now largely

replaced by the Panaflex.

Mix (1) Optical: A dissolve. (2) Sound: The mixing of several separate recording tracks.

Mixer (1) Chief sound recording technician. In charge of everything to do with sound recording. (2) The person who mixes or combines several separate soundtracks.

Model Shot Small models filmed to give the illusion that they are full-size.

Movement The main intermittent mechanism of a camera, printer or projector.

Moviola The trade name of an editing machine that allows picture film or films to be viewed synchronously with one or more sound films. Often used to refer to editing machines in general.

Multiple Image A number of images printed beside each other in the same frame, often showing different camera angles of the same action, or separate actions.

Mute A print with the picture image only, but no sound track.

Nagra Brand name of a widely-used portable sound tape-recorder, important in the development of *cinéma vérité* and direct cinema.

Narrative Film A film that tells a story.

Negative A film that produces an inverted record of the light and dark areas of the scene photographed.

Negative Cost The cost of a finished film, excluding projection prints, publicity, distribution and exhibition expenses.

Neorealism A major movement in Italian cinema which flourished around 1945–1950. The major directors in the movement were Rossellini, de Santis, de Sica and Visconti.

Neue Kino, Das German cinema since 1968.

New American Cinema The personal cinema of independent film-makers in the US since World War II. Marked by a lyric, poetic and experimental quality.

Newsreel Cinema film news report or any filmed actuality.

New Wave (1) Godard, Truffaut, Chabrol, Rohmer, Rivette and other film-makers who began as critics on *Cahiers du Cinéma* in the 1950s, and were influenced by André Bazin. (2) More loosely all the young French film-makers of the 1960s, or any new group of film-makers.

Novelization Making a novel from a film or screenplay.

One-Reeler A film ten to twelve minutes long.

Optical Effects Special effects such as fades, dissolves, superimpositions, freeze-frames, split-screens and wipes.

Optical Printer A machine that makes duplicate prints of a

film. Many other technical operations are carried out on the optical printer, including opticals, the balancing of colour values, and the correction of contrast.

Optical Sound Recording Converting electrical sound signals into light-beam intensity or width to be recorded on light-sensitive emulsion.

Outline The synopsis of a story intended to be developed into a screenplay.

Out Of Sync An expression meaning that sound and image are not synchronized.

Overcrank To speed up a camera. To shoot at more than the normal 24 frames per second, so that the resulting image appears in slow motion.

Overlap Sound A cut in which the cut in the sound-track is not at the same time as the cut in the image.

Pan The camera moves along a horizontal plane. With a flash, swish or blur pan the camera is moved very rapidly so that the filmed action appears on screen as a blurred movement.

Panavision Now the most widely used anamorphic process.

Parallel Action A narrative device in which two scenes are observed in parallel by cross-cutting.

Parallel Sound Sound that matches the accompanying image.

Photogram Still.

Picture Print Film print bearing positive images.

Pixillation An animation technique in which real objects, people or events are photographed in such a way that the illusion of continuous, real movement is broken, either by photographing one frame at a time, or later printing only selected frames from the continuously-exposed negative.

Plot Plant The technique, sometimes used in scripting a film, of planting early in the story an apparently trivial piece of information which gains importance later.

Poetic Film Non-narrative film, often experimental.

Point of View Shot A shot which shows the scene from the point of view of a character. Often shortened to 'pov'.

Porn or **Porno** Pornographic film exploiting sex.

Post-Synchronization Recording the sound after the picture has been shot.

Practical A lamp or other prop on the set that can be operated during the scene action.

Preview or **Trailer** A short film, usually made up of excerpts from another picture to be shown in some future programme, intended as an advertisement for that picture.

Print A positive copy of a film.

Process Projection A technique

of filming live action played in front of a screen on which the background view is projected.

Process Shot A shot of live action in front of a process projection.

Producer The person finally responsible for the making, shaping and outcome of a film. He is in charge of business activities involved in the film's production.

Programmer A B picture or minor film.

Protection Print or **Protective Master** A master positive print made from the assembled original and kept in case the original is damaged or lost.

Pull-Back Shot A tracking shot or zoom that moves back from the subject to reveal the context of the scene.

Pushover A type of wipe in which the next image appears to push the preceding image off the screen.

Ratings Classifications based on sexual or violence factors. The British Board of Film Censors gives three types of certificates: U (Universal); A (Adult, prohibited to children under 16 unless accompanied by an adult); and X (unsuitable for children under 16). In the US, the Motion Picture Producers of America (MPPA) rates films in four categories: G (General); PG (Parental Guidance suggested for children); R (Prohibited for persons under 18 unless accompanied by an adult); and X (Prohibited to persons under 18).

Reaction Shot A shot that cuts away from the main scene or speaker to show a character's reaction to it.

Realism An approach that emphasizes the subject as opposed to the director's view of the subject.

Record Film A film that provides a duplicate representation of the subject photographed, but makes no claim to artistic merit.

Reflex Camera A camera that has a mirrored shutter so that the cameraman can look at the scene through the taking lens rather than a separate viewfinder.

Relational Editing Editing of shots to suggest a conceptual link between them.

Release The general distribution of a film for public showing.

Release Print A composite print made for general distribution.

Re-recording Transferring several soundtracks, e.g. dialogue, music and effects, onto a single track, mixing them by controlling levels.

Rigging Positioning lamps in the studio according to the first lighting scheme.

Roll The movement of the camera around the axis that runs between the lens and the subject.

Room Sound, (1) The quality of sound in a particular location, mainly a result of reverberation and echoes. (2) The basic, underlying sound in a location.

Rough Cut Roughly edited film at the work-print stage.

Rushes Prints of takes that are made immediately after a day's shooting, for examination before the next day's shooting. Made quickly from negative, often without corrections. Also known as 'dailies',

Scenario (1) An outline for a screenplay. (2) A complete screenplay.

Scene A complete unit of film narrative. A series of shots (or a single shot) that take place in one location and deal with one action.

Schufftan Process A form of glass shot which makes use of mirror reflection to film composites of partially constructed full-size sets and miniatures that complete them.

Screenplay The script of a film, usually including rough descriptions of camera movements.

Screwball Comedy A type of comedy prevalent in the 1930s, marked by frenetic action, wisecracks and sexual relationships.

Script A written screenplay.

Second Unit A second film crew who shoot material such as foreign location backgrounds, not handled by the first unit.

Second Unit Director Director of location sequences involving spectacular action, 'casts of thousands', stunt men, etc., but not the actors in the film.

Semiology (of the Cinema) The study of film as a system of signs, involving a basic discussion of how film can be seen as a language.

Sequence An arrangement of shots or scenes which together provide a meaningful unit in the evolution of a film story.

Sequence Shot A long, normally complicated, shot, often including complex camera movements and action. Also called *plan-séquence*.

Serial A continuing story told in episodes, each with a specific place in the narrative. A serial has a definite beginning, middle and end.

Series A continuing string of films. Each episode shares the same situations and characters but is cut off from the others in its plot.

Set The location of a scene, usually built on a sound stage.

Set-Up A camera and lighting position.

Short A film usually less than thirty minutes long.

Shot A piece of film that has been exposed without cuts or interruptions in a single running of the camera.

Skip Frame An optical printing effect that cuts out selected frames of the original scene to speed up the action.

Slapstick A form of comedy, common during the silent era, depending on broad physical action and pantomime.

Slate Board A board recording written information such as production title and number, scene and take number, and director's and cameraman's names, photographed at the beginning or end of each take to identify them.

Slate, Electronic An electrical device synchronously exposing a few frames in the camera and providing an electric signal recorded on the magnetic tape, so that the two can be matched in editing.

Slow Motion The camera is overcranked, so that the film is fed through faster than the normal 24 frames per second. When it is later projected at normal speed the action will take longer than in reality.

Sneak Preview An unadvertised, usually surprise, public showing of a film before its general release or announced première. It is usually aimed to discover typical audience reactions to a film before its general exhibition.

Soft Focus Filters, vaseline or special lenses soften lines and points, usually to create a romantic effect.

Sound Effects All created sounds except dialogue or music.

Sound Speed Standard speed of filming and projecting at 24 frames per second, when the picture is synchronized with a sound track.

Sound Stage A special building in which sets can be built for studio filming.

Soundtrack Optical soundtracks operate by the modulation of a light beam that creates a band on the film that widens and narrows to encode the signal's information. Magnetic soundtracks, like tape recordings, encode the information electromagnetically on a specially prepared surface.

Spaghetti Western A European western, usually filmed in Spain or Italy. Popularized in the 1960s by the films of Sergio Leone.

Special Effects A wide range of techniques and processes, including some kinds of work done by stunt men, model shots, opticals, in-camera effects, matte shots, rear projection, negative image and others.

Splice The join between two pieces of film.

Split-Reel Two different short-subject films (each too brief for separate screening) spliced together on one 1,000-foot reel for movie-house exhibition in the silent era.

Split Screen Two or more separate images within the frame, not overlapping.

Spotlamp A general name for many studio lamps of similar design but different size, such as the baby, junior and senior.

Stand-In A substitute for an actor who, after a scene has been blocked out, repeats the actor's movements to allow the lighting and camera movements to be worked out for the actual shooting of the picture.

Steenbeck The brand name of a modern editing table that is more flexible than the old Moviola.

Stereoscopy Photography using two separate, twinned images–one for each eye–to re-create a sense of depth in the image.

Still A single photograph. More precisely, a frame enlargement or publicity photograph from a film. A photogram.

Stock Footage Film library footage of famous or typical places and situations, historical events etc., for use in different film productions.

Stock Shot An unimaginative or commonplace shot that looks as if it could be a library shot.

Stop Frame An optical printing effect in which a single frame image is repeated, appearing static when projected. Also, camera exposure made frame by frame rather than by continuous running.

Story Board A series of drawings and captions (sometimes like a comic strip) showing the planned shots and camera movements of the movie–its découpage.

Strip-Title or **Subtitle** A text near the bottom of the projected image, usually giving a translation of foreign language dialogue.

Structuralist Film A film in which the codes and structures of social arrangements are visible.

Studio The place where films are produced.

Subjective Camera A style allowing the viewer to look at events from the point of view of either a character or the author.

Subtitle See strip-title.

Superimposition Two scenes exposed on the same piece of raw filmstock, one on top of the other. Usually done in the printer, but can be performed in the camera, although this gives less control.

Surface Noise The random sound level in any recording method.

Surrealism (1) A movement in painting and film during the 1920s, best represented in film by the work of Salvador Dali and Luis Buñuel. (2) A film style reminiscent of that movement, fantastic or psychologically distorting.

Synchronous Sound Sound whose source can be seen in the frame of the image, or whose source can be understood from the context of the image.

Synchronous Speed Camera speed of exactly 24 frames per second synchronized with the sound recording.

Tail The end of a reel of film.

Take A scene or part of a scene recorded on film and/or sound tape from each start to each stop of a camera and/or recorder.

Technicolor The best-known, and probably most widely used, colour system.

Technirama A widescreen system developed by the Technicolor Company.

Telecine Equipment for producing a television signal from movie film.

Telerecording The technique of recording television images on photographic film.

Third World Cinema The cinema of the developing countries of Latin America, Africa and Asia.

3D The technique of filming and projecting movie pictures that give the illusion of being stereoscopic or three-dimensional.

Tie-In Any commercial venture connected to a film; usually the simultaneous release of a novelization and a film.

Tilt Camera vertical pivot. Sometimes called vertical panning.

Time-Lapse Photography Extreme fast motion. A typical speed might be one frame every 30 seconds so that 24 hours of real time would be compressed, when projected, into two minutes of film time.

Todd-AO A widescreen technique using 65mm film. It was developed by Dr. Brian O'Brien and exploited by Michael Todd and the American Optical Company.

Tracking Shot A shot in which the camera moves sideways in or out. The camera can be mounted on wheels that move on tracks or on a rubber-tyred dolly, or hand-held.

Trailer A short publicity film, usually giving information about a forthcoming programme.

Travelling Matte A complicated matte process in which backgrounds and foregrounds shot separately may be combined on an optical printer.

Travelling Shot See tracking shot.

Travelogue A film whose main purpose is to show scenes from exotic places.

Treatment A literary presentation of an idea for a film before a full script has been developed.

Tripack A single film base with three separate layers of photographic emulsion, for colour photography and printing.

Turret, Lens A revolving lens mount for between two and four lenses, allowing the cameraman to choose the lens quickly for the next shot.

Two-Reeler A film lasting

Further Reading

about twenty minutes. During the silent era very often a comedy.

Typage Eisenstein's theory of casting, which shuns professional actors in favour of 'types' or representative characters.

Undercrank To slow down a camera. To shoot at less than the standard 24 frames per second, so that the image, when projected at 24 fps, will appear in fast motion.

Underground Film Independent film, made without the usual sources of funding and distribution, usually on a small budget. Non-commercial cinema.

Variable-Area Track An optical sound track on which the electrical signals are recorded as the varying width of a constant-density image.

Variable-Density Track An optical sound track on which the electrical signals are recorded as the varying density of the image.

Viewfinder Device on a camera to show the exact area of the scene being photographed.

Vignette A masking device, often with soft edges.

Vistavision Paramount's response to Twentieth Century-Fox's CinemaScope in the 1950s. The negative was made on 70mm stock and reduced to 35mm during printing to reduce graininess.

Walk-Through First rehearsal on the set, for camera positions, lighting, sound, etc.

Weenie The object motivating the main action in a serial e.g. missing plans, lost city or buried treasure.

Widescreen Film presentation in which the picture shown has an aspect ratio greater than 1.33:1.

Wild Shooting without synchronized sound recording.

Wild Motor Camera motor that does not run at an exact synchronous speed. Usually can be adjusted for different speeds.

Wild Recording Recording sound separately from images, usually to obtain sound effects such as room sound.

Wild Walls The walls of a set that have been constructed so that they can easily be moved to facilitate the positioning of the camera. Camera angles can thus be obtained that would be impossible on a practical set.

Wipe An optical effect in which an image appears to wipe off the previous image. Very common in the 1930s.

Work Print A print built up from dailies. It is improved editorially from the assembly stage through rough cut to a fine cut.

General

The World in Frame Leo Braudy, Anchor Press/Doubleday, Garden City, N.Y., 1976

Understanding Movies Louis Giannetti, Prentice Hall, Englewood Cliffs, N.J., 1976

How To Read A Film James Monaco, O.U.P., New York, 1977

History

The Parade's Gone By Kevin Brownlow, Secker & Warburg, London, 1968 (Silent films)

The Liveliest Art Arthur Knight, Macmillan, New York, 1978

World Cinema David Robinson, Eyre Methuen, London, 1973

National Cinemas

Violent America: The Movies 1946–1964 Lawrence Alloway, Museum of Modern Art, New York, 1971

Japanese Cinema Joseph Anderson and Donald Richie, Grove Press, New York, 1959

A Mirror for England Raymond Durgnat, Faber, London, 1970

The Haunted Screen: Expressionism in the German Cinema Lotte Eisner, Secker & Warburg, London, 1969

The Italian Cinema Pierre Leprohon, Secker & Warburg, London, 1972

Kino: A History of the Russian and Soviet Film Jay Leyda, Allen & Unwin, London, 1960

Kings of the B's Todd McCarthy and Charles Flynn, Dutton, New York, 1975

The New Wave James Monaco, OUP, New York, 1976

The American Cinema Andrew Sarris, Dutton, New York, 1968

Hollywood England: The British Film Industry in the Sixties Alexander Walker, Michael Joseph, London, 1974

Industry, Production and Techniques

The American Film Industry edited Tino Balio, University of Wisconsin Press, 1976

Making Legend of the Werewolf Edward Buscombe, British Film Institute, London, 1976

Basic Motion Picture Technology Bernard Happé, Focal Press, London, 1975

The Magic Factory: How MGM made An American in Paris Donald Knox, Praeger, New York, 1975

Four Aspects of The Film: A History of the Development of Colour, Sound, 3–D and Widescreen Films James Limbacher, Brussel & Brussel, New York, 1968

Independent Filmmaking Lenny Lipton, Straight Arrow, New York, 1973

The Film Industries Michael Mayer, Hastings House, New York, 1973

The Movie Brats Michael Pye and Lynda Lyles, New York, Holt Rinehart and Winston, 1979.

A–Z of Movie Making Wolf Rilla, Studio Vista, London, 1970

Film and Society

Toms, Coons, Mulattoes, Mammies and Bucks: An Interpretive History of Blacks in American Film Donald Bogle, Viking, New York, 1973

The Sociology of Film Art George Huaco, Basic Books, New York, 1965

Popcorn Venus: Women, Movies and the American Dream Marjorie Rosen, Coward, McCann & Geoghagan, New York, 1973

Image and Influence: Studies in the Sociology of Film Andrew Tudor, Allen & Unwin, London, 1974

Film as a Subversive Art Amos Vogel, Random House, New York, 1975

Genres

Film Genre edited Barry Grant, Scarecrow Press, Metuchen, N.J., 1977

American Film Genres Stuart Kaminsky, Pflaum, Dayton, Ohio, 1974

Documentary Eric Barnouw, OUP, New York, 1974

The Crazy Mirror: Hollywood Comedy and the American Image Raymond Durgnat, Faber, London, 1969

Classics of the Horror Film William Everson, Citadel, Secausus, N.J., 1974

The World of Entertainment: Hollywood's Greatest Musicals Hugh Fordin, Doubleday, New York, 1975

Westerns Philip French, Secker & Warburg, London, 1973

The Silent Clowns Walter Kerr, Alfred Knopf, New York, 1975

Abstract Film and Beyond Malcolm LeGrice, Studio Vista, London, 1977

Studies in Documentary Alan Lovell and Jim Hillier, Secker & Warburg, London, 1972

Underworld USA Colin McArthur, Secker & Warburg, London, 1972

Film and Revolution James Roy MacBean, Indiana U.P., Bloomington, 1975

A Heritage of Horror: The English Gothic Cinema, 1946–1972 David Pirie, Gordon Fraser, London, 1973

Dreams and Dead Ends: The American Gangster/Crime Film Jack Shadoian, MIT, Cambridge Mass., 1977

Science Fiction Movies Philip Strick, Octopus, London, 1976

Auteur Directors

Ingmar Bergman edited Stuart Kaminsky, with Joseph Hill, O.U.P., New York, 1975

The Western Films of John Ford J. A. Place, Citadel, Secausus, N.J., 1974

Focus on Godard edited Royal S. Brown, Prentice Hall, Englewood Cliffs, N.J., 1972

Howard Hawks Robin Wood, Secker & Warburg, London, 1968

Hitchcock François Truffaut and Helen Scott, Secker & Warburg, London, 1968

The Magic World of Orson Welles James Naremore, O.U.P., New York, 1978

Film Aesthetics and Theory

The Major Film Theories J. Dudley Andrews, OUP. New York, 1976

Film Theory and Criticism edited Gerald Mast and Marshal Cohen, O.U.P., New York, 1974

Movies and Methods edited Bill Nichols, California U.P., Berkeley, 1977

Film as Film: Understanding and Judging Movies Victor Perkins, Penguin, Harmondsworth, 1972

Theories of Film Andrew Tudor, Secker & Warburg, London, 1974

Signs and Meaning in the Cinema Peter Wollen, Secker & Warburg, London, 1970

Reference

International Index to Film Periodicals edited for International Federation of Film Archives, St James Press, London/St Martin's Press, New York, annual since 1972

The Filmgoer's Companion Leslie Halliwell, 6th ed., Hart–Davis MacGibbon, London, 1977

The New Film Index: A Bibliography of Magazine Articles in English, 1930–1970 edited Richard Dyer MacCann and Edward Perry, Dutton, New York, 1975

A Biographical Dictionary of The Cinema David Thomson, Secker & Warburg, London, 1972

International Film Guide edited Peter Cowie, Tantivy Press, London, annual since 1964

INDEX

239

Acknowledgments

Photographs
Material reproduced in this book was obtained from the sources listed below whose assistance is gratefully acknowledged. Pictures are listed by page number, additional numbers read in order from top to bottom and left to right, taken together: i.e. top left first, bottom right last.

Don Allen 119/1
Architectural Association 94/1, 95/2 A H Jacobs, 95/3 Henri Savage
Artificial Eye 120/1, 194/1
Bananas 156/1
BBC 81/2
BFI 14/3, 15/1, 16/2, 17/3, 18/2, 19/1, 20/1, 20/2, 21/3, 24/1, 27/1,

27/3, 28/1, 28/2, 32/2, 34/1, 34/2, 36/1, 37/1, 37/2, 38/1, 39/1, 39/2, 40/1, 41/1, 41/2, 41/3, 42/1, 43/1, 43/2, 44/1, 44/2, 45/1, 45/2, 46/1, 47/1, 47/2, 48/1, 49/1, 50/1, 51/1, 52/1, 52/2, 54/1, 56/1, 56/2, 57/1, 58/1, 58/2, 59/1, 61/2, 63/1, 65/1, 65/2, 66/1, 68/1, 68/2, 69/1, 71/1, 73/1, 74/1, 74/2, 84/1, 85/1, 85/2, 86/2, 88/1, 91/1, 91/2, 96/1, 98/2, 108/2, 114/1, 115/2, 115/3, 118/1, 121/1, 123/1, 124/1, 125/1, 126/1, 126/2, 126/3, 127/1, 130/1, 132/1, 133/1, 136/1, 138/1, 139/1, 139/2, 140/1, 141/1, 141/2, 146/1,

148/1, 151/2, 151/3, 154/2, 155/1, 159/1, 159/2, 161/1, 161/2, 161/3, 183/1, 185/1, 187/2, 190/1, 191/1, 193/1, 196/1, 196/2, 198/1, 199/2, 200/1, 200/2, 200/3, 201/1, 201/2, 204/2.
Camera Press 109/1, 109/2, 112/1, 119/2, 119/3, 120/2, 128/2, 132/2, 152/1, 152/2, 153/1, 186/1, 186/2, 187/1
Cinegate 16/1, 77/1, 202/1, 202/2.
Complete Media Consultants 77/2
Contemporary 199/3
David Robinson 3/1, 4/1, 8/1, 8/2, 9/1, 10/1, 10/2, 11/1, 11/2, 12/1, 12/2, 12/3, 13/2, 14/2, 15/2,

17/1, 17/2, 17/4, 18/1, 19/2, 19/3, 21/1, 21/3, 22/1, 23/1, 23/2, 24/1, 25/2, 25/3, 26/1, 27/2, 29/1, 29/2, 30/1, 30/3, 31/1, 35/1, 35/2, 36/2, 84/2, 87/1, 92/1, 93/1, 93/2, 108/1, 139/3, 144/1, 199/1
EMI 92/2, 98/1, 157/1, 158/1
Mary Evans Picture Library 14/1
Golden Harvest Films 160/1
Granada 80/1, 81/1
Cecil H. Greville 128/1, 129/1
Neilson Hordell 137/1
John Kobal 25/1, 32/1, 50/2, 53/1, 60/1, 62/1, 64/1, 67/1, 67/2, 71/2, 73/2, 75/1, 76/1, 78/1, 86/1, 88/2, 89/1, 89/2, 90/1, 105/1, 110/1, 115/1,

118/2, 123/2, 131/2, 142/1, 143/1, 143/2, 144/2, 147/1, 149/1, 149/2, 151/1, 154/1, 157/2, 188/1, 188/2, 189/1, 191/2, 192/1, 192/2, 197/1, 203/1, 204/1, 205/1, 206/1, 207/1, 208/1
Kodak Museum 100/1, 101/1, 102/1
MCA 79/2, 79/3
Other Cinema 195/1
Pinewood 104/1, 104/2, 122/1, 129/2, 136/2
Paul Popper 113/1, 116/1, 116/2, 117/1, 192/3, 194/2, A-Z
Science Museum 13/1, 30/2
Thompson Org. 140/2
Walt Disney 38/2, 131/1, 163/1, 179/1
Warner Bros 70/1